THE EVOLUTION OF
THE HUMAN MIND

From Supernaturalism to Naturalism
An Anthropological Perspective

To Jane,
Intellectual companion
of sharp eye and penetrating
mind who, despite the flaws
she might find in these pages,
I hope never to lose as a warm
friend. With esteem and affection,

Bob

THE EVOLUTION OF THE HUMAN MIND

From Supernaturalism to Naturalism
An Anthropological Perspective

ROBERT L. CARNEIRO
American Museum of Natural History
New York, New York

ELIOT WERNER PUBLICATIONS, INC.
CLINTON CORNERS, NEW YORK

Library of Congress Cataloging-in-Publication Data

Carneiro, Robert L. (Robert Leonard), 1927-
    The evolution of the human mind : from supernaturalism to naturalism-an
    anthropological perspective / Robert L. Carneiro.
    p. cm.
    Includes bibliographical references and index.
    ISBN 978-0-9797731-1-2 (hardcover) – ISBN 978-0-9797731-2-9 (pbk.)
1. Human evolution. 2. Social evolution. 3. Brain – Evolution. 4. Thought
and thinking. 5. Naturalism. 6. Supernatural. I. Title.
GN281.C375 2009
599.93'8 – dc22

                                                        2008026261

ISBN-10: 0-9797731-1-3 (Hardcover)
ISBN-10: 0-9797731-2-1 (Paperback)
ISBN-13: 978-0-9797731-1-2 (Hardcover)
ISBN-13: 978-0-9797731-2-9 (Paperback)

Printed in the United States of America

To the memory of my mother and father

PREFACE

Not many authors, I suspect, can say exactly when the idea of writing their book came to them. If that is so, then this book is an exception to the rule, for I know precisely when and how the idea of writing it came to me.

I was on board a plane bound from New York to Ann Arbor, Michigan, on November 10, 2005, and was reading a printout of an article about Jean Buridan, a fourteenth century French cleric and scholar. What prompted my interest in Buridan was that unlike many of his contemporaries, he did not believe that God involved himself in the everyday running of the universe. Rather, he thought, "God may have given each of the heavenly bodies the impetus He desired at the time He created them, and they have been running of their own impetus ever since" (Dales 1989:111). I had once quoted this statement as an example of changing conceptions of God's role from that of a capricious deity, intervening repeatedly in the affairs of the world, to one who had—at the very outset—laid down a set of laws and thereafter allowed the cosmos to run according to these laws.

Buridan's contention, it seemed to me, afforded a striking example of the change undergone in human thinking, from a thoroughgoing belief in unalloyed supernaturalism toward an attitude in which naturalism played an increasingly greater role. This change was of fundamental importance in how the affairs of the world, and indeed of the universe, were deemed to run.

Yet as often as historians of ideas have noted this trend, I could not recall a single volume devoted entirely to tracing this change over the course of centuries. Certainly no book known to me followed this trend from the beginnings of supernaturalistic thinking (back in the Paleolithic) and carried it through the most advanced levels of scientific thought today. As an anthropologist interested in the religious beliefs of primitive peoples, as well as someone concerned with the philosophy of science, it occurred to me that I might have something to say on the subject. So, sitting in an aircraft at

34,000 feet, I decided to try to write a book that sought to trace the course of this intellectual evolution.

The title of this book—*The Evolution of the Human Mind*—occurred to me then as encapsulating its intended scope. Moreover, I wanted a title that was at once grandiose and presumptuous, provocative and intriguing—a title that would require a concerted effort in order to live up to it.

"The Mind of Primitive Man" has long been a subject of interest and concern to anthropologists. It was the title of Franz Boas's most famous book (1911) and it was the name of Leslie White's most popular course at the University of Michigan. But the word "mind" is ambiguous, and I need to make clear at the outset just what I mean by it. In the first place, this is not a book about human psychology. Psychology deals with the processes and mechanisms of thinking, even with the neuroanatomy that makes thought possible. This book, however, is not concerned with the structure and function of the brain, but only with its *contents*. That is to say, it deals with the thoughts—the ideas—that people have held over the course of millennia. More specifically, it deals with those ideas purporting to account for the origin of the world, how the world works, and humanity's place in it.

My exposition, I should note, does not presuppose any particular theory of brain function. It simply assumes the *correct* one. That is, it takes for granted how the brain actually works, how it has generated the ideas it has given rise to. But these ideas are not self-generating; they have not simply been excogitated. They have not been drawn from the inner workings of the human brain, the way a spider spins its web from material it draws from its spinneret, deep inside its body. The ideas that have emerged from the human brain have been very largely derived through the processing of experiences that people have had and have grappled with, using the intellectual tools available to them at the time—tools that were at first simple, crude, and limited.

A fair summary of what I mean by "mind" was once given by Julian Huxley and bears quoting.

> The brain alone is not responsible for mind, even though it is a necessary organ for its manifestion.... I would prefer to say that mind is generated by ... living matter, capable of receiving

> information of many qualities … about events both in the outer
> world and in itself, [and] of synthesizing and processing that
> information in various forms. (Huxley 1961:16–17)

I am not concerned here with whether, at bottom, the human "mind" operates in terms of dualities, dichotomies, or dialectics. I simply assume that the brain operates however it does. Again, what I am interested in are the concepts and ideas that were generated by cerebral activity as individuals sought to understand and interpret their experience of the world around them. And I am not concerned so much with the ideas of particular individuals—although I will of course cite them extensively as exemplifying these ideas—as I am in systems of ideas. As a cultural anthropologist, I am primarily interested in *culture*, which in one sense is the product of thought.

In searching for an analogy to illustrate the relationship between brain and mind, perhaps we can say that the brain "secretes" thought the way a polyp secretes coral. And my concern in this book is not with the polyp, but with the coral reef—the product of the polyp's accumulated secretions. Viewed over the course of time, those "accumulated secretions" constitute an evolutionary record. And the evolution of ideas can be studied in and of itself, quite independently of and apart from the organisms that gave rise to them.

As with evolution generally, the sequence of development of these ideas shows a distinct direction. And this direction is basically—strikingly—from a supernaturalistic interpretation of the world toward a naturalistic one. Moreover, this evolution has been marked not only by a direction, but by an *acceleration*. The trend toward naturalism has, unquestionably, been speeding up. The most dramatic changes in the interpretation of the world have come about during the last four hundred years of human history, more so by far than in the preceding forty thousand. In the pages that follow, I propose to track this evolution as well as it can be discerned, from the Paleolithic to the present. This means going back some tens of thousands of years to a murky, indistinct past and proceeding forward to the present time, when issues involving human understanding are more sharply delineated and the evidence for their transmutation is clearer and more abundant.

One of the notable features of this evolution is that its course is not strictly rectilinear, but (one might say) *sawtoothed*. Movement has been generally forward, but not always. Periods of stagnation or even retrogression have sometimes alternated with periods of advance. Particularly striking is the way in which, time and again, the new is intertwined with the old. Naturalistic and supernaturalistic attitudes are often intermingled in the same person. Indeed, it will be a leitmotif of this book that those individuals responsible for some of the greatest advances in naturalistic thinking—men like Copernicus, Kepler, and Newton—nevertheless retained palpable vestiges of supernaturalistic thinking. Only in recent decades are we beginning to find scientists in whom supernaturalism has been completely extirpated and whose naturalistic thought stands out distinct and uncompromised. But the story must begin with the first glimmerings about the fundamental questions of human existence. And these early glimmerings, as we are about to see, were suffused with supernaturalism. It could hardly have been otherwise.

ACKNOWLEDGMENTS

My overriding obligation in writing this book is to the hundreds of thinkers whose ideas about the great questions of existence, from the Paleolithic to the present, I have attempted to trace and interpret. But acknowledgments are usually made to the living, not to the dead. And although the former are far fewer in number, they nonetheless have been of inestimable value to me in pursuing the objectives that this book seeks to attain.

First among those to whom I owe a debt of thanks is Joyce Marcus. This marks the third book in which I have had the pleasure of expressing my appreciation to her. Despite her many more pressing concerns, she always found the time to read my manuscript with her unerring eye and give me the benefit of her keen insight, sound judgment, and warm encouragement. In a previous preface, I spoke of her support as being worth rubies; I would now raise that to diamonds.

Robert Bates Graber, my fellow evolutionist, friend, and comrade-in-arms, also read the manuscript and from his wit, wisdom, and deep knowledge of the history of science made many thoughtful comments, often forcing me to reconsider matters that I thought settled.

B. J. Brown, who on his own initiative has kept careful track of my published writings, used his powerful mind and unique perspective to offer a number of penetrating suggestions.

William Peace, fellow student of the works of Leslie White, and Seymour Baxter, friend since our college days, each read several chapters of the book and found something of value to contribute to their improvement.

This is the second volume in which Eliot Werner has been my editor. And I must report that my second experience with him in this role has only strengthened the opinion I voiced of him once before: that he is the kind of editor every author wishes he had. Let me just reinforce this by saying that any author who works with Eliot can expect the assurance—and indeed the satisfaction—that he is being held to the highest standards.

When we hit a particularly vexing problem in grammar or usage, about which we were uncertain or in disagreement, we turned to Gloria Brownstein of Marist College, whose wise and learned counsel we were almost invariably happy to follow.

Finally, I could not end my acknowledgments without conveying my thanks to my old friend and typist Clarissa Wilbur, who with skill, grace, and humor entered seemingly endless drafts of these chapters into her computer.

CONTENTS

THE EVOLUTION OF THE HUMAN MIND

From Supernaturalism to Naturalism
An Anthropological Perspective

CHAPTER 1

The Emergence of the Supernatural

No chimpanzee believes in God. Squaring the circle never troubles him, nor does he ever wonder how many angels could dance on the head of a pin. He certainly has never asked himself, "What is the meaning of existence?" Thus we may not know what a chimpanzee is thinking, but we know very well what he's *not* thinking. Questions like these simply cannot enter the mind of a subhuman, non-speaking, cultureless primate.

But a chimp's brain is by no means a void. Indeed, it might almost be said that a chimpanzee already has an *ontology* and an *epistemology* even if he is quite unaware of it himself. His reality is what he can grasp through his senses. A chimp "believes" in only what he can see, hear, smell, touch, and taste. That is to say, he believes only in those things that actually *exist*. He is thus at once an empiricist, a materialist, and a realist. To be sure, he is unable to engage in the high art of metaphysical speculation. He still cannot populate the world with phantasms—with things that *don't* exist. This ability became possible only after the ape brain had been supplanted by the hominid brain, which had evolved from it. In other words, none of this would have been possible until a certain neurological threshold in primate development had been reached and crossed.

The Symbolic Basis of Culture

According to the anthropologist Leslie A. White, that stage was reached when the continued evolution of the human brain gave rise to what he called the *symbolic faculty* (White 2005:22–39). This faculty consists of the ability to create symbols, the essence of a symbol being that it conveys a meaning that is not inherent in it. Meaning is arbitrarily *assigned* to a symbol by those who use it. The principal instrument for assigning and expressing meaning, of course, is language. Only with the existence of language—the means by which individuals could formulate, express, and exchange ideas, especially abstract ideas—could notions of a *supernatural* world, a world not perceivable by the senses, be entertained.

Language made at least two things possible. It permitted, first of all, communication between individuals about the natural world, the real world. But it also enabled humanity to create an *unreal* world—a world of immaterial, incorporeal, supernatural entities. Limited as they are in their mental capacity, chimpanzees are incapable of deceiving themselves in the same way that human beings can. People have this capacity in full measure and have expressed it unsparingly—most characteristically in the domain of religious beliefs. How did it all come about? What were the circumstances that led to the formation of the earliest supernatural beliefs? And what were these beliefs like?

As soon as we ask these questions, we find ourselves in an area of great uncertainty and even greater controversy. To those individuals who practice religion—more specifically to those who *believe in God*—the onset of religion entailed a *recognition* of something that existed. To the scientific student of the subject, however, skeptical of the truth of all religious beliefs, religion is an *invention*. It involved the creation of a class of entities that do *not* exist.

Is Religion Universal?

One of the great questions that confronted anthropologists when they first began to study religion among primitive peoples was whether it was universal among them. It was not uncommon during the nineteenth century for travelers who had returned from faraway places to report that there were tribes in remote corners of the world so simple and backward that not only did they not believe in God, but that they lacked "religion" in any form. Indeed, Sir John Lubbock (Lord Avebury) cited more than a dozen "trustworthy observers"—"sailors, traders, and philosophers, Roman Catholic priests and Protestant missionaries"—who reported the existence of such tribes (Lubbock 1870:121–122).

In introducing a discussion of this matter in his great work *Primitive Culture* (1871), E. B. Tylor asked a question: "Are there, or have there been, tribes of men so low in culture as to have no religious conceptions whatever?" (Tylor 1871:I, 377). Lubbock, as we just saw, believed that there were. Thus he wrote that "[a]s regards the lower races of men [i.e., the simpler peoples], it seems to me, even *à priori*, very difficult to suppose that a people so backward as to be unable to count their own fingers [as had been claimed to exist] should be sufficiently advanced in their intellectual conceptions as to have any system of belief worthy of the name of a religion" (Lubbock 1870:125).

But Tylor, who had a much broader knowledge of ethnography than Lubbock, did not believe that any such tribes—that is, tribes lacking any form of religion—actually existed. "The case," he wrote, "is in some degree similar to that of the tribes asserted to exist without language or without the use of fire; nothing in the nature of things seems to forbid the possibility of such existence, but as a matter of fact the tribes are not found" (Tylor 1871:I, 378). However, Tylor was quite ready to countenance the possibility that there had once been a *stage*—early in human history—when people did in fact lack any religious notions whatever. Accordingly, he declared that "no evidence justifies the opinion that man … cannot have emerged from a non-religious condition, previous to that religious condition in which he happens [to be found] at present" (Tylor 1871:I, 384). The fact that no societies known in Tylor's day lacked some form of supernatural beliefs could thus not be used to argue against an earlier stage when they *had* lacked such beliefs. "Nonreligious tribes may not exist in our day," Tylor argued, "but the fact bears no more decisively on the development of religion, than the impossibility of finding a modern English village without scissors or books or Lucifer-matches bears on the fact that there was a time when no such things existed in the land" (Tylor 1871:I, 384).

The current status of anthropological thinking on this issue is that either the early writers affirming the absence of religion had insufficient knowledge of the groups they were writing about, or that their conception of "religion" was too narrow or stringent. All such allegations, then, have proved false. *No* society ever studied by anthropologists lacked some form of supernatural beliefs.

The Search for the Origin of Religion

Nonetheless, if we regress back far enough through human history, there must have been a time—a stage—when no supernatural beliefs existed. How far back we must go before encountering such a stage is a matter of conjecture. But that there *was* such a stage can hardly be denied. Thus the question naturally arises: *when* did supernatural conceptions first emerge in the human mind, and *what form* did they take?

To be sure, some anthropologists regard it as fruitless to try to ascertain the earliest form of religion. More than a hundred years ago, Andrew Lang objected, "We have … in short, no opportunity of observing, historically, man's development from blank unbelief into even the minimum or most rudimentary form of belief," and he spoke of "the haze that covers great parts of the subject" (Lang 1898:53, 177). R. R. Marett, for his part, declared that "[f]or me the first chapter of the history of religion remains in large part indecipherable" (Marett 1914:viii).

More recently E. E. Evans-Pritchard, a leading contemporary student of primitive religion, betrayed the traditional British functionalist distaste for origins and for tracing the subsequent evolution of a phenomenon when he wrote, "To my mind it is extraordinary that anyone could have thought it worthwhile to speculate about what might have been the origin of some custom or [religious] belief, when there is absolutely no means of discovering, in the absence of historical evidence, what was its origin" (Evans-Pritchard 1965:101). To this objection he added, "I think that most anthropologists would today agree that it is useless to seek for a *primordium* in religion" (Evans-Pritchard 1965:104–105). He was particularly opposed to attempts at reconstructions that were based "on evolutionary assumptions for which no evidence was, or could be, adduced" (Evans-Pritchard 1965:108).

But to turn one's back by fiat on the study of origins and evolutionary tracks denies science the legitimate use of inference. And in fact Evans-Pritchard's injunction has been largely ignored by those intent on probing deeply into the question. Regardless of where and when religious beliefs first arose, undoubtedly there was a time before they made their appearance, followed by a time when they first did. For his part Lubbock believed in a primordial stage of atheism, "understanding by this term not a denial of the existence of a Deity, but an absence of any definite ideas on the subject" (Lubbock 1870:119).

Religion: Recognition or Invention?

Granting the reality of such a stage before any sort of religious beliefs began to appear, when did the first glimmerings of religion arise? And what were initial notions of it like? First of all, it is important to keep in mind (as stated before) that belief in God—the central focus of religion as generally understood today—is either a *recognition* of something that exists or an *invention* of something that does not. To a theist, of course, the first alternative is the correct one. Father Wilhelm Schmidt, a Catholic priest who was also an anthropologist, believed unquestioningly that religion was a divine revelation received by mankind. Believing in the truth of religion was not only accepting a *fact*, he contended, but it had an added benefit: it made one better able to study the phenomenon. "If religion is essentially of the inner life," wrote Father Schmidt, "it follows that it can be truly grasped only from within. But beyond a doubt, this can be better done by one in whose inward consciousness an experience of religion plays a part. There is but too much danger that the other [i.e., the nonbeliever] will talk of religion as a blind man might of colours, or one totally devoid of ear, of a beautiful musical composition" (quoted in Evans-Pritchard 1965:121).

If Father Schmidt was right, then one hardly needed a *theory* of the origin of religion. God revealed himself to man and that was that. This belief, of course, was not original with Schmidt. Writing a half-century earlier, Max Müller said that this view was "a legacy of another theory, very prevalent during the Middle Ages, that religion began with a primeval revelation" (Max Müller 1879:245).

Was There an Instinctual Basis to Religion?

According to another view of the matter, religion did not require a full-blown theory to account for it since supernatural beliefs were virtually instinctual. The nineteenth century Egyptologist Le Page Renouf, for example, considered religion "not the result of reasoning or generalizing, but an intuition as irresistible as the impressions of our senses" (Renouf 1880:103–104). And the German philosopher Friedrich Lange believed that "religion itself, quite apart from any revelation, must be reckoned among the natural impulses of man" (quoted in

Upton 1909:177). Again, G. C. Joyce, author of the article on deism in Hastings's *Encyclopaedia of Religion and Ethics,* spoke of "the inerad-icable religious instincts of mankind" (Joyce 1911:540). Even Evans-Pritchard maintained that "what instinct does for animals, religion does for man.... Ultimately it is a product of an instinctual urge, a vital impulse which, combined with intelligence, ensures man's survival and his evolutionary climb to ever greater heights" (Evans-Pritchard 1965:116).

The majority of anthropologists, however, holds a different view. For them religion was no divinely inspired epiphany, nor was it the manifestation of an instinct. Rather, it was a human construction, con-jured up as a result of reflection on the experiences of everyday life and applying to them the limited intellectual resources that human beings then had at their disposal. Wrote E. B. Tylor, "[A]s to the reli-gious doctrines and practices examined [in the pages of his *Primitive Culture*], these are treated as belonging to theological systems devised by human reason, without supernatural aid or revelation" (Tylor 1871:I, 386).

All told, many theories of the origin of religion have been pro-posed—far too many to discuss them all here. In general, though, we may group these theories into three main types: *psychological, sociological,* and *intellectual.*

Psychological theories look at religion largely as an emotional response, a projection into the external world of human fears, needs, aspirations, and desires. Sociological theories see religion as result-ing from the members of a society combining their efforts to exalt their group, to *deify* the society itself. Intellectual theories view reli-gion as the creation of spiritual entities as a way to explain the phe-nomena and events of human experience.

Psychological Theories of Religion

David Hume (1711–1776) may perhaps be placed among the first of the psychological theorists, since he held that religion arose "from a concern with ... the incessant hopes and fears which actuate the human mind" (quoted in Sorley 1965:182). Max Müller (1823–1900) likewise may be classified as a psychological theorist, since he believed that it was "awe at the extraordinary power of nature" that served as the basis of religion (quoted in Harvey 2005:11). But by far the best known psychological theorist was Sigmund Freud, who set forth his ideas on the subject most fully in *The Future of an Illusion* (1927).

Freud did not endear himself to ardent believers when he called religion "the universal obsessional neurosis of humanity" (Freud 1961:55). For him religion was "a store of ideas ... created, born from man's need to make his helplessness tolerable and built up from the material of memories of helplessness of his own childhood and the childhood of the human race" (Freud 1961:23). Freud went on to say that religious beliefs are in some sense automatic, almost instinctual: "Primitive man has no choice, he has no other way of thinking. It is natural to him, something innate, as it were, to project his existence outward into the world and to regard every event which he observes as the manifestation of beings who at bottom are like himself" (Freud 1961:27).

This feeling of helplessness, said Freud, led humans to invent supernatural beings as their protectors. Arguing powerfully against this theory, though, is the fact that among the first supernatural beings people invented—and with which they populated the world—appear to have been *bush spirits*, which were almost universally regarded not as benign but as malevolent. Thus, instead of comfort and succor, what they contributed to human experience were more dangers and greater uncertainties.

Another of Freud's theories about religion (elaborated in *Moses and Monotheism,* 1939) was that "the primal father was the original image of God, the model on which later generations have shaped the figure of God" (Freud 1961:54). The problem with this theory is that Freud wrote as if religion—at least theistic religion—had been invented only *after* civilization had emerged, since the attitude of reverence and awe that people would have had toward these gods would have been experienced only after they had been ruled by all-powerful monarchs who required complete obedience and respect. Clearly Freud was unfamiliar with what anthropologists, most notably Tylor and Spencer, had said about the origin of religion. Nor could he have had much acquaintance with ethnographic sources portraying the religious beliefs of primitive peoples, a considerable number of which had already accumulated.

Sociological Theories of Religion

Sociological theories of the origin of religion are most notably exemplified by Emile Durkheim. Durkheim, who never carried out fieldwork himself but who nevertheless had read widely about Australian aborigines, was convinced—erroneously, as it turned out—that clans represented the earliest form of human social groupings. Thus he believed that social organization based on clans was "the simplest we know." It followed, therefore, that "[a] religion so closely allied with the social system that is simpler than all others can be regarded as the most elementary [and thus the earliest] we can know" (Durkheim 1995:169). The form of religion Durkheim was referring to was *totemism*, the worship of animal ancestors, which he regarded as "the primordial religion of mankind" (Durkheim 1995:169). So fully did totemism cover the subject for Durkheim that in discussing religion he declared, "I have had no need even to say the words 'spirits,' 'genies,' or 'divine personage'" (Durkheim 1995:169).

If so, then where did God—spelled either with or without a capital "g"—fit into the picture? "Taking the word 'god' in a very broad sense," said Durkheim, "one could say that it is the god that each totemic cult worships. But it is an impersonal god, without name, without history, immanent in the world, different in a numberless multitude of things" (Durkheim 1995:191). It was in carrying out ceremonies, Durkheim held, that a society's members assembled, performed their rituals, and expressed their religious beliefs. Sociologists like Durkheim and his modern-day follower Guy Swanson, then, see religion as in some sense a projection of human society into the realm of spiritual ideas. Thus it is, says Swanson, that "social relationships inherently possess the characteristics we identify as supernatural" (Swanson 1964:22).

A few years after Durkheim, in an oft-quoted remark, the British anthropologist R. R. Marett—writing in his book *The Threshold of Religion*—echoed the notion that among the simpler societies religion was, first and foremost, a socio-ceremonial performance. "[S]avage religion," wrote Marett, "is something not so much thought out as danced out" (Marett 1914:xxxi). In these primeval performances, he thought that he could detect "phantasms teeming in the penumbra of the primitive mind, and dancing about the darkling rim of the tribal fire-circle" (Marett 1914:xiv).

Intellectual Theories of Religion

The third major category of theories purporting to account for the origin of religion sees it as arising from attempts to explain certain phenomena that human beings constantly experience, but lack the scientific basis to really understand. For the formal introduction of theories of this sort, we must go back to the nineteenth century, a period at the very beginning of scientific anthropology. Having immersed themselves in the rich ethnographic resources that were then becoming available, E. B. Tylor and Herbert Spencer—two of the great pioneers of this discipline—felt they could marshal convincing evidence of how the very first supernatural concepts arose.

There were, of course, qualifications to be uttered about the solidity of such theories. Spencer, for example, warned that "[t]o determine what conceptions are truly primitive would be easy if we had accounts of truly primitive men. But there are reasons for suspecting that men of the lowest types now known, forming social groups of the simplest kinds, do not exemplify men as they originally were" (Spencer 1901:95). Still, it seemed to him that existing primitive societies sufficiently reflected "primordial" conditions to allow him to make a reasonable surmise about those pristine times, when religious beliefs were first beginning to take form. It is true that at first glance the large corpus of ethnographic data showed no clear pattern on this score. However, as Spencer explained optimistically, "[A] loose mass of observations continues unsystematized in the absence of an hypothesis, but under the stimulus of an hypothesis, undergoes changes bringing about a coherent systematic doctrine" (Spencer 1901:123).

Operating independently of each other, Spencer and Tylor worked out schemes—alike in their essential features—that accounted for the rise of the earliest forms of religion. Tylor called his scheme *animism,* while Spencer labeled his the *ghost theory.* But the difference in name could not mask their near identity.

The Soul as the First Supernatural Concept

From their wide familiarity with ethnography, Tylor and Spencer knew that a universal feature in the supernatural systems of primitive peoples was the belief in a personal soul. And they came to regard this belief as the kernel out of which all other religious ideas had grown. But how had a belief in the soul arisen in the first place? Well, they asked themselves, what element was common to all human experience and at the same time present in all consciousness from the very beginning? The answer was *dreams*. Out of dreams, they thought, had come the notion of an immaterial, incorporeal double associated with every individual. It was this spirit essence, recognized as having an existence of its own, that came to be called the soul. As Spencer said simply, "The root of this belief in another self [i.e., the soul] lies in the experience of dreams" (Spencer 1877:416). In his own terse statement of the theory, Tylor remarked, "Stated shortly, this theory [animism] is ... that a conception of the Human Soul is a crude but reasonable inference by primitive man from obvious phenomena," principally dreams (Tylor 1877:142). And in their two great works—Tylor's *Primitive Culture* (1871) and Spencer's *The Principles of Sociology* (1876–1896)—they outlined in detail an impressive body of evidence to support their views.

Years later, summarizing this theory in his book *Anthropology*, Tylor wrote:

> What then is this soul or life which thus goes and comes in sleep, trance, and death? To the rude philosopher, the question seems to be answered by the very evidence of his senses. When the sleeper awakens from a dream, he believes he has really somehow been away, or that other people have come to him. As it is well known by experience that men's bodies do not go on these excursions, the named explanation is that every man's living self or soul is his phantom or image, which can go out of his body and see and be seen itself in dreams. (Tylor 1931:343)

Along the same lines, Spencer wrote:

> What then is the resulting notion? The sleeper on waking recalls various occurrences and repeats them to others. He thinks he has

been elsewhere; witnesses say he has not; and their testimony is verified by finding himself where he was when he went to sleep. The simple course is to believe both that he has remained and that he has been away—that he has two individualities, one of which leaves the other and presently comes back. He, too, has a double existence. (Spencer 1901:137)

To cite just one piece of supporting ethnographic evidence here, when A. W. Howitt asked an Australian aborigine if he thought his *yambo* (soul) could leave his body, the native replied, "It must be so; for when I sleep, I go to distant places, I see distant people, I even see and speak with those that are dead" (quoted in d'Alviella 1908: 536).

One could easily tire of similar ethnographic examples of this sort since there is such a plethora of them. However, let me cite just one more among the hundreds available. The Shavante of central Brazil are convinced that "[d]reams and hallucinations are ... explained as experiences of the soul during its periodic wanderings outside the body" (Maybury-Lewis 1971:289). Dreams, then, not only suggest but prove to the "primitive philosopher" that there *is* such a thing as a soul, that it is separable from his body and thus in some sense independent of it. As such, he further reasons, it is able to leave him in sleep and capable of surviving the death of his body and going to join others like it in the land of departed souls.

Other Bases for Belief in the Soul

Although dreams were foremost among the experiences that suggested the existence of a dual self (one material and the other not), other experiences reinforced this notion. Trances, visions, seizures, derangements, and the like all contributed to the idea that a person had a second self that was in some ways different from—yet at the same time the same as—the individual himself: an *alter ego*, in other words. Then there were other universal phenomena, like shadows and reflections, which Spencer argued offered additional evidence to primitive contemplation of the existence of such an immaterial double. As he put it, "Shadows are realities which, always intangible and often invisible, nevertheless severally belong to their visible and tangible correlatives;

and the facts they present, furnish further materials for developing both the notion of apparent and unapparent states of being, and the notion of a duality of things" (Spencer 1901:118).

Moreover, Spencer continued, "If the rude resemblances which a shadow bears to the person casting it, raises the idea of a second entity, much more must the exact resemblance of a reflection do this" (Spencer 1901:119). And it is "the reflection that generates a belief that each person has a duplicate, usually unseen, but which may be seen on going to the water-side and looking in" (Spencer 1901:119–120). Pursuing the same thought, Spencer continued, "Can he not, standing at the water-side, observe that the reflection in the water and the shadow on the shore, simultaneously move as he moves? Clearly, while both belong to him, the two are independent of him and one another; for both may be absent together, and either may be present in the absence of the other" (Spencer 1901:120). Finally, Spencer concluded, "[W]ith such knowledge of the facts as he has, this interpretation"— that he has an immaterial double which accounts for such experiences—"is the most reasonable the savage can arrive at" (Spencer 1877:417). So then the notion of the soul, an entity *aggregating* and *integrating* a number of separate observations (such as dreams, trances, shadows, reflections, etc.), thus rises to a satisfying, unifying concept.

Tylor's summary of the matter was as follows: "Here then in few words is the savage and barbaric theory of souls, where life, mind, breath, shadow, reflexion, dream, vision come together and account for one another in some such vague confused way as satisfies the untaught reasoner" (Tylor 1931:344). Tylor was well aware of the impact that this new view of the roots of religion—once accepted— was to have on Western thought. Thus he declared:

> It need hardly be said that such a view of the origin of fundamental theological ideas is revolutionary. If it, or anything like it, can be proved to the satisfaction of the educated world to be the true view, then the generally received systems of theology must either be developed into systems in harmony with modern knowledge, or they must after a time be superseded and fall into decay. (Tylor 1877:142)

Here was a warning to theologians and clerics, only lightly veiled, that a secular interpretation of the origin of religion was now abroad in the land, ready to challenge their traditional creed. It was a theory that denied the validity of revelation and scriptural texts explaining the rise of religion—including Christianity—and was thus sharply at odds with prevailing, entrenched, and passionately held interpretations.

Tylor and Spencer Dispute Priority

The first struggle over this theory, however, was not between anthropologists on the one hand and theologians on the other; it was between the two men who had put it forward. And the issue was not over minor differences in doctrine but over matters of priority, amounting even to charges of plagiarism. Tylor cast the first stone in his review of the initial volume of Spencer's *Principles of Sociology*, asserting that Spencer's discussion of animism "followed lines already traced" by Tylor himself in his major work *Primitive Culture*. An exchange of letters between the two men, in which each attempted to substantiate his claim to priority and independence, followed in the pages of scholarly journals.

At one point in the debate, Tylor had contended that "in its main principles, the theory [of animism] requires no great stretch of scientific imagination to arrive at it, inasmuch as it is plainly suggested by the savages themselves in their own accounts of their own religious beliefs. It is not too much to say that, given an unprejudiced student with the means ... of making a thorough survey of the evidence, it is three to one that the scheme of the development of religious doctrine and worship he draws up will be an animistic scheme" (Tylor 1877: 143).

Spencer quickly seized on this admission and replied as follows.

Thus it appears that though the view held by Mr. Tylor, with which he identifies mine, "is plainly suggested by the savages themselves in their own accounts of their own religious beliefs"; and though I had before me an immense accumulation of such accounts deliberately prepared for generalization; Mr. Tylor thinks I must have had recourse to his lectures for my conclusions. (Spencer 1877:426)

Then Spencer delivered the *estoque*.

> [Mr. Tylor] says it is three to one that this doctrine will be
> arrived at by "an unprejudiced student" "making a thorough sur-
> vey of the evidence"; and yet though I was in possession of
> abundant evidence from many parts of the world, classified and
> abstracted as no student of such evidence ever had it before, Mr.
> Tylor takes the one chance against the three, and prefers to think
> that I did not draw the inference myself, but plagiarized upon
> him. (Spencer 1877:426)

Although the intellectual swordplay between two of the early
giants of anthropology makes fascinating reading, an impartial
examination of the evidence points to a familiar conclusion: here is
but one more example, so common (and so significant!) in the history of science, of an essentially simultaneous and independent formulation of a new theory.

As evidence that such a theory could be developed independently by someone familiar enough with the facts, listen to Sir John
Lubbock, writing the year before Tylor and Spencer first published
their views on the roots of religion.

> Dreams are intimately associated with the lower forms of reli-
> gion. To the savage they have a reality and an importance which
> we can scarcely appreciate. During sleep the spirit seems to
> desert the body; and as in dreams we visit other localities and
> even other worlds, living as it were a separate and different life,
> the two phenomena are not unnaturally regarded as the comple-
> ment of one another. Hence the savage considers the events in
> his dreams to be as real as those of his waking hours, and hence
> he naturally feels that he has a spirit which can quit the body.
> (Lubbock 1870:126)

Elaboration of the Theory

Tylor and Spencer, then, had hit upon a theory—one that, in my
opinion, has yet to be improved upon—uncovering the very earliest
manifestation of supernatural beliefs. Of course, although this may
well have been the actual germ of religious thinking, it was still only

its rudimentary nucleus. A great deal of evolution lay ahead before a simple belief in human souls could be elaborated and enriched into the enormously varied and complex religious systems that eventually grew out of it. And both Tylor and Spencer were well aware of all the development that was to come.

In his book *Anthropology*, Tylor put it this way: "Animism, or the theory of souls, has thus been shown as the principle out of which arose the various systems of spirits and deities" (Tylor 1931:371). Expressing it a bit more fully, he noted that "the notion of a ghost-soul as the animating principle in man, being once arrived at, is extended by easy steps to souls of lower animals, and even of lifeless objects, as well as to the general conception of spirits and deities" (Tylor 1877:142). And summing up, Tylor said, "Thus the spiritual series, beginning with human souls, extends on into other special classes of spirits, of whom some are mere minor demons, angels, elves, &c., while some few rise to the rank of great deities, controlling man and nature. There is no real break in the whole series of conceptions which begins with the human ghost and ends with the highest divinity" (Tylor 1877:151).

Support for the Tylor-Spencer Theory

It seems to me that in the almost one hundred fifty years since Tylor and Spencer first proposed it, there has been less recognition and acceptance of this theory than it deserves. It would not be amiss, then, to review some of the evidence and arguments in its favor.

First of all, there is the universality of the phenomenon that initially gave rise to a belief in an incorporeal "double" to every human being—primarily (but not exclusively) *dreams*. Everyone dreams and does so every night. Moreover, dreaming seems to be an ancient mammalian trait, so it was a phenomenon already common in the experience of our earliest human ancestors. Furthermore, dreams are vivid experiences, rich in intricate detail. To the person having them, they seem at the time to be absolutely real experiences. Moreover, one always appears to be the protagonist of one's dreams, so that to the Ego experiencing them they appear to be actually happening to oneself. At the same time, dreamers are assured by those around them that regardless of what they may think, they have not moved from the spot. Yet *something* surely did. What was it? What could have the power to move so easily and travel so quickly and effortlessly?

A second line of argument in favor of the Tylor-Spencer theory of the primacy of soul beliefs is their universality. In *Primitive Culture* Tylor wrote, "[S]o far as I can judge from the immense mass of accessible evidence, we have to admit that the belief in spiritual beings [meaning, in this case, souls] appears among all low races with whom we have attained to thoroughly intimate acquaintance" (Tylor 1871:I, 384). And in *Anthropology,* written some years later, he noted that "the best proof [of] how the earlier ... soul-theory satisfied the uncultured mind is that to this day it remains substantially the belief of the majority of the human race" (Tylor 1931:345). What other religious belief has anywhere near the same universal currency?

And those observations have been corroborated and strengthened in the century or more since they were first put forward. As much as religious beliefs vary among tribes and regions, belief in a spiritual entity in each person—an entity that is immaterial and can separate itself from the body, specifically the soul—remains ubiquitous and unvarying.

At the same time, one can point to the *tenacity* of soul beliefs. It may have been the earliest supernatural belief entertained but it still remains firmly entrenched in the corpus of religious conceptions. No subsequent religious belief has replaced it. Indeed, a belief in the soul is probably the hardiest and longest lived abstract idea in the entire history of human thought! All of these attributes of the soul solidify its position as the leading candidate for being designated the primordial "atom" of religious notions, and the germ out of which all additional religious conceptions have evolved.

Neurological Prerequisites for Religious Beliefs

Many questions still remain to be answered about the soul. For example, when was such a belief first formulated? This, of course, is a very difficult question to answer. Although we will probably never know, we can still speculate. We may ask, for example, was the hominid mind capable of fashioning an Acheulian hand axe also capable of conceiving of an immaterial human double? And there is the equally thorny question of what neuroanatomical stage of development our hominid ancestors had to attain before the conception of an incorporeal entity, distinct from the physical body, could have entered their minds. But even beyond that, assuming we could establish when this neurological *capacity* came into existence, when was it *actualized* in the form of the cultural concept of the soul?

Another question that naturally arises is this: was there one origin of soul beliefs or several? Again it is a question whose answer can only be guessed at. It seems probable that the idea of a soul, being a concept that springs so easily to mind once a certain threshold has been reached, must surely have occurred to our thoughtful Paleolithic forebears more than once. But by the same token, it seems likely that the idea of the soul—once it occurred to one group of hominids—would have been taken up readily by neighboring groups in contact with them, impressed by its utility in explaining what happens in dreaming. In that way the idea of a soul could have spread far and wide, and relatively quickly. It would appear, then, that its present-day universality probably owes a good deal more to diffusion than to multiple independent inventions. That is to say, there would have been a ready pattern of diffusion, coupled with retention and transmission to succeeding generations. It can be argued that when man created the soul, his first supernatural creation, he created well. Indeed, he created for the ages, giving rise to an entity that became ubiquitous, universal, enduring, and practically indestructible.

The Counter-Theory of Animatism

Let us return to the point at which Tylor's animism and Spencer's ghost theory—which amounted to the same thing—had appeared in print. What was the scholarly reaction to it? By and large it can be said that animism, as the scheme accounting for the very origin of religion, established itself as a credible hypothesis. But not all students of religion were ready to endorse it. R. R. Marett, for one, was prepared to propose a counter-theory. Animism, he maintained, was not the earliest form of religion at all. There had been, he argued, a *pre-animistic* stage of religion that he called *animatism* (Marett 1914:14).

Nature, wrote Marett, in "its more startling manifestations, thunderstorms, eclipses, eruptions, and the like, are eminently calculated to awake in … [primitive man] an awe that I believe to be arrows or beaten to death with a club, what *does* happen to it when its body has ceased to exist? Some time after the concept of the soul was hit upon—and probably not long after that—human imagination began to formulate ideas regarding what the "afterlife" of the surviving soul might be like. And in fact ideas about the nature of an afterworld became so rich and varied that they warrant a separate chapter in this book (Chapter 4).

The Extension of Soul Beliefs: Bush Spirits

In this chapter I will examine how, starting out with only the simple human soul, the concept of spiritual beings was gradually developed and expanded in a variety of ways. The notion of the soul came to be extended beyond human beings, so that eventually a whole new class of spirit entities was created. Tylor and Spencer agreed that this next step in the evolution of supernaturalism was marked by the emergence of a bewildering variety of so-called "bush spirits."

Quite possibly the first step in this process was assigning spirit doubles to animals, especially to those considered noxious or dangerous. Accordingly, Indian tribes of Amazonia believe that such animals as the jaguar, anaconda, caiman, electric eel, king vulture, and vampire bat are—or have within them—spirits. Even when connected with animals not regarded as dangerous themselves, bush spirits are almost always thought of as hostile to human beings, capable of causing harm and even death.

At some point human imagination became unbridled and spirit beings were created and assigned on a wholesale basis. Spirits were conjured up that had no prototype or counterpart in the real world, but were just spirits. Some of these mythical beings were fanciful or bizarre. They had strange visages, extra appendages, peculiar appetites, and fearful dispositions. Almost invariably they were antagonistic to human beings and thus objects of fear.

If at all possible, therefore, encounters with bush spirits are carefully avoided, for merely seeing one may prove one's undoing. Typical in their attitude toward spirits are the Sirionó of Amazonia, who—according to Allan Holmberg—believe the universe to be "peopled with detached evil spirits called *abacikwaia,* which are responsible for most of the misfortunes that befall the human race"

(Holmberg 1969:239). Another Amazon group, the Shavante, paint a similarly forbidding picture of the *wazepari'wa*, their assemblage of evil spirits: "They appear in various disguises, all of them terrifying. Sometimes they are like ordinary mortals, but their long matted hair hangs down to their waists and partly conceals their faces, which are indescribably sinister" (Maybury-Lewis 1971:290).

It is important to bear in mind that while generally feared, bush spirits are not revered or propitiated. As a rule they are not worshipped and it is unusual for prayers to be directed to them or for sacrifices to be offered on their behalf. For the most part, then, spirits are to be avoided rather than courted.

Reverential attitudes and forms of behavior are reserved largely for a higher category of supernatural beings—beings powerful enough to have attained, or at least approached, the status of gods. Only when they reach this level do we find supernatural beings playing the role of creators, lawgivers, benefactors, or bestowers. For the most part, bush spirits are merely annoyers, disrupters, or destroyers. Still, their role should not be minimized in the history of supernatural beliefs. After all, they were the forerunners of the culture heroes and powerful deities to come, whom we will deal with in Chapters 3 and 6.

It is a curious and no doubt significant fact that even though bush spirits are often identified with particular animals, they are usually thought of—and indeed represented as—anthropomorphic. When during the course of fieldwork I asked my Kuikuru and Amahuaca informants to draw an *etseke* or a *yushí* (their terms, respectively, for their bush spirits), almost invariably they drew them as *people*. This would seem to bolster Tylor's and Spencer's contention that the concept of the *human* soul came first and only later was it extended to actual animals and beyond. Bizarre as they might be otherwise envisaged, therefore, bush spirits still reflect the form and attributes of their creators—that is, of human beings. From early in prehistory, people projected what they knew best (i.e., themselves) into whatever in the external world they little understood. Tylor was indeed correct when he noted that "[m]an habitually ascribed to his deities [including their bush-spirit prototypes] human shapes, human passions, human nature" (Tylor 1871:II, 224).

na impersonator who fails in his trust may be choked to death by his mask during the ceremony" (Bunzel 1965:444).

Katcinas may be more striking and colorful than the spirits of most tribes, but they share with other spirit beings the fact that they inspire fear because they can cause harm. "It is said more often of the katcinas than of other supernaturals," says Bunzel, "that they are dangerous. The katcinas inflict the most direct and dramatic punishment for violation of their sanctity" (Bunzel 1965:443–444).

The Shaman as Spirit Mediator

We come now to another important role of supernatural agents in people's lives: the part that they play in causing—and treating—disease. Disease, of course, is a universal worry of mankind and the concept of the soul has provided a major element in primitive peoples' etiology of illness. The loss of one's soul is universally regarded as bringing on sickness. But if *loss* of one's soul is thought to produce illness, its *retrieval* is the obvious way of restoring health. And it is at this point that the shaman comes into the picture. The shaman was the world's first religious practitioner. His concern, though, was not primarily with abstruse theological doctrines; rather, he was occupied with very practical matters, especially diagnosing the cause of an illness and effecting a cure. It was the existence of the soul—so often regarded as the vulnerable element through which illness was thought to strike—that in all probability provided the underlying conditions for the invention of the shamans.

The soul being immaterial and elusive, there had to be someone—a specialist—who could enter the realm of the supernatural, where the soul ordinarily resides, and deal with it on its own terms. Since the loss of one's soul was considered a major cause of illness, retrieving it and re-implanting it in the victim's body became the indicated method of treatment. Thus in his practice a shaman typically enters the spirit world, communicates with the spirits, enlists their aid in making the diagnosis, and then takes steps to bring about a cure. By this means he is able to restore the patient's missing soul, which more often than not has been stolen by an evil spirit.

Just as human societies created the very spirits so often blamed for causing illness, by creating shamans as well they devised a way to counteract and overcome these spirits' malign effects. However, entering the world of the spirits is not something easily done, even by a shaman. He must usually induce a trance in some way, as by taking a narcotic like peyote or *ayahuasca*. In much of Amazonia, it is also achieved by smoking tobacco and inhaling or even swallowing the smoke. Once the shaman has crossed the threshold and entered the domain of the supernatural, he comes face to face with a whole host of spirits. These spirits know many things and, if properly approached, can be induced to reveal what they know.

Wherever one looks in the primitive world—be it Amazonia or aboriginal Australia—the principal causes of illness are the loss of one's soul (as already noted) and by having had an intrusive object (a magical dart) shot into one's body. To the student of primitive religion, such a wide distribution of related beliefs points strongly to these beliefs being extremely old—going back, no doubt, deep into the Paleolithic. And since these beliefs were first conjured up untold thousands of years ago, they have had time to diffuse around the world to places as remote and distant from each other as Tasmania and Tierra del Fuego.

But we are not quite finished with soul loss. Taking advantage of a soul's temporary absence, an evil spirit (some people believe) may enter a person's body and take possession of it. Such a seizure may bring on illness or even death. In cases of spirit possession, a shaman may be called upon to deal with the unwelcome invader and expel it. It is worth noting, by the way, that a belief in spirit possession is by no means restricted to simple societies. Though loath to diagnose it as the cause of a person's derangement, the Catholic Church nevertheless still recognizes spirit possession as—in extreme cases—an actual cause of physical or mental illness. Furthermore, the Church allows for the treatment of spirit possession by the procedure known as *exorcism*. An attempt is made in such cases to drive out the demon (perhaps even the devil himself!) who is deemed to have entered a person's body and taken possession of it. Here again we see that ancient supernatural beliefs are still very much with us.

The Profound Influence of Supernatural Beliefs

One cannot overestimate the influence that supernatural beliefs continue to exert over human beings. So profoundly convinced may a person become that he is possessed by an evil spirit—or that he is the victim of a spell cast upon him by a witch—that he may literally *think* himself to death. The celebrated Harvard physiologist Walter B. Cannon published an article in the *American Anthropologist* (1942) entitled "Voodoo Death," in which he described the precise physiological chain of events that might ensue should a person believe himself the victim of sorcery. A succession of worsening states, Cannon argued, might eventually lead to death through purely natural physiological means induced by fear. Such is the power that supernatural beliefs may come to have over human beings. No chimpanzee has ever *thought* itself to death, but people have.

Finally, let us take a step back and examine spirit beliefs as part of primitive people's relationship with the supernatural world that they created. Perhaps the first thing to restate and emphasize is how real and pervasive supernaturalism has become in human experience. The imagined but unseen world forms a vigorous half of the dualism so characteristic of primitive peoples. The material world, of course, came first. Its existence had to be recognized—it could hardly be denied. And it had to be adapted to by practical, objective, empirical means if humanity were to survive. But there remained that other aspect of existence, an artificial half that human beings did not find ready made for them but had to devise wholly from their imagination. This new world arose in an effort to explain things for which human beings—given the limited intellectual resources then available to them—could not otherwise account.

Language and culture provided early societies with the ability to raise questions that they could not yet answer in any realistic way. But human curiosity is strong and, once aroused, must be satisfied. And so it was that spiritual beings—supernatural creatures—were created to provide *some* kind of answers to those questions. To be sure, this observation is no recent insight of social science. It was, for example, offered by David Hume two hundred fifty years ago. "No wonder, then," wrote Hume, "that mankind, being placed in such an absolute ignorance of causes, and being at the same time as anxious concerning their future fortunes, should immediately acknowledge a dependence on invisible powers possessed of sentience and intelligence" (quoted in Harvey 2005:4).

An explanation of any sort always involves casting the unfamiliar into the terms of the familiar. And what did primitive peoples know most fully and intimately? Themselves. The explanation of puzzling events and phenomena that they devised, then, was to make them the result of the actions of beings much like people themselves. The spirits whom they created, though more fugitive and less tangible than actual human beings, were still very similar to them— only more powerful. They were endowed with the ability to fulfill the functions for which they were mostly created, to account for the evils and misfortunes all around. A double world thus came into existence: a material world given by the senses, and an immaterial one that was a gift of the imagination.

The spirit world—devised to satisfy man's craving to know— became, over countless millennia, a progressively more embroidered tapestry. With the human soul as the germ and the prototype, all manner of spiritual beings were conjured up, mythical creatures who engaged in a variety of activities—more often than not, evil ones. From a strictly scientific point of view, these spirit beings were, of course, completely illusory. But the natives' own belief in their existence was implicit and unquestioning. And in a certain sense, they were correct. As the anthropologist Leslie White used to say in class at the University of Michigan, "The spirits are *real*, all right. The question is, is the locus of their reality in the mind or in the external world?" And this remains the underlying—and overriding—question as we deal with supernatural beliefs that we encounter today.

The so-called "bush spirits," the principal object of this chapter, were for a time the only supernatural entities thought to exist over and above the human soul. Eventually, though, bush spirits began to evolve into a greater class of spiritual beings. Some of them became powerful and exalted enough to warrant being called gods. (And we shall trace the evolution of the gods in Chapter 6.) Even after true gods made their appearance on the stage of human thought, however, bush spirits continued to exist. They may have become secondary in importance, playing a subservient role to the more elevated gods, but they still retained certain spheres of activity. Though in time exceeded in strength and status, bush spirits will always be able to claim the distinction of being the direct ancestors of the very gods who ultimately pushed them into a subordinate position in the realm of human beliefs.

CHAPTER 3

Origin Myths:
Accounting for Things as They Are

Two things can be said with certainty about early man: he was profoundly ignorant, but at the same time he was profoundly curious. Many things in the world around him he did not understand, but wanted to. And his curiosity drove him to try to explain things whether he could grasp them or not. When ignorance of the workings of nature prevented him from forming an accurate notion of how things worked or how they came to be, he called upon another human attribute—his imagination—to fill the gap. Thus when a *naturalistic* understanding of something was beyond his reach, he made good on the deficiency by conjuring up a *supernatural* explanation. The result was the creation of *origin myths*. "It will be found," wrote the British ethnographer and traveler Sir Everard Im Thurn, "that a very large proportion of the [Guiana Indian] stories are attempts to account for the features of the world in which the Indian lives" (Im Thurn 1883:376).

Thus it was that early in prehistory human societies began to develop a body of stories designed to explain all manner of occurrences. It was the belief of the English anthropologist R. R. Marett, on one side of the issue, that religion arose from "a common plasm of crude beliefs about the awful and occult" (Marett 1909:xiii). But there was a counter-view that held the opposite notion—that supernatural beliefs arose from attempts to explain not the unusual and the remarkable, as Marett held, but rather the commonplace, the everyday, the recurring events of human experience. Why is there a sun in the sky? Why does night follow day? What gave rise to human beings and what happens to them when they die?

For tens of thousands of years—indeed probably hundreds of thousands—people have been crafting answers to such questions.

Creators and transformers come in a multitude of shapes and sizes, with a variety of powers and proclivities. A few are regarded as omnipotent, like the God of the Bible, but with lesser abilities and limited in the scope of their actions. They performed their appointed tasks and then stepped aside. Such supernatural beings are usually called *culture heroes* rather than gods. No sharp dividing line, though, separates culture heroes from gods. Often culture heroes arrived on the scene with human beings already present. In fact, they are often regarded as human beings themselves—perhaps even ancestors—but nonetheless with extraordinary ability, knowledge, and intelligence. They created features of the landscape, bestowed many things on the human race, taught people useful arts, and so on. Then, their job done, they generally retired from the scene. They may continue to exist—most likely somewhere in the sky—but play no further role in human affairs.

Gods, on the other hand, usually do more outright creating and less bestowing and instructing. They are, moreover, likelier to remain concerned and involved in world affairs, exercising their powers robustly and conspicuously. Perhaps the best way to clarify the distinction between culture heroes and gods is to give some examples of each of them at work.

Like other Panoan-speaking Indians, the Amahuaca of the Peruvian Amazon (with whom I have done fieldwork) have no gods. They do, however, have a culture hero named Rantanka; it was he who taught them how to hunt, how to make stone axes and bows and arrows, how to plant crops, and many other useful things. Most informants, however, believe that he is no longer living. Dead or alive, Rantanka exemplifies culture heroes in their actions: while he bestowed all manner of gifts on his people, he no longer is concerned with their lives.

S'ributwe and Prine'a—two culture heroes of the Shavante of central Brazil—are also typical of the breed. According to David Maybury-Lewis, who studied the tribe in the field, these culture heroes "created many things before flying up into the sky" and the Shavante "do not think of these figures as exercising an influence over their day to day lives" (Maybury-Lewis 1971:287). As evidence that S'ributwe and Prine'a are not to be regarded as gods, the Shavante never invoke them, nor are they "held up for emulation nor turned to for assistance" (Maybury-Lewis 1971:286).

Culture heroes also tend to have limited powers and functions. Take, for example, Nhokpôkti (Sky Woman) of the Kayapó of the interior of Brazil. One day she came down from the sky and became the secret lover of a Kayapó man. Returning to the sky briefly, she came back to earth with cuttings of bananas, manioc, sweet potatoes, and yams, planting them in her lover's garden. From these plantings, the Kayapó say, came all the crops that they enjoy today.

Some culture heroes, though, do begin to take on the broader creative functions of a full-fledged deity. Raven, well known to the tribes of the Pacific Northwest, plays such a role. Thus Lewis Spence has written that the Athabaskan groups of that region "attribute the phenomena of creation to a raven, whose eyes were fire, whose glances were lightning, and the clapping of whose wings was thunder. On his descent to the ocean, the earth instantly rose, and remained on the surface of the water" (Spence 1911:127). Among the Tlingit of Alaska, Raven is not only said to have created the first human beings but also the first animals and the sun, moon, and stars.

While culture heroes—after making their contributions to human welfare—generally leave the scene, they do not always do so willingly and cheerfully. In the mythology of many peoples, their departure is provoked by some human blunder. Often the people he benefited displease him in some way, as by disobeying his commands or instructions, prompting him to leave them as punishment. And once he has gone, he seldom returns. Indeed, the stupid or willful offending of a supernatural benefactor is a recurring theme in primitive mythology and often serves to explain the misfortunes that have afflicted the human race ever since.

Creator Gods in Action

Gods (as already noted) usually engage in greater creative acts than culture heroes and fail to disappear thereafter. Let us take a close look at one such god.

"Throughout Polynesia the creation of the world is assigned to Tangaroa, the god of heaven" (Gray 1911:174). Tangaroa faced a more difficult task than most creators. When he appeared there was nothing on the face of the earth but water, so one of his first tasks was to provide dry land. At first he tried to fish up soil from the bottom of the ocean, but just as land was beginning to appear above the surface, his line broke and the accumulated earth slumped back into the sea. Thus he was forced to dive to the bottom repeatedly, coming up with handfuls of earth each time. With this slowly accumulating amount of soil, he proceeded to create the land that today makes up the islands of Polynesia (Gray 1911:174).

There are several variants of this myth. One of them current in Hawaii and Tahiti accounts for the Polynesian islands rather differently. Existing in the form of a bird, Tangaroa was for a long time "a prisoner ... in a gigantic egg. He finally broke out of his place of confinement, and the two halves of the egg shell formed the heaven and the earth, while the smaller fragments became the islands" (Gray 1911:174).

Either way, so great were Tangaroa's exertions in creating the world that according to some accounts, "the salt sweat which streamed from him formed the ocean" (Gray 1911:174). In performing his creative acts, Tangaroa is often thought to have been assisted by his wife, who is said to have been "an enormous rock named O-te-papa, by whom he became the parent of the gods, the planets, the sea, and the winds" (Gray 1911:174).

It is not surprising that having the vast expanse of the Pacific Ocean to contend with, Tangaroa's primary function should have been to create dry land. What *is* surprising is that this should also have been the primary task of Earthdiver, a culture hero or god recognized by many tribes of central North America. Even in mid-continent it was believed that the primeval world lay beneath the waters, and so under many different guises—a duck, a grebe, a coot, a falcon, a toad, and so on, depending on the particular version of the myth—Earthdiver repeatedly dived to the bottom of the ancient sea and came up with clumps of earth to create the land.

Despite the fact that they were performed by gods or culture heroes of great strength, such creative acts were generally carried out with *pre-existing* materials. The idea of a god creating something out of nothing—*ex nihilo*—through the power of his thought alone is ordinarily regarded as too demanding a feat for most deities. Thus Tangaroa and Earthdiver, great as they were, did not create the soil with which they worked; they dug it up from the bottom of the sea. It was already there for them to use. Rare indeed is the idea, as in Hindu theology, of a "self-existent god" who "with a thought, created the waters" and almost everything else (Cheyne 1910:216). Unusual as well is the Judeo-Christian God of Genesis, a creator who at times fashioned his own raw materials when there was nothing in place with which he could work.

Creators versus Transformers

If he worked only with pre-existing materials, then the role of a culture hero or god was really more that of a *transformer* than an outright creator. For example, it is said of the Teutonic gods that they "are not real creators, but organizers forming the desirable objects out of pre-existing elements" (Youngert 1911:178). Thus Odin, Vili, and Ve were said to have made the world from the body of the giant Ymir who—in the early stages of Teutonic mythology—was slain by other god-giants. "From Ymir's flesh they formed the earth; from his blood the rivers, lakes, and seas; from his teeth and smaller bones they made the rocks and pebbles; while from the larger bones they formed the mountains. With the eyebrows they surrounded this new-made earth ... the whole being overtopped by heaven which was made out of Ymir's skull.... From the giant's brains the gods made the flying clouds and the mists" (Youngert 1911:178).

Similarly, among the Bakairí Indians of south central Brazil, "[t]he place of a genuine cosmogony is taken by a number of myths, accounting not so much for the ultimate origin as for the more or less miraculous arrangement and regulation of observed phenomena through the power of culture-heroes" (Lowie 1911:171). A common feature of these transformative acts involved making animals into human beings—and sometimes the other way around. Again, what we see here is *metamorphosis* at work rather than pure creation.

The Physical Environment Created

Generally speaking, in accounting for things as they are, the physical environment needs to be created at the start, setting the stage for the arrival of the first human beings. The primeval conditions of the

pre-human world are not always described in detail in the mythology of primitive peoples, however. In the beginning things are usually thought to have been shapeless, unsettled, and even turbulent. Sky
and earth are often thought to have been one, so that darkness
reigned. In that case a culture hero's first task may well have been
to separate the two, thereby making the world habitable. However,
the mythic being who (according to some accounts) performed the
Herculean task of lifting the sky from the earth's surface usually
could not rest on his laurels. Often he had the responsibility of keeping the two halves apart. Occasionally—as one of the many vicissi-
tudes that befalls the human race in mythological times—the sky
falls again, frequently with disastrous consequences.

While in most primitive cosmogonies the world itself had somehow to be created, a few societies maintain that it always existed. The
Wapishana, a tribe of the Guianas, have no tradition of the creation of
the world, but start out with a ready-made earth composed of land and
water, air and sky, just as it is today. And the Brazilian ethnologist Curt
Nimuendajú tells us that among the Sherente, "[t]he earth, the heavens, the underworld … are represented as having always been in existence and always continuing to exist" (Nimuendajú 1942:84).

The Origin of Night and Day

While the earth itself may be thought of as pre-existing, present-day
conditions on it generally need to be accounted for. Since primitive
peoples are unaware that the earth's rotation is responsible for the alter-
nation of night and day, this recurrence must be explained in some
way. The Book of Genesis explains it as follows. "In the beginning …
the earth was without form, and void; and darkness was upon the face
of the deep…. And God said, Let there be light; and there was light"
(Genesis 1:1–3). According to the Bible, then, night preceded day—a
belief shared by the ancient Greeks, who thought that "[l]ong before
the gods appeared, in the dim past, … there was only formless confusion … brooded over by unbroken darkness" (Hamilton 1960:65).

The Kamayurá of central Brazil concur. In their mythology night
preceded day. Consequently, their myths describe the great discom-
forts that perpetual night occasioned for their early ancestors. It was
so dark, they say, that people could not see to hunt or fish or plant,

and so they were slowly starving to death. To add further to their discomfort, the birds in the trees kept defecating on their heads. But then the Kamayurá discovered that there was such a thing as day, and that the birds owned it. So the ancient ones decided to get it for themselves. By a subterfuge they succeeded in capturing the king vulture, chief of the birds, and after several failed attempts they finally forced him to let them have day, which came to them decked in the brilliant plumage of the red macaw.

This is only half the story, though. The other half is that some peoples believe just the opposite—that originally there was no night but *only* day. The sun then stood at zenith all the time, its rays glaring down unmercifully on the ancestors. Sleep was difficult (if not impossible) and people lacked the privacy that only darkness affords. According to a Tenetehara myth, night belonged to an old woman who lived deep in the woods and kept it well hidden in several clay pots. It was Mokwani, the Tenetehara's female culture hero, who finally obtained night from the old woman and gave it to the tribe.

The Maué, yet another Amazonian group, have a somewhat more colorful story to account for the origin of night. In ancient times, they say, night was owned by the rattlesnake, who at the time lacked poison. An ancestor named Uánham gave the snake some poison and, in exchange, received a little basket containing night. Rattlesnake had warned Uánham not to open the basket until he got home, but so anxious were he and his companions to see night for the first time that— while still on the trail to their village—they could not resist opening the basket. Immediately night poured out and engulfed them all. And in the darkness that followed, the disobedient Uánham was bitten by the fer-de-lance and stung by scorpions, spiders, and centipedes, to whom the rattlesnake had distributed some of the poison he had received. Thus is disobedience punished mythologically!

Thunder and Lightning, Earthquakes and Eclipses

Night and day were only two of the natural phenomena that had to be explained in terms primitive peoples could understand. A way also had to be found to explain such spectacular meteorological occurrences as thunder and lightning. According to both the Yanomamö and the Kayapó, a tapir played a leading role in how the two phenomena came into existence. For the Yanomamö thunder came about when Feifeiyomi, the brother of a mythological character, killed a tapir and brought it back to the village. In the distribution of parts of the animal, however, Feifeiyomi got only the pancreas. Angered by this slight, he threw the tapir's pancreas into the sky where it miraculously gave rise to thunder.

Infuriated at receiving only the tail of a tapir that he had helped kill, Bekororoti—a mythical Kayapó being—challenged the men of the village to a club fight. As he brandished his sword club menacingly in the air, the world's first thunder and lightning issued from it. Bekororoti then ascended to the sky and ever since has remained there as master of storms, casting them down in vengeance on his fellow tribesmen.

Earthquakes—which come suddenly and unexpectedly and whose cause is quite beyond the ken of primitive peoples—are often explained in similar ways. A widespread belief is that the world rests on the shoulders of a culture hero who occasionally shifts his burden, whereupon the earth shakes. Among the Muisca of highland Colombia, it was a mythical being named Chibekachua who—growing tired of the weight on his back—every so often moved the earth from one shoulder to the other, thereby causing an earthquake (Lowie 1911:170).

Another natural phenomenon whose cause is unknown to simpler societies, but which is universally feared by them, is an eclipse. In the case of a solar eclipse, the fear is that people will forever lose their source of light and warmth. Almost invariably it is thought that some celestial creature is eating the sun (or the moon) and the common response is to make a great deal of noise in order to scare off the offending creature.

Occasionally, though, the explanation given for an eclipse is a bit different. In the nineteenth century, Sir Everard Im Thurn witnessed an eclipse among some Guiana Indians and reported:

> On one occasion, during an eclipse of the sun, the Arawak men among whom I happened to be, rushed from their house with loud shouts and yells. They explained that a fight was going on between the sun and the moon, and that they shouted to frighten, and so part the combatants (Im Thurn 1883:364).

On the other side of the world, in aboriginal Australia, we find a somewhat similar explanation of an eclipse, but one involving amorous proclivities rather than belligerence between the two celestial bodies. The Walbiri of the central desert of Australia explain a solar eclipse as being

> the covering of the Sun-woman by the Moon-man as he makes love to her. On the other hand, a lunar eclipse occurs when the Sun-woman successfully forces her unwelcome attentions onto the Moon-man, who constantly tries to evade her by following a zigzag path through the sky. (Norris 2008:18)

In these two cases, curiously enough, we find more than an inkling of the true cause of an eclipse.

To those ignorant of its real cause, a striking occurrence like an eclipse remains a frightening spectacle. Moreover, fear of eclipses did not end with the tribal stage of human thought; indeed, it lasted well into the Middle Ages! As the year 1000 approached and the end of the world was being widely prophesied, an army marching into battle under the banner of the German Emperor Otto I "was so terrified by an eclipse of the sun, which it conceived to announce this consummation, as to disperse hastily on all sides" (Hallam 1897: 6859).

The Origin of Celestial Bodies

But eclipses are not the only celestial phenomena for which primitive peoples developed supernatural explanations. Ever visible in the sky, the Sun and Moon themselves—as well as the stars and constellations—are explained in a variety of fanciful ways. We now know that by and large the stars are older than the earth. Yet primitive peoples around the world think just the opposite. Constellations are almost invariably regarded as mythological persons or animals who, after undergoing a series of adventures here on earth, ultimately wound up in the sky. This is certainly true for almost every constellation recognized by Amazonian Indians. The Amahuaca, for example, see in the sky a monkey's eye, a tapir's foot, a caiman's jaw, a one-legged man, and many more such objects. Moreover, a

With celestial phenomena thus accounted for, let us turn briefly to myths explaining some familiar features of the earth—for example, water. With no water to drink, the Juruna of central Brazil say that their ancestors were always thirsty until the sons of their culture hero Sinaá broke open a box containing water and created the first rivers. On the other hand, the rivers of their region (say the Paressí) were formed when a mythological woman jabbed a piece of wood into her body and great quantities of water poured forth from the aperture (Lowie 1911:172). The Akuriyo of Suriname, for their part, say that a small bird discovered a spot of water and dragged it around the landscape by his beak, creating the rivers and streams that exist all around them today.

The Creation of Human Beings

Having set the stage, it is time now to see how in primitive mythology the human race is thought to have come into being. In the Book of Genesis, which provides the creation myth for the Judeo-Christian religions, God—after first creating heaven and earth, the fish of the waters, the birds of the sky, and the beasts of the field—turned his attention to the creation of man. "And God said, Let us make man in our image, after our likeness" (Genesis 1:26). (Parenthetically, it should be noted here that rather than regarding the traditional Judeo-Christian God as *anthropomorphic*, it would be more correct to say—if we take this biblical passage quite literally—that man is *theomorphic*!)

But back to the creation of humanity. After having "formed man of the dust of the ground, and breathed into his nostrils the breath of life," (Genesis 2:7), God realized that the job was only half done. So He said, "It is not good that the man should be alone; I will make him a help mate for him" (Genesis 2:18). And in order to do this, "the LORD GOD caused a deep sleep to fall upon Adam, and he slept; and he [God] took one of his ribs, and closed up the flesh instead [i.e., in place] thereof" (Genesis 2:21). "And [with] the rib, which the LORD GOD had taken from man, made he a woman" (Genesis 2:22). "And Adam called his wife's name Eve" (Genesis 3:20). When at last he finished his acts of creation, God gave man "dominion over the fish of the sea, and over the fowl of the air, and over the cattle, and over all the earth, and over every creeping thing that creepeth upon the earth" (Genesis 1:26).

Lacking such a powerful god, however, most primitive peoples have creation myths that are somewhat less impressive. The Umotina culture hero Aipuku, for example, created the first members of the tribe from *macaúba* palm nuts—the men from the long nuts and the women from the short ones. Some Polynesians say that "[f]rom the decaying leaves and tendrils [of a certain creeper] ... came worms, which Tuli [the daughter of Tangaroa] pecked in two with her beak, thus forming human beings" (Gray 1911:175). According to the Guiana Caribs, Makunaima, a culture hero, "breaking off twigs and pieces of bark from a silk-cotton tree ... threw them far and wide around him. Some, as they fell, became birds; others fell into the water and became fish; others fell on land and became beasts, reptiles, men, and women" (Im Thurn 1883:376–377). Another myth accounting for the fauna of the Arctic region is that of the Eskimo deity Sedna, who cut off her fingers, which turned into seals, whales, walruses, and other mammals of the north.

Some myths that account for the origin of the human race involve what might be termed "copulative irregularities." Among the Amahuaca, for example, Hindachíndiya (the first man) had no wife and lived with his mother. One day he copulated with a *sapalla* fruit but all the children thus produced rotted. He then told his mother to bring him a *xopá* fruit, with which he also copulated, the fruit again becoming pregnant. Finding it growing large and black, he put it into his hammock and told his mother to tend to it carefully. But she was careless and, while sweeping the house, allowed the *xopá* fruit to fall to the ground. It broke open and out of it came a boy and a girl. The boy died but Hindichíndiya's mother raised the girl, and when she was old enough, Hindachíndiya married her. Out of this bizarre incestuous union came the ancestors of all the Amahuaca living today.

In almost all primitive mythology, a close association exists between animals and people. For one thing different species—human and non-human—talk freely to each other, but a lot more than this takes place between them. Countless episodes tell of the transformation of human beings into animals or vice-versa. Animal-human matings occur with some frequency, the Greek legend of

Leda and the Swan being perhaps the most familiar but by no means the only one. Indeed, it is not uncommon for animals to be regarded as the precursors and progenitors of the human race—a crude foreshadowing, in a way, of the theory of organic evolution!

"Just So Stories"

Accounts of animal origins often contain details of how they acquired their distinctive characteristics—accounts that Rudyard Kipling called "Just So Stories." The Kaingáng culture hero Kadjurukre, for instance, "was making another animal which still lacked a tongue, teeth, and several claws, when the day began to break. As he was unable to complete the animal in the daylight, he quickly put a thin rod in its mouth and said, 'As you have no teeth, feed on ants!'" (Lowie 1911:173). Thus did the anteater come into being. The Amahuaca have a fanciful way of explaining the plumage color of various birds. According to one such myth, a number of birds once bathed in the blood of the dying ogre Yowashiko, whose blood was at the same time red, black, yellow, and blue.

Far more than the color of a bird's feathers is accounted for mythologically, however. Sexual proclivities may be similarly explained. Thus the Cuiva of the Colombian llanos say that in ancient times a man who repeatedly had sexual relations with his sister was turned into a tapir, an animal regarded as being highly sexed.

The Ba-Ila of Africa might well have served Kipling as a model for his "Just So Stories," since among them such stories abound. "How Skunk Came to Be a Helper of Men," "Why the Wart-hog Lives in a Burrow," "Why Bushbuck Came to Have a Red Coat," "How Rhinoceros and Hippopotamus Became Distinct," and "Why There Are Cracks in Tortoise Shells" are just a few examples of this type of story recounted by the tribe (Smith and Dale 1968:II, 358–373).

Reaching the Surface of the Earth

In a way, though, we are jumping ahead of the story. We have still to account for how human beings came to live on the surface of the earth. Three possibilities exist: (a) they were created on the surface (or have always lived there); (b) they originated in the sky but somehow managed to come down to earth; and (c) they originated underground and later climbed up to the surface. In the myths of primitive peoples, all three possibilities are realized. For those societies whose ancestors originated in the sky, the problem was twofold: first how to discover that there *was* an earthly world below, and then how to make their way down to it. Typical of such myths is that of the Warao of the Orinoco delta, which is worth recounting in some detail.

In the beginning the forebears of the Warao dwelt in an upper world among the clouds where there were only birds to hunt. One day a hunter shot at a bird with such force that his arrow pierced the ground of the sky world and reached the earth below. Curious to see where his arrow had landed, the Warao hunter enlarged the hole and peered through it. For the first time in his life, he saw the earth and marveled at the deer, peccary, and other animals disporting themselves on it. Determined to explore this new land so rich in game, he took a long cotton rope, attached it securely to a tree, and lowered himself until he reached the earth. After retrieving his arrow, he walked around looking at all the wondrous new things, unknown in the skyworld. He shot a deer, cooked it, and—finding its meat delicious—took some of it with him when he climbed back up the rope to the sky world. There he told everyone about the great and bountiful land he had discovered and, eager to see it for themselves, they began to descend after him.

One by one the Warao started climbing down the rope, many of them reaching the earth. But when the hunter's pregnant wife started her descent, she became stuck in the hole in the sky because of her great girth. Impatient to descend, the people above her began to tromp on her head, trying to push her through the hole. But the harder they tromped, the more firmly wedged she became. And there she stayed, stuck firmly in the hole, stopping it up forever, thus preventing the rest of the sky people from making their way down to earth.

In the Bororo version of this myth, the rope used to descend to earth is cut and those still clinging to it tumble to the ground. In most versions of this myth, in fact, communication between the sky world and the earth is severed in some way, never to be re-established.

A number of tribes, though, *reverse* the process of how human beings first reached the earth's surface. According to the Mandan myth:

> [T]he entire nation resided in an underground village near a great subterranean lake. The roots of a grapevine penetrated to their habitation, and some of the more adventurous of them climbed up the vine, and were rewarded with a sight of the earth, which they coveted because of its richness in fruits and plentifulness of buffalo meat. The pioneers returned laden with grapes, the taste of which so enchanted the people that they resolved to forsake their subterranean dwelling for the delights of the upper world. Men, women, and children clambered up the vine; but, when about half the nation had ascended, a corpulent woman who was climbing up broke the vine with her weight, and by her fall filled up the gap which led to the upper world. (Spence 1911:127)

Amazonian tribes have such a myth as well. The ancestors of the Karajá once lived in the underworld. One day, though, they happened to come up to the surface of the earth and liked what they saw. However, their leader Kaboi warned them that if they stayed there, they "could not live to the old age that fell to the lot of their own people, for in the underworld the Indians attained a very great age, and died only when they were too old to move any part of their body. In spite of this warning, the people preferred to stay above ground. Accordingly, while their fellow-beings in the lower regions are still in the prime of life, the descendants of Kaboi's companions are destined to die" (Lowie 1911:172). Thus do the Karajá explain not only life on the surface of the earth, but the origin of death as well.

A very similar explanation of death occurs among the Nilotic Nuer a whole continent away. According to them, initially there was no such thing as death. People could freely go up and down on a rope between the earth and the sky. If they felt death approaching, by climbing up into heaven people could apparently have their lives replenished and extended. One day, though, a hyena (a symbol of death to the Nuer) cut the rope and thereafter no further communication between heaven and earth was possible. Those people who were on earth at the time the rope was severed were from then on subject to dying (Evans-Pritchard 1974:10).

Primordial Good Times versus Primordial Bad Times

Whether from the sky world or from underground, when the first human beings managed to make their way to the surface of the earth, what sorts of conditions did they find? Mythologically speaking, there are two schools of thought on the matter. First, there is the view we may label "primordial good times," which can be equated in a general way with the biblical Garden of Eden. According to this view, the early period of human existence was a kind of "golden age." Life was easy, pleasant, and serene. There were no mosquitoes, crops grew rapidly, tools worked by themselves, discord was unknown, childbirth was painless, disease did not exist, and so forth. Life was everlasting, or if people did die, it was only (as among the Kayapó) when they grew tired of living. And if death came unbidden, the Kamayurá tell of a ceremony designed to restore the dead to life.

But those halcyon days were not destined to last. Something went wrong and travail, misfortune, suffering, and death have been the lot of humanity ever since. To be sure, the ills that today beset the human race are usually given some kind of specific mythological cause. Everything was fine, people say, until one day someone disobeyed a commandment or instruction—Eve's eating of the infamous apple, for example—and as a result the whole of humanity was punished and has continued to suffer ever since. So widespread is this notion that the "fall of man" was a result of some sort of human perversity that we can label it the "Pandora's box syndrome," after a familiar example from Greek mythology. According to the story, "The gods presented … [Pandora] with a box into which each had put something harmful and forbade her ever to open it." However, "Pandora, like all women, was possessed of a lively curiosity. She *had* to know what was in the box. One day she lifted the lid—and out flew plagues immeasurable, sorrow and mischief for mankind" (Hamilton 1960:74).

A similar myth motif—which, from the biblical instance of it, may be labeled the "Tower of Babel syndrome"—purports to explain the present-day mutual unintelligibility of human languages. Some tribes in Amazonia, for instance, believe that all Indians were once a single people, living together and speaking a common tongue. But then something happened. Among the Tikuna it was an event as trivial as the eating of two hummingbird eggs, and thereafter people began speaking different languages, split into separate groups and dispersed far and wide.

In contrast to the "golden age" concept, some peoples believe in just the opposite—the idea of "primordial hard times." According to this view, the earliest form of human existence was one of scarcity and hardship. The earth was bleak and barren, and with regard to human understanding, innocence and ignorance prevailed. Without animals to eat, the Cuiva went hungry. Without fire to cook their food, the Shavante were forced to eat wood soft enough to chew, while the Kayapó were reduced to eating palm pith and fungi. Without stone axes the first Amahuaca, at the cost of great effort, were forced to use rodent incisors to cut through tree branches. The Yanomamö ate dirt and worst of all, in primordial times before water existed, the Akuriyo had to drink their own urine.

Amazonian Indians were delivered from these wretched conditions by their various culture heroes, of whom we have already spoken. Typically culture heroes appeared on the scene when the early human ancestors were already in existence but at a time when they still were benighted and impoverished, lacking many of the essential arts and skills of life and struggling ineptly to survive. The role of the culture hero was to enlighten their minds and ease their toil by bestowing on them certain valuable cultural elements, teaching them how to perform various essential tasks and instructing them in the correct forms of belief and behavior.

The Theft of Fire

Culture heroes were indeed good to their beneficiaries. They gave them all sorts of things essential for living. But curiously enough one important element of culture was almost never given freely by a culture hero and had to be *stolen*. This element was fire. With striking uniformity in the world of origin myths, fire was the possession of a miserly owner who refused to share it with people. Accordingly, it had to be obtained through some sort of ruse or trickery. The theft of fire is, in fact, one of the most widespread motifs in the entire spectrum of primitive myths. Who is not familiar with the Greek version of this myth in which Prometheus stole fire from Zeus, who would not make it available to mankind?

The ancestors of the Choctaw had no fire because "the People of the East" were too stingy to share it with them. They decided, therefore, that Buzzard (from the Animal People) should be sent to steal some. Buzzard put a smoldering brand in his head feathers but his feathers were burned as he flew away with the treasured fire, and thus today buzzards have no head feathers—their heads looking red and blistered, a relic of their valiant deed.

A somewhat similar theft-of-fire legend was told to me by the Amahuaca. Fire (the Amahuaca say) was originally owned by Yowashiko, a stingy ogre who would not make it available to any-one else. In order to get some for his people, an Amahuaca turned himself into a parrot and flew to Yowashiko's house. The ogre was away at the time but his wife innocently gave the parrot a burning brand, with which the bird flew to the top of a dead tree. When Yowashiko returned home, he was furious at his wife for her misstep and sent heavy rains in a desperate effort to extinguish the burning brand, which the parrot still held tightly in its beak. However, many birds—especially large ones like vultures and eagles—hovered over the dead tree, their wings outspread to ward off the rain drops and keep the burning brand from being extinguished. In this way the Amahuaca were able to gain possession of fire. However (and here we have yet another "Just So Story," parallel to that of the Choctaw), the brand that the parrot had stolen and was holding in its mouth burned down so far that it blackened the bird's beak, a mark the par-rot bears to this day—forever signaling its gallant contribution to the Amahuaca and indeed, one might add, to the rest of humanity as well!

Finally, we can say that as a result of thousands of years of elabo-ration and embellishment, many origin myths have come to be things of great ingenuity, subtlety, imagination, and even beauty. In a word, they have become literature. But with all their literary merit, origin myths remain—in the eyes of science—failed efforts, for they did not account accurately for the many and varied phenomena of heaven and earth. However, they did provide the best explanations that human beings could devise at the time—a time when the intellectual tools available to the human race were rudimentary in the extreme.

CHAPTER 4

The Life of the Soul After Death

According to the theory we follow here, the soul—the very first supernatural conception entertained by human beings—was incorporeal and immaterial. Therefore it was not susceptible to any of the ills to which flesh is heir and could not die a natural death or be killed. Accordingly, it was able to survive the death of its body. E. B. Tylor, the co-originator of *animism* (the soul theory), wrote as follows of how primitive peoples must have regarded what happened to the soul after death—specifically, where it went.

> Savage religions, as they assume the existence of the ghosts of the dead ... have to deal with the question where is the land of souls, the abiding place of these ghosts. This question they answer in a number of ways. Perhaps the most primitive may be that the ghosts continue near the corpse, or hover about among the living.... But it is also believed by many tribes that the land of souls is in some distant part of the country, or on mountain-tops or remote islands, or down in some cavernous recess or under-world below the earth, or up in the sky. (Tylor 1877: 148–149)

In this chapter we will examine the range of answers that contemporary primitive peoples use to explain what happens to a dead person's soul. We can presume that the answers will shed some light on what these conceptions were like when people first contemplated the question many thousands of years ago.

Let us begin with the immediate problem posed by death. As people died something had to be done with their remains. The corpse had to be disposed of in some way; it could not be left to simply decompose. Accordingly, various methods were hit upon to get rid of it, interment and cremation being the principal ones. But this took care only of the material remains of the deceased. What about the *immaterial* remains—the soul—now suddenly freed from the body and become a ghost? The abrupt transition between life and death, marking a categorical change in a person's status, must have been noted. Among primitive peoples today, it is often recognized terminologically. Thus the Kuikuru call the soul of a living person *akuŋa*, but as soon as death occurs it becomes known as an *añá.*

As much as individuals were beloved during life, as soon as they die their soul becomes an object of apprehension and even dread. Almost universally a dead person's soul—a ghost—is regarded as potentially malevolent and therefore dangerous. Funerary rituals are in large part intended to ensure that the ghost will leave the area and not stay around to trouble the living. But after that the soul is expected to proceed to the afterworld, wherever that happens to be. Ghosts, understandingly resentful of their death, are often thought to be vengeful. So if not correctly buried, or if their graves are not properly tended thereafter, they are quite capable of returning to their community and haunting the living.

The Creation of the Hereafter

As Tylor suggested, in the early history of supernatural beliefs before afterworlds had been conceived of, ghosts (having nowhere to go) may have been thought to simply linger around the campsite. Eventually, though, their constant presence among the survivors became unnerving and even threatening, so some solution to the problem had to be devised. The answer was to create a *hereafter*— an afterworld—a place where dead souls were *supposed* to go, leaving the survivors alone and in peace. And since this afterworld was entirely a human invention, people were free to endow it with whatever attributes they wished.

Among a number of contemporary primitives, the soul of a dead person—reluctant to depart the scene—does not begin its journey to the afterworld immediately after burial. The Central Eskimo of Davis Strait, for example, "believe that … [the ghost] lingers for three days with the body" (MacCulloch 1920:825). Similarly, according to Zuni beliefs, "The ghost hovers round the village for four nights after death" (MacCulloch 1920:824). A few societies, like the Abipones of the Gran Chaco, are even reported not to have a definite afterworld to which their departed souls can go (MacCulloch 1920:819). But this is unusual; by far the greater number of societies believe in an afterworld of some sort. Our next step, then, is to consider what beliefs exist about the nature and location of this afterworld. In so doing I will draw heavily (as I have already) on J. A. MacCulloch's excellent survey of afterworld beliefs, presented in the article "State of the Dead" in Hastings's *Encyclopaedia of Religion and Ethics* (MacCulloch 1920).

The Location of the Afterworld

Societies differ widely in where they believe the afterworld to be. Most think of it as a village and locate this village in the sky, but there are many exceptions. A number of peoples place the afterworld somewhere on earth, usually in some distant spot. Thus according to the Naga Hill people of Assam, it is on "a high hill to the west"—a favored position with primitive peoples, according to Tylor, because that is where the sun sets (Tylor 1877:149). The Witoto of Amazonia also place the afterworld in the west (MacCulloch 1920:824), while the Toda of southern India not only locate it in that direction but also place it beneath the surface of the earth.

The Seri of Baja California are among those societies that also locate the village of the departed underground, believing that by going there dead souls are returning to where their ancestors originated (MacCulloch 1920:821). At death a Zuni soul heads for the "dance village," "the abiding-place of the council of gods, situated in the depths of a lake, and containing the great ceremonial house of the gods." From there the soul proceeds to a place deep underground, from whence—like the Seri—the Zuni believe they originally came (MacCulloch 1920:824).

Best known of all subterranean afterworlds is no doubt that of the ancient Greeks. Unlike most afterworlds, though, it was "a dismal, cheerless abode, hateful alike to gods and men" (Keller 1911:105). According to one scholar, "[T]he prevailing idea [in Homeric Greece] is that the dead, if they receive their due rites of fire and interment, abide, powerless for good or evil, in a shadowy *sheol* in the House of Hades." However, if the dead were not correctly buried, "they wander

Massim region of New Guinea, souls often fight—and if in one of these celestial combats a soul is killed, it dies for good (MacCulloch 1920:822). And not only may a Kuikuru soul perish by slipping off a log bridge, it may also be killed in one of the Kuikuru souls' recurring battles with the souls of the dead birds, whose village is nearby. Moreover, if a soul dies in this way, it is destined to be devoured by the dreaded double-headed vulture Ogomïgï, chief of the dead birds.

An easier and less eventful journey to the afterworld is enjoyed by the soul of an Omaha, who travels there along the Milky Way, considered to be the path of the spirits on their way to the hereafter. On this journey they are helped by an old man who directs "the spirits of the good and peaceable by a short route to the region of souls" (MacCulloch 1920:824).

The Choice of Afterworlds

However, when departed souls reach the sky, they do not all automatically end up in the very same place. The Kuikuru, for instance, say there are *three* villages of the dead. In addition to the one to which most souls are supposed to go, there are two others: one for those who died a violent death and one for those who died by poisoning. Since the latter two villages have many fewer members, they are anxious to increase their numbers. Accordingly, they try to entice new souls, walking along the path, to stay with them by gesturing and calling out to them as they wend their way toward the main village. Should the new soul look in the direction of the calls, instead of keeping its eyes fixed straight ahead, it is obliged to join those other souls and remain in their midst forever.

Sometimes the manner of dying determines the paths taken by a soul on its journey to the hereafter. Among the Trobriand Islanders, we are told, "[a]ccording to the causes of death—by magic, by poison, or in war—the spirit traverses a different road to Tuma [the spirit land, the path] for spirits of men killed in war being the best, by poison not so good, and by magic the worst" (MacCulloch 1920:826).

To those steeped in the Christian notion of the hereafter, with heaven being a place where good is rewarded and hell where evil is punished, it may be surprising to learn that according to most primitive societies, all souls by and large go to the same place. And if they do go to different places, just where they end up depends more on how they *died* than on how they *lived*. We have already seen this to be true of the Kuikuru. It is also true among the Nagas, where "those dying in battle go to one place; those who have their ears split to another; those dying in childbirth to a third" (MacCulloch 1920:824). And although all Hidatsa souls went to the same Ghost Village, suicides were said to occupy their own separate place in that village (MacCulloch 1920:824).

Rewards and Punishments in the Hereafter

Most societies, as we have seen, believe that all souls go to the same village of the dead regardless of how they behaved during their lifetime. The evaluation of a person's conduct here on earth, a Last Judgment in Christian terms, is not characteristic of simple societies. Generally speaking, it is a feature of complex cultures in which supernatural sanctions have been superadded to secular ones in an effort to effect stricter social control over the populace. Thus, for example, Sir Everard Im Thurn—who traveled among the Indians of British Guiana many years ago—wrote that "[a] belief in the reward or punishment of [human souls] ... after death for the good or evil which they did when in the body, is created only by religion at the moment when it begins to ... enforce morality; ... this stage has by no means been reached by the Indians of Guiana" (Im Thurn 1883:359). Evidently ancient Greece had not reached that stage either, for, writing of notions of the afterworld in Homeric times, the classical scholar Oskar Seyffert tells us that the early Greek "knows nothing of the future rewards of the righteous, or indeed of any complete separation between the just and the unjust, or of a judgment to make the necessary awards" (Seyffert 1995: 265).

There are, we should note, exceptions to this rule. In the beliefs of primitive peoples, we find occasional adumbrations of some kind of judgment being passed on a soul newly arrived in the hereafter. At first there is no official judge—no St. Peter—to decide who goes where. It "just happens." The souls of bad people somehow simply fail to make it to the afterworld. The Shavante of central Brazil, for example, "believe that evil-doers and wicked people never reach the village of the dead. They are destroyed on the way" (Maybury-Lewis 1971:289). Among the Temi of New Guinea, the resident souls there act as judges, deciding among themselves whether a new soul should be admitted to the afterworld or turned away (MacCulloch 1920:823).

The sixteenth century French missionary Jean de Léry gave the following account of what determines a Tupinambá's fate when it reaches the hereafter. "Some which have been virtuous, i.e., avenged them of their enemies and eaten many [the Tupinambá were redoubtable cannibals], fly beyond the mountains to join their ancestors, where they lead a joyous life in pleasant gardens. Souls of cowards, who did not care to defend their land, are violently carried away by Aygnan [an evil deity] and live in torment with him" (quoted in MacCulloch 1920:825).

An amusing—but at the same time instructive—example of a soul's purported judgment upon reaching the hereafter is described by Napoleon Chagnon for the Yanomamö. While on its journey to the land of the dead, a Yanomamö soul meets

> a spirit named Wadawadariwä, [who] asks the soul if it has been generous or stingy during mortal life. If the person has been stingy and niggardly, Wadawadariwä directs the soul along one path—leading to a place of fire: *Shobari Waka*. If the person was generous with his possessions and food, he is directed along the other path—to *hedu* proper, where a tranquil semi-mortal existence continues. The Yanomamö do not take this very seriously, that is, do not fear the possibility of being sent to the place of fire. When I asked why, I got the following kind of answer: "Well, Wadawadariwä is kind of stupid. We'll all just lie and tell him we were generous, and he'll send us to *hedu*. (Chagnon 1997:112–113)

This account leads me to make two observations. First, the passage shows that primitive peoples are not always overawed by their supernatural beings, bowing down to them unquestioningly. Nor are their spirit beings, whatever their attributes, always omniscient and discerning, but—as in this case—they can sometimes be fooled.

And second, the reported existence of a fiery "hell" sounds suspiciously as if the group might at some point have been exposed, directly or indirectly, to some Christian influence regarding the hereafter.

Christian Notions of the Afterworld

Here might be the place to discuss Judeo-Christian notions of the afterlife. To be sure, both Judaism and Christianity inherited from their prehistoric ancestors the very old belief in a separable soul and an afterworld to which it proceeds after death. The ancient Hebrews had the concept of *sheol*, a place not unlike the Underworld of the Homeric Greeks, to which it is often compared. Much like the afterworld presided over by the Lord of Hades, "Sheol is the place of departed spirits. Both the righteous and the wicked go there" (Harris 1975:1572). And this remained essentially the view of the hereafter described in the Old Testament.

In the New Testament, however, heaven and hell enter the picture as sharply distinguishable places, Christ himself discoursing on them. Heaven is where the souls go of those who have been worthy and whose names have been inscribed in the Book of Life. They are the righteous who go to dwell with God in unending happiness. As described in the Book of Revelation, in heaven "God shall wipe away all tears ... and there shall be no more death, neither sorrow, nor crying, neither shall there be any pain" (Revelation 21:4).

Hell, however, is quite another matter. If a person's name does not appear in the Book of Life—a ledger that records his or her good deeds while alive—the soul is destined for hell (Revelation 3:5, 20:12). Several passages in the Bible tell of the horrors of hell, "the terrible agonies of the soul as it suffers endless remorse in eternity to come" (Killen 1975:779). It is Christ who, in the New Testament, "gives the fullest teaching about hell" (Killen 1975:779). For example, Jesus says to John, "I ... have the keys of hell and of death" (Revelation 1:18).

The New Testament takes pains to itemize those most in danger of going to hell. They are "the fearful, and unbelieving, and the abominable, and murderers, and whoremongers, and sorcerers, and idolaters and all liars" (Revelation 21:8). As for the nature of hell kimos, in order to contrast their future life with the harsh conditions under which they normally live, say that their afterworld "abound[s] with deer which are easily caught, and there is neither ice nor snow, trouble nor weariness, and spirits there sing and play without end" (MacCulloch 1920:825).

Typical of an agreeable afterworld is the one that David Maybury-Lewis describes for the Shavante.

> Once the soul arrives in the village of the dead, its troubles are over. It is a huge village, situated at the "root of the sky" and as far to the east as it is possible to travel. It is built on the same pattern as those of the living, but with more houses than have ever been seen in a single community before. It is a place of abundance, where life is easy and food plentiful and the souls of the dead spend their time there singing and dancing. (Maybury-Lewis 1971:289)

Indeed, many accounts of the hereafter emphasize the singing, dancing, and feasting to which souls can look forward once they arrive there. The Pima, being among them, describe life in the land of departed souls as marked by unending rejoicing and gladness (MacCulloch 1920:822). The natives of Slade Island off the southeastern coast of New Guinea paint a particularly inviting picture of Bwebweso, the village of the dead in the sky. It is a place of eternal youth where husbands and wives are reunited, and where children are born and mature but never grow old (MacCulloch 1920:826).

Some societies presume to know a great deal about life in the hereafter. The residents of Sia Pueblo, for example, say that they learned these details from people who fell into a swoon, temporarily visited the afterworld, and (recovering) returned and reported back to the living what they had witnessed. The story they told was of a reverse afterworld, where the spirits of the dead sleep by day and work by night, following the subterranean course of the sun in the underworld (MacCulloch 1920:818, 824). The Kuikuru are likewise convinced that they know all about the hereafter since a living Kuikuru is said to have visited the village of the dead in the sky—invited there by his dead brother—and, after his return to earth, gave a faithful account of everything he observed.

Departed Souls Contact the Living

Once in the afterworld, the dead do not usually forget about the living. The Omaha say that "the dead still take an interest in the affairs of earth and can revisit it" (MacCulloch 1920:824). As a matter of fact, the ability of dead souls to return to earth and mingle with their living relatives is frequently cited. The *baloma*, the Trobriand spirits of the dead, "can revisit the earth from time to time, where they play tricks" on the living (MacCulloch 1920:826). The Shavante report that "[o]nce the soul has established itself in the community of the dead it can come and go with impunity. When it comes back to visit the living, Shavante are not afraid of it, since such souls are generally thought of as having the well-being of their kinsmen at heart." Indeed, the Shavante "seek and welcome the advice and assistance of the souls of their dead kin" (Maybury-Lewis 1971: 287).

On those occasions (reported at times by some tribes) when marauding souls come back to haunt the living instead of returning for a friendly visit, there are generally ways to combat the menace. In such cases, say the Hottentot, "a shaman may be called upon to exorcise the ghosts" (MacCulloch 1920:820).

Reincarnation and Transmigration

Reaching the afterworld is not always the end of the story, however. In some cases the soul may be said to undergo a further transmutation. It may, for example, be reincarnated into the body of another human being, especially that of an infant. According to the Oglala-Dakota, the soul of a deceased person ascends to the stars; each time a child is born, their god Skan takes one of these souls, plucks it out of the sky, and implants it in the body of the newborn babe (Radin 1985:xxxv).

Through the process of *transmigration*, the soul of a deceased may even enter the body of an animal. The ancient Egyptians are reported to have been the most thoroughgoing of all transmigrationists. It was their belief that the human soul "wandered through all the species of animals after the death of the body, returning to a human frame after three thousand years of transmigration" (Haeckel 1992:135).

Sometimes, as among the Dogrib of northern Canada, transmigration was considered a form of punishment and the soul of a wicked person was condemned to become a wolf (MacCulloch 1920:827). Among the Eskimo (firm believers in transmigration themselves), a woman would not eat walrus, for example, "because her [dead] husband's soul had adopted it as a temporary habitation." The *angakok* or shaman informed her what animal her late husband's soul had entered so she could avoid eating its flesh (MacCulloch 1920:827).

For the same reason, many tribes of western Amazonia will not kill a deer, since they believe that after a few temporary abodes (such as the body of an owl), deer became the ultimate repository of human souls. Curiously enough, the Mohave of North America also see the soul inhabiting the body of an owl after first having assumed the form of some other animal. Then—after dying for a third time—the soul becomes a water beetle, until changing at last into thin air (MacCulloch 1920:827). Not to be outdone, the soul of an Efate of the New Hebrides passes through no less than six stages before finally becoming extinguished (MacCulloch 1920:826).

But the most elaborate—and poetic—metamorphosis undergone by any human soul is perhaps that reported for the Jívaro (Shuar) of eastern Ecuador. The "true soul" of a Jívaro, the ethnologist Michael Harner tells us, "after existing for a span of years equivalent to a human lifetime, dies and changes into a certain species of giant butterfly … called wampan…. After a length of time about which the Jívaro are uncertain, the wampan finally has its wings damaged by raindrops as it flutters through a rainstorm, and falls to die on the ground. The true soul then changes into water vapor amidst the falling rain. All fog and clouds are believed to be the last form taken by true souls. The true soul undergoes no more transformations and persist eternally in the form of mist" (Harner 1972:151).

CHAPTER 5

The Later History of Soul Beliefs

The idea of the soul, the initial supernatural conception of humanity and the basis of all the religious beliefs that followed it, was carried over into Western thought. The soul was already a well-established part of early Greek folk beliefs long before it became the object of scrutiny and speculation by Greek philosophers. In journeying to the Underworld, the soul of an ancient Greek—after becoming detached from its body—came to the River Styx with its poisonous waters. Once it arrived there, it was ferried across the river by the boatman Charon, who had to be paid an *obol*—a Greek coin—for performing this service. Guarding the gates of the Underworld (which was presided over by the god Hades) was the three-headed dog Cerberus, who welcomed souls to the Underworld but barred them from ever leaving it should they attempt to do so. Thus the soul was destined to remain there, living a joyless—if not a miserable—afterlife.

The Concept of the Soul in Greek Philosophy

The existence of the human soul was a firm, universal, and unquestioned belief among the early Greeks of Homeric times. Even the early materialist philosophers such as Democritus (460–370 B.C.) and his follower Epicurus (342–270 B.C.) accepted the soul as real, although they insisted that it was no vaporous essence but was made up of small bits of solid matter. Thus they taught that "the soul consists of fine, round, smooth atoms like those of fire, very mobile and fluid, permeating the whole body" (Needham 1955:230), and it was "in their motions the phenomena of life arise" (Needham 1955; Tyndall 1874:4). More specifically, Democritus thought that "[t]here are channels in the eyes, ears, and nose along which the effluent atoms pass to collide with the atoms of the soul" (Campbell 1967:180).

69

The concept of a soul continued to be of interest to Greek philosophers, who elaborated it in a variety of ways. For instance, according to Bertrand Russell, Pythagoras (582–507 B.C.) "founded a religion, of which the main tenets were the transmigration of souls and the sinfulness of eating beans" (Russell 1945:31)!

But it was in the work of Plato (427–347 B.C.) and Aristotle (384–322 B.C.) that the soul received its closest scrutiny and greatest elaboration. Plato dismissed out of hand Democritus's notion that the soul was a material entity or that it had material constituents. For him it was an immaterial, incorporeal essence. As an idealist he found Democritus's materialist philosophy anathema, and in fact the story is told that in his old age, Plato "desired to collect all the works of Democritus and burn them to ashes" (Needham 1955:230).

Plato believed that people have two souls, one immortal and the other mortal. The immortal soul, he thought, was located in the head and the mortal one in the chest (Russell 1945:147–148). Furthermore, he professed to know a great deal about the characteristics and ultimate fate of human souls. He believed, for example, that one soul had been created for each star in the sky. Moreover, he was convinced that "[s]ouls have sensation, love, fear, and anger, if they overcome these, they live righteously, but if not, not. If a man lives well, he goes, after death, to live happily forever in his star. But if he lives badly, he will, in the next life, be a woman; if he (or she) persists in evil-doing, he (or she) will become a brute, and go on through transmigrations until at last reason conquers" (Russell 1945:145).

Aristotle too paid great attention to the soul. In fact, he wrote an entire book—*On the Soul*—about it. (It was he who coined the word *entelechy* to designate the soul, a term that, as we shall see, was to be resurrected two thousand years later.) Aristotle's notion of the soul derived basically from Plato, but he wrote more extensively about it than had his teacher. For example, Aristotle thought the soul was "located or at least concentrated in a central governing place in the body, the heart." At one point he, like Plato, held that human beings had two souls, one of which "becomes all things, just as light makes potential colors actual." The second soul is "separable, impassive, and unmixed, and only when it is separated does it have its true nature, immortal and eternal" (Kerferd 1967:158). Unlike Plato, however, Aristotle believed that the human soul was not capable of existence apart from the body with which it was associated.

It is significant, however, that Greek philosophers of every school accepted the existence of the soul. Beliefs may have varied about its *nature* but no one doubted that there actually was such a thing. Again, it is worth emphasizing that the soul was not only the first supernatural belief entertained, but also the most persistent and enduring.

The Roman poet Lucretius (99–55 B.C.) was a follower of Democritus and Epicurus and, like them, both an atomist and a materialist, and thus had a similar conception of the soul.

> Between the mind and the soul there is a close connection
> And they are made out of a single substance.
> (Lucretius 2005:79)

> [T]he mind and the soul
> Are material: for they propel the limbs
>
> . . .
>
> All the rest of the soul is diffused through the body
> And moves at the inclination of the mind.
> (Lucretius 2005:80)

Lucretius also believed that the soul was "subject to the laws governing the atoms and must perish accordingly with the body" (Needham 1955:231).

The Soul as Described in the Bible

In view of the degree of attention paid to it by Greek philosophers, it is surprising to find how little is said about the soul in the Bible, either in the Old Testament or the New. Its existence is simply taken for granted; virtually no interest is shown in substantiating its existence, describing its general nature, or specifying its particular features.

The first biblical mention of the soul appears in Genesis 2:7, in which we are told that God formed man out of dust "and breathed into his nostrils the breath of life, and man became a living soul." At this point no mention is made of a *spirit* distinct from the soul. Elsewhere in the Bible, though, there is an occasional suggestion that the two may have been considered separate entities. Thus I Thessalonians 5:23 distinguished between soul and spirit, while Hebrews 4:12 says that the word of God is "sharper than any two-edged sword, piercing even to the dividing asunder of soul and spirit." This passage implies that while the two may have been thought of as distinct, they were nevertheless regarded as very intimately connected.

The distinction between soul and spirit, however, is rarely made in the various books of the Bible. In fact, elsewhere in the Scripture when the word "spirit" occurs, it is used synonymously with "soul." Thus Ecclesiastes 12:7 tells us that on Judgment Day "the spirit shall return unto God who gave it." And again we read in Ecclesiastes 3:21: "[T]he spirit of man that goeth upward and the spirit of the beast downward to the earth" (see also Matthew 10:28, Romans 13:1, Hebrews 12:28, and I Corinthians 2:14). This latter passage, incidentally, clearly indicates that the author of Ecclesiastes believed that animals had souls too, even though they were destined for a lesser afterworld.

As to the very origin of souls, it was the view of Jerome (340–420), one of the Church fathers, that "God was daily making new souls to fit the new bodies which were being made by human generation" (Smith 1955:305). At the risk of repetition, let me point out that *one thing* all the major religions have in common—Christianity, Judaism, Islam, and Buddhism—is a belief in the *existence* of a soul. Buddhists are sometimes said not to believe in a god at all but they *do* believe in souls! Indeed, the Dalai Lama, the highest ranking Buddhist on earth, is thought to be the reincarnated soul of the Dalai Lama who immediately preceded him.

Ideas concerning the human soul proposed by the earlier Greek philosophers continued to be held long after them by thinkers of Greco-Roman times. The neo-Platonist philosopher Plotinus (205–270), for example, believed that "matter could not exist if soul had not created it, and, if soul did not exist, matter would disappear" (Russell 1945:293).

The Church Fathers Discourse on the Soul

For a good part of the Middle Ages, the ideas of Aristotle dominated much of Scholastic thinking. If the answer to a major question were not to be found in the Bible—and, as we have seen, the soul is scarcely mentioned there—it was to the writings of the great Aristotle that the Scholastics turned. Intense debates continued for centuries about just what Aristotle had meant by his various portrayals of the soul, with no real resolution forthcoming.

Several points of view regarding the soul were advanced by Church fathers such as Augustine. In *The City of God*, he painted man's existence on earth as a burden, troubled and transitory, the real goal of life being to leave it—thus allowing the soul to attain salvation in the hereafter where, unlike the soul of the ancient Greeks, it could count on spending a pleasant eternity.

It need hardly be said that the very existence of an afterworld, whether in Christianity or any other religion, *presupposes* the existence of souls—incorporeal entities that, once disengaged from their material counterparts, are free to proceed there. The physical bodies associated with these souls, on the other hand, inseparable from the material substance out of which they were made, cannot ascend to the afterworld. In Christianity it is generally believed that a bodily ascension to heaven is a privilege reserved to the religion's founder Jesus Christ and his mother the Virgin Mary, and is not vouchsafed to anyone else.

However, there is actually a difference of opinion in Christian circles about whether the material body can actually ascend into heaven, some believers holding that indeed it can. For example, E. B. Tylor quoted the following: "[O]n the 5th July, 1874, the Bishop of Lincoln preached against cremation, as tending to undermine the faith of mankind in a bodily resurrection" (quoted in Tylor 1877: 147).

In connection with the Catholic Church's prohibition on cremation—only recently rescinded—Bertrand Russell wryly observed, "It is apparently thought more difficult for Omnipotence to reassemble the parts of a human body when they have become diffused as gases than when they remain in the churchyard in the form of worms and clay" (Russell 1997:114).

Of the Church fathers, none had more to say about the soul than Thomas Aquinas. First of all, Aquinas reiterated the universal belief about the soul that it was immaterial: "By its very definition the soul is entirely form and not susceptible to any admixture of matter." But, he added, "[B]y reason of the nature of its own essence," the soul was capable of being united with a body (Aquinas 1993:204). It was no mere happenstance either, said Aquinas, that this should be the case: "[T]he capacity of union with the body is, on the contrary, essential to the soul and characteristic of its nature" (Aquinas 1993:204–205).

Moreover, Aquinas affirmed, the body was not a mortal coil to be despised and shucked off at death: "The body is not the prison of the soul, but a servant and instrument placed by God at its disposal; the union of the soul and the body is not a punishment of the soul, but a beneficent link by which the human soul will attain to its complete perfection" (Aquinas 1993:206).

The age of exploration brought with it an acquaintance with many native peoples, thus presenting an urgent problem to the Catholic priests who were sent to the New World to accompany the Conquistadors. Were the Indians human beings? And the question came down to the very practical matter of whether they had *souls*. If they did, here lay a vast field for missionizing—converting the Indians to Christianity so their souls could be saved and, following their death, could proceed to the hereafter and further populate heaven. An affirmative answer to the question of whether the Indians had souls, while assuring a life eternal to the souls of millions of Indians if they converted, did little to mitigate the plight of their bodies until they were separated from them.

Later European Conceptions of the Soul

With the coming of the Renaissance, a new materialism came to be added to—but not necessarily to supplant—the idealism that preceded it. This idealism was best exemplified by a continued belief in the soul. The new materialism, for its part, was partially exhibited by the philosophy of dualism, its most prominent exponent being René Descartes (1596–1650). Not only did Descartes continue to believe in the soul's existence, he actually pinpointed a specific seat for it within the human body. That location was the pineal gland, "a structure within the brain which, in his erroneous opinion, was not found in animals" (Singer 1955:148–149). In this gland the soul was able to make contact with the body and thus animate it (Russell 1945:561). However, while the soul might be lodged in a physical organ, it was nonetheless distinct from it. It could be likened, so to speak, to the spark plug that ignited the engine.

The exact location of the soul continued to interest—and puzzle—philosophers for years to come. Thus Immanuel Kant, "supported by the famous Frankfort anatomist, Sömmerring, sought the peculiar seat of the soul in the small quantity of ... watery serum which is found in the interior of the ... ventricles," a series of connecting cavities in the brain (Büchner 1891:257).

Francis Bacon (1561–1626) is credited with being the first modern philosopher of science. Yet he too believed implicitly in the existence of the soul. Indeed, he contended that "a man has two souls: one that is peculiar to human beings alone; the other, shared with all animals. The study of man's animal soul is part of science, but the higher soul is immaterial and cannot be investigated by the same techniques" (Cranston 1967:238). Again, as with Descartes, a basic dualism characterized the interpretation of human life.

Pierre Gassendi (1592–1665), a contemporary of both Descartes and Bacon, is generally regarded as a materialist. But while believing in the atomic theory of matter, he "maintained that atomic explanations did not extend to the human soul and ... accepted on faith the doctrine of the immortality of the soul" (Popkin 1967:272). He was after all, despite his generally materialist philosophy, a Catholic priest.

Julien La Mettrie (1709–1751) was a more thoroughgoing materialist than his predecessors. In opposition to the dualism of Descartes, he held that the soul owes its being to "specific organic forms" produced by a "*force motrice*" inherent in matter, and that this force was the basis of human mental faculties (Vartanian 1967a:380). Psychological phenomena, he held, were entirely dependent on organic changes in the brain and the nervous system. Accordingly, the soul ceased to exist as soon as the body died. In keeping with this belief, La Mettrie felt that the proper study of the soul fell to the natural scientist, not to the theologian or metaphysician (Vartanian 1967a:380).

The point to be emphasized here is that despite his materialism, La Metrie believed that there *was* such a thing as the soul. On this score, though, he differed from most of his contemporaries, stating that the soul was not some ethereal, disembodied essence but was grounded in and part of the anatomy and physiology of the human body. Still and all, so far was La Metrie from denying its existence that in 1745 he wrote a book entitled *A Natural History of the Soul.*

Since the few dedicated materialists of the age continued to believe in the soul, it is not surprising that the newly emerging English deists, whom we shall meet later in Chapter 9 and who sought to restrict the scope and power of God, "all recognized the soul of man" (Unsigned 1910a:936).

Some philosophers of the period, however, were not content merely to accept the concept of the soul in the form handed down to them by earlier thinkers. Instead they chose to speculate further about its origin and antiquity. One such philosopher was Gottfried Leibniz (1646–1716), who opposed the notion—taught by some—that the soul was not always the same but had evolved over time. On the contrary, Leibniz wrote in his book *Theodicy*, "[T]he souls which are destined one day to become human exist in the seed, like those of other species; … [thus] they … existed in our ancestors as far back as Adam—that is, since the beginning of the world" (quoted in Haeckel 1992:134).

This idea, known to biologists as *scatulation* and given a theological twist by Leibniz, was originally limited to heredity. It had been advanced by those who believed in the theory of *preformation*, according to which embryological development consisted of nothing more than the unfolding of what was already present, tightly enfolded in the form of a tiny homunculus. This homunculus, it was thought, resided within the egg or more likely the sperm. This theory was given greater specificity by the Swiss physiologist Albrecht von Haller (1708–1777), who "calculated that God had created … 6000 years ago—on the sixth day of his creational labors—the germs of 200,000,000,000 men, and ingeniously packed them all in the ovary of our venerable mother Eve" (Haeckel 1992:55). If genetic material could be thus encapsulated and transmitted, why not the soul as well? Thus, it was thought, the souls of present-day human beings were already reposing in the reproductive organs of Adam and Eve, to be passed on to untold thousands of generations.

The nature of the soul continued to be the center of intense and abiding attention among a wide range of intellectuals. In describing the soul beliefs of Bishop Joseph Butler (1692–1753), for example, the physicist John Tyndall wished to show that while Butler was very much a product of his time, his great concern for the soul was nothing new but in fact reflected a centuries-old interest in the subject. "Long previous to his [Butler's] day," Tyndall wrote, "the nature of the soul had been so favourite and general a topic of discussion, that, when the students of the University of Paris wished to know the leanings of a new Professor, they at once requested him to lecture upon the soul" (Tyndall 1874:34).

Professions of a belief in the soul—accompanied by a deep emotional attachment to it—were commonplace among European thinkers of every stripe, not just philosophers and theologians. Thus the celebrated mathematician Karl Gauss (1777–1855) was passionate about more than numbers, holding an abiding faith in the immortality of the soul and harboring no doubts about its ultimate and eternal repose in the hereafter (Pickover 2008:293). For his part the English essayist Joseph Addison (1672–1719) waxed lyrically, "There is not, in my opinion, a more pleasing and triumphant consideration in religion than that of the perpetual progress which the soul makes toward the perfection of its nature" (quoted in Lovejoy 1936:247).

Materialists Wrestle with the Soul

But there were those who took a less rapturous view of the soul. Prominent among them was the French *philosophe* Baron d'Holbach (1723–1789). Holbach rejected the common belief that the soul was separate and distinct from the body. Contrary to what Descartes had argued a century earlier, Holbach wrote, "It has been already sufficiently proved, that the soul is nothing more than the body, considered relatively to some of its functions" (Holbach 2006: 166).

This position he took repeatedly in his *System of Nature* (1770), saying of the average man, "[I]f, throwing aside error, he would contemplate his soul … he would be convinced that it forms a part of its body, that it cannot be distinguished from it, but by abstraction; that it is only the body itself" (Holbach 2006:93). And, he concluded, if the soul were coextensive "with the organs to which it gives impulse, it follows of necessity that this spirit must have extent, solidity, consequently distinct parts; [and] whenever a substance possesses these qualities, it is what we call MATTER" (Holbach 2006:91).

Accordingly, if the soul were material, the dearly held belief in it as an ethereal essence deserved to be ridiculed. Thus he wrote that if the soul is "so deprived of extent, so invisible, so impossible to be discovered by the senses ... by what means did the metaphysicians themselves become acquainted with it?" (Holbach 2006:89). Yet as *material* as the soul had to be for Holbach, its *existence* was not challenged.

It is perhaps not surprising that eighteenth century thinkers did not question the reality of the soul. What is surprising is that scientists of the latter half of the nineteenth century, even such a thoroughgoing materialist as the physicist John Tyndall (1820–1893), did not extricate themselves from the grip of this supernatural concept. What else can we conclude from Tyndall's statement that "[t]he problem of the connection of the body and soul is as insoluble in its modern form as it was in the prescientific ages" (Tyndall 1869:6)?

The German materialist physiologist and philosopher Ludwig Büchner (1824–1889), however, had no such difficulty connecting the soul and the body. He confidently affirmed that "[t]he brain is not only the organ of thought and of all the higher intellectual abilities, which have their exclusive seat in its gray layer, but it is also the only seat of the *soul*, taking that word as signifying the activity of the *whole* brain in all its parts" (Büchner 1891:255).

Ernst Haeckel Takes on the Soul

Another staunch German materialist, the biologist Ernst Haeckel (1834–1919), went to great lengths to expound the philosophy of materialist monism and was the first German scientist to champion the cause of Darwinism. In his famous book *The Riddle of the Universe* (1899), he devoted considerable attention to the soul. Haeckel made it clear that since for him the soul was a material entity, it was—contrary to the contentions of Descartes and Kant—quite capable of being studied by the methods of science. "What we call the soul is, in my opinion, a natural phenomenon; I therefore consider psychology [the science in which its study would fall] to be a branch of natural science" (Haeckel 1992:89). This being the case, he contended, "[I]t becomes one of the main tasks of the modern monistic psychology to trace the stages of the historical development of the soul of man from the soul of the brute" (Haeckel 1992:148).

Still, while granting it existence, Haeckel insisted that the soul was a material entity, the product of nervous tissue: "[T]he human soul is not an independent, immaterial substance, but, like the soul of all the higher animals, merely a collective title for the sum-total of man's cerebral functions" (Haeckel 1992:204). Accordingly, Haeckel had little sympathy with the ancient notion of the soul as some sort of insubstantial vaporous essence, and was quick to lampoon this belief.

> If, then, the substance of the soul were really gaseous, it should be possible to liquefy it by the application of a high pressure at a low temperature. We could then catch the soul as it is "breathed out" at the moment of death, condense it, and exhibit it in a bottle as "immortal fluid" (Fluidum animae immortale). By a further lowering of the temperature and increase of pressure it might be possible to solidify it—to produce "soul-snow." (Haeckel 1992:201)

It is curious that while Haeckel thought the soul to be just the product of the functioning of the brain, he nevertheless clung to the term as if it designated something that actually existed and was somehow different from the mind. But if he actually felt there was some subtle difference between the two, he failed to make clear what that difference was.

Theistic Scientists Embrace the Soul

If someone with the solid materialist (indeed atheistic) credentials of Ernst Haeckel could not divest himself of the soul concept, small wonder then that other scientists of the period—with far less allegiance to materialism—should have continued to believe in it.

Let us look, for example, at J. S. Haldane (1860–1936), the leading British biologist of the early twentieth century. Haldane had rather mixed feelings about the soul. In his general interpretation of biology, he was to a large extent a mechanist. Still, he felt there remained some residue of brain function that to be explained satisfactorily required the notion of the soul. Body and soul, however, were not two entirely separate and distinct entities. They were closely enmeshed, said Haldane, each being dependent upon the other and not readily separable. Moreover, he took pains to try to spell out the interdependence that existed between the two. In *The Sciences and Philosophy* (1929), he remarked:

> The supposed independent soul has turned out to be something which is dependent in every respect on the supposed physical body and environment. We cannot possibly separate their influence. If [on the other hand] we start with the provisional assumption that there is a physical or biological living body, with an independent soul to guide it, the facts lead us inevitably to a correction of this assumption. (Haldane 1929:117)

The belief in something like the soul quite separate from the body, which survived death and might be communicated with by the living, led in the latter half of the nineteenth century to the vogue of *spiritualism*. No one exemplified this movement better than Alfred Russel Wallace (1823–1913). In the 1860s Wallace came to the conclusion that natural selection was not enough to explain the great heights to which the human mind had risen. To account for it, he invoked an "overruling intelligence" that he thought lay behind "the development of mental and moral behavior" (quoted in Blum 2006:44).

Although Wallace's study of socialism—as expounded by Robert Owen—had "dispelled whatever glimmerings of the Christian faith there may have been latent in his mind," his biographer tells us, he still clung to a belief in a human soul that outlived the body (Marchant 1916:II, 182). Indeed, he believed in life after death "as the inevitable crowning conclusion to the long process of evolution" (Marchant 1916:II, 181).

In a letter to Marchant written the very year of his death, Wallace traced the development of his thinking in this regard: "The complete materialistic mind of my youth and early manhood has been slowly moulded into the ... spiritualistic, and theistic mind I now exhibit—a mind which is, as my scientific friends think so weak and credulous in its declining years." But despite what others might say, Wallace was ready to affirm in his last book *The World of Life* (1910) that "[t]he whole cumulative argument … is that *in its every detail* … [life] calls for the agency of mind … enormously above and beyond any human mind" (quoted in Marchant 1916:II, 181).

To see if he could engage in some communication with the dead, Wallace began attending séances. In 1866 he invited Thomas Henry Huxley to attend one of them with him, during which spirits were expected to appear and converse with the living. Huxley politely declined and, wearing his agnosticism on his sleeve, wrote, "It may be all true, for anything I know to the contrary"; but then, showing more of his true feelings in the matter, he added dismissively, "I cannot get up any interest in the subject. I never cared for gossip in my life, and disembodied gossip, such as these worthy ghosts supply their friends with, is not more interesting to me than any other" (quoted in Marchant 1916:II, 187). On another occasion Huxley spoke more fully and pungently on the subject.

> The only case of "Spiritualism" I have ever had the opportunity of examining into for myself was as great an imposture as ever came under my notice.… If the folk in the spiritual world do not talk more wisely and sensibly than their friends report them to do, I put them in the same category [as provincial old women and curates]. The only good that I can see in the demonstration of the "Truth of Spiritualism" is to furnish an additional argument against suicide. Better live a crossing-sweeper, than die and be made to talk twaddle by a "medium" hired at a guinea a *Séance*. (quoted in James 2008:76–77)

Darwin was even more caustic in this regard, becoming incensed at Wallace's seeming apostasy from the thoroughly naturalistic theory they had jointly proposed. In a letter he scolded him in these words: "You write like a metamorphosed (in retrograde direction) naturalist. I *defy* you to reject your doctrine" (quoted in Blum 2006:40). Later, in 1869, after reading an article on spiritualism written by Wallace, Darwin again wrote to him, "If you had not told me, I should have thought … [the comments] had been written by somebody else. As you expected, I differ grievously from you and I am very sorry for it" (quoted in Blum 2006:45).

Oliver Lodge Espouses Spiritualism

The physicist Sir Oliver Lodge (1851–1940) was another British scientist who believed that the human personality "persists beyond bodily death" and that at death the soul "leaves the terrestrial sphere, and enters on a discarnate existence" (Lodge 1905:103; 1912:163). Lodge had no doubts that "the soul of a thing is its underlying reality" (Lodge 1905:100). Indeed, he went on to say that the soul "may turn out to have a more permanent and therefore a more real existence than the temporary vehicle which served to manifest certain of those attributes and properties during man's short tenure of earth life" (Lodge 1912:73). How could Lodge be so sure of this? "We base this claim on the soul's manifest transcendence, on its genuine reality, and on the general law of the persistence of all real existence" (Lodge 1912:91).

But there was more. The soul or "spirit" of the deceased could revisit the earth and communicate with the living. Indeed, Lodge maintained that "[t]he possibility of phantasmal appearances [as in the course of a séance] is now well authenticated, and there is no need to discredit any of the testimony" (Lodge 1912:169). Thus he declared, "I do not feel constrained to abandon the traditional idea that the coming or the going of a great personality may be heralded and accompanied by strange occurrences in the region of physical force" (Lodge 1912:168).

William James Challenges the Soul—But Then Re-embraces It

Against these repeated espousals of the view that the soul is a real, undeniable, and indispensable element of human existence, there arose a challenge to it from a quite unexpected source: the philosopher and psychologist William James (1842–1910). James, who had long bridled at strict determinism and was an unabashed exponent of free will, nevertheless once delivered an incisive and impassioned critique of the concept of the soul. The occasion he chose for this dramatic disavowal was a series of lectures at Oxford in the days when it was still a bastion of German idealism. Here—where under Thomas Hill Green (1836–1882), F. H. Bradley (1846–1924), and Bernard Bosanquet

(1848–1923) the banner of idealism had been hoisted on high and still waved proudly in the air—James fearlessly argued his case. After warning all those arrayed before him that it was high time they began questioning idealism and looking more favorably on the hard-edged empiricism of Locke and others, James fired a powerful salvo against the human soul.

> [I]t is for no idle or fantastical reasons that the notion of the substantial soul, so freely used by common men and the more popular philosophies ... has no prestige in the eyes of critical thinkers. It only shares the fate of other unrepresentable substances and principles. They are without exception all so barren that to sincere inquirers they appear as little more than names masquerading. (James 1996:209)
>
> Souls have worn out both themselves and their welcome, that is the plain truth. Philosophy ought to get the manifolds of experience unified on principles less empty (James 1996:210).

Curiously, though, James failed to heed his own advice! For a quarter-century he was engrossed with the phenomenon of *spiritualism*, which in those days was enjoying enormous popularity. Spiritualism was, of course, nothing more or less than an attempt to communicate with departed *souls,* the very category of human conceptions James had found to be so "empty."

Throughout his career James seems to have vacillated as to just where he stood on this matter, alternately affirming and questioning the reality of spiritualism. While quite aware of all the quackery in the psychic field, he nonetheless believed in *"the presence,* in the midst of all the humbug, *of really supernnormal knowledge"* beyond that attainable through the ordinary senses (James 2008:82). On one occasion he even went so far as to assert that "[t]he concrete evidence for most of the 'psychic' phenomena ... is good enough to hang a man 20 times over" (quoted in Blum 2006:213).

Still, doubt was apparently never far from his mind. Thus he once wrote, "I confess that at times I have been tempted to believe that the Creator has eternally intended this department of nature to remain *baffling* ... so that, although ghosts and clairvoyances, ... and messages from spirits are always seeming to exist and can never be fully explained away, they also can never be susceptible to full corroboration" (James 2008:72–73). Thus the great psychologist remained, like so many leading thinkers before him, suspended uneasily between science and the supernatural.

But setting aside James's flirtation with spiritualism, and returning to his Oxford lecture on the soul, one can well imagine the stunned reaction that must have greeted his words. As an example of an unequivocal rejection of the validity and utility of the concept of the soul, it is hard to find its equal. Now one might have naively supposed that with someone of the stature and skill of William James having come out so strongly against its existence, the soul would have had received a severe wound—if not its quietus. Far from it! Not only is the soul by all odds the oldest one among them, it is certainly the hardiest perennial in the garden of supernatural beliefs. Without breaking stride it easily survived James's onslaught, continued to flourish, and is today alive and still warmly entertained by the earth's billions.

The Tenacity and Endurance of the Soul

It was E. B. Tylor who, many years ago, introduced the term "survivals" into anthropology, defining them as "processes, customs, opinions … which have been carried on by force of habit into a new state of society different from that in which they had their original home" (Tylor 1871:I, 15). However, since the concept of the soul retains very much the same meaning it did among those earlier hominids who first devised it—that is to say, it performs essentially the same explanatory function it did then—I would suggest we call the idea of the soul, as still embraced in the contemporary world, a *retention* rather than a *survival*.

Still, the rest of Tylor's characterization of survivals continues to be very apt when applied to present-day notions of the soul. Survivals remain, as Tylor maintained, proofs and examples of an older condition of society—one that at the time, as in the case of the soul, had no better explanation for recurring events in human experience (Tylor 1871:I, 15).

CHAPTER 6

The Birth and Evolution of the Gods

In 1928 the German ethnologist Günter Tessmann published a book on the Shipibo Indians of eastern Peru that he entitled *Menschen Ohne Gott* (*Men Without God*). And the title was indeed appropriate. The Shipibo, like other Panoan-speaking tribes of that region of Amazonia, believe in a large number of bush spirits—*yuhsi*—but none of them is powerful or exalted enough to be called a god.

And of the Indians of the Guiana region, another corner of Amazonia, Sir Everard Im Thurn wrote, "[T]here is nothing to suggest an affirmative answer to the question, [of] whether [these] Indians have any idea of a God" (Im Thurn 1883:366). Many other primitive peoples believe in a host of spirits that, important as they may be in the natives' mind, are likewise something less than gods. In fact, it is safe to say that in the history of religion, gods started out as spiritual beings of a lesser order. And gradually—and only in some places—did they evolve into full-fledged deities. In this chapter I propose to examine this evolution.

It should be kept in mind, though, that higher deities—when they finally rose to prominence—did not extinguish the lesser spiritual beings from whom they originated. Indeed, primitive peoples have populated the earth and the heavens with a bewildering and enduring variety of supernatural creatures, from lowly pixies, leprechauns, and hobgoblins to the Lord God of Hosts.

The bush spirits that Spencer and Tylor saw as derived ultimately from the human soul were creatures of relatively little power. They were generally troublesome—even dangerous—to human beings but too weak to perform great mythological tasks, such as lifting the sky from the earth or wiping out most of mankind with a great flood. However, as people felt the need to endow supernatural beings with the ability to perform more Herculean feats, they gradually built up their bush spirits, eventually strengthening them into a class of decidedly powerful supernatural beings. One such class was that of culture heroes, whose activities we have already explored in Chapter 3. These beings were powerful enough in their day to perform prodigious deeds for the benefit of humanity. Ultimately, though, culture heroes typically retired from the scene, in effect relinquishing their power. *Giti*, for example, the Kuikuru culture hero who became the Sun, created the "Wild Indians" and a few other things while still on earth, but then left it and rose to occupy his permanent place in the firmament. Now he travels across the sky every day, lighting and warming the world but no longer playing an active role in human affairs. Thus he cannot truly be called a god.

Bush Spirits Mutate into Gods

True, neither Tylor nor Spencer devoted many pages to describing just how souls became bush spirits or how bush spirits became gods. Here and there in their writings, though, they did suggest that this was indeed the transition that souls and spirits underwent. Tylor, for instance, said that "the conception of the human soul is the very 'fons et origo' of the conceptions of spirit and deity in general," and he added that human souls were "held to pass into the characters of good and evil demons, and to ascend to the rank of deities" (Tylor 1871:II, 224).

Accordingly, Tylor thought that he could detect in the high gods of the major religions traces of their animistic roots: "[A]s we consider the nature of the great gods of nations, ... it will still be apparent that these mighty deities are modeled on human souls, that in great measure their feeling and sympathy, their character and habit, their will and action, even their material and form, display throughout ... characteristics shaped upon those of the human spirit" (Tylor 1871:II, 224). And again he held to the view that "[t]he great gods of Polytheism, whose dominion thus stretches far and wide over the world, are ... [no] more than the lower spirits" magnified and embellished many fold (Tylor 1871:II, 225).

Lang Proposes Primordial Monotheism

For Tylor and Spencer, then, gods—fully formed and powerfully armed—were by no means primordial conceptions, springing full blown from the minds of Paleolithic theologians. Instead they were, like everything else, the product of an *evolution*. They had developed gradually over time out of simpler and more humble beginnings. And among anthropologists during the latter third of the nineteenth century, this was pretty much the reigning theory of the origin of religion. But in 1898, in his book *The Making of Religion*, the scholar and man of letters Andrew Lang challenged this view. He held that monotheism—the belief in a single "High God"—was no late arrival in the history of human beliefs, developing gradually in cultures that had already achieved a substantial degree of complexity. Rather, he argued, "the conception of a separable surviving soul of a dead man was not … essential to the savage's idea of his supreme god," adding emphatically that "the belief in a Supreme Being … is not derived from the theory of ghosts or souls at all" (Lang 1898:159). On the contrary, Lang held "that the idea of God … occurs rudely, but recognizably, in the lowest known grades of savagery, and therefore cannot arise from the later speculation of men … on the original datum of ghosts" (Lang 1898:175).

In a chapter entitled "High Gods of Low Races" (1898:187–200), Lang cited a number of cases—principally from aboriginal Australia but also among the Bushmen and the natives of Tierra del Fuego—of simple peoples having a belief in a relatively high, benevolent, moral god, which Lang believed could not have evolved out of soul beliefs at all. In fact, he insisted that "certain low savages are as monotheistic as some Christians" (Lang 1898:181).

Lang, then, was ready to *reverse* the accepted evolutionary sequence proposed by Tylor and Spencer, holding that "there would be nothing strange in the matter if the crude idea of 'Universal Power' came *earliest*, and was superseded, in part, by a later propitiation of the dead and ghosts" (Lang 1898:186). "If we can show," Lang continued, elaborating on his theory, "that the early idea of an eternal, moral, creative being does not necessarily or logically imply the doctrine of spirit, then this idea of an eternal, moral, creative being may have existed even before the doctrine of spirit was evolved" (Lang 1898:176).

How, then, was Lang to explain the fact that so many surviving primitive peoples believed in bush spirits and not in high gods? While he was loath to adopt the old degeneration theory—that is, that man had fallen from an initial lofty state—Lang nonetheless found himself somewhat in sympathy with certain elements of that theory. If accepted in a tempered form, he thought, it would help explain why most contemporary primitive societies lacked the concept of a high god that their ancestors had once held (Lang 1898:184). Thus, regarding those who still clung to the old idea of degeneration—of a "fall from grace"—he remarked, "I see what its advocates mean, or ought to mean, and the strength of their position" (Lang 1898:184).

Father Schmidt and Primordial Monotheism

Lang's thesis was later reaffirmed and extended far beyond what he himself had proposed. If Lang was uncomfortable with the idea that his Christian God had animistic roots, much less ready to accept this notion was Father Wilhelm Schmidt (1868–1954), an Austrian anthropologist who was also a Catholic priest. As Leslie White observed, Father Schmidt "seized upon Lang's idea and developed it in a six-volume work, *The Origin of the Idea of God*, in which he sought to prove that very primitive peoples were indeed monotheistic. In *Primitive Revelation* he accounts for primordial monotheism as an original revelation of God" (White 1987:345). And in an effort to prove this point, Father Schmidt cited some ethnographic evidence.

> [T]he really monotheistic character of their [primitive peoples'] Supreme Being is clear even to a cursory examination. This is true of the Supreme Being of most Pygmy tribes, so far as we know them; also of the Tierra del Fuegians, the primitive Bushmen, the Kurnai, Kulin, and Yuin of South-East Australia, the peoples of the Arctic circle, except the Koryaks, and wellnigh all the primitives of North America. (Schmidt 1965:23)

However, as White took pains to point out, "Father Schmidt had an axe to grind. He was a loyal and devoted priest and as such his ultimate goal was the service of theology" (White 1987:350). Schmidt believed that the monotheism of primitive peoples was no mere historical accident, or even an evolution out of simpler beginnings, but the result of divine revelation. Moreover, "evidence of this primordial revelation, according to Father Schmidt, would be found most clearly among the most primitive peoples of the world today, namely, the pygmies; hence the great concern of the Schmidt-Koppers school with those tiny people" (White 1987:350–351). And, White added, the conception of the Deity found among the Pygmies by Father Paul Schebesta (1887–1967), a disciple of Father Schmidt, was "virtually indistinguishable from the God of the Roman Catholic Church" (White 1987:350–351).

But was this really true? Was this actually the Christian God in rain forest garb? It so happens that here we have a test case since, years after Schebesta, Colin Turnbull—an anthropologist with no connection to a religious sect—studied the same Pygmies. And in his well-known book *The Forest People* (1961), Turnbull makes no mention at all of Father Schebesta's contention that the Bambuti (the largest group of Pygmies) believe in a monotheistic high god. Unlike Schebesta, Turnbull lived in intimate contact with the Bambuti for months, but (like Schebesta) he inquired into their religious beliefs. On one occasion, speaking with a Pygmy informant named Moke, Turnbull reported:

> He told me how all Pygmies have different names for their god, but how they all know that it is really the same one. Just what it is, of course, they don't know, and that is why the name does not matter very much. "How can we know?" he asked. "We can't see him; perhaps only when we die we will know and then we can't tell anyone. So how can we say what he is like or what his name is? But he must be good to give us so many things. He must be of the forest. So when we sing, we sing to the forest"—in what the Pygmies term the *"molima* ritual." (Turnbull 1961:92–93)

This hardly sounds like the distinct, personalized, anthropomorphic high god whom Schebesta so readily attributed to the Pygmies. In fact, in their almost worshipful attitude toward the forest (a feature of Pygmy belief that Turnbull makes a point of emphasizing), there seems to be more than a touch of pantheism: God and nature coalescing into one. But if he was aware of this, Father Schebesta could hardly have been expected to point it out, for—as we shall see in Chapter 11—the idea of pantheism is anathema to Catholic doctrine.

In championing his thesis, Father Schmidt had to face the same hard fact Lang felt compelled to reckon with. If the first religious belief was a pristine monotheism, how was it that so many primitive peoples no longer held such a belief? And Schmidt answered the question in much the same way Lang had, by proposing a modified form of the degeneration theory. Humanity, he held, had lapsed into a bewildering variety of supernatural beliefs after somehow losing its original clear-cut monotheism.

Yet arguments could easily be raised against Schmidt's contention. Even if a large number of contemporary primitive peoples held to a strict monotheism, that in itself would prove nothing. After all, eons had passed since human beings first began to entertain supernatural beliefs, so that whatever religious ideas they held— even those of the Pygmies, or Fuegians, or aboriginal Australians— while they might be considered *primitive*, were not necessarily *primordial*. Thus their ideas told us nothing about human beliefs, say, a hundred thousand years ago.

In passing, I might point out that in a cross-cultural study, J. W. M. Whiting found that of 81 hunter-gatherer societies in his sample, only 28 of them (35 percent) believed in a high god (cited in Wilson 2006:560). Moreover, it should be stated that Tylor made no blanket denial of the existence of monotheism among certain contemporary primitives, writing that "[t]here have existed in times past, and do still exist, savage or barbaric peoples who hold such views of a highest god" (Tylor 1871,II: 336).

Anthropological judgment of Schmidt's hypothesis has been uniformly negative. "Apart from the research of Father Schmidt and his disciples," wrote the sociologist Guy Swanson, who has made a detailed study of primitive religion, "there is no support for Schmidt's judgment that those societies which have the simplest form of organization are also worshippers of high gods" (Swanson 1964:59). And E. E. Evans-Pritchard, a close student of primitive religion, concluded that the Schmidt school "has disintegrated since his death; and I doubt whether today there are many who would defend his reconstructions" (Evans-Pritchard 1965:104).

Tracing the Evolution of the Gods

We are now in a position to begin tracing the evolution of supernatural beings, conjectural as it may be, starting with those rudimentary forms that are essentially bush spirits. We shall track this development until we reach the stage at which supernatural beings can unequivocally be considered gods. This does not mean, of course, that there has been a single, universal trajectory that all societies have followed in the development of their religious beliefs. The paths to godhood were many and varied. But the history of this trajectory must surely begin with simple, unpretentious spirit beings, limited in both scope and power. Those first-generation spirits were, in all likelihood, associated with particular localities and restricted in their spheres of action.

The next stage in this evolution may have seen these spirits become disassociated from their initial particularities and become more generalized and far ranging in their activities. In this process they gradually increased their powers as they widened their functions. In some cases they came to exercise control over specific natural phenomena, such as thunder and lightning—for example, Tupã of the Tupíans and Sharpo of the Yoruba. And when manifesting such control, supernatural beings may have exhibited a potency of such magnitude as to warrant calling them gods.

Another route to godhood may have been through origin myths. We have seen that as people sought to account for more and more aspects of the world around them (both terrestrial and celestial), they devised culture heroes specifically designed to do just that. For the most part, these culture heroes retired from active service after creating certain features of the environment or having taught some essential arts and skills of life, but nothing beyond this. In such cases the pathway of theological evolution that gave rise to them proved to be a side spur and a dead end. Culture heroes remained culture heroes and nothing more.

Still, to suggest that this was always the case might be giving culture heroes too short a shrift. In some cases the evolutionary track leading to gods perhaps *did* run through culture heroes who chose *not* to retire. Indeed, they remained active and did not forsake their earlier powers, but managed to retain and even enhance them. And once they were strong enough to bring daylight or rivers or fire into existence, such supernatural beings might thereby have staked a claim to being gods.

At any rate, and in whatever manner they arose, once full-fledged gods were in existence they tended to expand in particular ways. A few succeeded in concentrating power in their own hands, dwarfing other gods who had arisen or crowding them out of the pantheon altogether. The culmination of this trend was, of course, the emergence of monotheism, the rise of a supreme deity, an almighty god—omnipotent, omniscient, and unchallenged. Writing vividly of the pathway leading to the attainment of such theological primacy, Tylor declared (in loftier language than he was accustomed to employ), "High above the doctrine of souls, ... of local nature-spirits, of the great deities of class and element, there are to be discerned in savage theology shadowings, quaint or majestic, of the conception of a Supreme Deity, henceforth to be traced onward in expanding power and brightening glory along the history of religion" (Tylor 1871:II, 302).

The Gods Continue to Evolve

As Tylor indicates, in their development higher gods exert a kind of centripetal force that over time concentrates more and more power in themselves. This process can be seen at work, for example, in the evolution of the sun into a major deity among the ancient Hindus. According to Max Müller, a specialist in Hindu religion, in the verses of the Vedic poets, "The sun is no longer the bright Deva [supernatural being] only, who performs his daily task in the sky, but he is supposed to perform much greater work; he is looked upon, in fact, as the ruler, as the establisher, as the creator of the world. We can follow in the Vedic hymns, step by step, the development which changes the sun from a mere luminary into a creator, preserver, ruler, and rewarder of the world" (Max Müller 1879:255).

Given the sun's tremendous physical power and commanding presence, which manifests itself day after day, it is little wonder that in time it became a major deity in the pantheon of several early civilizations. In that role it was known, for example, as Ra among the ancient Egyptians and Inti among the Incas.

The Gods Demand Worship

As gods gain in magnitude, strength, and prestige, they attract—indeed *demand*—greater veneration. So insistent and menacing may they become that new ways must be devised to placate them and curry their favor. To ward off their anger and acquire their benevolence, they must be appealed to in convincing ways. And to do so successfully they must be approached with a sense of awe, reverence, and submission—attitudes generally *not* characteristic of the religious beliefs and practices of the simpler peoples. So as gods become "high gods," prayers—almost never directed at bush spirits—are addressed to them. They are thanked, propitiated, and even adored. Sacrifices are made in their name, including the ultimate one—human sacrifice. Thus among many ancient cultures, the sacrifice of individuals was a not uncommon way to gain the favor of the gods. The belief reigned that taking the life of a human being, often an enemy captive, was somehow pleasing to the gods. Especially was this true among warlike societies that often had in their pantheon a distinct and implacable god of war, a god whose demand for blood was insistent and insatiable.

High gods are often given honorific titles that emphasize their power, extol their greatness, or praise their benevolence. These epithets, sometimes piled one on top of the other, often refer to the broad spectrum of the god's activities. The Ba-Ila of southern Africa, for example, call their high god the creator, the molder, the constructor, the omnipresent, he-from-whom-all-things-come, the giver, the rain giver, the flooder, the deliverer-of-those-in-trouble, he-who-cuts-down-and-destroys, and so on (Radin 1985:340–341).

It often happens, though, that a high god—as he becomes more grandiose and essential to human welfare—becomes more difficult to reach and influence. As with kings who become increasingly exalted and inaccessible to the average citizen as they gain in power, supreme beings likewise tend to become more aloof and remote and harder to move. However, just as this is occurring—indeed *because* it is happening—a body of religious specialists (priests) conveniently emerges to carry out this very function. Ostensibly they do this for the benefit of the entire society; in practice they benefit greatly from it themselves.

Along with priests—flesh-and-blood individuals dedicated to their service—high gods tend to develop a coterie of lesser supernatural beings to assist them in carrying out their various functions. In the Christian religion, angels were once thought to play an active role in propelling the planets around in their orbits and ensuring that they stayed on course, thereby relieving God of this onerous if routine task.

In a high god's evolution, says Paul Radin, "His character becomes correspondingly ennobled and to his ethical attributes are added omnipotence and omniscience," thus removing him further from the reach of people (Radin 1985:353–354). As an example of this from his own fieldwork, Radin cites "Earthmaker [the supreme deity of the Winnebago] ... [who] never holds direct communion with men. He acts only through the intermediaries he has created" (Radin 1985:362). Addressing prayers to the Virgin Mary—or to a particular saint—instead of to God directly is a familiar example of approaching a deity indirectly through a subordinate supernatural being.

Another distinctive feature of some high gods is that their nature sometimes surpasses human understanding. Take, for instance, the various gods of the Oglala Dakota, who "had no beginning though some existed before the others and some bear the relation of parent and offspring to one another. No person can understand this contradiction for it is *akan*, a mystery" (Radin 1985:331). Many religions exhibit a number of such paradoxes, as if to put the gods even higher above mere mortals by placing them beyond the realm of comprehension.

By making the gods so inscrutable, mysteries like those cited above provide a more stringent test for true believers. But beyond that, they require the intercession of priests or other religious specialists who claimed to understand the enigmatic words and wishes of the gods. By acting as interpreters of a god's obscure pronouncements and desires, priests were able to harness the power of the gods for everyone's benefit. And of course by so doing the priests gained power, enhancing their aura and status. As a body they became an institution, developing a hierarchy and elaborating a corpus of doctrine. Temples were built in which to carry out their devotions. And these temples sometimes became a *sanctum sanctorum*, a place too sacred for any but initiated members of their fraternity to enter. We are told by the Egyptologist Le Page Renouf, for example, that "[a]t no period of the Egyptian religion were the public admitted to the temples as worshippers. All the temples we know were royal offerings made to the divinity of the locality, and none but the priestly personages attached to the temple itself had free access to its precincts" (Renouf 1880:86).

Polytheism as a Precursor of Monotheism

Polytheism is often regarded as the forerunner of monotheism. Tylor, for example, affirmed that "[t]he doctrine ... which opens to ... [the simplest peoples] a course tending [in the direction of monotheism] is polytheism culminating in the rule of one supreme divinity" (Tylor 1871:II, 302). According to this view, what began as multiple gods eventually narrowed down and coalesced into one. In the process the sole surviving deity incorporated and concentrated within himself the powers of the various other deities whom he successfully vanquished and absorbed. For Sigmund Freud this course had been neatly exemplified by the history of the Judeo-Christian religion. He believed that monotheism was the end point of a logical progression in which the Hebrew Deity Yahweh was "one of the divine beings into which, in our civilization, all the gods of antiquity have been condensed" (Freud 1961:24).

To those who—as a matter of faith—wholeheartedly believe in a single supreme being, *monotheism* is not only the glorious culmination of religion; it is its direct *fons et origio,* as Tylor would have said. No other source was required, no preceding stable of lesser gods. Others, though, regard *polytheism* as a precursor, a necessary stepping stone to monotheism. The great Scottish philosopher David Hume, for one, while convinced that Christian monotheism was humanity's highest religious conception, nonetheless held that polytheism was an essential early stage on the road to a belief in a single god. "It appears to me," he wrote, that "if we consider the improvement of human society, from rude beginnings to a state of greater perfection, polytheism ... was, and necessarily must have been, the first and most ancient religion of mankind" (Hume 1927:254). And again he asserted that "in enquiring concerning the origin of religion, we must turn our thoughts towards polytheism, the primitive religion of uninstructed mankind" (Hume 1927:258–259).

As convinced as he was that polytheism had led to monotheism, Hume nevertheless had little regard for the collection of gods that he thought constituted this earlier stage of religious belief. "[T]he gods of the polytheists," he scoffed, "are no better than the elves and fairies of our ancestors, and merit as little ... pious worship and veneration" as they did (quoted in Huxley 1908:186).

In this appraisal, however, Hume was wide of the mark. If we examine the multiple gods of the early civilizations, we find them to be several notches above elves and fairies. Indeed, they exercised an impressive degree of power, even though it was generally restricted to their assigned spheres of action. Hume was also wrong in another regard. Polytheistic gods, as we have seen, can hardly be considered the first supernatural beings to emerge in primitive consciousness. Their eventual high status was not one that they initially enjoyed but something they had to "grow into," step by step, during the course of their evolution.

Celestial Structure Reflects Social Structure

Students of religion have long held that the structure a society assigns to its supernatural world closely reflects the structure of the society itself. Tylor put it this way: "[H]uman society and government became the model on which divine society and government were shaped. As chiefs and kings are among men, so are the great gods among the lesser spirits. They differ from the souls and minor spiritual beings ... but the difference is rather of rank than of nature" (Tylor 1871:II, 225).

The renowned Egyptologist James Breasted is often credited with being the first to suggest that monotheism arose most readily out of a strong monarchy in which a single absolute ruler stood unchallenged at the top of his kingdom (Swanson 1964:75–76). The omnipotence often assigned to a monotheistic god thus mirrored, said Breasted, the power manifested by a supreme political leader. Later in this chapter we will examine an apparent example of this development—quite possibly the very instance that led Breasted to formulate his theory.

There is yet another way in which what goes on in heaven mirrors what takes place on earth. It is this: as societies grow larger, more varied, and more complex, so do the activities assigned to their various deities and the number of gods required to carry them out.

Thus advanced societies tend to develop a kind of celestial specialization—a divine division of labor. Here is how Leslie White summed up this development: "The growth of division of labor in society finds its counterpart in division of labor among the gods: farmers, fishermen, and various handicrafts, and social classes such as merchants, each has its patron deity; in some cultures even thieves have their own god" (White 1987:353).

Commenting on polytheism in ancient Rome, Hume offered these instances of celestial specialization: "Juno is involved at marriages; Lucina at births. Neptune receives the prayers of seamen; and Mars of warriors. The husbandman cultivates his field under the protection of Ceres; and the merchant acknowledges the authority of Mercury. Each natural event is supposed to be governed by some intelligent agent" (Hume 1927:261).

If the simpler societies—with no full-time specialists—have supernatural beings that can pass muster as gods, what they are placed in charge of are usually natural phenomena. Such a society may thus have a god of rain, a god of thunder, a god of wind, and the like. In more complex societies, however, we begin to find gods in charge not only of natural phenomena, but (as White noted) of certain occupations and activities. No better way of illustrating the polytheistic division of labor comes to mind than by presenting examples of a few such cases, drawn from the pantheons of four well-known pre-industrial civilizations: those of the Egyptians, Hindus, Greeks, and Aztecs.

SUN	**MOON**
Egyptian—*Aten, Ra*	Egyptian—*Thoth*
Hindu—*Surya*	Hindu—*Soma*
Greek—*Helios*	Greek—*Selene*
Aztec—*Tonatiuh*	Aztec—*Meztli*

FIRE	**CREATION**
Egyptian—*Bast*	Egyptian—*Khnum*
Hindu—*Agni*	Hindu—*Brahma*
Greek—*Hephaestus*	Greek—(none)
Aztec—*Xiuhtecuhtli*	Aztec—*Quetzalcoatl*

FERTILITY, AGRICULTURE
Egyptian—*Min*
Hindu—*Sarasvati*
Greek—*Demeter*
Aztec—*Tonantzin*

WAR
Egyptian—*Bes*
Hindu—*Kartikeya*
Greek—*Ares*
Aztec—*Huitzilopochtli*

WISDOM, KNOWLEDGE
Egyptian—*Ptah*
Hindu—*Brahma*
Greek—*Athena*
Aztec—*Quetzalcoatl*

Nor were these polytheistic deities in any way vague creatures or abstract principles. On the contrary, they were described in very concrete terms, readily capable of visualization and depiction. Some polytheistic deities—such as Ganesh, the Hindu elephant god—had animal form. And in the mythology of ancient Egypt, according to G. F. Moore in his *History of Religions*, each god was said to have had an animal prototype: "Khnum ... was a ram, Hathor a cow, Nekhhbet a vulture, Bast a cat, Horus a falcon, Anubis a jackal, Sobek a crocodile, Thoth an ibis, and so on" (quoted in Garvie 1918:113). An early rattlesnake god of the Aztecs became, in time, the great feathered serpent deity Quetzalcoatl. The majority of the ancient gods, though, were—from the beginning—anthropomorphic.

Human Roots and Attributes of Gods

Proof of the human derivation of polytheistic gods is the fact that despite their great power and exalted status, these early deities are often thought of as having very familiar human attributes, including everyday foibles and frailties. Of the gods of ancient Egypt, for example, it was said that "they have both parts and passions; they are described as suffering from hunger and thirst, old age, disease, fear and sorrow. They perspire, their limbs quake, their head aches, their teeth chatter, their eyes weep, their nose bleeds.... They may be stung by reptiles and burnt by fire. They shriek and howl with pain and grief" (Renouf 1880:89).

And we are all familiar with how faithfully the Greek gods of antiquity reflected the Greeks themselves. As the sociologist Albert Keller described them, "The Homeric gods were men of a larger being and power" but withal had all the familiar vulnerabilities. "They had human form, they had weight, could fall, could be bound with chains, could feel intense physical pain, and they could be, if not mortally, certainly very painfully wounded, even by men" (Keller 1911:108).

Indeed, the very human failings of the Greek gods led them to engage in unending quarrels. Altogether these shortcomings of their gods could be taken as reflecting relations among the Greek city-states themselves, which—rather than well-integrated, harmonious entities—were forever engaged in squabbles, disputes, and outright wars.

All this allows us to raise the question again: to what extent was a society's supernatural world a reflection or projection of the things that went on in its own midst? The constant wars of the ancients, with their succession of victories and defeats and the resulting shifts in political fortunes, seems to have left an indelible mark on the theological canvas of these societies. As a result the identities of their gods became confused and intermixed. Sometimes the very names of the gods were conflated with one another. At one time each of the leading cities in Babylonia had its own patron deity: in Eridu it was Ea, in Nippur it was Enlil, and in Uruk it was Anu. However, when a new dynasty became dominant in the region with Babylon as its capital, the patron deity of that city (Marduk) supplanted the other deities in authority. Indeed, "[i]n one hymn the other gods are treated as only variant names of Marduk in his varying functions" (Garvie 1918:113).

A similar transformation took place in ancient Egypt. One reason for the rise of its extensive polytheism was the existence of many local deities, each town or district usually having its own set of gods. Egypt was divided into 42 *nomes* or provinces, each of which had its principal deity as well (Renouf 1880:84). When the military conquests that led to the political unification of Egypt threw all these gods together into a heterogeneous and bewildering pantheon, the various deities vied with each other for recognition—if not supremacy. According to Renouf, "The Egyptian deities are innumerable. There were countless gods in heaven and below the earth. Every town and village had its local patron. Every month of the year, every day of the month, every hour in the day and of the night, had its presiding divinity," thus bringing about "inextricable confusion" among the Egyptian deities (Renouf 1880:89, 93).

To make matters even more confusing, Renouf continues, "Not only are some inferior deities mere aspects of the greater gods, but ... several at least of the greater gods themselves are but different aspects of one and the same" (Renouf 1880:91). "It happened frequently that in the same town one god was worshipped under different aspects, or as proceeding from different localities, and treated as though there were different divine persons of the same name" (Renouf 1880:87).

And as in Babylonia, so too in Egypt: when cities gained prominence, so did their once-local deities. As Renouf noted, "It is most probable that neither Ptah nor Amon were originally at the head of lists, but obtained their place as being chief divinities of the capitals Memphis and Thebes" (Renouf 1880:91–92).

The tendency also existed for lesser gods to be assimilated into the manifestation of greater ones. "On comparing these lists together," Renouf observes, "it is again plain that Mentu and Tmu, two of the great gods of Thebes, are merely aspects of the sun-god Ra" (Renouf 1880:91). And in ancient Egypt this tended to happen repeatedly: "[A]s the political importance of the provincial cities increased, their local cults could not be suppressed, and each deity was in turn identified with Ra, and appropriated his attributes" (Garvie 1918:113). Indeed, this process became almost a *reductio ad absurdum*, so that "[i]n the Litanies of the god Ra, which are inscribed on the walls of the royal tombs at Biban-el-moluk, the god is invoked under seventy-five different names" (Renouf 1880:90).

The organization of celestial beings may become so complex, in fact, that tiers or echelons of gods may develop, with the greater gods directing the activities of the lesser ones. This bewildering variety of deities, however, may have contained within it the seeds of its own destruction. And the process of polytheistic dissolution or subordination may have occurred somewhat as follows. In heaven a perfect democracy seldom reigns. Just as in civil society competition for leadership tends to arise among various aspirants for power, so in celestial society the gods are inclined to compete vigorously with one another for supremacy. The outcome of such a struggle, therefore, may actually be determined by the relative influence and effectiveness of the particular priesthood devoted to each deity; it may also reflect the power, here on earth, of the secular backers of each contending god. And the results of such earthly struggles manifest themselves most visibly in how the contending gods come to be ranked in the firmament.

The Drift Toward Monotheism

At first in this theological competition there might be a kind of "power-sharing" agreement in which the leading deities distribute the various godly functions and responsibilities more or less evenly among themselves. The Hindu religion, for example, has a trinity of sorts, with Brahma being the creator, Vishnu the sustainer, and Shiva the destroyer, while in Babylonia "[a]n attempt at systematic theology appears in the partition of the universe among those three gods; Anu rules in heaven, Enlil in earth and air, and Ea in the waters" (Garvie 1918:114).

Running counter to this sharing of authority, however, is always the tendency—terrestrial and celestial—to concentrate the greatest power in the hands of a single ruler. As Hume noted more than two centuries ago, "It may readily happen ... that though men admit the existence of several limited deities, yet there is some one God, whom, in a particular manner, they make the object of their worship and adoration" (quoted in Huxley 1908:189). This theological conception is sometimes termed *monolatry*, a belief in several gods but the recognition of one of them as being distinctly superior to the rest. Odin, for example, was the greatest of the various Teutonic gods and is sometimes called the father of the gods (Youngert 1911:178). Among the Greek gods, this condition was particularly well exemplified by Zeus, who— despite having to contend with a number of fractious fellow-gods— had nonetheless become paramount over all of them.

> It was Zeus who rained, who thundered, who snowed, who hailed, who sent the lightning, who gathered the clouds, who let loose the winds, who held the rainbow. It is Zeus who orders the days and

nights, the months, seasons, and years. It is he who watches over the fields, who sends rich harvests, and who tends the flocks. (Max Müller, quoted in Tylor 1871:II, 234)

Heavenly Reflections of Society Once More

Herbert Spencer made the observation that in the Greek pantheon, Zeus stood "exactly in the same relation that an absolute monarch does to the aristocracy of which he is the head" (Spencer 1901:193). We have referred more than once to the view that the religious order thought to reign in heaven reflects, in a general way, the social order that prevails on earth. Already in antiquity Aristotle, in his *Politics*, very astutely remarked that "all people say that the gods also had a king because they themselves had kings either formerly or now; for men create their gods after their own image, not only in regard to form; but also with regard to their manner of life" (quoted in Evans-Pritchard 1965:49).

Two thousand years later, Leslie White made much the same point: "A pastoral culture may find its image in a Good Shepherd and his flock; an era of cathedral building sees God as a Great Architect; an age of commerce finds Him with a ledger, jotting down moral debits and credits" (White 2005:254). But on the other hand, White also noted that "[a] cultural system based upon a wild food technology could hardly have a conception of 'Great God our King,' or 'Christ, the Royal Master'" (White 1987:346).

The Triumph of Monotheism

Zeus was surely a power in the firmament of ancient Greece, but he was still something of a *primus inter pares* rather than an absolute, all-powerful, and uncontested ruler. Dominant as he was, he still fell short of being totally supreme. As Greek mythology vividly reveals, Zeus was repeatedly unsuccessful in constraining the actions of his strong-willed subordinate deities. Thus he lacked the *omnipotence* that comes only with serene and unchallenged monotheism.

Father Schmidt (as we have seen) would not have us believe that modern-day monotheism—Christian monotheism—is a phenomenon that gradually evolved out of obscure and inchoate beginnings.

Nor would he have us believe that monotheism grew out of the consolidation of an established and well-ordered polytheism. Rather, for him monotheism was a sudden revelation made to man by God. The facts adduced in this chapter, however, point to a different conclusion. When we examine the theological ideas of early pre-Christian civilizations, we find that virtually all of them believed in multiple deities. The Babylonians, Egyptians, Hindus, Greeks, and Romans, for example, were all polytheists. And in the New World as well, the Aztecs, Mayas, and Incas believed in a multiplicity of gods.

When all is said and done, polytheism appears to be an essential *stage* in the evolution of religion, a *precursor* to monotheism. Even if one chooses to regard monotheism as a higher and nobler theological conception, a supreme culmination of the religious sentiment, one is not obliged to consider it a revelation from God. It is not necessarily an idea divinely inspired and implanted—full grown and finely polished—into the human mind. Rather, monotheism was a *development* that like all evolving phenomena had *roots* and *stages*. And in its evolution the immediate antecedent of a triumphant monotheism seems ineluctably to have been a variegated and complex polytheism.

We have noted that in polytheistic societies, after an initial proliferation of gods, there comes a recurring tendency toward a concentration of divine power in fewer and fewer hands. A purely egalitarian polytheism, then, is unusual and unstable. And as a result of this lack of equilibrium on the part of the contending gods, monotheism seems to be peering over the theological horizon. Indeed, in the very book that proclaims the unchallenged authority and unity of the Christian God, traces of an earlier Hebrew polytheism may be discerned. In the struggle for dominance among the earlier Hebrew deities, Yahweh (Jehovah) eventually emerged triumphant and supreme. Nonetheless a tiny vestige of the competitors that preceded his ascendancy in the Hebrew pantheon can be gleaned from the words of the Decalogue in which true believers are told, in no uncertain terms, "I am the Lord thy God" and enjoined that "thou shalt have no other gods before me." Not that no other gods *exist*, mind you, but only that none should command anywhere near the allegiance and respect due to Yahweh. In attempting to obliterate all traces of an earlier polytheism, the compilers of the Old Testament somehow failed to expunge this single telltale bit of evidence of its prior existence!

Of the titanic struggles that must once have ensued among the various Hebrew deities, the Bible is silent. The victory had been won and all glory to the victor. The losers were to be eradicated from history without even a mention. If we can reduce the matter to secular terms, the priesthoods that stood as proxies for the various gods must have battled each other savagely before one of them emerged triumphant. Moreover, we can surmise that the competition must have been intense and prolonged. And it most likely involved not only fierce theological debates, but also clashes of arms on the battlefield as occurred among the secular representation of each deity.

Something of the nature of the theological wars involved—and the difficulty monotheism must have faced before ultimately being crowned with success—is provided by an experiment that took place in Egypt many centuries before the rise of Christianity. In one of his essays, Leslie White traced in minute detail this remarkable episode. It was during the reign of a pharaoh of Middle Kingdom Egypt (1409–1369 B.C.) that the events leading to an abortive introduction of monotheism took place. As summarized by White:

> Very early in the reign of Amenhotep IV the worship of a supreme god, Aton, was inaugurated. Aton was none other than the old sun-god, Re [or Ra], in a new role. Other gods were tolerated for a while, but with the growing resentment of the priesthoods, particularly that of Amon, Amenhotep IV built a new city-capital, Akhetaten, for his god, changed his name to Ikhnaton, closed the temples of the other gods, dispossessed the priesthoods, confiscated their lands and revenues, and set to work to establish his new regime, both religious and political. (White 2005:248)

This radical theological innovation, however, did not long survive Ikhnaton's death. His successor, who ascended the throne at the age of nine, soon fell afoul of the priesthoods of those other gods who for time had been brusquely thrust aside. As White continues to recount events:

By now the priestly party [that had been deposed by Ikhnaton] was growing rapidly in strength. The new king soon realized that he could stay on the throne only if he "came to terms with the supporters of the traditional faith," i.e., the priests.... He was compelled to abandon the heresy of Ikhnaton and to "acknowledge himself officially as an adherent of ... Amun." (White 2005:249)

Thus was the upstart monotheism of pharaonic Egypt overthrown and the old polytheism re-established. To curry favor with the old gods and the priests who served them, the young king who succeeded Ikhnaton—the celebrated Tutankhamun—"made monuments for all the gods, ... restoring their sanctuaries [as well as] ... providing them with perpetual endowments" (White 2005:249).

And so the heroic experiment in monotheism had failed. The traditional gods (that is to say, their *priesthoods*) proved too strong. And once the pharaoh who had instigated this revolutionary innovation was no longer on the scene to enforce it, it was swept away. Ra continued to occupy a high place in the Egyptian pantheon, but once more he became just one of several great gods. It would be many centuries before circumstances were again such that monotheism could once more emerge triumphant. And this time it established itself on a much firmer basis. Through the agency of Christianity, Judaism, and Islam, this new monotheism has succeeded in making its way in the world and establishing the worship of a single deity (God, Jehovah, Allah) in the farthest corners of the globe.

Yet in a curious way, it has been argued that Trinitarian Christianity is really polytheism rather than the strict monotheism it purports to be. The German biologist and scholar Ernst Haeckel contended that with the Catholic Church raising the Virgin Mary to near-godlike status, there arose a *fourth* Christian deity to accompany the Father, the Son, and the Holy Ghost in the heavenly firmament (Haeckel 1992:283–284). Indeed, Haeckel went so far as to argue that in modern Catholicism, with its plethora of saints, we have "the most extensive branch of Christianity, a rich and variegated polytheism that dwarfs the Olympic family of the Greeks" (Haeckel 1992:284).

* * * * * *

Here we come to the end of our survey of the evolution of religion. We turn next to a consideration of that mode of thought— science—that posed a direct challenge to supernatural thinking. And from here on we will trace, in considerable detail, the ensuing struggle between these two modes of thought, a struggle that continues to this day.

CHAPTER 7

The Rise of Scientific Thinking

One of the fundamental elements of scientific thought is the concept of causation. No one can say when this concept first arose in the human mind. It certainly long predates the ancient Greeks. Indeed, as the work of anthropologists has clearly shown, the search for causes is a universal feature of the way primitive peoples examine events.

However, among preliterate peoples the chain of causation is usually longer than with practitioners of science today. A tree falls and kills a man. Our analysis is satisfied when we attribute its fall to a strong wind. Primitive peoples, though, are seldom content with this explanation. They want to know *who* sent the wind. Their view of causation almost always involves the element of *personal* causation. There are two ways in which personal causation manifests itself. First, an occurrence is thought to be the result of the actions by an actual human being, generally someone regarded as a witch. The other interpretation of the cause of an event is that it came about through the actions of a being, not entirely human but anthropomorphic in appearance and malevolent in intent—in other words, an essentially supernatural creature, often a bush spirit. It took many thousands of years before the concept of purely *impersonal* causation, with the human factor eliminated from the equation, became recognized as a way of envisioning causation. And of course the idea of personal causation has by no means been eradicated from human thought. It continues to abide with us, as when some natural catastrophe is assigned to a personal agency, such as the will of a god—"an act of God" in legal terminology.

The attitude that led people to look for what lay behind natural occurrences had its positive side as well. The power of curiosity and imagination that prompted primitive peoples to invent notions of souls, spirits, and gods also led to a stage that we can consider the forerunner of scientific thinking. This stage saw the formulation of *origin myths,* which are essentially *hypotheses* about how things came to be what they are. Their formulation thus constituted the first element in the great triumvirate of scientific conceptions, the other two being *empiricism* and *verification.* Empiricism must of course have been present from the very beginning. Life could not have been lived successfully without a high degree of reliance on sense perceptions and on the empirical testing of inferences drawn from those perceptions.

However, some degree of reliance on empiricism did not prevent the rise of non-empirically based ideas. Thus it was that supernatural notions arose, filling in the gaps between the islands of empirical knowledge. And in time such notions came to dominate large parts of human thinking. This new mode of thought—involving such things as intuition, inspiration, excogitation, and eventually revelation—introduced ways of looking at the world that went far beyond what sense impressions alone could provide.

Unlike the framing of hypotheses, *verification*—the third element in the triumvirate—is limited to, or at least most characteristic of, science. It calls for testing hypotheses and not simply accepting them on faith, authority, or tradition. As such, verification on a broad scale came *late* in the history of thought. Still, its arrival was of supreme importance.

Science and Philosophy in Ancient Greece

So much for the concepts involved in ancient ways of interpreting nature and experience. Let us jump ahead to the state of thought in ancient Greece.

The earliest Greek thinkers inherited a full-blown pantheon of gods from Greece's prehistoric past, but they also went on to develop a number of scientific concepts that set the gods to one side and attempted to account for events of the world without them. By the sixth century B.C., Greece was already a complex society with a marked division of labor. In a number of Greek city-states, especially Athens, *teachers* were already in evidence. They were men who taught in the academies and had the time to reflect on how to interpret nature. Speculative philosophy began when these thinkers started breaking away from traditional beliefs and proposing alternative hypotheses. One of the things several of the early pre-Socratic philosophers questioned was belief in a universe created by the gods and continuing to be ruled by them. Even later thinkers like Plato, who did not abandon the idea of gods, still thought of them in more abstract terms rather than in the very concrete human ways in which Greek mythology portrayed them.

Schools of philosophy began to emerge that took some bold and innovative steps. Most significantly, some of them dispensed with the gods altogether. Leucippus and his disciple Democritus, who flourished in the city of Abdera in the late fifth century B.C., worked out the first clear conception of matter—the fundamental stuff out of which (they held) everything was made (Campbell 1967:180). Not only were Leucippus and Democritus materialists, they were also "strict determinists, who believed that everything happens in accordance with natural laws" (Russell 1945:66). A thoroughgoing philosophy of science had thus begun to develop. And not only was the *philosophy* of science emerging, but also its *practice*.

Several of the ancient Greeks made genuine contributions to the body of scientific knowledge that was beginning to accumulate. Aristarchus, for example, proposed that the sun—and not the earth—was the center of the solar system, and that the earth was merely one of several planets that revolved around it. (Copernicus later acknowledged his indebtedness to Aristarchus for this hypothesis.) And Archimedes, though not primarily a theorist or a philosopher, made many notable contributions to scientific understanding and was responsible for several significant mechanical devices based on principles derived from observation and experimentation.

There was, however, another philosopher-scientist whose influence on the thought of his day—and for centuries thereafter—was not quite so easy to categorize. Aristotle was a classifier and a systematizer, but he had a tendency to decide things by fiat and dictum instead of observation. For instance, according to the nineteenth century physicist John Tyndall, Aristotle "determined *a priori* how many species of animals must exist, and shows on general principles why animals must have such and such parts" (Tyndall 1874:15). Furthermore, as part of his system of philosophy, Aristotle devised rules of thought—syllogisms—for trying to prove things by logic rather than by empirical means of observation.

John Stuart Mill once asserted, "Few will doubt that had there been no Socrates, no Plato, and no Aristotle, there would have been no philosophy for the next two thousand years" (Mill 1930:612). However, one can argue precisely the opposite. Had these men *not* lived, not only would there have been philosophy just the same; but had later thinkers pursued the empiricism, materialism, and determinism of Leucippus and Democritus instead of the idealism of Plato and the "a priorism" of Aristotle, philosophy would have advanced faster and gone further!

In his famous Belfast Address to the British Association for the Advancement of Science, John Tyndall offered a severe indictment of the scientific work of Aristotle.

> As a physicist, Aristotle displayed what we should consider some of the worst attributes of a modern physical investigator— indistinctness of ideas, confusion of mind, and a confident use of language, which led to the delusive notion that he had really mastered his subject, while he had as yet failed to grasp even the elements of it. He put words in the place of things, subject in the place of object. He preached induction without practicing it, inverting the true order of inquiry by passing from the general to the particular, instead of from the particular to the general. He made of the universe a closed sphere, in the centre of which he fixed the earth, proving from general principles, to his own satisfaction and to that of the world for near 2,000 years, that no other universe was possible. (Tyndall 1874:14–15)

And in the same address, Tyndall spoke dismissively of Socrates, Plato, and Aristotle, "whose yoke," he said, "remains to some extent unbroken to the present hour" (1874:10). It is interesting to note that Voltaire anticipated Tyndall in his harsh judgment of Aristotle's teacher, Plato: "O Plato," he wrote, "so much admired! I fear that you have told us only fables, and have never spoken except in sophisms. O Plato! You have done more harm than you know" (quoted in Lovejoy 1936:253).

I quote this assessment of Aristotle's philosophy because of the powerful influence it continued to exert on Western thought throughout the Middle Ages and well into the Renaissance. As Bertrand Russell noted, "Whether there are people at the antipodes, whether Jupiter has satellites, and whether bodies fall at a rate pro-portional to their mass, were questions to be decided, not by obser-vation, but by deduction from Aristotle" (Russell 1997:16).

Behind this logical deduction there lay a set of general princi-ples from which conclusions about the behavior of things were to be deduced. These principles were so fundamental as to be, if not self-evident, then at least accepted without question. Donald Longmore described this aspect of Aristotle's thinking as follows.

> In Aristotle's universe things moved because of "inherent ten-dencies." Objects fell to the ground, for instance, because all matter possessed an inherent tendency to seek the centre of the universe (the centre of the earth). The stars, the sun, moon, and planets, locked fast in their crystal spheres, rotated about that same centre because rotation was "inherent" in all spheres. (Longmore 1971:18)

Thus Aristotle's hold on the European mind had first to be broken and then transcended before science could take firm hold and begin to make significant advances.

Aristotle's stultifying influence, however, should not be allowed to overshadow the contributions to scientific thinking made by a few other thinkers of the Greco-Roman world. There was, to be sure, Lucretius's great naturalistic poem *De Rerum Natura,* which, "written to propagate the philosophical materialism of Democritus and Epicurus, devoted considerable space to the mechanistic theory of life and, of course, argued in its favor" (Needham 1955:230). In Lucretius's atomism, materialism, and belief in the reign of natural law, there was no need—indeed no room—for the gods. Atoms, falling freely in parallel lines, occasionally veered off course, col-lided, and adhered to each other, and it was in this way that larger objects were formed. And in Lucretius's scheme all this happened without divine assistance. Crude as it was, here was a clear state-ment of a materialist interpretation of things, pointing ahead to what was to come centuries later. These tendencies, though, were soon stifled and snuffed out by the official Christian theology adopted by the Roman Empire after the conversion of the Emperor Constantine in the year 313.

One of the most striking advances in the early history of science was that of the Greek astronomer Ptolemy. With the early Greek empiricists, there began an age during which observation came to be stressed over excogitation, and this attitude was reflected particularly in astronomy. During studies of the motions of the planets, it had been observed that at times some of them seemed to show *retrograde* motion in the sky, as seen against the starry background. The planets would move in one direction and then appear to reverse course for a time and move in the opposite direction, after which they would resume their forward motion.

Astronomical observations, especially *anomalous* ones like this, called for an explanation. And to explain this puzzling planetary behavior, Ptolemy developed the idea of *epicycles*. He proposed that each planet traveled in an orbit around the earth (as was already generally believed), but that in addition to this primary orbit, each planet had a smaller secondary orbit that it described as it circled around a central point along its primary orbit. When planets were in a certain phase of this smaller orbit, they appeared from earth to be moving *backward*. But even though Ptolemy's scheme did in fact account for the observed retrograde motion of the planets, it was so complicated that when Alfonso X of Castile ("the Sage") had it explained to him many years later, he remarked that had God consulted *him* when he was setting up his celestial system, he could have advised the Almighty how to design it better (Dreyer 1953: 273)!

Nevertheless Ptolemy's system was a distinct advance over what had preceded it since it not only explained the planets' mysterious retrograde motion, but it did so without invoking the need for a supernatural agent to push them around as they moved through the sky.

The Bible and Aristotle in the Middle Ages

Jumping ahead to the Middle Ages, the most salient point to note is that there were two sources of knowledge on which the Schoolmen of that period relied. If the answer to an important question was not found in the Bible, they would turn next to the writings of Aristotle. The authority that resided in his texts was used to resolve almost every issue left in dispute. Any attempt to appeal to nature directly by means of observation and experimentation was deemed beneath the Schoolmen's dignity.

It is reported that one of Galileo's contemporaries refused to look through his telescope because—the man argued—there was no need to reopen a question (specifically, whether the earth revolved around the sun) "which had already been settled by Aristotle" (Jeans 1961:124). And though the Church Father Augustine was willing to grant that the earth was round, he refused to countenance the idea that men, whose "heads do grow beneath their shoulders" (as Shakespeare put it in *Othello*), were living in the antipodes. Augustine's argument against this possibility was that the existence of such creatures was not mentioned in the Bible—the other unimpeachable source of medieval knowledge.

And when neither reference to the Bible nor to Aristotle was found sufficient to settle an argument, recourse was had to logic, which was valued more highly than mere observation. Thus the Middle Ages proliferated dozens of ingenious—but alas unavailing—logical proofs of the existence of God. (We may perhaps offer here the contrasting case of the native Polynesians, who did not waste their time trying to *prove* the existence of Tangaroa, but simply accepted it as a fact and went about their business. As usual, faith proved more economical of thought than doubt!)

The great change in Western thinking that ultimately saw empiricism and materialism enthroned was fundamentally the result of science. The best exemplification of this came from the work of Galileo and its beginning can be dated to around 1600, or slightly earlier. At about the same time, the systematic, reflective thought that underlay this experimental work—that is to say, the philosophy of science—was being given voice by others. These were men who, while sympathetic to the cause of science, were not (for the most part) scientists themselves. We will consider their ideas in this chapter, saving for the next the actual work of the early scientists.

Not surprisingly, Leonardo da Vinci (1453–1517) was, along with his other accomplishments, an early proponent of the ways of science. According to Sir James Jeans, his contribution was as follows.

> Perhaps Leonardo's greatest service to science was his exposition of the principles which ought to govern scientific research.

1967:237). And "when the Royal Society of London was founded in 1667, forty-one years after Bacon's death, many regarded it as realizing the kind of scientific brotherhood that Bacon had idealized and fought for in his *New Atlantis*, a utopian state dedicated to pure scientific study" (Urbach and Gibson 1994:xii).

René Descartes

René Descartes (1596–1650) was the leading philosopher of the first half of the seventeenth century. According to the historian of science Charles Singer, "The Cartesian philosophy was the first complete and coherent system of modern times. It rapidly found adherents and spread in every country and was popular for several generations" (Singer 1955:149). Our interest in it here is as a part of the movement in human thought away from supernaturalism and toward naturalism. Still, in this regard Descartes—like so many other thinkers—had a foot in each camp. The most distinctive feature of Descartes's philosophy was his *dualism*. The world was composed, he thought, of two fundamentally different kinds of things: *matter* and *mind* (or soul). The world of matter consisted of solid, palpable substance; it had *extension* and could therefore be measured. The world of mind, however, was immaterial and was neither connected to—nor derived from—matter.

Descartes's world of mind or soul was thus a holdover from the familiar and ancient regime of thought that we have traced back to its beginnings. This part of his philosophy, then, looked back toward the age of supernaturalism, while his materialism and mechanism looked forward toward the scientific advances still to come. Let us look first at those aspects of Descartes's philosophy that earned him a place among those seventeenth century thinkers who stood in the vanguard of science.

Descartes was part of that century's great revolt against Aristotleianism. In his *Discourse on Method* (1637), he asserted that "the first step is to wipe away all earlier and accepted authority and to start with a clear and unbiased mind" (Barnes 1937:723).

Except for mind (or soul) and God, the world consisted of matter in motion. In fact, Descartes declared, "Give me matter and motion and I will construct the universe" (quoted in Stebbing 1958:157). Prior to Descartes "Aristotleianism had viewed the world in terms of qualities (earth, air, etc.); now it was viewed in terms of quantities—which [having extension] could be measured" (Strathern 1997:30). And measurement yielded numbers, which could then be manipulated mathematically. Referring to mathematics, Descartes maintained, "I am convinced that it is a more powerful instrument of knowledge than any which has been bequeathed to us by human agency" (quoted in Barnes 1937:725). And indeed it was Descartes who created that branch of mathematics known as analytic geometry. And it was he who invented the graph, more formally known as "Cartesian coordinates," a technique of representing the relationships between two variables that today graces the pages of every scientific journal. Summing up, one biographer observed that "[i]t will be evident from Descartes's conception of the physical world that his aims for scientific explanation are that it should be entirely mechanical ... and that mathematical physics should emerge as the fundamental science" (Williams 1967:352).

This was, of course, the *materialist* side of Descartes's dualism. The other side of his philosophy was the one that recognized immaterial, incorporeal phenomena as having a separate and independent existence. Here then was the spiritual world, "whose essential nature lay in conscious thought undetermined by causal processes" (Campbell 1967:182). It was *thought* that played a paramount role in this half of Descartes's philosophy. Few maxims are better known than Descartes's *cogito ergo sum* ("I think, therefore I am"). And he argued forcefully that "this *I*, which thinks, is an immaterial substance which has nothing corporeal about it" (quoted in Williams 1967:348). Since Descartes stressed reason over experience as a source of knowledge, he was more of a rationalist than an empiricist. To prove his own existence and that of mankind, he resorted to thought rather than observation.

In Descartes's system, mind and soul were not clearly distinguishable. Indeed, it seems that thought was the product of the soul, which Descartes located in the pineal gland. He chose this locus for it since this gland was a single, unpaired structure deep in the brain, which he supposed unique to the human species—Descartes erroneously believing that it occurred in no other animal (Williams 1967:353). But though Descartes placed the soul within a physical organ, in its function he regarded it as independent of the body and thus not accessible to study through mechanical means, as was the rest of the body (Barnes 1937:689). "The picture Descartes offers of the behavior of the body is that of the soul directly moving the pineal gland and thus affecting the animal spirits which he considered the hydraulic transmission system of mechanical changes in the body" (Williams 1967:353).

Not all actions of the body, however, needed to be initiated by the soul. In instances of reflex action, as when someone throws out a hand to keep from falling, the body—Descartes maintained—acted purely mechanically, "without the intervention of the soul" (Williams 1967:354). And unlike the belief commonly held in primitive societies that death occurs when the soul leaves the body, Descartes believed that the body died first, and only then did the soul depart from it (Williams 1967:353).

Descartes, who remained a good Catholic throughout his life, never questioned the existence of God. In fact, he was much interested in devising proofs of the Deity's existence, including one patterned after St. Anselm's famous ontological argument (Williams 1967:350). However, he did not envision God as the familiar anthropomorphic Christian Deity, but—as one writer put it—as "a continuous, all-embracing unity of existence" (Harald Höffding, quoted in Barnes 1937:724). Along with the soul, Descartes affirmed, God was immune from the kind of mathematical analysis that could properly be applied to physical entities.

Despite his generally mechanistic view of things, Descartes rejected the theory that atoms are the indivisible, elemental building blocks of nature, arguing that "it was absurd to suppose that God, if he so pleased, could not divide an atom" even further (Tyndall 1874:21). Descartes also maintained that God had not only created all the matter constituting the universe, but also that he had given it its qualities, such as mobility and divisibility.

In the evolution of the human mind that we are attempting to trace, Descartes's thinking represents an advance since it brought the human body under the reign of purely mechanical principles. But at the same time, he was unable to break away entirely from the traditional Christian view of the world. He had, after all, been well schooled by the Jesuits to believe that the individual had a soul that was beyond the reach of physical causation and thus of scientific study.

Thomas Hobbes

Thomas Hobbes (1588–1679) is best known to the world as a political philosopher who saw humanity—in its early days—living in a state of nature and waging "the warre of all against all," which resulted in a life that was "nasty, brutish, and short." But Hobbes was also much interested in science, contributed to scientific philosophy, and numbered among his acquaintances men of like mind such as Galileo, Harvey, and Gassendi.

With regard to epistemology and ontology, Hobbes was firmly in the camp of empiricism and materialism. Furthermore, he held that matter existed independently of our perception of it. Indeed, in his *History of Modern Philosophy,* Harald Höffding went so far as to say that Hobbes "instituted the best thought-out attempt of modern times to make our knowledge of natural science the foundation of all our knowledge of existence" (quoted in Barnes 1937:725). Hobbes's basic position was that "all that exists is body (matter); all that occurs is motion" (Barnes 1937:726). By so arguing he repudiated the dualism of Descartes and thus greatly diminished and limited the sphere of the supernatural. According to Harry Elmer Barnes, Hobbes "eliminated the supernatural from his scheme of physical analysis. Physics deals with bodies in motion: in the supernatural world there are no bodies in motion. Hence, we cannot extend physical analysis ... to the supernatural world" (Barnes 1937: 726).

As a materialist Hobbes thought that the notion of an incorporeal substance "was a contradiction in terms. He thus rigorously excluded theology from philosophy" (Peters 1967:44). What about God, then? Like every philosopher and scientist of his age, Hobbes remained a theist. He was unable to dispense with the concept of God. But if—according to his philosophy—only matter existed, where did that leave God? When Bishop Bramhall once asked him what he took God to be, Hobbes replied, "I leave him to be a most pure, simple, invisible, spirit corporeal" (quoted in Peters 1967:36).

Though relegated to a thin, diaphanous, barely material existence in Hobbes's philosophy, God nevertheless had not lost his original and underlying power. In *Leviathan* (1651)—the last two hundred pages of which are devoted to religion—Hobbes maintained that God was the cause of the world, "that is, a first and eternal cause of all things; which is that which men mean by the name of God" (quoted in Peters 1967:44). However, Hobbes seemed to feel that the era of divine revelation, which had been in active ferment during biblical times, had long since passed. Thus if someone claimed to have had a revelation from God, Hobbes insisted that it was far more likely the person had *dreamed* it than that the revelation had actually occurred!

In his political writings, Hobbes had repeatedly shown great deference to the authority of the king and made him the arbiter of virtually all things, including those ordinarily thought of as theological. But as one commentator remarked, it is difficult to avoid the suspicion that Hobbes's suggestion "that the sovereign should pronounce on such matters as the creation of the world" was, in point of fact, "a subtle piece of irony, a pious protestation to protect himself against the charge of atheism" (Peters 1967:45).

Pierre Gassendi

The last of the four seventeenth century thinkers to be considered here as espousing the philosophy and methods of science is Pierre Gassendi (1592–1655). Although Gassendi received the degree of doctor of theology, took holy orders, and remained a priest all his life, he contributed a good deal more to the advancement of science than to that of religion. If not a pure materialist—he believed, after all, in an immaterial, rational, and immortal soul capable of free will—he was at least a thoroughgoing empiricist. Gassendi "shared to the full the empirical tendencies of the age" (Adamson 1910:503). His favorite saying was "there is nothing in the intellect which has not been in the senses" (Adamson 1910:503). Gassendi became interested in Epicurus's theory of atomism and (it has been said) his presentation of it "as a hypothesis or model for explaining the phenomenal world had a great and lasting impact on the development of modern scientific theory" (Popkin 1967:272).

Like Bacon, Gassendi stressed the importance of observation and experimentation in fostering the progress of science. He was, moreover, in the forefront of those who pointed out the stultifying effects of continuing to adhere to Aristotleian thinking. Indeed, he "expounds clearly, and with much vigour, the evil effects of the blind acceptance of the Aristotleian dicta on physical and philosophical study" (Adamson 1910:503). As enthusiastically as he embraced the ways of science, Gassendi "followed with interest the discoveries of Galileo and Kepler" (Adamson 1910:503).

But, withal, Gassendi was a Catholic priest with a strong allegiance to the Christian God. And while his interest in theology lessened with time, he never completely overcame its hold on him. This can be seen in his attitude toward atomism. As one observer remarked, "To bring the Epicurean system into closer conformity with Christian doctrine, he claimed that the atoms are not eternal but [were] created. They are finite, not infinite, in number and are organized in our particular world by a providential determination of initial conditions" (Campbell 1967:181). Moreover, in opposition to Epicurus, Gassendi believed in "the doctrine of an immaterial rational soul, endowed with immortality and capable of free determination" (Adamson 1910:504).

Arguing in the manner of the ancient skeptics, Gassendi "tried to show that all that we can know is how things appear, not how they really are in themselves" (Popkin 1967:207). This assertion is at once an advance and a retrogression. By seeming to deny that there is some readily perceptible "spiritual double" underlying all material things, it is an *advance*. But in appearing to imply that beyond the material appearance of things there is something that actually exists but which we can never get at, it represents a *retrogression*.

Scientific Thinking Forges Ahead

In his article "Materialism" in *The Encyclopedia of Philosophy*, Keith Campbell summarized the period that we have been discussing.

> From the close of the classical period until the Renaissance the church and Aristotle so dominated Western speculation that materialist theories virtually lapsed. The revival of materialism is attributable to the work of two seventeenth-century philosophers, Gassendi and Hobbes, who crystallized the naturalistic and skeptical movements of thought which accompanied the rediscovery of antiquity and the rise of natural science. (Campbell 1967:181)

However, while the four men whose work we have examined in this chapter wrote incisively about science and characterized it as the pre-eminent path to knowledge, it was the actual work of scientists themselves that really redirected European thought to a more naturalistic view of the world. Thus it is to the concrete advances made by these scientists that we now turn.

CHAPTER 8

The Impact of the Physical Sciences

Medieval Europe is popularly thought of as languishing in intellectual stagnation. This notion, however, is not strictly true. Underneath an exterior of quiescence, conditions were beginning to show signs of ferment. The idea of a uniformity in the processes of nature, guiding the way the world worked, was beginning to take root. And it was forcing itself with increasing insistence on more thoughtful minds. According to the British historian Herbert Butterfield, a specialist in this period of history, "In the later Middle Ages men had become more conscious of the existence of the machine, particularly through mechanical clocks. This may have prepared them to change the formulation of their problems. Instead of seeking the essence of a thing, they were now more prepared to ask, even of nature, simply: How does it work?" (Butterfield 1960a:6).

It was not only mechanical contrivances, however, that were making people wonder about how things worked. Mathematical tools of increasing power and sophistication were coming into use and, by the beginning of the seventeenth century, were making it possible to express the relationship among things more precisely. Now these relationships could be expressed quantitatively instead of just qualitatively. This advance contributed not only to practical mechanics, but also made possible what can properly be called theoretical physics. As regularities were discovered in the behavior of nature, they began to be formulated as *laws*. The model for this use of the word "law" in scientific discourse was that of manmade rules that—in principle, at least—allowed for no exceptions.

Copernicus and the Heliocentric Theory

When Copernicus began his observations, the reigning theory in astronomy was that the earth was at the center of the solar system and that the sun and the planets revolved around it. Moreover, the mysterious retrograde motion of some of the planets, which at times made them appear to move backward against the background of the stars, continued to be explained according to a theory first proposed in the second century A.D. by the Greek astronomer Ptolemy. This explanation, as we have seen, involved a series of epicycles or circular orbits, which each planet was supposed to describe as it moved along its main orbit around the earth. Ptolemy's system correctly predicted the observed movements of the planets but was incredibly complex. Still, so satisfied was he with his ingenious scheme for accounting for the peculiar movements of the planets that Ptolemy crowed exuberantly, "When I trace at my pleasure the windings to and fro of the heavenly bodies, I no longer touch the earth with my feet. I stand in the presence of Zeus himself and take my fill of ambrosia" (quoted in Tyson 2003:77).

The heliocentric theory of the solar system, which Copernicus now proposed to replace Ptolemy's cumbersome geocentric one, was by no means original with him. It was first proposed by the Greek astronomer Aristarchus in the third century B.C. But then Ptolemy, around the year A.D. 130, "rejected the view of Aristachus and restored the earth to its privileged position at the centre of the universe. Throughout later antiquity and the Middle Ages, his view remained unquestioned" (Russell 1997:20–21). However, toward the end of the Middle Ages, the heliocentric theory again began to be advanced—as simpler and more plausible—by several medieval scholars, including Jean Buridan and Nicholas of Cusa.

"Such late scholastic thinkers ... had perceived the theoretical virtues and explanatory power of the heliocentric principle," but for scriptural reasons they still fell back on the geocentric theory. Nevertheless they gave a fuller exposition of the heliocentric theory than had any of their predecessors since Aristarchus (Hanson 1967:220). However, according to the British astronomer Sir James Jeans, the geocentric theory—with its complicated Ptolemaic epicycles—"was still the official astronomy of the universities and of the Church" (Jeans 1961:117–118).

The Polish astronomer Nicolas Copernicus (1473–1543) was nonetheless led to believe that Ptolemy's system of epicycles contained a fundamental flaw. He argued that "the observational intricacies of planetary motion were not real, but merely apparent." He explained the seeming retrograde motions of the planets by interpreting these motions "not as something the planets 'really' did 'out there,' but as the result of ... [the earth's] own motion" in its path around the sun, which made "other circling objects sometimes appear to move backward in relation to the fixed stars" (Hanson 1967:220, 221).

This explanation of retrograde motion, coupled with the heliocentric theory's placing of the sun in its rightful spot at the center of the solar system, greatly simplified the understanding of how the system worked. Copernicus had taken the intricate and disparate pieces of a complicated astronomical theory and reduced them to a single, simple, readily intelligible system.

To be sure, Copernicus's discoveries had a devastating impact on the prevailing human conceit of being at the center of things. As Sir James Jeans summed it up, after Copernicus "Man could no longer claim that his home was the fixed center of the universe around which all else revolved; it was one of the smaller of the planets, and like the other planets, it revolved around a far larger sun" (Jeans 1961:124). The blow to human dignity—to human arrogance—was bound to be profound and, as Jeans added with a touch of sarcasm, "If, as man had hitherto believed, he was himself the climax and crown of all creatures," then he must have been dismayed to find that he had been "assigned a home in space which was quite incommensurate with his importance, a home, indeed, which stood 'in the same proportion to the universe as a point does to a clod'" (Jeans 1961:124).

Now if Copernicus had thus demoted man, he had also demoted God, since the heliocentric theory greatly reduced the Deity's astronomical functions in guiding the planets along their complex epicycles. It also ran counter to the long-established teachings of the Catholic Church. So threatening, in fact, did the Church regard Copernicus's views that it banned the teaching of the heliocentric theory and—by order of the Pope—placed any volume advocating it on the Index of Prohibited Books (Russell 1997:38). Not until 1822, Jeans tells us, did "the Roman Church give formal permission for the Copernican system to be taught as the truth, and not as a mere hypothesis" (Jeans 1961:125).

It was not only Catholics, though, who found the new astronomical findings distasteful. Commenting disparagingly on Copernicus, Martin Luther wrote:

> People give ear to an upstart astrologer who strove to show that the earth revolves, not the heavens or the firmament, the sun and the moon. Whoever wishes to appear clever must devise some new system, reverse the entire science of astronomy; but sacred Scripture tells us that Joshua commanded the sun to stand still, and not the earth. (quoted in Russell 1997:22–23)

The great irony, though, was that Copernicus was himself devoutly religious and dedicated his great book *De Revolutionibus Orbium Codestum* (1530) to Pope Clement VII (Russell 1997:22). Again and again we shall meet in the pages that follow instances of scientists whose discoveries lessened the necessity for God's intervention in the workings of the world, but who nevertheless proclaimed that their discoveries were made for God's greater glory.

Copernicus's discoveries were, at the same time, a blow to Aristotelian teachings. Others were to follow. Twenty-nine years after Copernicus's death, Aristotle's strictures were again challenged. He had held the view—and the Schoolmen continued to teach—that the heavens were fixed and unchanging. But on October 11, 1572, the Danish astronomer Tycho Brahe observed a star in the constellation Cassiopeia suddenly flare up as bright as Jupiter in the night sky. It was a supernova. As Jeans noted, "The Aristotelians had taught that everything in these outer regions of space was perfect, and therefore unchanging.... Tycho, by showing from direct observation that these regions were no more immune from change than the regions nearer to the earth, had dealt a shattering blow to the Aristotelian cosmology" (Jeans 1961:128). This occurrence, added to Copernicus's discoveries, had greatly diminished the role of God in the universe. The most poignant statement of this effect came not from an astronomer, but from one who appeared to voice it with a pang of nostalgia and regret. More than two centuries later, the German romantic poet Goethe wrote:

> Of all discoveries and opinions, none may have exerted a greater effect on the human spirit than the doctrine of Copernicus. The world had scarcely become known as round and complete in

itself when it was asked to waive the tremendous privilege of being the center of the universe. Never, perhaps, was a greater demand made on mankind—for by this admission so many things vanished in mist and smoke!

Galileo Challenges Aristotle and the Church

Even heavier blows were to follow. At the time Galileo began his experiments, he was still very much in the grip of Aristotelian ideas—ideas that although already shaken, continued to dominate European thought. The teachings of Aristotle had fostered an "a priorism" that had stunted and stifled the investigation of nature. Nonetheless this mode of thinking, with its heavy reliance on tradition and authority, was beginning to give way. Galileo (among others) turned away from received wisdom to *observation* and *experimentation* in order to determine what nature was really like. "Throughout the 2,000 years from Aristotle to Galileo," Bertrand Russell tells us, "no one had thought of finding out whether the laws of falling bodies are what Aristotle says they are" (Russell 1997:35). Galileo's famous experiment, conducted from the top of the Leaning Tower of Pisa, "showed in the most public manner the error of the Aristotelian view that treated the rate of fall as a function not of the period of fall but of the weight of the object" (Singer 1955:136–137). In addition to this, Galileo's *Sermones de Motu Gravium* contained "a number of objections to Aristotelian teaching" (Singer 1955:136).

As Galileo gained in scientific stature, he met increasing opposition from the Church. His critical attitude toward Aristotle, "the bulwark of the scholastic system, earned him the virulent enmity of the academic classes. Immediately it cost him his chair. He had, however, made the first definitive breach in the Aristotelian armour" (Singer 1955:137).

"Galileo believed that the Natural World was a vast system consisting of motions of matter in space and time, describable completely and solely in the language of mathematics" (Stebbing 1958:157). In addition, he accepted Copernicus's view that the earth was not fixed in space but revolved around the sun, which *was* fixed. Thus "[e]very one of the foundations of the Aristotelian system had been undermined by Galileo and their place taken by an intelligible mathematical relationship. From now on scholastic Aristotelianism was as much an embarrassment to official religion as the narrative of miracles became at a later date" (Singer 1955:145).

The Catholic clergy of the day, finding Galileo's pronouncements to be opposed to the teachings of the Church and inimical to its interests, vigorously resisted them. Of Galileo's findings the Inquisition declared, "The first proposition, that the sun is the center and does not revolve about the earth, is foolish, absurd, false in theology, and heretical, because expressly contrary to Holy Scripture"; and "the second proposition, that the earth is not in the center but revolves about the sun, is absurd, false in philosophy, and, from a theological point of view at least, opposed to true faith" (quoted in Smith 1955:312). But that was a mild reproach compared with the words of Pope Urban VIII: "The opinion of the earth's motion is of all heresies the most abominable, the most pernicious, the most scandalous; the immovability of the earth is thrice sacred; argument against the immortality of the soul, the existence of God, and the incarnation, should be tolerated sooner than argument to prove that the earth moves" (quoted in Smith 1955:313).

But Galileo fought back. "In matters of faith, he considered himself a devout and sincere Catholic" and thought his findings to be "completely congruous with a belief in the teachings of the Bible and of the Church Fathers" (Holton 1960:56). In a letter Galileo wrote that "the holy Bible and the phenomena of nature proceed alike from the divine Word, the former as the dictate of the Holy Ghost and the latter as the observant executrix of God's commands" (quoted in Holton 1960:56). In trenchant support of empirically based knowledge, Galileo argued that God "would not require us to deny sense and reason in physical matters which are set before our eyes and minds by direct experience or necessary demonstrations" (quoted in Holton 1960:57). Moreover, he did not hesitate to say that the Bible was not always to be taken as the last word on every subject. This belief he expressed by stating that the Bible "is not chained in every expression to conditions as strict as those which govern the physical effects; nor is God any less excellently revealed in Nature's actions than in the sacred statements of the Bible" (quoted in Holton 1960:57).

Outspoken statements like these, coupled with his advocacy of the heliocentric theory, brought Galileo into conflict with the Catholic Church and led to his trial for heresy, in which powerful ecclesiastical guns were leveled against him. During his trial in 1615, for example, Cardinal Roberto Bellarmine, the Church's guardian against heterodoxy, declared that "[t]o assert that the earth revolves around the sun is as erroneous as to claim that Jesus was not born of a virgin."

For centuries Galileo's views continued to be anathema to the Church. Three hundred years after his conviction, the report of a Vatican Biblical Commission—which had been appointed specifically to confront the problems of Scripture and science—dealt deftly with the issue by stating, "Of those methods which form the primary object of the teaching of natural sciences, God taught nothing to man by the intermediary of the sacred writers, since such instruction would not be of any use for their eternal salvation" (quoted in Holton 1960:57–58). In other words, the Bible was no longer to be regarded as a source of infallible knowledge of the physical world, since its concern was only with loftier matters!

In an essay entitled "On Transformation and Adaptation in Scientific Thought," the Austrian physicist Ernst Mach assessed Galileo's contribution to the advancement of science.

> It was toward the close of the sixteenth century that Galileo with a superb indifference to the dialectic arts and sophistic subtleties of the Schoolmen of his time, turned the attention of his brilliant mind to nature. By nature his ideas were transformed and released from the fetters of inherited prejudice. At once the mighty revolution was felt, that was therewith effected in the realm of human thought. (Mach 1943:214).

Kepler and His Three Laws

As the historian of science Gerald Holton observed, "[I]t was in the physical sciences, and particularly in celestial mechanics, that modern scientists first found themselves in conflict with theologians on a large scale" (Holton 1960:52). Following Copernicus, Tycho Brahe, and Galileo, the astronomical work of Johannes Kepler

(1571–1630) brought still another challenge to the theologians' and Scholastics' way of thinking about the cosmos.

Mindful of the attendant consequences, Kepler at one point remarked, "It must be confessed that there are very many who are devoted to Holiness, that dissent from the judgment of Copernicus, fearing to give the Lye to the Holy Ghost speaking in scriptures, if they should say that the earth moves and the Sun standeth still" (quoted in Jeans 1961:125). Nonetheless, in his first major astronomical work *Mysterium Cosmographicum* (1596), Kepler strongly supported the heliocentric theory. However, his defense of the theory was based in a strange way on religious grounds, since he conceived of the entire universe as being heliocentric, with God the Father represented by the sun!

But if Kepler supported Copernicus's views in one respect, he challenged them in another. Before Kepler it was thought that the orbits of the planets were circular. Why? Because since the time of the Greeks, it had been held a priori that the circle was the most perfect figure and the planets had to conform to it in their motions. As Bertrand Russell explained, "Although the Greeks knew a great deal about ellipses, and had carefully studied their mathematical properties, it never occurred to them as possible that the heavenly bodies could move in anything but circles or complications of circles, because their aesthetic sense dominated their speculations and made them reject all but the most symmetrical hypotheses" (Russell 1997:29). However, by observation and theoretical calculations, Kepler was able to show that planetary orbits were, in fact, *ellipses* (Hanson 1967:221).

Kepler's major contribution to astronomy was the formulation of his three laws of planetary motion. Here again was another irony. These laws, as well as Kepler's others scientific achievements, he thought had been inspired by God. Thus he wrote, "I believe that Divine Providence intervened so that by chance I found what I could never obtain by my own efforts. I believe this all the more because I have constantly prayed to God that I might succeed" (quoted in Pickover 2008:58). Indeed, he regarded his scientific discoveries "as a process of the revelation of the greatness of the Creator" (Singer 1955:145). Kepler had originally trained for the ministry and he wrote in his first book, *Mysterium Cosmographicum*, "I wanted to become a theologian." Failing that he found other compensating satisfactions. Said he, "Now, however, observe how through my efforts God is being celebrated in astronomy" (quoted in Holton 1960:53). After formulating his Second Law of Planetary Motion, Kepler exulted that he was in "sacred ecstasy," writing that "I have stolen the golden vases of the Egyptians and raised a tabernacle for my God, far away from the land of Egypt" (quoted in Holton 1960:55).

When Kepler succeeded in formulating his Third Law of Planetary Motion—the greatest of them all—after years of intense and dedicated effort, his exuberance overcame his modesty and he exulted, "The problem which inspired my lifelong devotion to astronomy ... I have solved at last.... The book [containing it] may be read now or by posterity, it does not matter. If it must wait a century to be read, I care not, since God himself has had to wait six thousand years" (quoted in Kramer 1974:I, 245–246). Elsewhere Kepler expressed the conviction that "God created the solar system according to mathematical pattern" (Losee 1993:49) but had left it to human beings to figure out just what that pattern was. And Kepler believed that *he* was God's chosen instrument to do so!

What Kepler must have felt in this regard was summed up by Ronald Hepburn: "In Kepler, ... nature appears as the realm of the quantitative, a realm amenable to mathematical study and, indeed, to more precise study than ancient philosophy ever demonstrated. Such a view of nature could coexist with a religious interpretation of things, for the mathematical structure could be taken as supplied and sustained by the mind of God" (Hepburn 1967:455).

Kepler had asserted, "I take religion seriously, I do not play with it" (quoted in Holton 1960:53). And he left no doubt of this when he declared, "In all science there is nothing which could prevent me from holding an opinion, nothing which could deter me from acknowledging openly an opinion of mine ... except solely the authority of the Holy Bible" (quoted in Holton 1960:53).

The history of science offers scarcely a better example of a life dedicated to science and achieving a great scientific triumph, while at the same time revealing a man held firmly in the grip of religion and unable to free himself from it—or wishing to. Indeed, he saw his own achievements as merely laying bare God's grand plan, thereby bringing him even greater glorification.

The Coming of Isaac Newton

As majestic as Kepler's three laws of planetary motion were, they all turned out to be deducible from a single master law—the law of universal gravitation. And the man who formulated that master law, of course, was Isaac Newton. It is important to emphasize that in achieving his great synthesis, Newton had intellectual forebears. He was the beneficiary of the work of those men who had preceded him, notably the three men we have just discussed—Copernicus, Galileo, and Kepler. And he readily acknowledged his debt to them. "If I have seen a little farther than others," he wrote, "it is because I have stood on the shoulders of giants" (quoted in Strathern 1997:9). But he stood tall nonetheless and his magnificent accomplishment was succinctly extolled in an epitaph written by his contemporary, the poet Alexander Pope: "Nature, and nature's laws lay hid in night, / God said, *Let Newton be!* And all was light."

When he began his astronomical work, Newton had in front of him Kepler's Third Law of Planetary Motion, which expressed a mathematical relationship between the periods of revolution of the planets and their distance from the sun. This relationship was true but it was also complex. Did some simpler law underlie it?

In addition to Kepler's laws, there was also Galileo's law of falling bodies to take into account. Could the two sets of laws be united and integrated into a single master principle? In the words of the historian of science Charles Singer, "It had not yet ... been shown that the natural laws that governed the heavenly bodies were in relation to the laws that govern earthly phenomena. To prove that that relation amounted to identity, to show that the force that causes the stone to fall is the same as that which keeps the planets in their path, was the achievement of Newton" (Singer 1955:149).

Newton's Master Synthesis

Some skepticism had been expressed about the force that Newton labeled gravity—enough, in fact, to lead him to insist that "gravity does really exist, and act[s] according to the laws which we have explained, and abundantly serves to account for all the motions of the celestial bodies, and of our sea" (quoted in Stebbing 1958:156).

Yet despite his conviction that it existed, this physical force of gravity was somehow not enough to completely satisfy Newton. Perhaps he was, underneath his sense of triumph, a bit disturbed that this new force had displaced the angels whose traditional function had been to drive the planets around in their orbits (Smith 1955:330). The *action at a distance* that was strikingly characteristic of gravity—so different in operation from, say, the act of one billiard ball striking another—bothered him enough that he felt compelled to introduce an additional factor to explain its operation and thus complete the picture.

> And now we might add something concerning a certain most subtle Spirit which pervades and lies hid in all great bodies; by the force and action of which Spirit the particles of bodies mutually attract one another at near distances, and cohere, if contiguous. (quoted in Stebbing 1958:156)

The *natural*, therefore, was not quite enough for Newton. It had to be supplemented by something that sounded suspiciously like the *super*natural. And these suspicions could be easily confirmed, for Newton had suggested that in his design of the universe, "God was responsible for giving the planets their initial velocities in orbit, without which the planets would have fallen into the Sun" (Pickover 2008:112).

There was, moreover, another reason why Newton felt the need to introduce supernatural elements into his system. Newton believed that the density of the *ether* was about 1/700,000th that of air. This medium, through which the planets were then believed to move, was thin enough, he said, "so that there would be no sensible alteration [in] the motions of the planets through frictional resistance even after 10,000 years. Over very long periods of time, however, the planets would gradually be slowed down and motion in general would be lost from the universe through frictional effects" (Mason 1962:205–206). The cosmos, in effect, was in danger of running down, and Newton feared that his celestial mechanics could not accommodate this supposed loss of motion. But here God, acting as a veritable *deus ex machina*, came to the rescue. "Newton therefore suggested that the Deity constantly replenished the motion lost by friction from the universe" (Mason 1962:206).

But another astronomical problem arose to perturb Newton, one with which he wrestled unsuccessfully. Observation had detected anomalies in the orbital movements of the planets Saturn and Jupiter, and these anomalies Newton could not satisfactorily explain by means of the laws of celestial mechanics. The irregularities were slight and of short duration, eventually ironing themselves out. Nonetheless they existed and had to be accounted for in some way.

So strong a hold did theology have on Newton's mind that rather than deciding this discrepancy must be due to some natural factor, hitherto undetected and thus not allowed for, Newton chose to invoke the hand of God. The Deity, he felt, "was always present in the universe" and was ever ready to step in and correct such irregularities as might occur and thus return the planets to their proper courses (Mason 1962:294).

It was more than a century later that the mystery was solved. The solution was provided by the great French mathematician and astronomer Pierre-Simon de Laplace. Using an improved form of the calculus, devised principally by Lagrange, Laplace was able to show that the anomalies in the orbits of Saturn and Jupiter were caused by their gravitational interactions, which were magnified when the trajectories of the two planets around the sun brought them relatively close to each other (Harré 1967:392; Mason 1962:294). The hand of God could thus be dispensed with.

This achievement of Laplace, little noted today, was nonetheless a great step forward in the history of human understanding. It showed that despite Newton's occasional lapses into the supernatural, the solar system could be shown to operate entirely according to the laws of celestial mechanics, with no need whatever for divine intervention.

Newton's introduction of God into his system where he thought that he needed his assistance was not at all surprising. After all, he was a devout—indeed an almost mystical—Christian who spent hours poring over the Bible and who, for example, "researched the prophetic utterances of Daniel and St. John for a chronology of the future, and carefully concluded that Satan's spell over the world would be broken in the year 1867" (Updike 1998:120).

Newton clung to the biblical six days of creation but was convinced from reading the New Testament in the original language that translations of it had corrupted the text. In fact, he came to the conclusion that "the idea of the Trinity (Father, Son, and Holy Ghost) was a complete hoax, a fraudulent conception foisted on Christianity by scheming deviants. Christ had not been *divine*" (Strathern 1997:59). Therefore, Newton insisted, Jesus was not to be regarded as an intercessor and God should be prayed to directly.

Newton could not find words strong enough to praise the Lord and his achievements. In an oft-quoted passage, he declared that "this most beautiful cosmos could only proceed from the counsel and dominion of an intelligent and powerful Being" (Newton 1934:544). Nor was this an isolated passage. From his knowledge of nature Newton felt ready to assert, "And these things being rightly dispatch'd, does it not appear from Phenomena that there is a Being incorporeal, living, intelligent, omnipresent, who in infinite Space, as it were in his Sensory, sees the things themselves intimately, and thoroughly perceives them, and comprehends them wholly by their immediate presence to himself?" (quoted in Stebbing 1958:62).

Newton, indeed, never seemed to tire of heaping encomiums on God. To cite just one more:

> The Deity endures for ever [sic] and is everywhere present, and by existing always and everywhere, he constitutes duration and space.... [He] governs all things and knows all things that are, and can be done.... Who, being in all places, is more able by His will to move the bodies within His boundless uniform sensorium, and thereby to form and reform the parts of the Universe, than we are by our will to move the parts of our body? (quoted in Mason 1962:206)

And Gerald Holton recounts the following story.

> [Richard] Bentley [1662–1742] had been appointed to the Robert Boyle Lectureship; its warrant being "to prove the existence of God by arguments drawn from nature.... In order to be able to use, in his last two lectures, arguments from Physics, Bentley turned to Newton himself for advice. Newton replied in four letters, the first of which starts with the sentence: 'Sir,

When I wrote my Treatise about our System, I had an Eye upon such Principles as might work with considering Men, for the Belief of a Deity; nothing can rejoice me more than to find it useful for that Purpose."' (quoted in Holton 1960:59)

Ironically, then, he whose work did more than anyone else to displace God from his traditional task of running the universe was actually a pious, dedicated, and unquestioning theist for whom this displacement was furthest from his intentions. So striking is this contradiction that it has been emphasized repeatedly by historians of science. John Greene, for example, noted that "[t]he Newtonian conception of nature as a law-bound system of matter in motion, when pushed to its logical conclusion, proved irreconcilable with belief in miracles, special providence, prophecies, and the like" (Greene 1960:255). Similarly, Gerald Holton wrote that "[a]s science has pushed back the frontiers of the unknown, it has made untenable the position of theologians who argued as Newton did [i.e., that God ultimately pulled the strings], and has left fewer and fewer chores for the Deity in the everyday functions of the world" (Holton 1960:60).

But it did not take modern-day historians of science to recognize the profound theological impact of Newton's celestial mechanics. His contemporaries clearly perceived it. Gottfried Leibniz, Newton's archrival, was not long in pointing out the implications of extending naturalistic explanations to the workings of the solar system. He asserted that with his formulation of the law of gravitation, Newton "had robbed the Deity of some of his most vital attributes and had sapped the foundations of Natural Religion" (Levy 1938: 128).

Newton's excessive piety, however, is merely an idle curiosity in the overall history of science. Immeasurably above it in importance stand his contributions to the scientific understanding of the heavens. With Newtonian celestial mechanics, it became possible for the first time to calculate the precise workings of the solar system. Thus eclipses—which not long before were regarded as diabolical manifestations, striking panic into the hearts of common folk throughout the world—now not only came within rational comprehension, but were capable of being predicted with a striking degree of accuracy.

Comets: From Objects of Dread to Predictable Phenomena

Less well known, but still affording an impressive measure of the intellectual progress made in human thought over the course of just two centuries, was the interpretation of comets. In 1456 a comet streaked across the heavens, causing terror throughout Christendom. Worried by what this strange apparition might portend, as well as by the relentless march of the Ottoman Turks up the Balkan peninsula, Pope Calixtus III ordered that prayers be offered to ward off the dire threats. A bit later, when comets had begun to be interpreted as normal astronomical phenomena, Martin Luther—still clinging to the old fear about them—was led to remark, "The heathen write that the comet may arise from natural causes, but God created not one that does not foretoken a sure calamity" (quoted in Russell 1997:47).

The reappearance of this comet a little more than two hundred years later provided a dramatic demonstration of the predictive power that science had by then attained. By 1682 astronomy had advanced to the point where, when a comet appeared in the night sky in August of that year, it was no longer cause for general alarm. The English astronomer Edmund Halley, observing this comet and calculating its orbit, concluded that it was the very same one that Kepler had observed in 1607. Estimating its period at about seventy-five years, Halley decided that it must also be the same comet that had terrified Europe in 1456 and had been seen again in 1531 (Laplace 2007:5–6; Newcomb 1932:226–227).

On the basis of the calculated length of its period—a little over seventy-five years—and applying to it Newton's laws of celestial mechanics, Halley predicted that the comet (today known by his name) would reappear in late 1758 or early 1759. Since Halley was born in 1656, he would be long dead by then and—the skeptics said—quite safe from being proved wrong.

Halley died in 1742, but as the predicted date approached for the comet's return, the French mathematician Alexis Claude Clairaut—intent on verifying Halley's prediction—applied the laws of celestial mechanics and was able to calculate the effect that would be produced by the action of Jupiter and Saturn on the comet's orbit.

"He found that this action would so delay its return that it would not reach perihelion [the point at which its orbit brought it closest to the sun] until the spring of 1759. It appeared according to the prediction," actually reaching perihelion on March 12, 1759 (Newcomb 1932:227).

Thus in a little more than two centuries, human thought had evolved to the point where an event that had once terrorized the world was now greeted with equanimity, and indeed whose recurrence had actually been forecast with great exactitude.

CHAPTER 9

The Attenuation of the Concept of God

We begin this chapter with the God of the Bible already fully fledged and sharply delineated. The Deity was then further elaborated and defined by the early Church fathers, especially Augustine and Thomas Aquinas. Here was a God with powers plenipotentiary—creator of all the world and its inhabitants, omnipotent, omniscient, and benevolent. He was also the formulator of the rules of moral conduct and was ready to punish any transgression of these rules—if not in the here and now, at least in the hereafter. In form and visage, he was clearly anthropomorphic … and as "Our Father," unequivocally male.

We shall see, however, that over the ensuing centuries this conception of God was successively modified into something markedly different. During much of the seventeenth and eighteenth centuries—at the hands of certain philosophers—the sharp contours of the God of orthodox Christianity were gradually softened, blunted, and blurred. Starting as a supernatural being of solid substance, he began to lose some of these characteristics and in time turned into more and more of a rarified essence.

Even during the dark days of the Middle Ages, faith alone sometimes failed to satisfy the few thoughtful Christians who, as a way to bolster their simple faith, began to look for rational arguments for God's existence. Thomas Aquinas had already favored formulating such carefully reasoned proofs. Two hundred years later, Nicholas of Cusa proposed several "proofs" that God existed. (A *proof*, one may note, is usually called for only after faith alone is no longer deemed sufficient.) The most famous medieval proof of God's existence was that devised by St. Anselm. Briefly put, Anselm claimed that he was thinking of the most perfect God imaginable, and since such a God would be more perfect if he existed than if he did not, he *had* to exist! Though no longer taken seriously even by theologians, in Anselm's day it was thought to be an ingenious and convincing proof. Today one is inclined to regard it as either disingenuous or charmingly naive.

Miracles versus the Laws of Nature

At the same time, a degree of uneasiness began to develop regarding the authenticity of miracles. Thomas Hobbes characterized something as a miracle "if when it is produced, we cannot imagine it to have been done by natural means, but only by the immediate hand of God" (Hobbes 1997:318). Miracles had, of course, appeared in great profusion in the Bible. But as time went on, they were no longer reported nearly as frequently or as convincingly. The credulity of the faithful began to be seriously tested, if not severely strained, by being asked to believe in them.

Also at the same time, a certain dissatisfaction was beginning to emerge with a God who was supposed to have limitless power, yet who felt compelled to intervene at every turn in order to make sure the world ran as he wished. As a corrective to this view, already in the fourteenth century the concept of a God who decreed that the world should run according to laws he himself had laid down—and then continued to allow it to run that way—began to appeal to advanced thinkers. If this new limited form of divine control did not yet apply to human affairs, at least it manifested itself in keeping the stars and planets on course. One of the earliest expressions of this idea was by the French scholar and cleric Jean Buridan, who suggested around the year 1350 that "God may have given each of the heavenly bodies the impetus He desired at the time He created them, and they have been running of their own impetus ever since" (Dales 1989:111).

In assigning this circumscribed role to the Deity, Buridan was ahead of his time, anticipating by some four hundred years the English astronomer John Nichol, who "hailed the advent of the comprehension of Nature through discoverable Laws and rejoiced at the disappearance of the capricious ways of Providence," feeling that it "added greatly to the dignity of God to think that He governed the world through Laws and not through unpredictable willfulness" (Peckham 1959:30).

But while some believed that an extension of the operation of natural law increased the glory of God, others disagreed. They felt that it diluted the firm conception of God given to the world by Holy Writ. Nonetheless a slowly growing rationalism led to greater skepticism with regard to miracles—which were, after all, violations of those laws. And these apparent violations contributed to a questioning of religious authority. The skepticism that this bred led to a harder look at those miracles sprinkled liberally and unabashedly throughout the Bible. Had Jonah actually been swallowed by a whale and survived? Did the sun actually stand still on Joshua's command? Did Moses, in fact, part the Red Sea? Had Methuselah really lived nine hundred years? Did Lot's wife literally turn into a pillar of salt? Miracles—events that ran counter not only to natural law but also to everyday experience—now began to be seen as seriously challenging the very laws that God had laid down. They came, therefore, to be regarded with increasing suspicion.

Skepticism Begins to Spread

Only around 1600, however, with the introduction of scientific thinking on a broad scale and its heavy reliance on empiricism and experimentation rather than revelation and authority, did traditional religious beliefs begin to be seriously questioned. The skepticism engendered by science continued to spread and resonate throughout Europe, even among those thinkers concerned primarily with theological matters. The very fact that the eminent classical scholar Richard Bentley (1662–1742) was appointed to the Robert Boyle Lectureship, and given the specific assignment "to prove the existence of God by arguments drawn from nature," strongly suggested that sufficient doubts along these lines had already arisen (Holton 1960:59).

In addition to such skepticism, a new and different stream of evidence helped broaden the perspective and deepen the questioning mood of those European thinkers concerned with matters of religion. As described by G. C. Joyce:

> Travelers were bringing home from recently discovered, or rediscovered countries reports of imposing civilizations, in which the sanctions of civil order were provided by religions of the utmost diversity in origin and character. In this way materials for the study of comparative religion began to be collected, and it

became possible to form some conception of the bewildering
multiplicity of religious customs, ceremonies, and doctrines
throughout the world. No philosophic explanation of man and
man's religious faculties could claim to be adequate which left
all this mass of new material out of account. (Joyce 1911:533)

The strict religious doctrine that for centuries had reigned in
Europe, against which these new foreign ideas began to clash,
demanded unquestioning belief in the God of the Bible. Whatever
modifications the Church fathers had made in how God was perceived and portrayed were merely refinements of the biblical
account of the Deity. Being divinely inspired, the words of the Bible
were not to be challenged and revelation was not to be disputed.
Every miracle described in the Holy Book was regarded as literally
true and thus had to be believed.

The beginnings of the great revolution in human thinking that
was to breach the walls of religious orthodoxy can be dated to
roughly the year 1600. Early in the seventeenth century, Galileo's
investigations were uncovering striking regularities in the behavior
of nature. And around the time that the experimental science of
Galileo and others was yielding such notable results, the philosophical underpinnings of that science were beginning to be enunciated.

Francis Bacon (1561–1626) was piecing together—at about that
time—the first closely reasoned philosophy of science, disdainful of
what had previously passed for genuine knowledge. On the one hand,
he argued, "The Schoolmen, with their love of disputation, only
passed from one question to another, without ever reaching knowledge," and on the other he insisted that "[t]he Renaissance humanists
were so much in love with the style of the classical writers that they
had come to cultivate eloquence for the sake of eloquence and thus
to 'hunt after words more than matter'" (Cranston 1967:237). Yet
Bacon's reproach of the Schoolmen was tempered by the fact that he,
like all men of his age, retained a fairly orthodox conception of God.

The Rise of Deism

All in all, Bacon may be said to have broken the philosophical
ground that others were to sow. The movement that he led, which

involved a formal questioning of many of the certainties of traditional Christianity, came to be given the name *deism*. One student of the movement, G. C. Joyce, dates its beginning as contemporaneous with the English Revolution of 1688 (Joyce 1911:533). The same writer, however, felt that already in the writings of Bacon's contemporary Thomas Hobbes (1588–1679) one could detect stirrings toward deism, and that "the tendency of the *Leviathan* was in the direction of a thoroughgoing infidelity" (Joyce 1911:534). Indeed, according to Joyce, "As much as any other single writer ... [Hobbes] gave the impulse to religious speculation, and, by helping to shake the old confidence in tradition, contributed to the removal of one of the main obstacles to the introduction of Deism" (Joyce 1911:534). Coming a little later, and regarded as the father of British empiricism, John Locke (1632–1704) can also be counted among the intellectual forerunners of deism.

It should be kept in mind, though, that as skeptical as they were about many elements of Christianity, the deists were by no means atheists. They all believed in God and were simply looking for surer ways of gaining trustworthy knowledge of him. It was that the formerly accepted ways of doing so no longer satisfied them.

Faith as the cornerstone of religious belief—that is, the unquestioned acceptance of the word of Scripture, without asking for evidence to support it—was being undermined. It was an age that increasingly required argument and evidence before it would embrace any proposition wholeheartedly.

Nevertheless expressing religious dissent in late seventeenth century England—as openly professing deism was deemed to be—was risky business. The Press Licensing Act of 1662 "very effectively prevented the publication of heterodox works" (Bury 2007:110). True, in 1695 this law was allowed to lapse, but there were still the Ecclesiastical Courts to contend with. These courts had the power to imprison anyone for a period of six months for the offenses of "atheism, blasphemy, heresy and damnable opinions" (Bury 2007:110). Nonetheless, in 1696 John Toland, sometimes considered the father of deism, published a tract entitled *Christianity Not Mysterious* in which he argued that "[n]either God himself or any of His attributes are mysterious to us." All his ways, Toland believed, were clearly manifest and open to rational inspection. Toland's book elicited many attempts at refutation and was deemed heretical enough to be condemned by the Irish Parliament and ordered burned (Joyce 1911:535). Indeed, Toland had to leave Ireland "to escape arrest by the prosecution" (Sorley 1965:146). In a second book, *Amyntor* (1699), he cast doubt on certain historical passages in the Bible, maintaining that they were "the offspring of superstition and credulity" (Joyce 1911:535).

"Reason" was the watchword and touchstone of the deists. Toland virtually deified it. Nothing contrary to reason could be part of a purified Christianity (Sorley 1965:146). "What man could not comprehend," he contended, "was, on that account, to be rejected" (Joyce 1911:535). Miracles were therefore denied out of hand. Humanity was to be guided by reason and reason alone. Still, the fact should not be lost sight of that in spite of his unrelenting emphasis on reason, Toland professed "some form of theism here and in subsequent writings" (Mossner 1967:141).

Another deist of the period, Matthew Tindal (1657–1733), likewise affirmed that nothing belonged to "true Christianity" except that which "after a strict scrutiny ... our reason tells us is worthy of having God as its author" (quoted in Joyce 1911:536). God, then, was still very much in the picture, but there had to be a pruning away of invalid ways of getting to know him or ascertain his will. As long as these reservations were kept in mind, the practice of religion was still considered a legitimate enterprise.

In deism, prayer, revelation, miracles, and other such forms of communication between the individual and God were reduced to a minimum—if not severed entirely. The God of the deists became more distant and therefore less accessible; he was, so to speak, held at arm's length. Writing in 1704, Samuel Clarke—an enemy of deism—characterized its advocates as those who "pretend to believe [in] the existence of an external, infinite, independent, intelligent Being; at the same time ... they fancy God does not at all concern himself in the government of the world, nor has any regard to, or care of, what is done therein" (quoted in Sorley 1965:149n).

Thus according to the deists, instead of God's presence being verified by observing the performance of miracles that were carried out irregularly and at unexpected times, there was to be a different way of judging how he worked. He was still acknowledged as having created the world, but then he was thought to have laid down rules by which it was to run—by natural law—ever after. It thus became unnecessary for him to intervene, from time to time, in order to have things run properly. God still retained the *power* to intervene but he seldom needed to exercise it. Only occasionally, as Newton held, did he involve himself so as to regularize the motions of the planets when they happened to get out of kilter. Such intervention might be tantamount to a violation of his preferred way of doing things, but it occurred only rarely.

In a way the God of the eighteenth century deists was reminiscent of the otiose culture hero of many primitive societies. He had carried out important work early in the history of the world, determining how it was to be structured and how it was to run, but then had withdrawn from the scene. Today he lived remote and aloof, an interested spectator to be sure, but no longer an active participant.

Invoking natural law rather than divine intention to account for whatever transpired on earth was becoming more and more common. Skeptics became increasingly suspicious of any alleged instance of God having set aside natural law and imposed his capricious will on mankind. Most critics, however, were careful not to malign God or deny his ultimate authority—let alone his existence. Even a redoubtable skeptic like David Hume (1711–1776) reined in his skepticism when it came to God's existence or his power. Thus he affirmed that "[t]he whole frame of nature bespeaks an intelligent author; and no rational enquirer can, after serious reflection, suspend his belief a moment with regard to the primary principles of genuine Theism and Religion" (Hume 1927:253). And again, after contemplating the unity of nature, Hume remarked that "[a]ll things in the universe are evidently of a piece. Everything is adjusted to everything. One design prevails throughout the whole. And this uniformly leads the mind to acknowledge one author" (quoted in Huxley 1908:170).

One of the concepts that emerged from—or at least was strengthened by—deism was that of "natural religion." The underlying premise of natural religion was, again, that the only valid basis for believing in God was through the application of reason. Revelation was no longer to be regarded as admissible evidence of the Almighty. Religion therefore was not abolished, but there was an insistence that *true* religion sprang only from a *reasoned* interpretation of what nature caused to be part of human experience. As a source of truth, then, Reason trumped Revelation. In fact, it was thought that the existence of God could be established quite independently of Revelation, and indeed a number of deists attempted to do just that.

Thomas Paine: The Quintessential Deist

At this point it might be worth presenting in some detail the ideas of the best known of the latter-day deists, Thomas Paine (1737–1809), as set forth in his celebrated book *The Age of Reason* (1794, 1796), of which the British historian John Bury wrote, "This book is remarkable as the first important English publication in which the Christian scheme of salvation and the Bible are assailed in plain language without any disguise or reserve" (Bury 2007:135).

Despite the fact that Theodore Roosevelt is said to have called him a "dirty little atheist," Paine did not deny God's existence. He adhered pretty strictly not only to God, but also to monotheism. "I believe in one God, and no more," he said (Paine 2006:18). Indeed, if atheism were to be imputed at all, Paine argued, it was not to himself but to Christianity! In a striking turn of accusations, he wrote:

> As to the Christian system of faith, it appears to me as a species of atheism; a sort of religious denial of God. It professes to believe in a man [Jesus] rather than in God. It is a compound made up chiefly of man-ism with but little deism, and is as near to atheism as twilight is to darkness. It introduces between man and his Maker an opaque body, which it calls the redeemer. (Paine 2006:42)

Clearly, then, Paine was no Christian. "I do not believe in the creed professed by the Jewish church, by the Roman church, ... by the Protestant church, nor by any church that I know of. My own mind is my own church" (Paine 2006:18). Thus while Paine did believe in God, he insisted that "[t]he only idea man can affix to the name of God, is that of a first cause" (Paine 2006:39). And like a good deist, he added that "[i]t is only by the exercise of reason, that man can discover God" (Paine 2006:39).

It was Paine's belief that God had created the universe not for his own pleasure, but for humanity's edification. By studying the universe, people could determine the rules by which it ran—rules that God had imparted to it at the very beginning. Accordingly, he wrote, "The Almighty lecturer, by displaying the principles of science in the structure of the universe, has invited man to study and to imitation. It is as if he had said to the inhabitants of this globe that we call ours, I have made an earth for man to dwell upon, and I have rendered the starry heavens visible, to teach man science and the arts. He can now provide his own comfort" (Paine 2006:44).

The Founding Fathers of the United States—who were well acquainted with Paine's writing—were, to a significant extent, deists. Indeed, none of the first five presidents was an orthodox Christian.

> John Adams, a Unitarian, did not accept the notion of the trinity or the divinity of Christ. In 1804, Thomas Jefferson used a razor to remove all passages of the King James Version of the New Testament that had supernatural content—such as the virgin birth, resurrection, or turning water into wine. About one-tenth of the bible [sic] remained, which he pasted together and published as *The Philosophy of Jesus of Nazareth*. (Pickover 2008:106)

It is a great irony that Thomas Jefferson, the chief architect of the U.S. Constitution and third president of the United States, were he running for the office today and were these facts made generally known (as surely they would be), would stand very little chance of being elected!

"Natural Religion" and the Undermining of Christianity

One can trace a gradual evolution in the tenets adhered to by the deists. At first they remained within the ambit of Christianity and tried merely to rid it of those elements—especially miracles and divine revelation—that ran counter to everyday experience and the dictates of common sense. With the passage of time, however, the deists came more and more to diverge from traditional Christianity, distance themselves from the Bible, and espouse "natural religion," which contained much less of the supernatural element. They held fast to the view that all things were completely understandable through the application of reason alone. At the same time, God himself, if not stripped of his powers altogether, had had them diminished in strength and reduced in scope. Moreover, he was seen as exercising these powers less frequently and through the agency of "nature" rather than directly by his own personal involvement.

G. C. Joyce provided a clear summary of what became the deists' position in its later stages.

> [God had brought the world] into being and ordained its laws. He imparted to it once for all the energy which serves as the driving power of the stupendous mechanism. The Deist recognizes in God the ultimate source of matter and motion, and, consistently with this conception, admits the possibility of occasional interferences on the part of the Deity. But, though the possibility of such interferences is granted, the probability is called in question. It seems more in accordance with the principles of Deism that Nature should be left to work itself out in obedience to laws originally given. (Joyce 1911:541)

Deism and the French *Philosophes*

Although deism originated in England, it is more commonly associated with France. In fact, it has been said that "[i]n France the conceptions characteristic of Deism found a soil more favorable to their rapid developments than England had ever afforded them" (Joyce 1911:538). And in that country they were most prominently advanced by the *philosophes* of the Enlightenment.

Curiously enough, deism's entry into France occurred through Voltaire (1694–1778). During his exile in England from 1726 to 1729, Voltaire became acquainted with the writings of the English deists and was impressed by them. Despite the fact that he is often called a deist, Voltaire did not consider himself to be one. He believed in God the Father, epitomizing his views by saying that "the existence of a watch proves the existence of a watchmaker," thereby anticipating William Paley in proposing the now familiar argument from design. Voltaire may have believed in God but he was decidedly not a Christian. Indeed, he renounced any connection with Christianity and "considered the establishment of Christianity a grievous aberration of the human mind" (Torrey 1967:267).

While he believed that God had created the universe, Voltaire thought there were definite limitations to his power. God, he asserted, could not be omnipotent and benevolent at the same time. With approval he quoted the famous remark attributed to Epicurus: "Either God can remove evil from the world and will not, or being willing to do so, cannot; or he neither can nor will; or he is both able and willing. If he is willing and cannot, he is not omnipotent. If he can but will not, he is not benevolent. If he is neither willing nor able, he is neither omnipotent nor benevolent" (quoted in Torrey 1967:265). This conundrum has remained a thorny problem for Christian theologians—and true believers—down to the present day.

Voltaire thus found it impossible to reconcile God's alleged omnipotence and benevolence with great tragedies, such as the Lisbon earthquake of 1755 that killed 60,000 persons and inspired him to write his biting satirical novel *Candide,* ridiculing the notion of God's goodness. Why, he wondered, had so many people died inside the churches of Lisbon while the brothels of that city had been spared (Torrey 1967:265)?

The *Encyclopédie,* the great product of the French Enlightenment, has been called "an organ of deism" (Unsigned 1910a:937). Its pages did in fact reflect a skeptical, deterministic, materialistic tone and it was a strong voice in combating superstition, religious orthodoxy, and clerical authority. For that reason it was banned for a time by both the church and the state. The high purpose of its editors—principally Denis Diderot—was "[t]o change the general way of thinking," and indeed the *Encyclopédie* proved to be extraordinarily influential in transforming the intellectual climate of Western Europe (Wilson 1967:506).

Despite the overall secular approach of the work, in an article entitled "Irreligieux" Diderot identified the moral law—the *jus naturae* to which many articles in the *Encyclopédie* referred—with "the universal law that the finger of God has engraved upon the hearts of all" (Wilson 1967:507). From this statement we can perhaps conclude that while Diderot found it unnecessary to regard the Bible as providing the moral compass people needed to guide their everyday lives, he nonetheless believed that such a compass existed and that God had implanted it deep within every human soul. This view was thus strikingly reminiscent of Immanuel Kant's belief in a "categorical imperative," an instinctive spur to right conduct in every human being. But this view was not original with either Diderot or Kant. It had been enunciated nearly a century earlier by the Earl of Shaftsbury (1671–1719) who believed that morality did not depend on religion at all, but rather that man's "ethical standard was determined by the dictates of an intuitive moral faculty, forming part of the essential endowment of human nature" (Joyce 1911:538).

The Rejection of the Trinity

The deists were primarily concerned with the functions of God, seeking to curtail them and insisting that they be manifested through law and not through caprice. At the same time, there was a critical examination of the traditional ways in which the *personality* of God—or of his son—was to be conceived. Most prominent in this regard was the position maintained by Thomas Paine of denying outright the divinity of Christ. This, of course, amounted to a rejection of the Holy Trinity.

One of the principal challenges to orthodox Christianity, in fact, came over the very subject of the Trinity. Among the great mysteries of Christianity was how God could be one person and three simultaneously. This idea proved troublesome (indeed "unscriptural") to a number of "Christians" and their response was an espousal of Unitarianism. God was God. Jesus—a man—had lived and died like any other mortal, but there had been no Resurrection of his physical remains. He had been a great prophet, indeed a great man, but that was all.

This belief, of course, represented an ominous threat to traditional Christianity and was met in England—a nation where the state and the church were virtually one—with the passage of the Statute of 1698. This law provided that "any person educated in the Christian religion" who "shall by writing, printing, teaching, or advised speaking deny any one of the persons in the Holy Trinity to be God" was prevented from holding public office after a first conviction, and lost his or her civil rights and went to prison for three years following a second (Bury 2007:111). Unitarianism, therefore, was declared outside the pale and Unitarians became an embattled and beleaguered minority.

While cutting themselves loose from what they deemed to be the less tenable precepts of Christianity, Unitarians still retained the central core of the religion—a belief in God. Moreover, they continued to retain many of the trappings of organized religion and to welcome as communicants people who, while not atheists, no longer felt comfortable in either a Protestant or Catholic setting.

Those who subscribed to Unitarian principles did not find that their new religion demanded a rigid and uniform acceptance of a definite creed. Indeed, they had been driven away from other sects precisely because of such demands. American Unitarians, for instance, were said to have turned their backs on "the pessimism and morbidity of Calvinist religion," just as Joseph Priestly—the early English Unitarian—had done in England years before them (Kurtz 1967:86).

Needless to say, strict Christians (such as the Methodists) considered Unitarians to be an abomination. Replying to a tract by Priestley in which he had attacked their fervid evangelism, the Methodists rebutted him with a hymn enjoining their own deity to smite the false believers.

> Stretch out thy hands, thou Triune God:
> The Unitarian fiend expel
> And chase his doctrine back to Hell.
> (Priestley 1965:17)

It was the Unitarians' softening of the doctrinal demands placed on their supporters that led Erasmus Darwin to call Unitarianism "a feather-bed to catch a falling Christian" (quoted in Ward 1943:28). What united Unitarians, besides a heavy reliance on reason in the interpretation of Scripture, was a greater latitude of thought in all matters of religious belief. While there might be an acceptance of the divinity of the Christian God, such a belief was accompanied by an insistence on the full humanity of what others took to be the son of God. Consequently, this offshoot of Christianity could no longer be regarded as truly Christian. By embracing this new faith, and cutting off the Son and the Holy Ghost, Trinitarianism had become Unitarianism.

The "Higher Criticism" and the Waning of Belief

But now this God, whose existence Unitarians continued to accept (even if with stipulated limitations on his powers), was himself undergoing a change in how he was being perceived. The traditional Christian view of the person of God, of course, was that of an anthropomorphic deity. And not only was he human in form and countenance, but also unmistakably male. By the late eighteenth century, however, those philosophers not ready to dispense with the idea of God altogether were nonetheless moving away from picturing him as a solemn masculine figure with a flowing white beard. And his other human attributes were being dissolved away as well.

Somewhat later, biblical scholarship began to subject the Bible itself to rigorous scrutiny. While accepting the historicity and in some cases even the divinity of Christ, the "Higher Criticism" (as it was called) was carried out principally by German scholars and concerned itself largely with the ordering and dating of the books of the Gospel. Nonetheless this careful scholarly analysis had the effect of weakening the authority of the Bible over practicing Christians.

But this parsing of passages in the Bible was largely the concern of minutely focused scholars. Theologians and philosophers continued to concern themselves more broadly with the general concept of God. And as God began losing his shape and the distinctness of his features, he was being transmuted into someone or something less recognizably human. And as he became less anthropomorphic, he became more amorphous and ethereal—in fact, more an *essence* than a *being*. According to the German philosopher Johann Gottlieb Fichte, God was now "without consciousness and personality" (Case 1911:230). This striking denaturing of God will be explored more fully in the next chapter.

CHAPTER 10

The Rise and Demise of Idealist Philosophy

As we have seen, the notion that an immaterial, incorporeal world underlies the material, observable one is long standing. At times it has even attained considerable prominence, its advocates proclaiming that appearance is not the basic reality after all, but merely a mask for covering something deeper and more fundamental—the real stuff of existence—that lies below it.

The view that what we see is not truly real, but only a pale reflection of reality, did not begin with Western philosophy, as is often assumed. The belief is found in the primitive world as well. The Dakota, for example, held this old idealist notion, believing that we do not perceive the real world at all but only its *tonwanpi*, which Paul Radin—in *Primitive Man as Philosopher*—translated as "divine resemblance" (Radin 1985:252–253). *That,* and only that, is truly real. We saw in Chapter 2 that the Jívaro Indians of Ecuador have a similar conception, and we quoted Michael Harner to the effect that among the Jívaro, "[t]he normal waking life is explicitly viewed as false or a lie, and it is firmly believed that truth ... is to be found by entering the supernatural world or what the Jívaro view as the real world" (Harner 1972:134).

Despite such exceptions, however, primitive peoples' conceptions of the world—while at times highly imaginative and fanciful—tend not to be excessively rarefied or abstract. Notions like "pure essence" or "transcendent ideas" do not generally arise among them, living as they do close to the hard facts of nature. Such ideas are more likely to be a product of the leisure-time musings of philosophers dwelling comfortably in complex societies, who do not have to spend their days hunting deer or planting corn and can afford to devote their time to idle speculation. The best known and most elaborate early Western system of thought which taught that the realm of ideas is the highest reality was that of the Greek philosopher Plato.

The Platonic Basis of Western Idealism

Still, the metaphysical groundwork had to be laid for Plato's system to be erected. Before the notion of the world as *ideas* could be advanced, the concept of *mind* had first to be established. After all, everyone agreed, ideas were the product of the *mind* and—as the generator of ideas—the mind had initially to be given formal recognition. The Harvard philosopher Ernest Hocking has argued that "[m]atter is at first so obvious, the mind so intangible ..., that mind had to be *discovered* for metaphysics, as a part of reality" (Hocking 1939:219), and this discovery he assigned to the earlier, pre-Socratic philosophers Heraclitus (540–475 B.C.) and Anaxagoras (500–428 B.C.). The latter conceived of mind as "a very fine and diaphanous substance disseminated throughout limitless space" (Hocking 1939:219). In keeping with this sweeping but diffuse conception of mind, Plato (427–347 B.C.) saw the things of the world as consisting of

> a system of immaterial beings, the "ideas," which appear to be "embodied" in the particular shapes we see by becoming as it were entrapped in matter, and compromised by association therewith, but which in reality remain unsullied in their own unchangeable realm. The ideas are perfect and eternal; their visible images are defective and passing. (Hocking 1939:219–220)

Such archetypes or spiritual templates of the tangible objects accessible to perception did not, however, exist in and of themselves; they had been created by God. Since the Christian God that followed a few centuries after Plato could also not be perceived through the senses but had to be grasped through the mind, Plato's idealistic philosophy proved quite congenial to later Western theologians and their philosophical congeners. And so it is that an interest in Plato's ideas has continued to occupy—if not dominate—philosophers' thoughts almost to the present day. Indeed, Alfred North Whitehead went so far as to declare that "the safest general characterization of the European philosophical tradition is that it consists in a series of footnotes to Plato" (quoted in Lovejoy 1936:24).

Still, there was also a certain practical, barefoot materialism to primitive Christianity that could not be denied. To be sure, Christian dogma did call for a belief in the reality of the spiritual, but at the same time Christians accepted—without much question—the independent existence of matter. For them matter did not require, as it did later for Bishop Berkeley, to be *observed* in order to exist! The writers of the Gospels were certainly not swayed by the powers of the mind. After all, did the Bible not ask with a touch of skepticism, "Which of you by taking thought can add one cubit onto his stature?" (Matthew 6:27).

During the Middle Ages, Scholastic philosophers (being theologians at heart) were much devoted to problems that by their very nature could not be solved by observation, but only through logical argument—in effect through *excogitation*. How else could one possibly determine, for example, how many angels could dance on the head of a pin? Indeed, a belief in the privileged reality of ideas that regarded them as finer, more subtle, and more noble than mere matter carried over into later Western thought. And this continued to be the case even after scientific thinking began making serious inroads into Western philosophy. Thus Pierre Gassendi (1592–1655), who had a higher regard for matter than most of his contemporaries, who advocated empiricism as the best road to genuine knowledge, and who was a friend of Galileo and Kepler, nonetheless thought of physical appearance as only second best. "[A]ll we can know," he argued, "is how things appear, not how they really are in themselves" (quoted in Popkin 1967:270). A thread of idealism, then, ran through even that element of European thought represented by Gassendi and generally labeled materialist.

The Subjective Idealism of Bishop Berkeley

The classic expression of idealist philosophy was that of a bishop of the Anglican Church, George Berkeley (1685–1753). Berkeley's extreme subjective idealism denied the independent existence of matter. Only when material objects entered someone's mind as perceptions could they be said to exist. A tree, for example, would have no existence unless someone was actually observing it. To the objection that a tree might then actually cease to exist if no one happened to be looking at it, Berkeley replied that "God always perceives everything" (quoted in Russell 1945:647). As Berkeley himself put it:

> All the choir of heaven and furniture of earth, in a word all those bodies which compose the mighty frame of the world, have not any substance without the mind.... So long as they are not actually perceived by me, or do not exist in my mind, or that of any other created spirit, they must either have no existence at all, or else subsist in the mind of some Eternal Spirit." (quoted in Jeans 1947:171)

This was not, then, *absolute* idealism. Though it required someone to observe it, matter could nevertheless be real, could still exist. This insistence on observation—human or divine—on Berkeley's part led Ronald Knox to compose a parody in limerick form of the bishop's philosophy.

> There was a young man who said, "God
> Must think it exceedingly odd
> If he finds that this tree
> Continues to be
> When there's no one about in the Quad."
>
> REPLY
> Dear Sir:
> Your astonishment's odd:
> *I* am always about in the Quad.
> And that's why the tree
> Will continue to be,
> Since observed by,
> *Yours faithfully*,
> God.
> (quoted in Russell 1945:648)

A pure idealism, however, was hard to sustain in the world of physical reality. Practical men like Samuel Johnson would have none of it. James Boswell tells us that one day he and Johnson were coming out of church discussing Berkeley's view of the world. "I observed that though we are satisfied his doctrine is not true, it is impossible to refute it. I never shall forget the alacrity with which Johnson answered, striking his foot with mighty force against a large stone, till he rebounded from it. 'I refute it *thus*'" (Boswell 1952:129). At the same time, in the hands of some thinkers influenced by Berkeley, the sharp outlines of an anthropomorphic God began to blur and his substance to dissolve. Thus the Deity became progressively less concrete and more abstract.

German Metaphysical Idealism

Although Berkeley had expounded a philosophy of subjective idealism in which matter enjoyed only a subordinate status, still and all he was an Anglican priest. Accordingly, he had to maintain a certain allegiance to a rather tangible Christian God and could not very well forsake him for a pure abstraction. It was left to the German philosophers of the latter half of the eighteenth century—several decades after Berkeley's death—to further erode the concept of God, transforming it into something indistinct in form and elusive in substance. At the hands of these German idealists, God became more and more an *Idea* and less and less a recognizable anthropomorphic Being. This new concept of the Deity, however, was not depersonalized altogether. It was often referred to as the Absolute with a capital "A," in order to retain for it something of the aura and dignity befitting the author and sovereign of the universe—a God of sorts who could still be respected and perhaps even worshipped.

Thus we have Schelling's "doctrine that the One, the absolute substance, cannot be described, since description is limitation.... The Absolute Being is beyond the distinctions of mind and matter" (Hocking 1939:446). Moreover, according to Hocking, the Absolute Being of the German idealists "could not be supposed subject to emotion, ... it could neither be angry, nor pleased with prayer and praise, nor be moved by any sentiment of love for finite creatures— it would certainly not be identical with the God of historical religion" (Hocking 1939:371–372).

Fichte's notion of the Absolute was much the same. It was so amorphous and abstract, in fact, that it struck officials at the University of Jena (where Fichte taught) not only as alien to the

Christian God for which they officially stood, but even as showing
atheistic tendencies, and they therefore dismissed him from his post
(Cohen 1930:294). The struggle here was thus between the traditional anthropomorphic God of Christianity and the new, highly rarefied, metaphysical God of the idealist philosophers.

It is true that most interpreters of Hegel today agree that for him
the Absolute was God in metaphysical disguise, so that in fact his
conception of the Absolute was at bottom theology masquerading as
philosophy. But those in power at German universities showed little
interest in such subtleties. They were quite ready to suppress what
they deemed to be departures from religious orthodoxy among their
faculty.

Since what they espoused was so nebulous, it is not surprising
that the Absolute idealists traded charges of incomprehensibility
among themselves. Thus Hegel said of Schelling's Absolute that it
"had no positive ascertainable features," and Schelling retorted that
Hegel's Absolute was "nothing but an array of abstract categories"
(quoted in Acton 1967:7). The fact of the matter was that both dis-
putants were right! Indeed, the genus "German idealism" contained
many different species, finely sliced into minute distinctions by its
expositors, but for all practical purposes appearing to the outside
world as one and the same.

One element of German idealist philosophy was Immanuel
Kant's distinction between *noumenon* and *phenomenon*. A phenomenon was the outer, perceptible characteristic of a thing, but beneath
this empirically observable level was the noumenon, the *Ding-an-
sich*, the "thing-in-itself," the *real* object. And this reality was
beyond perception, inaccessible to ordinary human cognition, and
so ultimately "unknowable." In effect, the noumen was the *soul* of
an object and thus very much like Plato's ideal archetypes or templates, which impressed themselves on things and thereby brought
them to life.

This concept of the noumenon, a peculiar entity that lay outside
the purview of science, was criticized for its uselessness by Thomas
Henry Huxley.

Since Kant is never weary of telling us that we know nothing
whatever, and can know nothing, about the noumenon, except as

the hypothetical subject of any number of negative predicates;
the information that it is free, in the sense of being out of reach
of the law of causation, is about as valuable as the assertion that
it is neither gray, nor blue, nor square. (Huxley 1908:226–227)

But to some thinkers the idea of the noumenon proved attractive,
even seductive, by virtue of its very elusiveness. It thus surfaced
again and again among a number of philosophers, providing one
more demonstration that the mere coinage of a word—*entelechy* by
Aristotle or *noumenon* by Kant—created the presumption that there
must be *something* there to correspond to the word. After all (it was
reasoned), if you can name something, you can talk about it; and if
you talk about it, it must exist.

Philosophy, however, has not been the only discipline to suffer
from this delusion. Science has too. *Caloric, phlogiston,* and the
ether, once considered reputable scientific concepts that labeled
something real in the external world, turned out not to be so.
Happily modern science has for the most part learned to avoid chas-
ing such will-o'-the-wisps.

Although under attack by the academic authorities in their
home country, the idealist perspective of these eighteenth century
German philosophers—men like Schelling, Fichte, Hegel, and
Kant—nevertheless managed to cross the Atlantic. Here it was able
to influence the newly emerging Transcendentalism, which became
the first coherent philosophical movement to develop in the United
States. As we shall see in the next chapter, the Transcendentalists
recoiled from the crass empiricism of John Locke and his followers, since for them "the universe was far richer and deeper than
empirical philosophy would allow" (Kurtz 1967:86). Accordingly,
"[in] the area of metaphysics, the Transcendentalists were idealists.
Emerson's early essay *Nature* (1836) presented their general position. The world is divided into two realms. On the one hand, there
is the unreal world of appearances and sensations that is the object
of empirical science. Ultimate reality, however, is founded upon the
unseen transcendental world in which mind, spirit, and the oversoul
prevail, and this world can be discovered only through poetry and
philosophy." Such was their fundamental belief. And indeed, for the
most part these Transcendentalists "were poets and mystics who

believed that truth is attained through subjective intuition" (Kurtz 1967:86).

German Idealism Crosses the English Channel

Influential as it became in America, the place where German idealism took firmest hold and had the greatest impact was—surprisingly enough—England. Here, despite that country's long empiricist tradition stretching from Bacon, Hobbes, and Locke, to Darwin, Huxley, and Spencer, idealism sprang up with the vigor of a rank weed in the British universities, especially Oxford. As Thomas Case noted in his long article on metaphysics, "Before the beginning of the 19th century, Kant had made his way to England in a translation of some of his works…. [Then] after a period of struggle, the influence of Kant gradually extended … as we see in the writings of Coleridge and Carlyle," until it finally "secured an authority over English thought almost equal to that of Hume" (Case 1911:244). The joke then making the rounds in England was that "[g]ood German philosophers, when they die, go to Oxford" (Saleeby 1906:342).

Irritated beyond measure by the strength of this foreign invasion, Professor Henry Jones of Cambridge declared that "[t]he Rhine has flowed in the Thames…. The stream of German idealism has been diffused over the academical world of Great Britain. The disaster is universal" (quoted in James 1996:53, 54).

The source of annoyance was easy to see for anyone whose philosophical feet were planted squarely on the ground. Absolute idealism was indeed a rarefied theology/philosophy in which reality had been distilled to the point of vaporization. But while the notion of a diluted God may have been congenial to Oxford undergraduates, it was anathema to those of their elders who remained orthodox Christians. Bristling at the idealist philosophy that had become so fashionable among young Oxonians, a philosophy which he felt had reduced God to an impalpable essence, Mark Pattison— rector of Lincoln College—complained that by the teachings of the metaphysicians, the idea of God had been "defecated to a pure transparency" (quoted in Harrison 1884:496–497).

Later philosophers who, while still religious believers, were by no means traditional Christians likewise found the decorporealization of God not at all to their liking. William James, for example, wrote, "I can hardly conceive of anything more different from the absolute [of the German idealists] than the God, say, of David or of Isaiah. *That* God is an essentially finite being *in* the cosmos ... I hold to the finite God" (James 1996:111). And again he wrote, "When I read in a religious paper words like these: 'Perhaps the best thing we can say of God is that he is *the Inevitable–Inference*,' I recognize the tendency to let religion evaporate in intellectual terms. Would martyrs have sung in the flames for a mere inference, however inevitable it might be?" (James 1994:546n).

The Spanish philosopher Miguel de Unamuno can also be classified among those who favored a God of more solid substance than that of the idealists—a Deity whom he referred to derisively as a "Nothing God." "[S]uch a fleshless abstraction," he declared, "cannot be the answer to the cravings of the human heart" (quoted in Edwards 1967a:176). Perhaps the most biting critique of this denaturing of the Deity was offered by Sigmund Freud in *The Future of an Illusion*.

> Philosophers stretch the meaning of words until they retain scarcely anything of their original sense. They give the name of "God" to some vague abstraction which they have created for themselves; having done so they can pose before all the world as deists, as believers in God, and they can even boast that they have recognized a higher, purer concept of God, notwithstanding that their God is now nothing more than an insubstantial shadow and no longer the mighty personality of religious doctrines. (Freud 1961:41)

But let us return to the English idealists. F. H. Bradley (1846–1924), Thomas Hill Green (1836–1882), and Bernard Bosanquet (1848–1923) were, by their combined efforts, able to "spread a kind of Hegelian orthodoxy in metaphysics and in theology throughout Great Britain" (Case 1911:244). As one commentator on British philosophy of the period expressed it, the appeal went out to "Englishmen under five-and-twenty to close their Mill and Spencer and open their Kant and Hegel" (Sorley 1961:43).

The idealists seem to have had little doubt that they were bringing to British philosophy something not only profound but unprecedented. This at least was the opinion of G. J. Warnock, another Oxford philosopher who followed the idealists by a half-century and who believed that their aim had been to convey a "general impression that they were concerned with far deeper questions, and concerned with them far more seriously and intently, than any of their predecessors" (Warnock 1958:53–54).

Little doubt was left about just what these philosophers were proclaiming. Bradley, for example, ended his *Appearance and Reality* (1893) with "the essential message of Hegel: Outside of spirit there is not, and there cannot be any reality; and the more that anything is spiritual, so much more is it veritably real" (quoted in Laird 1936:50). Still, abstract, metaphysical, and un-Christian as these pronouncements might seem, hiding behind the vaporous essence that the British idealists had created shone the familiar countenance of the God of their childhood. William James, who lectured in England during those years and saw this idealist philosophy at close range, remarked that the functions performed by the Absolute of Bradley and his cohorts were "identical with those of the theistic God" (James 1996:71).

Some years later Julian Huxley also thought that he saw through the subterfuge and wrote, "[S]ome idealist philosophers [assert] that the ground of all reality is wholly spiritual, and then ... [christen] this hypothetical ground the Absolute.... Such a God is only a dummy divinity, a theatrical *deus ex machina* dropped onto the religious stage through the trapdoor of metaphysics" (Huxley 1957:51).

William James Trumpets the Return of Empiricism

The candle of German idealism burned brightly in England for a time, but its flame was soon greatly dimmed—if not altogether extinguished. In his Hibbert Lectures given at Manchester College in 1908, William James bore witness to the ebbing of this tide and gladly wrote its obituary: "The prestige of the absolute has rather crumbled in our hands," he said. "The logical proofs of it miss fire; the portraits which its best court-painters show of it are featureless and foggy in the extreme" (James 1996:133). And summing up his own feelings about the movement, he commented wryly that "the stagnant felicity of the absolute's own perfection moves me as little as I move it" (James 1996:48).

However, James thought he saw an antidote for the malaise that idealism had cast over English philosophy.

> Oxford, long the seed-bed, for the English world, of the idealism inspired by Kant and Hegel, has recently become the nursery of a very different way of thinking. Even non-philosophers have begun to take an interest in a controversy over what is known as pluralism or humanism. It looks a little as if the ancient English empiricism, so long put out of fashion here by nobler sounding Germanic formulas, might be repluming itself and getting ready for a stronger flight than ever. (James 1996:3)

James foresaw the resurgence of the empirical tradition as being a reaction against the nebulosity and vacuity of what had, for a time, passed in British philosophy as coin of the realm. The contributions that science—with its allegiance to empiricism, materialism, and determinism—was making every day were so large and visible that idealism, with no tangible results to show for all its rhetoric, began to shrink and attenuate by comparison. And James happily tolled the death knell of the movement: "If Oxford men could be ignorant of anything, it might almost seem that they had remained ignorant of the great empirical movement towards a pluralistic panpsychic view of the universe, into which our own generation has been drawn, and which threatens to short-circuit their methods entirely and become their religious rival" (James 1996:313–314).

Though his pronouncements on the subject of spirits varied at times, on more than one occasion James came out foursquare for science and against metaphysics. Thus in *The Varieties of Religious Experience*, he wrote, "The sciences of nature know nothing of spiritual presences, and on the whole hold no practical commerce whatever with the idealistic conceptions" (James 1994:533).

Sir Oliver Lodge Fights on for Idealism

Diminished as it might be, however, idealism (along with its close congener, spiritualism) was by no means completely defunct. Certain individuals who had some philosophical—and even scientific—pretensions continued to maintain and expound this doctrine.

Although among its advocates (as we saw in Chapter 5) one can list several prominent figures, such as Alfred Russel Wallace, I will examine here the opinions of only one of its adherents, Sir Oliver Lodge (1851–1940). Lodge, a physicist with notable professional accomplishments in the field of electromagnetism, chose not to remain entirely within the realm of physics but to pursue psychical research as well. This endeavor led him to affirm his belief in the possibility of communicating with the dead. More broadly, though, he attempted to reconcile science and religion.

Though a trained physicist, Lodge was ready to assert that while "[t]here is plenty of physics and chemistry and mechanics about every vital action, ... for a complete understanding of [life] ... something beyond physics and chemistry is needed" (Lodge 1912: 78). Some kind of vital principle or "mind," he thought, must be involved and about it he wrote:

> The essence of mind is design and purpose. There are some who deny that there is any design or purpose in the universe at all: but how can that be maintained when humanity itself possesses these attributes? Is it not more reasonable to say that just as we are conscious of the power of guidance in ourselves, so guidance and intelligent control may be an element running through the universe, and may be incorporated even in material things? (Lodge 1905:102–103)

The nature and qualities of mind, Lodge insisted, should be probed more deeply. "Whether such things as intuition and revelation ever occur is an open question. There are some who have reason to say that they do. They are at any rate not to be denied offhand" (Lodge 1912:101).

Since mind was incorporeal, it could and did transcend physical life: "Personality persists beyond bodily death," Lodge affirmed. And he added that "the evidence—nothing new or sensational, but cumulative and demanding prolonged serious study—to my mind goes to prove that discarnate intelligence, under certain conditions, may interact with us on the material side" (Lodge 1912:103).

Lodge was, of course, going well beyond the bounds of established science when he declared, "Mysticism must have its place, though its relation to Science has so far not been found" (Lodge 1912:101). And he was really only expressing a fond hope when he proclaimed his "conviction that occurrences now regarded as occult can be examined and reduced to order by the methods of science carefully and persistently applied" (Lodge 1912:103).

Finally, Lodge did not wish to leave his readers with any doubt that—for him—his investigations and observations seemed to point to the Deity. And so he concluded one of his books with these lyrical words: "[W]e are deaf and blind therefore to the Immanent Grandeur, unless we have insight enough to recognize in the woven fabric of existence, flowing steadily from the loom in an infinite progress towards perfection, the ever-growing garment of a transcendent God" (Lodge 1912:106). So much for Sir Oliver Lodge.

Idealist Elements Imputed to Modern Science

We have seen from the words of Bishop Berkeley that an idealist philosophy frequently had a strong subjectivist element. This may be understandable when the spokesman for it was a cleric, but it is a little surprising when the theorist in question was a scientist with little or no regard for the Deity. Yet this was the case with the Austrian physicist and philosopher Ernst Mach (1838–1916).

Mach, one of the founding fathers of the logical positivist movement, was an avowed empiricist. Experience was the one and only basis of knowledge, he contended. But experience came through the senses, and in his ontology Mach emphasized the primacy of sense impressions over and above the objects that gave rise to them. Especially was this true if those objects were not (in Mach's day at least) directly observable. "It is well known," we are told by Werner Heisenberg, "that Mach did not believe in the existence of atoms, on the grounds that they cannot be observed" (Heisenberg 1972:34). The counter-argument to this, of course, is that genuine knowledge derives not only from direct perceptions, but also from *inferences* drawn from these perceptions. And arguing as he did, Mach left himself open to criticism by other physicists—including Heisenberg himself, who held that "inferring concepts and things from sense impressions is one of the basic presuppositions of all our thought. Hence, if we wanted to speak of nothing but sense impressions, we should have to rid ourselves of our language and thought. In other words, Mach rather neglects the fact that the world really exists, that our sense impressions are based on something objective" (Heisenberg 1972:65).

Moreover, speaking of discoveries about nature, Heisenberg added that "the mere fact that we could never have arrived at these [discoveries] by ourselves, that they were revealed to us by nature, suggests strongly that they must be part of reality itself, not just our thoughts about reality" (Heisenberg 1972:68). Accordingly, V. I. Lenin—whose materialist philosophy led him to criticize anything that seemed even vaguely like a statement of idealism—tried to tie Mach's thinking to that of Bishop Berkeley. "[T]he clear and indisputable fact," wrote Lenin, is "that Ernst Mach's doctrine of things as complexes of sensations is subjective idealism and a simple rehash of Berkeleianism. If bodies are complexes of sensations, as Mach says, or combinations of sensations, as Berkeley said, it inevitably follows that the whole world is but my idea. Starting from such a premise, it is impossible to arrive at the existence of other people besides oneself: it is the purest solipsism" (Lenin 1943:109).

Jeans and Eddington: Idealism in British Science

To be sure, Mach was not the only scientist who could be tied to the idealist camp. While they might not have been entirely happy at being so classified, Sir James Jeans (1877–1946) and Sir Arthur Eddington (1882–1944), two distinguished British physicists and astronomers, clearly deserved it. In fact, well into the twentieth century they sailed under the full canvas of idealism.

Eddington's idealist metaphysics apparently derived from a study of Immanuel Kant (Nerlich 1967:461). Indeed, one might say that Eddington was actually more of an idealist than Bishop Berkeley. For while Berkeley was at least willing to grant objective existence to matter *as long as it was being perceived*, Eddington would not allow it even that sort of tenuous contingent existence. The whole of the universe was "mind-stuff," matter being nothing but a *concept* of that "mind-stuff." "To put the conclusion crudely," he wrote in *The Nature of the Physical World* (1928), "the stuff of the world is mind-stuff" (Eddington 1948:276). Accordingly, one would have to characterize astronomy—by Eddington's conception, the study of universal mind-stuff—as a kind of celestial psychology!

Jeans had a similar notion of the universe. Thought—Eddington's "mind-stuff," essentially—was again enthroned. "[T]he universe," Jeans wrote, "can be best pictured, although still very imperfectly and inadequately, as consisting of pure thought," adding that "[i]f the universe is a universe of thought, then its creation must have been an act of thought. Indeed, the finiteness of time and space almost compel us, of themselves, to picture the creation as an act of thought" (Jeans 1947:168, 181). And if thought *created* the universe, thought must surely be what continued to *guide* it: "Again we may think of the laws to which phenomena conform in our waking hours, the laws of nature, as the laws of thought of a universal mind" (Jeans 1947:175).

It was ineluctable, of course, that if the universe were *thought*—since thought is the product of *mind*—it had to be entertained in *someone's* mind. And to no one's surprise, that "someone" turned out to be God. This God, however, was no ordinary thinker. Since the laws that governed the universe were beautiful mathematical equations—Jeans himself was a distinguished mathematician—he felt that "we must describe" the great celestial thinker "as a mathematical thinker" (Jeans 1947:168). Thus Jeans no doubt would have approved of the notion of the old German idealists, Schelling and Hegel, "that the world is an absolute thought in an infinite mind" (Case 1911:231).

Curiously enough, Jeans's conception of the universe was strongly similar to that expressed by Pythagoras more than two thousand years earlier, for whom *numbers*—which constituted a separate and privileged mode of existence—were the real stuff of the universe.

Conclusion

In concluding this chapter, it is safe to say—and is also a measure of the advance of astronomy since the days of Eddington and Jeans—that no professional astronomer today entertains such a tenuous metaphysical conception of the universe. Indeed, I cannot name a scientist of any standing who holds such a view of the nature of existence. He or she is much more likely—along with Dr.

Johnson—to kick the stone and refute idealism that way than to engage in some arcane recital about "mind-stuff."

Philosophical idealism is so alien to everyday experience—especially in an age when science is successfully probing deeper and deeper into the study of matter without finding a trace of anything like "absolute ideas" underlying it—that idealism as a coherent and vigorous philosophy is virtually extinct.

Or to put it slightly differently, science has rendered both organic and inorganic phenomena so precisely delineated, so specific, so well understood, so "real," that the notion of their being simply the creation, manifestation, or reflection of "mind"—either humanity's or God's—has lost virtually all its plausibility and appeal. Thus *idealism* as a philosophical system no longer has any standing in the world of serious thought.

CHAPTER 11

The Expansion of Naturalism

D uring the early days of Christianity, when the biblical God was at the height of his powers, he was ready on any occasion to intervene in the affairs of the world. Personal and direct intercession by the Deity, exercising his unquestioned authority, was how many events were explained. The idea of *nature* as somehow separate from God and capable of acting on her own was scarcely entertained. Nature was recognized, of course, but was always considered subservient to God—his handmaiden, so to speak.

With accumulating human experience, however, the belief began to impinge on more thoughtful minds that events occurred with a regularity, consistency, and predictability that seemed at odds with the notion of direct interventions by an often willful and capricious God. Thus the idea of nature as a system of interlocking laws and principles, operating on its own, gradually began to gain acceptance. To be sure, it was usually thought to be *God's* nature, a subordinate and obedient order of things dutifully at work on his behalf. Although capable of functioning pretty much on her own, nature was ultimately responsible to God and thus under his overall command and control.

Naturalism was thus still closely conjoined with supernaturalism and became an alternate (but not necessarily conflicting) way of explaining why things happened as they did. In time, though, naturalism became an alternative—and even a competing—way of accounting for things and events. And as the centuries unfolded, the relative proportion of occasions when one or the other of the two types of explanation were invoked changed conspicuously. And the change was in nature's favor. It is in fact the tracing of this great trend over the course of human history that this book attempts to document. We have already pointed out a number of examples of this trend. In this chapter additional instances of its trajectory will be presented.

Skepticism Points Ahead to Naturalism

Christian theology, which had dominated the Middle Ages, began to show fissures with the coming of the Renaissance. A new skepticism was abroad and it began to show its effects on religious belief. The interpretation of events, which heretofore had been solely or largely in terms of the supernatural, now began to be examined more carefully and critically. Thus miracles, which were by definition acts contrary to the laws of nature, began to be questioned more sharply. More and more, events began to be accounted for as being due to purely natural causes. Biblical stories—especially the more dramatic and implausible ones—once taken as literally true now began to tax credibility ever more severely. In an effort to combat this trend toward skepticism and retain the authority of the Bible, improbable events started to be thought of not as actually having happened precisely as described in the Bible, but as *allegories*.

In previous chapters we saw the effect of this growing skepticism as *weakening* the strength of God. In this one we will focus on the obverse of the process—the *strengthening* of naturalistic interpretation. One characteristic of naturalism is that it repudiates the view that "there exists or could exist any entities or events which lie, in principle, beyond the scope of scientific explanation" (Danto 1967:448). We shall now proceed to examine how this repudiation came increasingly to be invoked.

From a broad perspective, one can say that there was nothing unpredictable about the emergence and florescence of naturalism. As the sociologist Lester Ward put it a century ago, "It was perhaps the inevitable outcome of the reaction, which began with the Renaissance, against the medieval domination of mere authority" (Ward 1911:274).

Still, centuries before the Renaissance, the Church father Augustine had already begun clearing the ground for the acceptance of the concept of nature as virtually autonomous and a full partner with the Almighty when he wrote, "God the Author and Creator of all natures does nothing contrary to nature; for what is done by Him who appoints all natural order and measure and proportion must be natural in every case" (quoted in Miller 2008:162). And much later another Church father, Thomas Aquinas, sought to reinforce this view by holding that "if God exists, he is the author of nature itself, and the cause of causes. Therefore, finding a natural cause for any phenomenon does not take it out of the realm of divine providence" (quoted in Miller 2008:162).

Nonetheless it is undeniable that a vigorous naturalism was the philosophical offspring of the spectacular advances made in the physical sciences by the likes of Copernicus, Galileo, Kepler, and Newton (as we saw in Chapter 8). Whether they intended it or not—and they, in fact, did not—the work of these men had the effect of reducing the will of God to the laws of nature. We might even go further and say, putting the matter in Newtonian terms, that for every *advance* in naturalism there was an equal and opposite *retreat* from supernaturalism.

The conception of the universe that emerged during the Renaissance proved itself capable of doing something theology had never been able to accomplish: it was able to make verifiable predictions. More than once since the beginning of Christianity, religious zealots had solemnly forecast the end of the world—and nothing had happened! Now, with the powerful tool of Newtonian celestial mechanics, it became possible for the first time to predict eclipses with ease and accuracy. The fears that religion had instilled in people, and on which it had thrived, science was able to dispel. And of course the net effect of this was to enhance the mechanical, naturalistic view of the universe.

Seeking to resist this increasing tendency to diminish the role of God in running the world, Reverend Thomas Burnet (1635–1715)—a friend of Isaac Newton—tried to use science against itself. He did so by invoking Newton's laws, not as lessening God's stature but as augmenting it. This Burnet did by presenting the Almighty as the master artificer of the universe, reasoning as follows: "We think him a better artist that makes a clock that strikes regularly at every hour from the springs and wheels which he puts in the work, than he that so made his clock that he must put his finger to it every hour to make it strike" (quoted in Gould 1999:23). As we have seen, this argument had already become the dedicated theist's way of coping with the spectacular success of scientific explanations. If God's role had become less powerful by such advances, at least he was now more predictable, more closely associated with nature. He was in fact seen as working hand in glove with her.

Deism: Curtailing the Power of God

The deists of the Enlightenment, as we have seen, were intent on setting strict limits on God's powers and the ways in which he could exercise them. Conceding that God may have laid down the laws of nature at the time of creation, the deists nevertheless held that he was now bound by them himself. No longer was he allowed to interfere capriciously in events—either human or celestial—by suspending or transcending these laws. He had learned to respect them, allowing them fully and frankly to take their course unimpeded.

Another way in which some deists expressed the matter was to say that God had installed nature as his lieutenant, with amplified powers and responsibilities. He had in effect placed her in charge of carrying out the day-to-day activities, thus freeing himself from the routine chores of running the business of the world. This, it was thought, gave the world greater stability and predictability. As the historian James Harvey Robinson put it, "The eighteenth-century Deists never tired of praising a God of immutable law" (Robinson 1965:122).

So salient in the mind of Immanuel Kant was the lawfulness of the universe that at times it seemed as if his main reason for believing in God was to have a way to account for and ensure its precise operation. Such an exquisite mechanism, he reasoned, required a Supreme Intelligence to design it, set it in motion, and keep it running smoothly. Accordingly, in his *Universal Natural History and Theory of the Heavens* (1755), he wrote:

> Matter, which is the primitive constituent of all things, is therefore bound to certain laws.... It has no freedom to deviate from this perfect plan.... It must necessarily have been put into such harmonious relationships by a First Cause ruling over it; and [thus] there is a God just because nature ... cannot proceed otherwise than regularly and according to order. (quoted in Crowe 1994:370–371)

The prevailing view, then, was that God had created nature for a purpose, and having done so was now content to act through her, distancing himself from her everyday activities. Still, he kept a watchful eye on her to make sure she continued to run things properly. In the apt words of Auguste Comte, the deists' God was pictured "as a sovereign who reigns but does not govern" (quoted in Frank 1945:62).

The French Enlightenment and the *Encyclopédie*

The French Enlightenment virtually enthroned nature, especially in the pages of its "house organ," the great *Encyclopédie*. That work was a landmark in the compilation and systematization of human knowledge, particularly regarding the workings of nature. Moreover, the *Encyclopédie* stressed *materialistic* kinds of knowledge. Indeed, the work of its editor Denis Diderot and his fellow *philosophes* and contributors represented, as one critic put it, a "further stage in the downward transition from Deism towards Materialism." Of Diderot himself it was said that "[w]ith him even that residue of natural religion which Voltaire would have retained became a mere superfluity" (Joyce 1911:539).

When the philsosophers of the French Enlightenment talked enthusiastically about "the progress of the human mind," what they were actually referring to was an increase in the sum of verified empirical knowledge—especially that provided by the operation of mechanical devices. The pages of the *Encyclopédie* were in fact lavishly illustrated with all manner of machines through which the forces of nature, now increasingly well understood, were being harnessed and put to work for the benefit of humanity.

The most materialist and empirical of all the Encyclopedists— and thus the most naturalistic—was Baron d'Holbach, whom we will discuss in detail in Chapter 15. For the *Encyclopédie* Holbach wrote or translated "a large number of articles on chemistry and mineralogy, chiefly from German sources" (Unsigned 1911a:577). Reduced to its simplest terms, Holbach's philosophical stance was this: if God cannot be perceived through the senses, we are not obliged to believe in his existence. For Holbach, then, there was nature and *only* nature. For him any beings that man's fancy "pictures as above nature, or distinguished from her, are always chimeras," because "there is not, there can be nothing, out of that Nature which includes all beings" (Holbach 2006:19).

No other *philosophe* went quite that far. Nevertheless together these men made the *Encyclopédie* "a symbol of the intellectual predominance of France in the 18th century." The "*Encyclopédie* contributed greatly to the strengthening of the rationale of scientific hypothesis and scientific method," and in his introduction to the *Encyclopédie*, d'Alembert "laid the methodological foundation of empiricism, which became the cornerstone of the great science of the age" (Dilthey 1972:193). The *philosophes* inveighed against the sort of metaphysics that sought to embody in "the great rationalistic schemes of the seventeenth century, the systematic philosophy of Descartes, Malebranche, Spinoza, and Leibniz" (Wilson 1967:506). Much of their philosophical fire was thus directed at this form of rationalism, which was seen as a close kin of idealism.

Not surprisingly, the *philosophes* were decidedly opposed to the French establishment. And because of the challenge that many articles in the *Encyclopédie* presented to the country's political and religious institutions, that work aroused the wrath of the monarchy and the Church. Several articles were critical of the miracles described in the Bible, treating them "in a way that secularized and modernized historical techniques" (Wilson 1967:507). Many orthodox Christians were offended, for example, by the sharply worded opinions expressed by Diderot in his article "Irreligieux," in which he asserted categorically that "morality can exist without religion, and religion can coexist, and often does, with immorality" (Wilson 1967:507).

The writings of the *philosophes* cannot be cited without some mention of Voltaire, who typified the determinism and secularism of the age by insisting that "[e]verything happens through immutable laws, … everything is necessary" (quoted in Edwards 1961:120). But Voltaire did not stop there. Late in his life, he launched a spirited attack against Christianity. Pointing an accusing finger at the religious fanaticism that underlay the Inquisition, he declared, "Those who can make you believe absurdities can make you commit atrocities" (quoted in Torrey 1967:266).

The Signal Achievement of Pierre-Simon Laplace

The most profound intellectual challenge to the traditional Christian God, however, came not from the radical writings of Diderot or

Voltaire or even Holbach but from the work of an astronomer. In Chapter 8 we noted that one of the great triumphs of naturalism occurred when Pierre-Simon de Laplace was able to show that Newton's laws were entirely adequate to account for the apparent irregularities that at times marked the orbits of Jupiter and Saturn. Contrary to what Newton himself believed, Laplace demonstrated that no supernatural intervention was required to explain either the deviations in the courses of these planets or the subsequent corrections of those deviations.

Laplace was again the protagonist in one of the most celebrated incidents highlighting the contrast between supernaturalism and naturalism. The story is as follows. Laplace had been one of Napoleon's instructors when the latter was a student at the École Militaire in Paris. Years later, after the publication of Laplace's epochal work the *Mécanique celeste*, he presented a copy to Napoleon, by then emperor of France. After reading it Napoleon told Laplace how strange he found it that in a book devoted to the workings of the universe, there should be no mention at all of God—to which the astronomer replied, "Sire, I have no need of that hypothesis" (Russell 1997:58).

So convinced was Laplace of the universe's total conformity to natural law that he set forth what is, by all odds, the strongest statement of universal determinism ever penned. Imagining a supreme intelligence, gifted with unlimited powers of calculation, Laplace argued the case for determinism, beginning as follows.

> We ought ... to regard the present state of the universe as the effect of its antecedent state and the cause of the state that is to follow. An intelligence knowing, at a given instant of time, all forces acting in nature, as well as the momentary positions of all things of which the universe consists, would be able to comprehend the motions of the largest bodies of the world and those of the lightest atoms in one single formula, provided his intellect were sufficiently powerful to subject all data to analysis; to him nothing would be uncertain, both past and future would be present to his eyes. (quoted in Stebbing 1958:160)

In a later chapter of this book, we shall assess the current standing of Laplace's bold assertion.

A striking confirmation of his belief in a strictly determined—and thus fully predictable—universe, based on the laws of celestial mechanics, appeared some two decades after Laplace's death. In 1846 the English astronomer John Couch Adams and the French astronomer Urbain Leverrier independently predicted the existence and location of a heretofore unknown planet. While previous calculations had already determined the orbit of Uranus, close observations of the planet showed that it sometimes reached its expected position *before* it was supposed to, and sometimes *after*. Working separately, Adams and Leverrier calculated that this anomaly in Uranus's actual path could be entirely explained by positing the existence of a previously unsuspected planet with a certain mass and a specified location. When apprised of these predictions, observational astronomers trained their telescopes on the precise location designated by Adams and Leverrier and a new planet—Neptune—was discerned at that very spot (Duncan 1946:249).

Describing the impact made at the time by this discovery, the physicist Freeman Dyson noted, "The successful prediction of the presence of an unseen planet was one of the great events of nineteenth-century science. It impressed the educated public of that time as a spectacular demonstration of the power of human reason to uncover Nature's secrets" (Dyson 2004:30–31).

The Mixed Contributions of Auguste Comte

Such striking successes in the physical sciences may well have led another French thinker—Auguste Comte (1798–1857)—to survey the history of thought and discern in its course what he deemed to be a dominant trend. This trend Comte encapsulated in what he called the Law of the Three Stages: the Theological, the Metaphysical, and the Positive. In the Theological stage, Comte stated, everything is explained as being caused by supernatural agents. In the Metaphysical stage, supernatural agents are replaced by abstract forces. (For example, in this stage of thought, sleep is said to be produced by a *soporific principle*, while stones are thought to result from the *congelation of lapidific juices*.) Finally, in the Positive stage, supernatural agents and metaphysical forces are eliminated altogether and things are explained in terms of the workings of natural laws.

Comte thought that the progression of human ideas had been from the first of these stages to the second, and from the second to the third. In his *Cours de philosophie positive* (1830–1842), he launched the new science of sociology, which attempted to set forth the laws that governed the progress of society. But then, in his *Système de politique positive* (1851–1854), he proposed something very different. In one of the strangest reversions from science back toward religion to be found in the history of human thought, Comte set forth a scheme designed to uplift the condition of society by establishing what he called a Religion of Humanity. Greater social benevolence, he argued, "can only be reached by a heartier develop-ment of the sympathetic instincts," and these "sympathetic instincts can only be developed by the Religion of Humanity" (quoted in Morley 1910:821).

This proposed new religion retained many of the trappings of Catholicism, including a priesthood, calendar of saints, and hierar-chy of sacraments. "Catholicism *minus* Christianity" it was dubbed by one of its detractors, while others thought it was "the wanderings of a deranged mind" (Hubert 1931:152). The Religion of Humanity was indeed a peculiar concoction. "The particularities of its wor-ship, [included the] minute and truly ingenious re-adaptation of sacraments, prayers, reverent signs, down even to the invocation of a New Trinity" (Morley 1910:821). Comte himself was to be its high priest and the religion had holidays and a new assemblage of saints—including the likes of Dante, Shakespeare, Adam Smith, and Frederick the Great. The scheme, however, was not theistic in any strict sense, since in its body of doctrine the conception of a tan-gible God was superseded by the abstract notion of humanity, envi-sioned as a kind of diffuse personality (Morley 1910:821).

In England the Religion of Humanity was roundly criticized and derided. Huxley had nothing but scorn for it, referring to Comte as the "Moses of Positivism" and his new religion as "eviscerated papistry" (Huxley 1896a:256, 255). He was quite content, said Huxley, "to leave to the Comtists the entire monopoly of the manu-facture of imitation ecclesiasticism" (Huxley 1896a:211).

In fairness to Comte, the Religion of Humanity was a product of his declining years, when senility had dulled the sharp edges of his positivism. Of course this must be counted as a regression back to something like the Theological stage. It was, in fact, a recrudescence of what he had meant to banish from modern thought. Indeed, it was the revisitation of a now familiar virus, coming back in diluted and attenuated form to be sure, but nonetheless recognizable for what it was.

John Stuart Mill and Thomas Henry Huxley

Crossing the English Channel, it is time now to examine the fate of naturalism at the hands of two of the leading British intellects of the day, John Stuart Mill (1806–1873) and Thomas Henry Huxley (1825–1895).

It is not generally known that despite the publication in 1840 of his *System of Logic*, the first rigorous and meticulous analysis of the scientific method to be penned, Mill was at heart a theist. For example, he asked "[w]hether there was not something antecedent to the whole series of causes and effects that we term Nature, and for [the lack of] which Nature itself would not have been." And replying to his own question, Mill declared that "[t]he only answer which has long continued to afford satisfaction is Theism" (Mill 1998:134). But Mill did not wish to appear to turn his back on science, and so on the very next page he reaffirmed his belief that "the theory, which refers the origin of all phenomenon of nature to the will of a Creator, [is] consistent with the ascertained results of science" (Mill 1998:134).

However, Mill was not prepared to entertain any capriciousness on the part of his Deity. The only theological doctrine he found consistent with the findings of science "is the conception of a God governing the world by invariable laws" (Mill 1998:135). And on this point he was emphatic: "The phenomena of Nature do take place according to general laws. They do originate from definite natural antecedents. Therefore if their ultimate origin is derived from a will, that will must have established the general laws and willed the antecedents. If there be a Creator, his intention must have been that events should depend upon antecedents and be produced according to fixed laws" (Mill 1998:135–136). Mill's God therefore had to operate within pretty strict limits. Clearly by now the tenets of the deists in this regard had become fixed principles among British intellectuals.

Deeming his scientific readers to be more or less satisfied on this score, Mill then proceeded to court his orthodox readers, assuring them that "Science contains nothing repugnant to the supposition that every event which takes place results from a specific volition of the presiding Power." But at the same time, he again reassured secularists that such could only be the case "provided that this Power adhere in its particular volitions to general laws laid down by itself" (Mill 1998:136). Mill thus made it clear that he would not countenance a willful, capricious, and interventionist Deity. He insisted that God abide by his own laws, with no exceptions allowed. In short, we find in John Stuart Mill a theist to be sure, but not an entrenched and dedicated one. Still, he was a theist who, while an avowed advocate of naturalism, at times was not quite ready to embrace it wholeheartedly.

With Thomas Henry Huxley, the case was rather different. Huxley was clear and uncompromising in his naturalism. At times he may have flashed the badge of his agnosticism (a term he himself had coined), but what most distinguished him was the assurance—indeed almost the ferocity—of his assertions of naturalism. Consider the following example.

Charles Darwin was too modest or too cautious to enter readily into the spirited controversies that followed the publication of his great book. Huxley, however, was always ready to wield his broadsword in its defense. In 1860, in reviewing *The Origin of Species* in the pages of the *Westminster Review*, he wrote, "It is true that if philosophers have suffered [in defense of scientific theories] their cause has [nevertheless] been amply avenged. Extinguished theologians lie about the cradle of every science as the strangled snakes beside that of Hercules, and history records that whenever science and dogmatism have been fairly opposed, the latter have been forced to retire from the lists, bleeding and crushed, if not annihilated; scotched if not slain" (quoted in Browne 2002:106).

Huxley's antipathy toward the clergy was profound and he seldom missed an opportunity to voice it. Thus in his *Autobiography* he spoke of his "untiring opposition to that ecclesiastical spirit, that clericalism, which in England, as everywhere else is the deadly enemy of science" (Huxley 1909:13–14).

Summing up the many advances of science, Huxley said, "Anyone who is acquainted with the history of science will admit, that its progress has, in all ages, meant, and now, more than ever, means, the extension of the province of what we call matter and causation, and the concomitant gradual banishment from all regions of human thought of what we call spirit and spontaneity" (quoted in Stebbing 1958:147).

One of the main tenets of Huxley's philosophy of science was that the objective of studying nature was the "elimination of the notion of mystery or creative interference" (quoted in Browne 2002:106). As an example of this philosophy, Huxley reiterated the argument first set forth by Laplace that—thanks to an overriding cosmic determinism—a supreme calculator would have a prevision of any future state of the universe.

> If the fundamental proposition of evolution is true, namely, that the entire world, animate and inanimate, is the result of the mutual interaction, according to definite laws, of forces possessed by the molecules which made up the primitive nebulosity of the universe; then it is not less certain that the present actual world reposed potentially in the cosmic vapour, and that an intelligence, if great enough, could from his knowledge of the properties of the molecules of that vapour have predicted the state of the fauna in Great Britain in 1888 with as much certitude as we say what will happen to the vapour of our breath on a cold day in winter. (quoted in Thomson 1911:141–142)

Naturalism, then—as well as determinism—had no greater champion than Thomas Henry Huxley.

Pantheism Makes Its Appearance

We turn now to another aspect of the clash between naturalism and supernaturalism: the tendency of some thinkers to attempt to make the two philosophies overlap, or even coincide. This movement, which aimed to blur the line between God and nature—indeed to fuse the two into one—is generally labeled *pantheism*. This view was exemplified, for instance, by Johann Gottlieb Fichte (1762–1814), according to whom "all distinctions disappear in the ultimate nature of things. The divine is identified with this ultimate distinctionless merging of nature and spirit, a unity more fundamental than any of the differences of the merely empirical world" (MacIntyre 1967:34).

In the more robust forms of this philosophy, God is made identical with—or at least indistinguishable from—nature. Another way to characterize pantheism is to say that according to its tenets, God is one with the universe. Or as it is sometimes expressed, grandiosely if nebulously, "God ... manifests himself as an infinite multiplicity of particular modes" (Unsigned 1911b:683); or yet again, "that everything that exists constitutes a unity and that this all-inclusive unity is divine" (MacIntyre 1967:34).

Although a vague sort of pantheism was espoused by some Greek Stoics, it was not until many centuries later that the doctrine was given a formal exposition. It began to gain popularity in Europe after the sixteenth century, perhaps because—by diluting God and robbing him of his sharp outlines and distinct personality—it somehow elevated the status of humanity, something found gratifying by some Renaissance thinkers. During the eighteenth century, especially in Germany, the view began to be expressed that "[i]nstead of the old belief that God made the world for man, philosophers began to fall into the pleasing dream, I am everything, and everything is I— and even I am God" (Case 1911:231).

As might be expected, however, the organized institutions of Christianity—which had a vested interest in maintaining the God of the Bible just as he was, a discrete and concrete personage—were strongly opposed to any pantheistic portrayal of him, which necessarily diffused and attenuated his being. The Church (Protestant or Catholic) wanted nothing to do with some vague, amorphous deity, coextensive with the whole of nature and thus indistinguishable from it. The traditional Christian God was distinct in his person and clearly separate from the world that he ruled. He was, at all costs, to be retained in his traditional form as an anthropomorphic deity of solid substance.

For this reason those few individuals who initially were drawn to pantheism had invariably found themselves severely rebuked by their church. John Scotus Erigena, a ninth century philosopher, wrote a work *De Divisione Naturae* that was deemed pantheistic and was

unequivocally condemned by Pope Honorius III in 1225 as "pullu-
lating with worms of heretical perversity" (quoted in MacIntyre
1967:32). And centuries later among the various heresies attributed
to Giordano Bruno (1548–1600) was his advocacy of a kind of pantheism that the Catholic Church considered a grave offense and a
challenge to its teachings. Indeed, the Church was intent on making
it clear that "[r]eligion meant nothing unless the Creator was distinct from His creation" (Jeans 1961:129–130). The pantheistic
heresy of Giordano was in fact one reason why he was burned at the
stake.

Pantheism continued to be anathema to the Catholic Church. As
late as 1864, Pope Pius IX issued his infamous "Syllabus of Errors" in
which he listed no fewer than eighty doctrinal mistakes that he thought
had been made by modern thinkers. And at the top of his list, as if this
were the greatest and most dangerous error of them all, was pantheism. The essence of this erroneous belief, according to Pius IX, was
the assertion that "[t]here exists no Supreme, all-wise, all-powerful
Diving Being, distinct from the universe." Instead these perverse
minds think that "God is identical with the nature of things … [A]ll
things are God and have the very substance of God and God is one and
the same thing with the world." Such a view was to be uncompromis-
ingly opposed and, if at all possible, ruthlessly eradicated.

The European philosopher best known for his supposed allegiance to a form of pantheism was Baruch Spinoza (1632–1677),
for whom God penetrated all creation. Spinoza actually "considered
his doctrine basically identical with both that of the ancient Hebrew
writers and of St. Paul." Nevertheless that "did not save him from
condemnation by the synagogue in his lifetime, let alone from condemnation by the Catholic Church afterward" (MacIntyre
1967:33–34). Reflecting organized religion's repugnance of this
philosophy, Schopenhauer once called pantheism "a polite form of
atheism" (quoted in Haeckel 1992:291).

Transcendentalism: An American Philosophy

A form of pantheism manifested itself again many years later in the
United States. This time, though, the consequences faced by its
adherents were nowhere near as dire. This philosophical movement,

which took place in the first half of the nineteenth century, was known loosely as Transcendentalism. To find its roots, we must go back to Europe. By the seventeenth and eighteenth centuries, philosophy—as represented by such men as Spinoza, Leibniz, Kant, and Hegel—was no longer strongly dominated by traditional Christian theology. To be sure, it was still firmly rooted in the idea of God, but the Deity was not to be conceived of as distinctly anthropomorphic. But while becoming nearly incorporeal, God nevertheless still retained the human attributes of mind, purpose, and will.

Adopting this attenuated notion of God, German philosophy was thus poised to embrace a species of pantheism. As Alasdair MacIntyre explained it in his treatment of the subject, "With the increased questioning of Christianity, accompanied by an unwillingness to adopt atheistic positions, pantheism became an important doctrine, first for Goethe and Lessing, both of whom were influenced by Spinoza, then for Schleiermacher, and finally for Fichte, Schelling, and Hegel" (MacIntyre 1967:34). Indeed, among the most profound intellectual influences on the Transcendentalism that arose in New England were these selfsame German idealists. All the Transcendentalists, in fact, made a serious effort to acquaint themselves with the works of contemporary German philosophers (Moran 1967:479).

There was, however, another equally important component to Transcendentalism. Rather than deriving from the subtleties and high-flown rhetoric of German idealism, this was a romantic and artistic strain that reflected more the "personalized and poetic expressions of ... Wordsworth, Coleridge, and Carlyle" (Moran 1967:479).

In addition to these elements, there lay behind the emerging Transcendentalism a desire to relax the religious strictures that had once weighed so heavily on many educated Americans. The first step in this liberation was a turning away from the dour, harsh Calvinism of their fathers. This sea change was reflected in "the anguished former Calvinists like Hawthorne and Melville—those who, in Melville's words, 'could not believe but could not be comfortable in disbelief '" (Applegate 2006:271).

Along with a rejection of the narrow precepts of orthodox Christianity, there came a turning toward the more liberal tenets of

Unitarianism, then led in America by two Unitarian ministers William Ellery Channing (1780–1842) and Theodore Parker (1810–1860). In Boston in 1841, Parker delivered a fiery sermon entitled "The Transient and Permanent in Christianity" in which he "denied the necessity of believing in Biblical inspiration and miracles." This fervid pronouncement "led Emerson to nickname Parker 'the Savonarola of transcendentalism'" (Moran 1967:479). Of Channing it was said that "[t]he path to transcendentalism lay through Unitarianism, and it was Channing who helped pave the way" by rejecting the "irrational and unscriptural doctrine of the 'Trinity'" (Bartlett 1967:80).

The thinkers who were to be known as Transcendentalists generally moved beyond Unitarianism. But while taking on the trappings of pantheism, they did not do away with all the traditional notions of God. They still clung to him, but as a Deity who manifested himself in a diffused and diluted form. In essence what they did was to transfer his divinity from the distinct and discernable anthropomorphic entity of old to a rather depersonalized nature. Ralph Waldo Emerson, for example, is said to have "portrayed Christ as a set of ideal teachings rather than as the actual son of God" (Applegate 2006:274). Those thinkers who now found an anthropomorphic God implausible and unacceptable sought to resolve their difficulties by transforming the Deity from a single personage with a distinct form to the vast entirety of an impersonal nature.

Still, Emerson was by no means prepared to dispense completely with the traditional figure of God, especially if the alternative were the impersonal determinism offered by Laplace and like-minded French materialists. He felt strongly that their doctrine "rejected the hope and consolation of man" that the Christian God had always provided. The French astronomers, he declared, mistakenly "adopted the belief of an eternal Necessity, as if that very eternal necessity was anything else than God" (quoted in Crowe 1994:377).

As budding—or blooming—pantheists, the Transcendentalists chose to focus more on the ubiquity of God and the grandeur of his works than on the delineation of his person. If the notion of an identifiable God were to be retained at all, then he would have to be everything and everything had to be he. However, the Transcendentalists were not all of one stripe. If some tended to see God every-where, others tended to see him nowhere. After all, they were in large measure free thinkers, Unitarians or ex-Unitarians concerned more with actuality than theology. It is inaccurate, therefore, to regard Transcendentalism as "primarily a movement within the Christian church. For its outcome, as the works of Emerson and Thoreau, for example, amply testify, was essentially secular and humanist in the widest sense" (Moran 1967:480).

It should be noted, though, that the Transcendentalists were by no means rigorous thinkers with hard-edged concepts carefully hammered out and systematically welded into a rigid structure. Rather, having freed themselves from the strict tenets of orthodox Christianity, they extended their arms toward a more amorphous, abstract, and pleasing notion of the Good and the Beautiful. It was, when closely examined, more a movement *away* from biblical Christianity than *toward* the mental toughness and rigor of science.

In her biography of Henry Ward Beecher, Debby Applegate gives a fine assessment of the movement.

> Transcendentalists did not share a single philosophical or religious system; instead they shared a liberal habit of thought. It was characterized by an appreciation for provocative new ideas, a fascination with the way the mind works, a determination to throw off the constraints of society and tradition, and a Romantic emphasis on strong, intuitive feeling. Transcendentalism deliberately turned Calvinism on its ear. Where the Calvinists believed in a deep divide between a superior, supernatural God and an innately corrupt human nature, the Transcendentalists insisted that the divine coursed throughout the natural world, and especially the human heart. They had an optimistic faith in mankind's "infinite worthiness," as Emerson put it, in humanity's—and society's—ability to transcend our lower natures by cultivating the sublime within ourselves. (Applegate 2006:272)

In general, the practitioners of Transcendentalism were characterized by "the placing of imagination over reason, creativity above theory, action higher than contemplation, and a marked tendency to see the spontaneous activity of the creative artist as the ultimate achievement of civilization" (Moran 1967:480). Prompted to express in broadly defining terms the principal features of the movement, Emerson once said that "whatever belongs to the class of intuitive thoughts, is popularly called at the present day *Transcendentalism*" (Moran 1967:479).

Perhaps its leading voice, Emerson remarked at one point that "[w]hat is popularly called Transcendentalism among us, 'is Idealism; Idealism as it appears in 1842'" (quoted in Moran 1967:479). And adopting a word that had become something of a shibboleth among the German idealists, Emerson liked to speak of an "Oversoul," by which he meant—in all its vague diffuseness— the "transcendent unity which embraces subject and object, mind and matter, and in which all the differences in virtue of which particular things exist are absorbed" (Unsigned 1911c:384).

Emerson was much given to flowery excesses in describing whatever he espoused. Thus after quoting a passage from him in which he fulsomely extolled the role of the Great Man in history, the anthropologist Leslie White observed, "Thus wrote the man who provided the intelligentsia of America with the verbal reflexes called 'thought' for so many years" (White 2005:279).

Without a doubt, much of what was put forward in the name of Transcendentalism was wordy and windy. Pointing to the flowery vacuities of some Transcendentalists, the *Brooklyn Eagle* joked, "When a speaker talked so that his audience didn't understand him, and when he said what he didn't understand himself—that was transcendentalism" (quoted in Applegate 2006:272).

For all its fuzziness, though, the most significant feature of Transcendentalism from our perspective was the fact that it distanced itself from biblical Christianity. In doing so it transferred its allegiance—one might almost say its veneration—to the all-encompassing world of nature. But this natural world was by no means the highly determined, mechanical universe of Newton or Laplace. Rather than being an impersonal machine, running with clocklike precision, it was "an organism, a symbol and analogue of mind" (Moran 1967:480). The pantheism that was such a notable element of Transcendentalism may have been far removed from what Schopenhauer once called "only a polite form of atheism" (Handy 1967a:401). But it did represent a major break with traditional

Christianity and showed a readiness to look at the natural world with fresh and appreciative eyes. And what it saw was decidedly not a carefully choreographed stage play, manipulated by strings carefully jiggled by supernatural hands. Rather, pantheism of the kind professed by the Transcendentalists may be thought of as a halfway house or way station between orthodox Christianity and a materialistic and deterministic view of the world fostered by science.

Spencer: Advancing the Cause of the Knowable

No one in the nineteenth century did more to promote the cause of naturalism in the interpretation of phenomena than Herbert Spencer. History, though, has not been kind to Spencer. If today he is remembered at all, it is mostly for his conservative political philosophy—especially his advocacy of "Social Darwinism." His great contributions to science, especially social science, are all but forgotten or ignored. Yet during his lifetime Spencer was enormously influential in demonstrating the power of science when applied to the study of all aspects of nature.

We have seen that along with E. B. Tylor, Spencer was co-expounder of what we consider the most persuasive explanation of the origin of religion. Moreover, as we will see in the next chapter, he played a leading role in advancing the cause of evolution, both organic and social. But Spencer did take a step backward, becoming entrapped in metaphysical quicksand when he engaged in an intellectual flirtation with the concept of the Unknowable—a purportedly parallel domain of existence, imperceptible and inaccessible to study (as will be described in Chapter 15). However, the practical effect of Spencer's propounding of the Unknowable was virtually nil. The philosopher William Ernest Hocking had a clear perception of this.

> When the agnostic says that we cannot know anything about the reality beyond nature or experience, he implies that there is such a reality; and some, like Spencer, clearly accept this inference. To this extent they are not pure naturalists.... [W]e can know nothing of supernature, we have nothing to do with it either in thought or conduct—we can manage our lives as if it did not exist. (Hocking 1939:136)

And that is precisely how Spencer proceeded. In 1862 he wrote a landmark volume entitled *First Principles,* intending to introduce and develop the general doctrine of evolution preliminary to applying it rigorously to various domains of phenomena in his *Synthetic Philosophy,* several volumes of which were to follow. This ambitious undertaking was meant to unify all knowledge by treating everything as having developed out of simpler forms, through an entirely natural process that at no point involved the supernatural. Moreover, Spencer insisted that his was an interpretation of the facts—objective and incontrovertible—acceptable to anyone regardless of his or her metaphysical views. To underscore this point, in an early chapter of *First Principles*, Spencer asserted that in the later pages of the book he would lay out "an orderly presentation of facts," adding that this

> interpretation of the facts is nothing more than a statement of the ultimate uniformities they present—the laws to which they conform. Is the reader an atheist? The exposition of these facts and these laws will neither yield support to his belief nor destroy it. Is he a pantheist? The phenomena and the inferences as now to be set forth will not force on him any incongruous implication. Does he think that God is immanent throughout all things, from concentrating nebulae to the thoughts of poets? Then the theory to be put before him contains no disproof of that view. Does he believe in a Deity who has given unchanging laws to the Universe? Then he will find nothing at variance with his belief in an exposition of these laws and an account of the results. (Spencer 1937:106)

And in a succession of volumes forming part of a coordinated series—the *Synthetic Philosophy*—Spencer put these pronouncements into practice. Chief among these works were *The Principles of Biology* (two volumes, 1864–1867), *The Principles of Psychology* (two volumes, 1870–1872), and *The Principles of Sociology* (three volumes, 1876–1896). With an impressive command of the data of biology, psychology, and sociology/anthropology and a readiness to examine them from bold new perspectives, along with unsurpassed powers of generalization, Spencer took on the salient facts of those fields and skillfully traced their evolution from rudimentary beginnings to their present state.

That the phenomena constituting these fields could be studied rigorously along purely naturalistic lines and be made to yield illuminating results was the message Spencer meant to convey. And to a large extent, it was a message readily absorbed and embraced by educated minds. Moreover, some of the highly literate among them went on to reflect his view of the world in their own writings. No better summation of Spencer's profound influence in promoting naturalism in American letters, for example, can be found than in Vernon Parrington's *Main Currents in American Thought*.

> The appeal of Spencer to the generation born after the Civil War was extraordinary. Ardent young minds, for whom the candles of theology were burnt out and who were seeking new light to their feet, were drawn to him irresistibly. Young rebels who had thrown off the guidance of their elders and were bent on discovering fresh paths through the tangle of dead faiths—independent souls like Hamlin Garland and Jack London and Theodore Dreiser who were to become leaders of the realistic revolt against the genteel traditions in life and letters and faith—went to [Spencer's books] ... to prepare themselves for the great work of freeing the American mind from the old theological inhibitions.... Everywhere the influence of the great Victorian penetrated, and wherever the influence spread, the old theological presuppositions disintegrated. (Parrington 1930:197–198)

Such was Spencer's contribution—so little appreciated today—to the advancement of human inquiry and understanding.

The Challenge to the Anglican Church

In Chapter 9 we described the attenuation that took place in the concept of God the Father. Correspondingly, there followed a diminution in the stature of God the Son. As we have seen, this was a prominent element in the arguments raised by the deists, especially Thomas Paine. But more was to follow. There came the so-called Higher Criticism (mentioned earlier) that involved the careful, critical examination of the biblical portrayal of Jesus Christ. Of this close scrutiny, initiated largely by German scholars, the British historian J. B. Bury wrote, "Modern criticism of the New Testament began with the stimulating works of [Bruno] Bauer and of [David Friedrich] Strauss, whose *Life of Jesus* (1835), in which the supernatural was entirely rejected, had an immense success and caused furious controversy" (Bury 2007:156).

In his introduction to J. R. Seeley's *Ecce Homo*, a British historian's parallel attempt to portray Christ as purely human, Sir Oliver Lodge spoke of "the shock experienced when an historian set to work to deal with the life of Christ as he would deal with any other history" and noted that this endeavor "struck devout persons as almost blasphemous" (Lodge 1908:viii).

As expected, a strong reaction to this biblical criticism ensued, ecclesiastical and academic authorities objecting strenuously to what they perceived as an undermining of the wellsprings of Christian belief. And as Bury remarked in his *History of Freedom of Thought*, "The havoc which science and historical criticism have wrought among orthodox beliefs during the last hundred years was not tamely submitted to.... Strauss was deprived of his professorship at Tübingen, and his career was ruined. [Joseph] Renan, whose sensational *Life of Jesus* (1863) also rejected the supernatural depiction of him, lost his chair in the Collège de France. Büchner was driven from Tübingen (1855) for his book *Force and Matter,* which, appealing to the general public, set forth the futility of supernatural explanations of the universe. An attempt was made to chase Haeckel from Jena" (Bury 2007:158).

In England as well as on the continent, the supernatural elements of Christianity came under meticulous examination. In 1860 a group of seven scholars at Oxford University, including the classicist Benjamin Jowett (famed for his translation of Plato), published a volume entitled *Essays and Reviews* forthrightly challenging—in the theological writing of the day—the "abominable system of terrorism which prevents the statement of the plainest fact" (quoted by Bury 2007:163). Radical as the book seemed at the time to staunch believers, what its seven scholarly contributors advocated was certainly mild enough. "It is not a useful lesson," they argued, for the young student of the Bible in examining difficult passages "to make formal reconciliations of discrepancies which he would not think of reconciling in ordinary history" (quoted in Bury 2007:163). Nevertheless, despite the moderate tone of their remarks, the scholars came to be branded as the "Seven against Christ."

Notwithstanding such a characterization, these Oxford scholars did their best to present themselves to their readers as being safely within the Christian fold. For one thing they maintained that the Thirty-Nine Articles, a litany of faith to which every Anglican minister was required to subscribe, permitted one to accept as "parable or poetry or legend" (rather than as strictly factual) any miraculous occurrence described in the Bible—as, for example, a donkey speaking with the voice of a man or one of water, not in the form of ice, somehow standing in a solid heap (Bury 2007:164).

Difficulty in accepting such biblical stories as literally true (they held) no longer needed to constitute an impassable barrier for a questioning Christian. It was now enough to accept them as *parables*. The position of the seven Oxford scholars was that any biblical story that might be "incapable of being ascertained or verified [as history], may yet be equally suggestive of true ideas with facts absolutely certain" (quoted in Bury 2007:164–165). In other words, as Bury put it in plain English, "they may have a spiritual significance although they are historically false" (2007:165).

As moderate as the assertions in *Essays and Reviews* now seem to us, at the time the book appeared they were roundly denounced by Anglican bishops. Indeed, two of the more outspoken of the seven contributors to the book were brought up before the Ecclesiastical Court and charged with offenses against the Church of England. They were convicted on several counts and suspended from their clerical duties for one year.

However, the two men appealed their conviction to the Privy Council of Great Britain and the council—after carefully examining the evidence—reversed the Ecclesiastical Court. In stating the decision of the council, chief judge Lord Westbury declared that henceforth it was unnecessary for an Anglican clergyman to believe in eternal punishment, as had previously been required of him. This opinion, which was widely quoted and publicized, led one waggish observer to remark of Lord Westbury (who was then about to retire) that "[t]oward the close of his earthly career he dismissed Hell with costs and took away from Orthodox members of the Church of England their last hope of everlasting damnation" (quoted in Bury 2007:165).

From our point of view, two aspects of this episode stand out. First, critical thinking in England had reached the point where few educated persons were ready to accept as literally true the miracles scattered so liberally throughout the Bible. And second, the judgment of the Privy Council constituted a striking example—almost unprecedented in England up to that time—of secular opinion peremptorily overriding religious authority. And with that a new, powerful, and promising trend was clearly foreshadowed.

CHAPTER 12

The Coming of Evolution

In all likelihood no single event in the history of Western thought has done more to advance the cause of naturalism—and at the same time deal a heavy blow to supernaturalism—as the formulation by Charles Darwin of the theory of organic evolution by natural selection. Evolution, of course, did not appear on the intellectual landscape full blown: evolution itself evolved. Before describing the effect exerted by Darwin's theory when it was first presented to the world, therefore, it seems appropriate to trace the trajectory of its development.

One reason a theory of organic evolution was so long in coming—and met with such stiff resistance when it arrived—was that the reigning explanation of how the world and its creatures had come into being was the biblical account of special creation. The scriptural story had thus been firmly in place for two millennia. Moreover, the institution whose mission it was to uphold that explanation—the Church, first Catholic and then Protestant—was prepared to vigorously defend it against any competing explanation. But that is getting ahead of the story.

The notion that things came to be what they are by a gradual process of development, rather than by a sudden and miraculous act of creation, was already found in a rather inchoate form among certain early philosophers. In a sense the Greek atomists can be regarded as evolutionists, since they conceived of atoms as being not only the *elemental* but also the *primordial* building blocks out of which everything else in the universe had been formed. And if all present-day objects started out as uniformly small, simple atoms, the process by which their complex structures had been built—that is, the successive stages in the aggregation of matter—must necessarily be evolutionary. Still, this was evolution only in a broad, general sense.

Foreshadowings of Evolution in Antiquity

The two Greek philosophers whose names are linked with this form of evolution are Anaximander (611–547 B.C.) and Anaximenes (585–525 B.C.). In his history of the theory of evolution, *From the Greeks to Darwin* (1929), Henry Fairfield Osborn wrote that Anaximander's "explanation of the metamorphosis of 'aquatic men' into 'land men' is the first dim adumbration of a belief in slow anatomical transformation rather than in the immediate attainment of anatomical perfection," as called for in various religious accounts of divine creation (Osborn 1929:48–49). Anaximander's successor Anaximenes "introduced the idea of primordial terrestrial slime, a mixture of earth and water, from which, under the influence of the sun's heat, plants, animals, and human beings were directly produced" (Osborn 1929:50).

In a "Historical Sketch" added to later editions of *The Origin of Species,* Charles Darwin named thirty-four individuals who—to one degree or another—had anticipated him in thinking that animal organisms had not always been the same but had changed over time. "Passing over [without further comment] allusions to the subject in classical writers," said Darwin, he nevertheless supplied a footnote in which he quoted the following passage from Aristotle: "Wheresoever, therefore, all things together ... happened like as if they were made for the sake of something, these were preserved, having been appropriately constituted by an internal spontaneity; and whatsoever things were not thus constituted, perished, and still perish"—a very rough portrayal of natural selection at work (quoted in Darwin 1970:53).

In tracing early foreshadowings of the theory of evolution, we next jump ahead to the Roman philosophical poet Lucretius (96–55 B.C.) and his remarkable poem *De Rerum Natura*. A follower of Epicurus, and like him an atomist, Lucretius regarded "the primitive atoms ... as seeds of which individual things are developed. All living and sentient things are formed out of insentient atoms" (Mitchell 1910:24). In Lucretius's account the natural motion of atoms was to fall downward through space in vertical parallel fashion. Occasionally, though, one atom would veer off course and fall diagonally, striking another atom and uniting with it, giving rise to a more complex object. "Verily not by design," Lucretius wrote, "do the first beginnings of things station themselves each in his right place, ... but because after trying motions and unions of every kind, at length they fall into arrangements, such as those out of which this our sum of things has been formed" (quoted in Osborn 1929:93–94). Once the earth was fashioned in this way, life followed in due course.

> The new earth shot out grass and shrubs at first
> And then went on to produce the mortal animals,
> Great numbers of them, starting in various ways.
> The animals cannot have fallen from the sky
> Nor those that live on land have come out of the sea.
> No wonder therefore the earth is called our mother
> Since every creature came out of the ground.
> (Lucretius 2005:158)

The process, said Lucretius, continued as follows:

> Then it was the earth first gave forth races of animals
> For at that time the ground was wet and warm.
> And so, wherever there was a suitable spot
> Were breeding-places attached to the earth by roots
> And the young came out when they were ready to come.
> (Lucretius 2005:158)

Lucretius seems also to have formed some rough notion of natural selection, for he wrote:

> Many species will have died out at this period,
> Not having the capacity to continue their race.
> For wherever you see a creature which has survived
> It is craft or strength or mobility that has saved it,
> Affording protection from the very beginning.
> (Lucretius 2005:160)

In *From the Greeks to Darwin*, Osborn characterized Lucretius's place in the history of evolutionary thinking in this way: "We cannot truly speak of Lucretius as an evolutionist, in the sense of gradual development by descent, although he believed in the successive appearance of different forms of life. His nearest approach to true evolution teaching was in his account of the development of the faculties and arts among the races of men" (Osborn 1929:96).

Biblical Creationism Becomes Official Dogma

When the biblical story of creation—as portrayed in the Book of Genesis—became the official dogma of the Roman Empire following Constantine's conversion to Christianity in 313, speculative thought regarding the origin of man and his fellow creatures essentially ceased. Occasionally, through the ensuing centuries, enlightened thinkers expressed their doubts about the sudden and spontaneous creation of life as set forth in the Bible. For instance, Descartes was quoted by John Dewey as saying, "The nature of physical things is much more easily conceived when they are beheld coming gradually into existence, than when they are only considered as produced at once in a finished and perfect state" (quoted in Dewey 1979:308). But this was hardly a strong demurral to the prevailing Christian account.

With the burgeoning of the physical sciences—especially the astronomical discoveries of Copernicus, Galileo, Kepler, and Newton—beginning around 1600, a naturalistic view of causation began to gain ascendancy and became more prominent in Western thought. Slowly but irresistibly naturalistic explanations of the workings of the cosmos began to push aside traditional supernaturalistic ones.

A Clockwork View of the Universe

The mechanical interpretation of the world, however, was limited in its application. What it stood for may be termed a *clockwork* view of the universe, which explained well enough the repetitive movements of the planets and stars but was not readily translatable to human biology and behavior. Moreover, in the mechanical model of the solar system, the motions of the objects were seen only as cyclical and recurring. Non-recurring, *directional* changes in things over long periods of time—the essence of evolution—had not yet become a scientific formulation. The universe was conceived of as essentially *non-evolving.* Indeed, according to Bertrand Russell, "Newton ... seemed to favour a sudden creation of the sun and the planets as we know them, and to leave no room for cosmic evolution" (Russell 1997:53). There was no question, then, about organic matter having undergone significant transformations and assuming a succession of different forms.

To be sure, biblical creation—being in itself a dramatic transformative act—had introduced novelty into the world. But because that act had been a sudden, special, and unique event rather than one involving many steps in a lengthy process, the world and its creatures had remained essentially the same from that point forward. Writing in 1759, the Abbé Pluche was emphatic about what could be expected to transpire in the future: "Nothing more, therefore, will be produced in all the ages to follow. All the philosophers have deliberated and come to agreement upon this point" (quoted in Lovejoy 1936:243). In the abbé's opinion, then, the Schoolmen and theologians of an earlier period had already concurred that stasis was the future of the world.

Yet during the Middle Ages, the concept of a Great Chain of Being was slowly taking shape. And according to this view, "[A]ll organisms can be put in a continuous line from the simplest to the most complex, from monad to man, as people often said.... In itself the chain was not evolutionary—it was more a fixed ladder than a moving escalator—but it was pointed in the right direction, for those who were so inclined" (Ruse 2005:29).

Beginning in the seventeenth century, the extraordinary advances in physics and astronomy showed what a powerful tool the method of science could be. Even the clergy—at least the more enlightened members of it—could not help but be impressed. Stephen Jay Gould offered an example of this in the person of the Reverend Thomas Burnet (1635–1715). According to Gould, Burnet "accepted the scriptural account as a rough description of actual events, but he insisted upon one principle above all: the history of the earth cannot be regarded as adequately explained or properly interpreted until all events can be rendered as necessary consequences of invariable natural laws, opening with the knowable regularity recently demonstrated for gravity and other key phenomena by his dear friend Isaac Newton" (Gould 1999:18).

Eighteenth Century Glimmerings of Evolution

As great a scientist as he was, Newton was no evolutionist. His was a clockwork universe, as we have seen, marked by recurrences and the restorations of equilibria that had been temporarily disturbed. In fact, the first man to look at the structure of the heavens, and to conceive of them as the result of an unfolding evolutionary process, was … Immanuel Kant! In his *General Natural History and Theory of the Heavens* (1755), Kant proposed "the notion of gradual development [of the universe] from an almost undifferentiated primal distribution of matter throughout space." "This is the first serious attempt," wrote Bertrand Russell, "to substitute evolution for sudden creation" on a cosmic scale (Russell 1997:56).

As the eighteenth century drew to a close, the attitude of demanding that events conform to law was becoming commonplace among those who were intent on studying natural phenomena. It was at this juncture that the notion of *social* evolution began to command attention. Condorcet's famous *Sketch of a Historical Table of the Progress of the Human Mind* (1799) had portrayed the transformation of society from primitive simplicity to the complexity of the present day, and this depiction stood as a model for biologists to contemplate as they studied life and its unfolding. Might not *organisms*, they reasoned, also have undergone a similar sort of transformation?

"Evolution": The Term and the Concept

It was in biology—specifically in the field of embryology—that the word "evolution" first made its appearance. A fierce controversy was raging about how it was that an embryo developed. On one side stood the *epigenesists,* who believed that the embryo began as a virtually formless bit of germ plasm and only gradually differentiated into successively more complex forms. The adversaries of the epigenisists, led by the Swiss naturalist Charles Bonnet, held the opposite view: that the embryo consisted of a tiny but perfectly formed "homunculus" and that development in the womb involved only the unfolding and subsequent growth of that minuscule being. Those who held this latter view were called *preformationists*, and the process by which they believed development took place Bonnet termed *evolution.*

Using the word "evolution" in this sense seemed appropriate enough since it reflected the original Latin meaning of *evolūtio,* which was "unrolled." This term was applied especially to Roman books—rolled-up manuscripts of parchment—which, in order to be read, had to be unrolled or *evolved.*

Cuvier and Buffon: Biologist Adversaries

The battle between the epigenesists and the preformationists, however, was restricted to the narrow field of embryology. The larger argument between those who believed in the fixity of species, and those who argued for their transformation over time, was a separate issue that as yet had barely surfaced. When it finally did emerge into prominence, the two greatest naturalists of the age found themselves aligned on opposite sides.

On one side was the renowned anatomist Georges Cuvier (1769–1832), generally regarded as the father of comparative anatomy, who also almost single-handedly had founded the science of paleontology. Cuvier claimed that he could reconstruct an entire animal by examining a single bone (Davies 1947:107). When it came to the question of how animal species had arisen, though, Cuvier looked backward to biblical creation for the answer. As a paleontologist he was of course aware of the existence of fossils— animals that no longer roamed the earth but whose existence was proved by the testimony of the rocks. And these fossils had to be accounted for. The issue placed Cuvier on the horns of a dilemma, one neatly encapsulated by Isaac Asimov.

> Cuvier, however, was a pious man who could not accept the possibility of evolutionary changes. He adopted instead an alternative view that although the earth was indeed ancient, it underwent periodic catastrophies during which all life was wiped out. After each such catastrophe, new forms of life would appear, forms that were quite different from those that had previously existed. Modern forms of life (including man) were created after the most recent catastrophe. In this view, evolutionary process-

es were not needed to explain the fossils, and the biblical story, supposed [by Cuvier] to apply only to events after the last catastrophe, could be preserved. (Asimov 1964:44)

On the other side of the issue—the side that believed in the transmutation of species—we can cite, first of all, Cuvier's countryman Georges Buffon (1707–1788). Buffon composed a monumental 44-volume *Histoire naturelle*, in Volume 9 of which he had spoken of "the quickness with which species vary" and "the ease with which they alter their nature by taking on new shapes" (quoted in Ward 1943:27)—without, however, suggesting any mechanism to account for such a transformation (Darwin 1970:53–54).

This opinion, however, was expressed in the 1750s just before the Age of Enlightenment had dawned, a period during which the Catholic Church still held a stranglehold on French thought. Buffon's heretical views were condemned by the Church and he was forced to retract what he had written. Accordingly, in a later volume of his *Histoire naturelle,* Buffon abjured his former views, holding that in his previous writings "I had no intention to contradict the text of Scripture; that I believe most firmly all therein related about the creation, both as to order of time and matter of fact; I abandon everything in my book respecting the formation of the earth, and generally, all that may be contrary to the narrative of Moses" (quoted in Russell 1997:62). Just as in Galileo's case, the power of the Church had forced a grudging and humbling recantation.

Erasmus Darwin and Lamarck: Early Transformationists

Next among the early transformationists was Erasmus Darwin (1731–1802), the grandfather of Charles Darwin, who acknowledged his debt to "the ingenious Mr. Buffon" (Ward 1943:27) and went on to compose several works—most of them in verse—in which he championed a vague form of organic evolution. In one such work, *The Temple of Nature* (1803), he wrote these portentous lines:

[W]ould it be too bold to imagine that all warm-blooded animals have arisen from one living filament, which THE GREAT FIRST CAUSE endued with animality, with the power of

acquiring new parts ..., and thus possessing the faculty of continuing to improve by its own inherent activity, and of delivering
down those improvements by generation, to its posterity, world
without end! (quoted in Ward 1943:421)

Erasmus Darwin's undisguised reference to "THE GREAT
FIRST CAUSE" showed clearly that he, like his fellow biologists,
was no atheist. In fact, writing in his most famous work *Zoonomia*
(1794) of the series of natural laws through which he thought God
had striven to produce these momentous changes, he remarked,
"What a magnificent idea of the infinite power of *The Great
Architect! The Cause of Causes! Parent of parents*" (quoted in Ruse
2005:33).

The third of the early evolutionists was Jean Baptiste Lamarck
(1744–1829), who drew inspiration from his two predecessors.
"Lamarck borrowed Buffon's ... idea that species change by adjusting to changed conditions, and expanded [Erasmus] Darwin's conjecture about the operation of needs and desires in producing the
change" (Ward 1943:431). Indeed, Charles Darwin was led to
remark, "It is curious how largely my grandfather ... anticipated the
views and erroneous grounds of opinion of Lamarck in his
'Zoonomia'" (Darwin 1970:54). Initially Lamarck had accepted the
fixity of species, but around 1800 he came to believe in *transmutation,* as evolution was then generally called (Ward 1943:431). In his
most famous work, *Philosophie zoologique* (1809), Lamarck avoided using the word "evolution," in all likelihood because of the specific—and erroneous—meaning that the term had already been
given by Bonnet.

As early as 1802, in his *Recherches sur l'organisation des corps
vivant,* Lamarck had expressed his conviction that gradual transformation—not a single act of creation or even a succession of them,
as Cuvier believed—accounted for the variety of life forms on
earth. "Ascend from the simplest to the most complex," Lamarck
wrote, "leave from the simplest animalcule and go up along the
scale to the animal richest in organization and facilities; conserve
everywhere the order of relation in the masses; then you will have
hold of the true thread that ties together all of nature's productions,
you will have a just idea of her *marche* and you will be convinced

that the simplest of her living productions have successively given rise to all others" (quoted in Ruse 2005:30–31).

By 1809, in his *Philosophie zoologique*, the mechanism that Lamarck was ready to use to explain the long-term changes in species was this: the inheritance of acquired characteristics. He explained its operation as follows.

> [G]reat changes in the conditions [in which they live] cause, for the animals, great changes in their needs, and such changes in the needs necessarily cause changes in their actions. Now, if the new needs become fixed or permanent, the animals then acquire new habits, which are as permanent as the needs which have originated them. (quoted in Ward 1943:429)

These needs and habits, in turn, brought about morphological changes in the bodies of these animals in order to enhance their ability to accomplish the necessary adaptations. Thus the giraffe's need to feed higher on acacia trees caused it to develop a longer neck.

Here we may summarize Charles Darwin's assessment of Lamarck's role in the coming acceptance of evolution, and the influence—or lack of it—that Lamarck's views had on him. One of Darwin's first encounters with Lamarck occurred while he was still a student at Edinburgh, during a conversation with a zoologist named Robert Grant: "He one day, when we were walking together, burst forth in high admiration of Lamarck and his views on evolution. I listened in silent astonishment, and as far as I can judge, without any effect on my mind" (Darwin 1929:13).

Even before this conversation with Dr. Grant (Darwin wrote in his *Autobiography*), "I had previously read the *Zoonomia* of my grandfather, in which similar views [to Lamarck's] are maintained, but without producing any effect on me. Nevertheless it is probable that the hearing rather early in life such views maintained and praised may have favoured my upholding them under a different form in my *Origin of Species*" (Darwin 1929:13).

Despite Lamarck's failure to hit upon natural selection as the mechanism of organic evolution, Darwin considered his overall contribution to fostering a belief in evolution to have been decidedly positive: "He first did the eminent service of arousing attention to the probability of all change in the organic, as well as in the inorganic world, being the result of law, and not of miraculous interposition" (Darwin 1970:54).

At this point in our effort to trace the development of the theory of evolution, we must return to the physical sciences—this time to geology. Unlike physics, which dealt with recurring processes, geology dealt largely with non-repetitive events that had occurred over vast stretches of time. And indeed it was geology that played a major role in weakening a belief in the traditional biblical chronology—a chronology that, according to Archbishop James Ussher (1581–1656), placed the creation of the world in the year 4004 B.C.

Charles Lyell Introduces Uniformitarianism

In the hands of Sir Charles Lyell (1797–1875), however, geology did more than enormously expand the age of the earth. Lyell laid down the principle that "no causes whatever have from the earliest time to which we can look back, to the present, ever acted, but those *now* acting; and that they never acted with different degrees of energy from that which they *now* exert" (quoted in Ward 1943:72). Every geological feature—mountains and valleys, lakes and rivers, and the like—could be explained by the operation of natural causes, with no recourse to miracles. This dictum, which became known as the doctrine of Uniformitarianism, was most fully expounded by Lyell in his three-volume work *Principles of Geology* (1830–1833).

Opposed to this view was the earlier doctrine of Catastrophism, according to which the world had been subjected to periodic episodes of violent upheaval, often of a miraculous kind, as described in the Bible. The effect of Lyell's work, if not its intent, was to undermine the Bible as an authoritative guide to the history of the earth (Browne 2002:22). This aspect of *Principles of Geology* thus served the cause of evolution, which required a long span of time for it to operate—to say nothing of a perfectly natural set of causes by which to act. Lyell's argument exerted a strong influence on Charles Darwin, for as Isaac Asimov noted, "Darwin had read Lyell's first volume on geology ... before starting out [on the voyage of the *Beagle*] and had a clear realization of the antiquity of the earth and of the long ages through which life had had time to develop" (Asimov 1964:61).

Lyell's *Principles,* however, was by no means consistent in its advocacy of naturalistic interpretations. This was especially true when it came to the history of life on earth. True enough, Lyell emphasized "the adequacy of known causes" in interpreting the past, and indeed in most chapters of Volume I of *Principles* he preached the "unchanging uniformity of natural law." But in Chapter 9 this uniformity was abruptly overridden, Lyell finding himself unable to go the whole way with a naturalistic account of life's origin and evolution. His deep Christian roots prevented him from doing so. As Thomas Henry Huxley put it, "Lyell, who most strenuously argued in favour of the sufficiency of natural causes for the production of the phenomena of the inorganic world, held stoutly by the hypothesis of creation in the case of those of the world of life" (Huxley 1896a:277).

This was most true of the human race. In Volume I of *Principles*, Lyell felt compelled to admit that "the creation of man was a breach in the uniformity of natural law, but a breach in a very lofty sphere— in the creation of a moral being." Now, in Volume II, he was obliged to concede that every species had been specially created. "He was peppering his grand uniformity with millions of mysterious 'creations,' and implying that a 'creation' was a divine interference with natural law" (Ward 1943:102). Indeed, Lyell wrote the second volume of *Principles* "for the express purpose of proving that there had *not* been any progressive development in organic life" (Ward 1943:433). In this regard Lyell was a special creationist, pure and simple, writing in Volume I of his *Principles of Geology*, "There is no foundation for the popular theory of the successive development of the animal and vegetable world" (quoted in Ward 1943:75).

Nevertheless, looked at in its totality, *Principles of Geology* represented a major step forward in the replacement of supernaturalistic with naturalistic explanations in accounting for the present state of the world. Said Huxley, "I cannot but believe that Lyell, for others as for myself, was the chief agent in smoothing the road for Darwin. For consistent uniformatarianism postulates evolution as much in the organic as in the inorganic world. The origin of a new species by other than ordinary agencies would be a vastly greater 'catastrophe' than any of those which Lyell successfully eliminated from sober geological speculation" (quoted in Ward 1943:435). And indeed Lyell's tomes, widely read as they were, caused great discomfort to the orthodox.

Vestiges of the Natural History of Creation

Despite Lyell's expressed opposition to organic evolution, there is no doubt that as early as the 1830s that idea was already "in the air." W. C. Wells in 1813 and Patrick Matthews in 1831 wrote pieces that although unnoticed at the time, were later recognized by Darwin himself as having caught at least a glimmer of evolution by means of natural selection (Darwin 1970:55, 56). Then, in 1844, an anonymous work appeared that did catch the public's eye.

Vestiges of the Natural History of Creation offered no compelling theory to explain how the transmutation of species had occurred, but it did propose to abandon the biblical story of creation, substituting for it an account of this great change invoking only natural causes. Its author saw the succession of animal forms as having taken place somewhat as follows: "From reptiles we advance to birds, and then to mammals, which are commenced by marsupials, acknowledgedly low forms in their class. That there is thus a progress of some kind, the most superficial glance at the geological history is sufficient to convince us" (quoted in Ruse 2005:49). "*The Vestiges* rested the case for evolution," wrote J. W. Burrow in his introduction to a recent reprint of *The Origin of Species*, "chiefly on the assertion that the fossil series, from most ancient to the most recent geological strata, demonstrated a gradual 'ascent.' It also employed arguments from the existence of rudimentary and vestigial organs from embryology" (Burrow 1970:29).

The author of *Vestiges* turned out to be a Scottish editor and publisher named Robert Chambers (1802–1871). The reason Chambers chose to publish the book anonymously was that he "was aware of the storm that would probably be raised at the time by a rational treatment of the subject and did not wish to involve his firm in the discredit that a charge of heterodoxy would bring with it" (Unsigned 1910b:821). Despite—or, more likely, because of—the controversy that it generated, the book remained popular and altogether went through twelve editions. In explaining the threat that *Vestiges* was seen to pose to orthodox Christian belief, Henshaw Ward, one of Darwin's biographers, wrote:

> An argument that the wonderful adaptations of animals had been brought about by natural causes was supposed to be a denial of God's design in His creation, and so to be atheistic. Worse still, an argument for the development of one species out of another was sure to indicate that human beings are not a special creation. (Ward 1943:229)

But Chambers was no atheist. Indeed, despite his denial of special creation, he thought that his book ultimately served to elucidate "the works and ways of God" (quoted in Lanham 1968:168). In the tenth edition of *Vestiges,* printed in 1853, Chambers "gives as his final opinion that the animal series is the result, *first,* of an *impulse,* imparted by God, advancing all the forms of life, through the various grades of organization from the lowest to the highest plants and animals" (Osborn 1929:315). Countering the argument of his opponents that the idea of the evolution of the human species out of earlier, simpler forms was degrading, Chambers wrote, "It has pleased Providence to arrange that one species should give birth to another, until the second highest, give birth to man, who is the very highest" (quoted in Lanham 1968:167).

Still, Chambers made it clear that he was ready to set aside the biblical account of creation. Thus he asked, "In what way was the creation of animated beings effected?" and answered, "The ordinary notion ... [is] that the Almighty author produced the progenitors of all existing species by some sort of personal or immediate exertion. But how does this notion comport with what we have seen of the gradual advance of species from the humblest to the highest?" (quoted in Miller 1999:282).

Vestiges caused a sensation when it appeared. In nine years, from 1844 to 1853, it went through ten editions. By most reviewers the book was alternately ridiculed and vilified. "The *Vestiges* was saturated with errors of biological fact and interpretation, ranging from the trivial to the fantastically absurd, and was savagely attacked by many biologists" (Lanham 1968:168). Adam Sedgwick, professor of geology at Cambridge, was particularly virulent in his assault on it. "From the bottom of my soul," he wrote, "I loathe and detest the *Vestiges*" (quoted in Miller 1999:283). But his objections to the book were more theological than scientific. He fulminated that "if the book be true, the labours of sober induction are in vain; religion is a lie; human law is a mass of folly, and a base injustice; morality is moonshine" (quoted in Burrow 1970:29). Sedgwick warned that if the "serpent coils" of the philosophy of *Vestiges* were accepted, "What then will follow? The reader can judge for himself: I can see nothing but ruin and confusion in such a creed.... If current in society it will undermine the whole moral and social fabric, and inevitably will bring discord and deadly mischief in its train" (quoted in Lanham 1968:169).

The reaction to *Vestiges* by the two great evolutionists of the future, Darwin and Huxley, was somewhat more tempered. Darwin wrote to Hooker in 1844, "I have also read the *Vestiges*, and have been somewhat less amused at it than you appear to have been: the writing and arrangement are certainly admirable, but his geology strikes me as bad, and his zoology far worse" (quoted in Lanham 1968:169–170). For his part Huxley wrote, "As for the Vestiges, I confess the book simply irritated me by the prodigious ignorance and thoroughly unscientific habit manifested by the writer. If it had any influence at all, it set me against evolution" (quoted in Lovejoy 1959:359). Years later, in 1887, reassessing the influence that the book had on him at the time, Huxley remarked, "I must have read the "Vestiges" ... before 1846, but if I did, the book made very little impression on me, and I was not brought into serious contact with the 'species' question until after 1850" (quoted in Lovejoy 1959:359).

Nevertheless, despite its infelicities and shortcomings, the overall effect of *Vestiges* on the idea of organic evolution must be judged as positive. Henry Fairfield Osborn summarized it as follows: "The great sensation which this book caused and its rapid sale through ten editions are proof that the truth of Evolution was ready to burst forth like a volcano and that the times were ripe for Darwin" (Osborn 1929:313).

Though lacking the sure touch of a professional naturalist, Chambers's book at least brought the idea of evolution boldly before the British public and kept it alive there. It is said that Alfred Russel Wallace read *Vestiges* and found its thesis to be "an ingenious glorious hypothesis," and that "from that time on his mind dwelt much on the origin of species" (Ward 1943:285). Darwin himself later wrote of it, "In my opinion it has done excellent service in this country in calling attention to the subject, in removing prejudice, and in thus preparing the ground for the reception of analogous views" (Darwin 1970:58). More recently Michael Ruse has noted, "Even if *Vestiges* was wrong, the idea of evolution … was now a familiar fixture on the intellectual and popular landscape. By the 1850s in Britain … evolutionary ideas were becoming known and less threatening" (Ruse 2005:53).

Finally, it is worth pointing out two positive effects that *Vestiges* appears to have had on Darwin, indirectly if not directly. Writing critically to Lyell in 1845 about Sedgwick's intemperate review of Chambers's book, Darwin remarked—already thinking ahead to his own future work on the subject—that in spite of its overall evolutionary message, "[I]t is a grand piece of argument against mutability of species, and I read it with fear and trembling, but was well pleased to find that I had not overlooked any of the arguments, though I had put them to myself as feebly as milk and water" (quoted in Lanham 1968:170).

The possibility that the adverse reviews of Chambers's book might have had a cautionary—and salutary—effect on Darwin has been supported by the biologist Uri Lanham: "It may be," he wrote, "that the reception of the *Vestiges* showed Darwin that it was an extremely bad time to come out with another book on evolution. Quite likely his work would have been misinterpreted and lost in the maelstrom of criticism that was swallowing up the scientific reputation of the author of the *Vestiges*" (Lanham 1968:170).

In his introduction to the 1969 reprinting of *Vestiges*, Gavin de Beer was more emphatic about the book's delaying influence on Darwin. Said he, "In 1844, the same year as that in which *Vestiges* appeared, Darwin had finished his Essay on evolution by natural selection; but seeing how the ideas in *Vestiges* raised the hackles of scientists and theologians alike, he held his hand and kept his secret to himself" (quoted in Miller 1999:283). That Darwin felt great apprehension about revealing his theory to the world is shown by his letter to Joseph Hooker early in 1844, in which he remarked that making it public would be "like confessing a murder" (quoted in Eldredge 2005:43).

Spencer and the Concept and Process of Evolution

The first explicit and detailed elucidation of the concept of evolution is generally thought to have been made by Charles Darwin, but such was not the case. Darwin, in fact, did not even use the word "evolution" in the first five editions of *The Origin of Species*. It was Herbert Spencer who formally introduced the term into nineteenth century biology—and into scientific discourse in general—and gave it a carefully formulated definition. This aspect of the story of evolution is today very little known and deserves to be presented here in some detail.

Spencer had virtually no formal schooling, but his father—a former schoolteacher—inculcated in him from an early age an attitude that inclined him toward science. Of his father's influence, Spencer wrote, "Always the tendency in himself, and the tendency strengthened in me, was to regard everything as naturally caused; and I doubt not that while the notion of causation was thus rendered much more definite in me than in most of my age, there was established a habit of seeking for causes, as well as a tacit belief in the universality of causation. Along with this there went absence of all suggestion of the miraculous" (Spencer 1924:I, 89).

Unlike Darwin, Spencer apparently never held any fixed religious beliefs. He relates that at the age of twenty he received a letter from his father that "called my attention to religious questions and appealed to religious feelings—seeking for some response." But no such response was forthcoming. As Spencer later wrote:

> The acquisition of scientific knowledge, especially physical, had cooperated with the natural tendency thus shown [a dislike for authority and ritual]; and had practically excluded the ordinary idea of the supernatural. A breach in the course of causation had come to be, if not an impossible thought, yet a thought never entertained. Necessarily, therefore, the current creed became more and more alien to the set of convictions gradually formed in me, and slowly dropped away unawares. (Spencer 1924:I, 152–153)

While still in his early twenties, Spencer became interested in geology and paleontology and purchased a copy of Lyell's *Principles of Geology*, of which he noted in his *Autobiography*:

I name this purchase chiefly as serving to introduce a fact of considerable significance. I had during previous years been cognizant of the hypothesis that the human race had been developed from some lower race; though what degree of acceptance it had from me memory does not say. But my reading of Lyell, one of whose chapters was devoted to a refutation of Lamarck's views concerning the origin of species, had the effect of giving me a decided leaning to them. Why Lyell's arguments produced the opposite effect to that intended, I cannot say. Probably it was that the discussion presented, more clearly than had been done previously, the conception of the natural genesis of organic forms.... My inclination to accept it as true, in spite of Lyell's adverse criticisms, was, doubtless, chiefly due to its harmony with that general idea of the order of Nature toward which I had, throughout life, been growing. (Spencer 1924:I, 176).

Then, in the course of his reading in 1851, Spencer recounted in his *Autobiography*,

I came across von Baer's formula expressing the course of development through which every plant and animal passes—the change from homogeneity to heterogeneity.... [T]his phrase of von Baer expressing the law of individual development, awakened my attention to the fact that the law which holds of the ascending stages of each individual organism is also the law which holds of the ascending grades of organisms of all kinds. And it had the further advantage that it presented in brief form, a more graphic image of the transformation, and thus facilitated further thought. (Spencer 1924:I, 384–385)

The following year—1852—Spencer published in a new periodical called *The Leader* his pioneering article "The Development Hypothesis." Writing with what Darwin was to call "remarkable skill and force" (Darwin 1890:xix), Spencer openly rejected special creation as an explanation of the diversity of animal species and espoused instead the process of organic evolution through successive bodily modifications.

In 1858, shortly after reading this essay, Darwin wrote to Spencer, "Your remarks on the general argument of the so-called development theory seem to me admirable. I am at present preparing an Abstract of a larger work on the changes of the species [*The Origin of Species*]; but I treat the subject simply as a naturalist, and not from a general point of view, otherwise, in my opinion, your argument could not have been improved on, and might have been quoted by me with great advantage" (Darwin 1959:I, 497).

As he continued to think about the question, Spencer became increasingly convinced of the truth of organic evolution. Thus in 1855 he wrote, "Life under all its forms has arisen by a progressive, unbroken evolution ... out of the lowest and simplest beginnings ... and through the immediate instrumentality of ... natural causes" (Spencer 1896a:I, 465n).

Spencer had met Thomas Henry Huxley in 1852, and in their many conversations the subject of evolution continually arose. We have from the pen of each man a most revealing account of those discussions. First the words of Herbert Spencer:

> Involved as the hypothesis of organic evolution was in most of my thinking, it not unfrequently cropped up in our talk, and led to animated discussions in which, having a knowledge of the facts immensely greater than mine, he habitually demolished now this and now that argument which I used. But though continually knocked down, I continually got up again. The principle which he acted upon was that of keeping judgment in suspense in the absence of adequate evidence. But acknowledging though I did, the propriety of his course, I found myself in this case unable to adopt it. There were, as it seemed to me, but two imaginable possibilities—special creation and progressive development; and since the doctrine of special creation, unsupported by evidence, was also intrinsically incredible, because incongruous with all we know of the order of Nature, the doctrine of development was accepted by me as the only alternative. Hence, fallacious as proved this or the other special reason assigned in support of it, my belief in it perpetually revived. (Spencer 1924:I, 505)

Huxley, for his part, took his familiar position of keeping a definitive opinion in abeyance until more facts were available.

> Many and prolonged were the battles we fought on this topic. But even my friend's rare dialectic skill and copiousness of apt

illustration could not drive me from my agnostic position. I took
the stand upon two grounds:—Firstly, that up to that time, the
evidence in favour of transmutation was wholly insufficient; and
secondly, that no suggestion respecting the causes of transmutation assumed, which had been made, was in any way adequate to
explain the phenomena. Looking back at the state of knowledge
at that time, I really do not see that any other conclusion was jus-
tifiable. (quoted in Huxley 1900:I, 180; Spencer 1924:I, 390)

When Darwin's *On The Origin of Species* (the original title)
appeared in 1859, Spencer welcomed it warmly, finding in it massive support for the general theory that he himself had long upheld.
Darwin supplied what Spencer had not: a satisfactory mechanism—
natural selection—to account for evolution. Somewhat chagrined at
having failed to hit upon the principle of natural selection himself,
Spencer made an attempt to account for this failure.

One [reason] was my espousal of the belief that the inheritance
of functionally-produced modifications suffices to explain the
facts. Recognizing this as a sufficient cause for many orders of
changes in organisms, I concluded that it was a sufficient cause
for all orders of changes. There are, it is true, various phenomena which did not seem reconciliable with this conclusion; but I
lived in the faith that some way of accounting for them would
eventually be found. Had I looked more carefully into the evidence, and observed how multitudinous these inexplicable facts
are—had I not slurred over the difficulties, but deliberately contemplated them; I might perhaps have seen that here was the
additional factor wanted. (Spencer 1924:I, 390)

As it was, in an essay entitled "A Theory of Population Deduced
from the General Law of Animal Fertility" published in *The
Westminster Review* in 1852—seven years before *The Origin of
Species*—Spencer, according to the biologist J. Arthur Thomson,
"came within an ace of recognizing that the struggle for existence
was a factor in organic evolution" (Thomson 1917:17). Discussing
the reasons for the differential survival of individuals among human
populations, Spencer noted:

For as those prematurely carried off must, in the average of cases, be those in whom the power of self-preservation is the least, it unavoidably follows, that those left behind to continue the race are those in whom the power of self-preservation is the greatest—are the select of their generation. So that, whether the dangers to existence be of the kind produced by excess of fertility, or of any other kind, it is clear, that by the ceaseless exercise of the faculties needed to contend with them successfully, there is ensured a constant progress toward a higher degree of skill, intelligence, and self-regulation. (Spencer 1852:500)

Spencer's contributions to the propounding of evolution, however, went far beyond the realm of biology. He saw evolution as a master principle, a general process operating universally not only among organic and inorganic phenomena but also in the cultural sphere. In the course of writing several articles on specific manifestations of it, he had already identified various aspects of the evolutionary process. Then in *First Principles*, a volume published in 1862, Spencer carefully formulated the overall concept of evolution, building it up stone by stone, culminating in his famous "formula" of evolution.

Evolution is a change from an indefinite, incoherent homogeneity, to a definite, coherent heterogeneity; through continuous differentiations and integrations. (Spencer 1862:216)

Because of Spencer's exhaustive treatment of many aspects and illustrations of the process, Darwin was later led to hail him as "the great expounder of the principle of Evolution" (Darwin 1890:4).

In three subsequent works—*The Principles of Biology* (1864–1867), *The Principles of Psychology* (1870–1872), and *The Principles of Sociology* (1876–1896)—Spencer surveyed these fields of knowledge from the point of view of evolution, a process that he thought revealed itself at work in all domains of nature.

I have devoted considerable space to tracing Spencer's role in developing the idea of evolution because today his role in doing so is minimized, if not altogether forgotten. It is quite the contrary with Darwin, whose role in promoting the theory of organic evolution by means of natural selection is exceedingly well known. It has been told and retold so many times (e.g., Bowlby 1991; Browne 2002; Desmond and Moore 1991; Eldredge 2005; Milner, 1994; Quammen 2006; Ward 1943; West 1938), and in such full measure, that there is no need here to recount it again. Rather, I will pick up the story with Darwin's theory already having been laid out in full detail in *The Origin of Species* and describe the impact of that book—as well as the idea of evolution itself—on the intellectual world on which it had suddenly been let loose.

CHAPTER 13

The Impact of Evolution

One of the reasons for Darwin's slowness in getting his theory into print—he delayed almost two decades in doing so—was his realization that much of what it contained undermined widely held and deeply felt religious convictions. For the better part of two thousand years, the Bible had been the touchstone of truth on almost every subject with which it dealt. Matthew Arnold, for instance, wrote that before the publication of *The Origin*, the prevailing opinion among Christians in England was that "[e]very verse of the Bible, every word of it, every syllable of it, every letter of it, is the direct utterance of the Most High" (quoted in Huxley 1896a:304).

This, of course, was something of an overstatement. Still, there was more than an element of truth to it. For example, it was said of Michael Faraday—by all odds the leading experimental scientist of the mid-nineteenth century—that "[h]e accepted every word of the Bible as literal truth" (Pickover 2008:271).

Thus it was a foregone conclusion that Darwin's theory—when it finally appeared—would suddenly pose a powerful, immediate, and direct challenge to Christian faith. In natural selection Darwin had found, and expounded with vigor and depth, an alternative hypothesis of the origins of life to the one presented in the Book of Genesis. It was a theory skillfully argued and buttressed by exhaustive evidence, painstakingly gathered and assembled. It was therefore an open provocation to traditional Christian beliefs, beliefs that were not only firmly enshrined in Scripture but also preached daily from every pulpit in the land. And so strongly held were these beliefs that anything running counter to them was to be opposed with the greatest vigor.

Clergymen were quick to see what even some scientists—made uncomfortable by the fear of social disapproval—were often at pains to deny: that when it came to accounting for the origin of the

215

earth and its inhabitants, the theory of evolution rendered the notion of a Creator unnecessary and therefore superfluous. As Bertrand Russell noted, "[T]he theologians were quicker to perceive the consequences of the new doctrine than were its advocates, most of whom, though convinced by the evidence, were religious men, and wished to retain as much as possible of their former beliefs" (Russell 1997:76).

Recognizing the danger to their cherished tenets, religious leaders quickly grew hostile and antagonistic to evolution. "If the Darwinian theory is true, Genesis is a lie, the whole framework of the book of life falls to pieces, and the revelation of God to man, as we Christians know it, is a delusion and a snare," wrote one clergyman (quoted in White 1899:I, 71). "[I]f Darwin be right in his view of the development of man out of a brutal condition, then the Bible teaching in regard to man is utterly annihilated," wrote another (quoted in White 1899:I, 74). The dean of Chichester, in a sermon delivered at Oxford, informed his listeners that "those who refuse to accept the history of the creation of our parents according to its obvious literal intention, and are for substituting the modern dream of evolution in its place, cause the entire scheme of man's salvation to collapse" (quoted in Russell 1997:78). And the outspoken Thomas Carlyle, more noted for the pungency of his prose than for the subtleties of his arguments, called Darwin the "apostle of dirt-worship" (quoted in Russell 1997:78).

Henry Cardinal Manning, a leading Catholic clergyman, "declared his abhorrence of the new view of Nature, and described it as 'a brutal philosophy—to wit, there is no God, and the ape is our Adam'" (quoted in White 1899:I, 71). Finally, speaking with the religious authority of the throne of St. Peter, Pope Pius IX berated the theory of evolution as "[a] system which is repugnant at once to history, to the tradition of all peoples, to exact science, to observed facts, and even to Reason herself, would seem to need no refutation, did not alienation from God and the leaning toward materialsm, due to depravity, eagerly seek a support in all this tissue of fables" (quoted in White 1899:I, 75n). Pius IX proceeded in his denunciation of organic evolution, fearing what its effects would be. He was convinced that its proponents, "after rejecting the Creator of all things and proclaiming man independent, wishing him to be his own king, his own priest, and his own God," would abandon humanity to a rampant atheism (White 1899:I, 75).

British and American Scientists React to Evolution

Moving from clerics to those with a scientific turn of mind, Darwin might well have expected the strong support of John Stuart Mill, whose book *A System of Logic*—first published in 1843—was the leading treatise on the scientific method of the entire nineteenth century. But if Darwin expected Mill's enthusiastic backing, he was to be sorely disappointed. What Mill wrote about *The Origin of Species* was, at best, lukewarm. To be sure, in his *Three Essays on Religion* Mill remarked that "the analogies which have been discovered in experience, favourable to the possibility [of evolution by natural selection], far exceed what anyone could have supposed beforehand." But he quickly added that "[w]hether it will ever be possible to say more than this, is at present uncertain. The theory if admitted would be in no way whatever inconsistent with Creation" (Mill 1998:174). Indeed, Mill retained a certain partiality toward the Argument from Design. Thus, while stating ruefully that "it must be acknowledged that [evolution by natural selection] ... would greatly attenuate the evidence for it" (Mill 1998:174), he recovered enough of his acceptance of design to conclude with these words: "I think it must be allowed that, in the present state of our knowledge, the adaptations in Nature afford a large balance of probability in favour of creation by intelligence" (Mill 1998:174).

Nor was Mill the only scientific thinker not immediately converted to the notion that natural selection could supplant God as the true mechanism to account for the origin of the human species. Darwin's fond hope of persuading Charles Lyell "to renounce his faith in creation and accept evolution" was to be largely dashed (Ward 1943:434). Still, Lyell strove valiantly to create an umbrella broad enough to accommodate both the orthodox believer and his friend's master theory. In a hopeful—if unsuccessful—straddling of the fence, he wrote, "They who maintain that the origin of ... a species or a genus can be explained only by the direct actions of the creative cause [i.e., God], may retain their favorite theory compatibly with the doctrine of transmutation" (Lyell 1863:505–506).

Similarly, the leading physicists of England were by no means quick to jump on Darwin's bandwagon. Of the two greatest, James Clerk Maxwell (1831–1879) and William Thomson (Lord Kelvin; 1824–1907), it has been said that they "not only embedded their new natural philosophy in the culture of Presbyterianism but had also been ready to deploy that natural philosophy in the service of Christianity" (Brooke 2003:203). In fact, at one point Lord Kelvin threw consternation into the Darwinist ranks.

Darwin, of course, needed a considerable span of time to accommodate the entire course of events that evolution required. On the basis of rates of deposition and weathering, Darwin had calculated that a certain sedimentary formation in southeastern England known as the Weald was about three hundred million years old. Therefore, he reasoned, the earth as a whole had to be considerably older (Lindley 2004:170).

Lord Kelvin, however, had come to a very different conclusion. Based on calculated rates of cooling for the earth, he estimated that before one hundred million years ago, the earth would have been in a molten state and thus unfit for the existence of life—let alone its evolution (Lindley 2004:170). Kelvin's argument for a relatively young earth confronted Darwin "like an odious spectre" and he admitted that Kelvin's views on the matter, backed by his considerable authority, "have been for some time one of my sorest troubles" (quoted in Lindley 2004:174). Another physicist, Peter Guthrie Tait (1831–1901), professor of natural philosophy at the University of Edinburgh, went Kelvin one better, allowing the habitable earth no more than fifteen million years—a figure that Darwin regarded as "monstrous" (quoted in Lindley 2004:177). Further research, of course, showed the earth to be billions rather than millions of years old, providing more than ample time for the full range of Darwinian evolution to unfold.

Even Darwin's loyal friend and confidant, the American botanist Asa Gray, could not completely endorse Darwin's theory. While Gray was ready to accept the truth of natural selection, he still clung tenaciously to a belief in a creator and to intelligent design by that creator. As a solution to his dilemma, Gray proposed to Darwin a middle course. In personal letters and published reviews, he volunteered what he thought was a compromise solution. He proposed the idea that variations were produced by God and that natural selection then acted upon them, the ensuing competition among variations giving rise to the succession of species that the fossil record revealed. Gray considered that he was giving Darwin's mechanism its due by allowing it—instead of God—to make the final selection and thus ultimately determining the outcome of the process (Browne 2002:175).

But as much as the kindly Darwin was disposed to accommodate his friend, he would not yield the point. Writing to Gray in 1862, he said, "I grieve to say that I cannot honestly go as far as you do about design" (quoted in Browne 2002:175). Darwin may not have denied the existence of God outright (as we will see in the next chapter), but after having carefully excluded the Deity from playing any role in the evolutionary process, he was not about to allow him back into the workings of nature through any such well-intentioned subterfuge as Gray was proposing.

If Asa Gray could be regarded in some ways as a friendly critic of Darwin, his Harvard colleague Louis Agassiz—the foremost American naturalist of his day—was a hostile one. According to William James, another of Gray's Harvard colleagues, "Agassiz's view of Nature was saturated with simple religious feeling" (James 2008:13). For Agassiz a species was not so much a biological entity as an "archetype," "a metaphysical construct," "a thought of the creator"(Dupree 1959:151). Consequently, Agassiz was greatly troubled by Darwin's book, which relieved the creator of any role in the transformation of animal species, including *Homo sapiens*. Reporting on a conversation he had overheard while on a visit to America, John Tyndall noted that Agassiz had "[e]arnestly, almost sadly, … turned, and said to the gentlemen standing around, 'I confess that I was not prepared to see this theory received as it has been by the best intellects of our time. Its success is greater than I could have thought possible'" (Tyndall 1874:45).

Nor was Agassiz the only American scientist opposed to Darwin's theory. The Yale paleontologist Edward Drinker Cope (1840–1897) was a supporter of Lamarckianism "because the theory allowed [him] … to argue that there was something inherent in each organism that drove it to evolve. For Cope, that internal mechanism was placed in each organism by God" (Francis 2007:71–72).

There were many American thinkers, though, who tried hard to reconcile evolution with the basic precepts of Christian theology. Thus in rather elliptical prose, the philosopher Charles Peirce declared, "[A] genuine evolutionary philosophy, that is, one that makes the principle of growth a primordial element of the universe, is so far from being antagonistic to the idea of a personal creator that it is really inseparable from that idea" (Peirce 1955:350).

Back in England certain other scientists likewise failed to be won over to the theory of organic evolution. In 1860 Richard Owen, considered the leading anatomist in England at the time, opposed natural selection while entertaining his own vague metaphysical notions of "archetypes" of the vertebrate skeleton, about which he wrote, "The archetypal idea was manifested in the flesh … upon this planet, long prior to the existence of those animal species that actually exemplify it" (quoted in Darwin 1970:58). Herbert Spencer dismissed Owen's archetypes out of hand: "I could not accept his Platonic notion of an ideal vertebra, of which he considered each actual vertebra an embodiment" (quoted in Duncan 1908:II, 316). Irreconcilably hostile to Darwin's theory of natural selection, Owen wrote a harsh review of *The Origin of Species* that appeared in the prestigious *Edinburgh Review* and brought the book wide attention.

Harshest of all the critiques by a scientist, though, were the remarks of Adam Sedgwick, Darwin's former geology professor at Cambridge. Asked by the archbishop of Dublin for an assessment of *The Origin* and its theory of organic evolution, Sedgwick expressed his "detestation of the theory because of its unflinching materialism" (Sedgwick 1979:222). Indeed, he called *The Origin* "a dish of rank materialism cleverly cooked" merely "to make us independent of a Creator" (quoted in Smith 1955:369). Despite Sedgwick's position as a geologist, it is evident that the underlying basis of his criticism of the book was theological, since he was also a devout Christian. Nevertheless he tried to give his critique a veneer of scientific respectability by saying, "Darwin's theory is not *inductive*—not based on a series of acknowledged facts pointing to a *general conclusion*—not a proposition evolved out of the facts" and, he concluded, "I look on the theory as a vast pyramid resting on its apex, and that apex a mathematical point" (quoted in Hull 2003:168).

But Sedgwick could not remain on that philosophical plane for very long. He attacked the principle of natural selection, which he found so uncongenial because it failed to acknowledge "that there is exterior to, and above, the mere phenomena of Nature a great prescient and designing cause" (Sedgwick 1979:221). And ultimately Sedgwick was convinced that *The Origin* would not stand because "[t]he author of Nature will not permit His work to be spoiled by the wanton curiosity of Man" (Sedgwick 1979:220–221).

In Defense of Darwinism

Darwin was stung by Sedgwick's criticism of his theory, especially by his assertion that the concept of natural selection was poor science. However, instead of replying to Sedgwick himself, Darwin chose to ask his mentor and longtime friend John Henslow to convey to his Cambridge colleague his vexation at being accused of failing to practice proper science. Complained Darwin, "I can perfectly understand Sedgwick or any one saying that nat. selection does not explain large classes of facts, but that is very different from saying that I depart from right principles of scientific investigation" (quoted in Hull 2003:179).

Darwin disliked public controversy and shrank from it. Fortunately for his cause, some of those near him were ready to take up the struggle on his behalf. Foremost among them was Thomas Henry Huxley who, taking pride in being "all beak and claws," styled himself "Darwin's bulldog" (quoted in Browne 2002:104–105). The very day of *The Origin*'s publication, anticipating the titanic struggle that was bound to ensue, Huxley wrote to Darwin, "And as to the curs which will bark and yelp, you must recollect that some of your friends are endowed with an amount of combativeness which may stand you in good stead" (quoted in Ward 1943:296). Indeed, with typical Huxleyan zeal he told Darwin, "I am ready to go to the Stake if required in support of Chap. IX of *The Origin*," which dealt with the imperfections of the geological record (Darwin 1993:390). Moreover, speaking of *The Origin* as a whole, Huxley was convinced that it would encounter wide opposition since, he said, "[o]ld women of both sexes considered it a decidedly dangerous book" (quoted in Milner 1994:71).

With evident glee Huxley goaded his benighted opponents, declaring, "The doctrine of biblical infallibility ... was widely held by my countrymen within my recollection: I have reason to think that many persons of unimpeachable piety, a few of learning, and even some of intelligence, yet uphold it. But I venture to entertain a doubt whether it can produce any champion whose competency and authority would be recognized beyond the limits of the sect, or theological coterie, to which he belongs" (quoted in Greene 1960:257).

Speaking of the more enlightened among his ambivalent adversaries, Huxley wrote that "the publication of the Darwin and Wallace papers in 1858, and still more that of the *Origin* in 1859, had the effect upon them of the flash of light, which to a man who has lost himself in a dark night, suddenly reveals a road which, whether it takes him straight home or not, certainly goes his way" (quoted in Ward 1943:298)

In the many battles on Darwin's behalf that Huxley fought against clergymen and theologians, the best known and most dramatic one was without doubt his passage at arms with Bishop Samuel Wilberforce at a meeting of the British Association for the Advancement of Science in Oxford in 1861. Again, it is too familiar an incident to need recounting here. Ten years later, though, at the Exeter meeting of the British Association, as related by an eyewitness, "[a]gain there was a bitter assault on Darwinism, this time by a Scottish doctor of divinity; and smiling serenely Huxley smote him hip and thigh" (Tuckwell 1908:57).

And the same eyewitness to the British Association meeting at Exeter in 1870, quoted above, wrote that "the audience, hostile or cold at Oxford [in 1860 was] here ecstatically acquiescent. The decade had worked its changes: Darwin and evolution fighting in their courses against Inscience and Prejudice, had subdued the popular mind" (Tuckwell 1908:57). In the meantime, in 1863 Huxley had published *Man's Place in Nature*, "giving new and most cogent arguments in favour of evolution by natural selection" (White 1899:I, 74).

Charles Darwin and Karl Marx

Praise for Darwin and support for his epoch-making theory came from an unexpected source: Karl Marx. In December 1860 Marx read *The Origin of Species* and wrote to Friedrich Engels, "[A]lthough elaborated in a crude English manner, this is the book that contains the biological basis of our conception" (quoted in Rubel and Manale 1976:169). Two years later he again wrote to Engels saying, "It is remarkable how Darwin rediscovers among beasts and plants the society of England, with its division of labour, competition, opening up of new markets, inventions, and the Malthusian struggle for existence" (quoted in Browne 2002:187–188).

The Darwin-Marx connection has a curious sequel. When the second German edition of *Das Kapital* came out in 1872, Marx sent a copy to Darwin, whose work he had always admired as a scientific corroboration of his own materialist philosophy. Darwin acknowledged receipt of the book in a courteous note, written on October 1, 1873, modestly hinting that the work was beyond his competence to understand.

> Dear Sir: I thank you for the honour which you have done me by sending me your great work on Capital; and I heartily wish that I was more worthy to receive it, by understanding more of the deep and important subject of political economy. (quoted in Padover 1978:211)

Years ago the account took root and became widely accepted—indeed, became part of academic folklore—that Marx had once offered to dedicate *Das Kapital* to Darwin, but Darwin had declined the offer. The story, however, turned out to be untrue, but only during the last twenty years was the source of the error uncovered and the facts of the matter set straight (see Wheen 2001:363–368).

When the earlier battles over Darwin's theory had been pretty well won, Huxley looked back and counted as the positive outcome of the struggle, "the revolution in natural knowledge set afoot by the publication of 'The Origin of Species' … the rapid and complete change which has been effected both inside and outside the boundaries of the scientific world in the attitude of men's minds toward the doctrines which are expounded in that great work" (Huxley 1896a:244).

To be sure, other writers besides Huxley had assisted in the fight for evolution, including Herbert Spencer. Years later, with Darwin dead and Huxley in failing health, when Lord Salisbury wrote an article attacking evolution by distorting the principle of natural selection, Spencer undertook to refute him and did it so effectively that it drew praise from Alfred Russel Wallace (Wallace 1905:II, 32). But while others helped, the brunt of explaining and defending *The Origin of Species* had fallen largely to Huxley, and his contribution to this task was appreciatively summarized by his friend, the physicist John Tyndall.

> [T]he work needed an expounder; and it found one in Mr. Huxley. I know nothing more admirable in the way of scientific exposition than those early articles of his on the origin of species. He swept the curve of discussion through the really significant points of the subject, enriched his exposition with profound original remarks and reflections, often summing up in a single pithy sentence an argument which a less compact mind would have spread over pages. (Tyndall 1874:38–39)

Perhaps another word or two would not be out of place regarding the siege under which the religious community felt itself by the coming of the theory of evolution. Besides his Oxford encounter with Huxley, Bishop Wilberforce also figured in another famous incident stemming from the controversy over evolution. Benjamin Disraeli, the conservative politician and two-time prime minister of England, had accepted an invitation from Wilberforce to attend a diocesan congress of Anglican clergymen at Oxford, an assembly of men whom Disraeli surmised to be "every one a potential Tory voter." At the rhetorical climax of his address to this group, Disraeli asked the question "Is man an ape or an angel?" and delighted his clerical audience—as well as bequeathing to posterity a celebrated phrase!—by declaring, "I am on the side of the angels'" (quoted in Browne 2002:252).

Disraeli, though, was not the only British prime minister to cast aspersions on Darwinian evolution. Mindful of the effect on "celestial politics" that *The Origin of Species* was bound to have, William Ewart Gladstone remarked, astutely if regretfully, "Upon grounds of what is termed evolution God is relieved of the labour of creation; in the name of unchangeable laws he is discharged from governing the world" (quoted in White 1899:I, 76).

Theists Come to Terms with Evolution

It must be pointed out, though, that a few members of the clergy sought an accommodation with the new theory. And such attempts proved significant in the history of the controversy. The case of the Reverend Charles Kingsley, once chaplain to Queen Victoria, is illuminating in this regard.

Kingsley began reading *The Origin of Species* with great trepidation, writing to Darwin in 1859 of having "the clear intuition, that if you are right, I must give up much that I have believed and written" (quoted in Darwin 1959:II, 81). But he gritted his teeth and persisted anyway. "Let us know what *is*," he asserted stoically, "follow up the villainous shifty fox of an argument into whatsoever unexpected bogs and brakes he may lead us" (quoted in Darwin 1959:II, 81). In the end, though, Kingsley succumbed in part to Darwin's "shifty fox of an argument" and wrote to him:

> I have gradually learnt to see that it is just as noble a conception
> of Deity, to believe that He created primal forms capable of self
> development into all forms needful … [as it is] to believe that
> He required a fresh act of intervention to supply the lacunas
> which He himself had made. I question whether the former be
> not the loftier thought. (quoted in Darwin 1959:II, 82)

Kingsley came to Darwin's aid on another occasion. The naturalist Philip Gosse, impelled by an "ardent desire to reconcile faith and science," proposed in his book *Omphalos* that God had purposely put fossils into the rocks in order to give the false impression of great antiquity, but at the same time preserving the biblical chronology of creation. The Reverend Kingsley, however, would have none of it. He could not conceive, he declared, that God would perpetrate such an "enormous and superfluous lie" (quoted in Browne 2002:22).

The wrenching effect on his faith produced by the acceptance of evolution was most poignantly expressed by the biologist—and lapsed Catholic—G. J. Romanes (1848–1894): "When at times I think … of the appalling contrast between the hallowed glory of that creed which once was mine, and the lonely mystery of existence as now I find it—at such times I shall ever feel it impossible to avoid the sharpest pang of which my nature is susceptible" (quoted in Unsigned 1910c:828). And he also remarked wistfully, "I am not ashamed to confess that with this virtual denial of God, the universe has lost to me its soul of loveliness" (quoted in Edwards 1967a: 187).

But not all members of the British intelligentsia grew reconciled to Darwinian evolution, grudgingly or otherwise. George Bernard Shaw (1856–1950), for instance, was repelled by it, writing, "[W]hen its significance dawns on you, your heart sinks ... within you. There is a hideous fatalism about it, a ghastly and damnable reduction of beauty" (Shaw 1977:32).

The Impact of Evolution on Western Thought

With almost every passing year, the conviction grows that *The Origin of Species* brought about a fundamental revolution in human thinking. Not just in the present day, but even in the days of its novelty, this positive assessment of the theory of evolution—and the volume that first presented it to the world—was already being made. Thus at the time of the book's publication by John Murray, rival publisher John Chapman wrote in his diary that it was "likely to effect an immense mental revolution" (quoted in Browne 2002:263).

Of *The Origin* Thomas Henry Huxley, its staunchest defender, wrote that "[i]t is doubtful if any single book, except the 'Principia' [of Newton] ever worked so great and so rapid a revolution in science, or made so deep an impression on the general mind" (Huxley 1896a:286). And in much the same words did Alfred Russel Wallace assess the impact of *The Origin of Species*: "[T]he greatness and completeness of Darwin's book caused a vast change in educated public opinion.... Probably so complete a [reversal] on a question of such vast difficulty and complexity, was never before effected in so short a time" (quoted in Milner 1994:67). More recently the philosopher John Herman Randall has declared that "all our present-day philosophizing is still profoundly influenced by the intellectual consequences of accepting Darwinian evolution" (Randall 1979:316).

What the theory of evolution did (among many other things) was to remove purpose—human or divine—from playing any role in the organic development of animal species. Purpose, underlaid by *intent*—which is necessarily the product of *mind*—was replaced by an impersonal mechanism, the process of natural selection, which could account for the transformation of species and the unfolding of the world without recourse to supernatural agents or forces. The celestial entity, which had heretofore been thought the sole architect and engineer of all major changes that the world had undergone, now found itself displaced and supplanted by a purely natural phenomenon. Human thought was freed from the need to scan the face of God in looking for answers to the great questions of existence. The understanding of earthly processes now became graspable through the ordinary senses, requiring no reliance on unquestioning faith or divine revelation. A greater step in the history of human comprehension can hardly be imagined.

CHAPTER 14

The Religious Views of Charles Darwin

The theory of organic evolution by means of natural selection had an enormous impact on the religious thinking of the Western world. It also had a profound effect on the religious views of the man who formulated it. However, we have no complete and forthright statement by Darwin of his mature beliefs about God and religion since—as he himself said—he was "in some degree unwilling to express myself publicly on religious subjects" (Darwin 1929:40).

Darwin once spoke of this unwillingness, and the reasons for it, in an 1880 letter to Edward Aveling: "[T]hough I am a strong advocate for free thought on all subjects, yet it appears to me ... that direct argument against christianity [sic] and theism produce hardly any effect on the public; & freedom of thought is best promoted by the gradual illumination of men's minds, which follow from the advance of science. It has, therefore, always been my object to avoid writing on religion, & I have confined myself to science" (quoted in Wheen 2001:365).

Nevertheless Darwin was less reticent about expressing his feelings about God in his private correspondence. And it is thanks to this, as well as to his occasional allusions to religion in his *Autobiography*, that it is possible to reconstruct how his thinking on this subject evolved. And evolve it did.

Darwin's Attitude Toward Religion

Devout Christians of the Victorian age who might turn the pages of *The Origin of Species* with mounting apprehension that they would find it to be the work of a dedicated atheist, would have been surprised—and no doubt relieved—to read in the famous concluding passage of all later editions of the book, "There is grandeur in this view of life, with its several powers, having been originally breathed

by the Creator into a few forms or into one" (Darwin 1958a:450).
However, had they read a letter that Darwin wrote to Joseph Hooker
in 1863, four years after the appearance of *The Origin*, they would
again have had serious misgivings, for in that letter Darwin told
Hooker, "I have long regretted that I truckled to public opinion, and
used the Pentateuchal term of *creation*, by which I really meant
'appeared' by some wholly unknown process" (quoted in Ward
1943:339).

The fact is that Darwin's mature belief about religion was a rather
ambivalent agnosticism. In a letter written to J. Fordyce in 1879, he
noted, "[M]y judgment often fluctuates.... [However] in my most
extreme fluctuations I have never been an Atheist in the sense of denying the existence of God. I think that generally (and more and more as
I grow old), but not always, that an Agnostic would be the more correct description of my state of mind" (Darwin 1929:139).

Shortly before his death, in a conversation with the staunch
materialist Ludwig Büchner, Darwin "maintained his agnosticism
against his opponent's atheism" (Case 1911:228). Still, this agnosticism meant that while he was not ready to deny the existence of
God, neither was he ready to assert it.

In his *Autobiography* Darwin repeatedly confessed his inability
to reach a conclusive opinion about the existence of a Creator.
Indeed, toward the end of his life he confided to Joseph Hooker,
"My theology is a simple muddle" (quoted in Bowlby 1991:28). It
is not surprising, therefore, that Darwin should have concluded that
"[t]he mystery of the beginning of all things is insoluble by us, and
I for one must be content to remain an Agnostic" (Darwin 1929:
149).

Darwin never fancied himself a philosopher and thus felt incapable
of dealing with—let alone resolving—the great question of Existence.
Broad metaphysical issues did not appeal to him as a fit subject for
speculation. He much preferred to deal with concrete things, even if
only lowly earthworms and barnacles. Thus, writing to Francis
Ellingwood Abbott—an American philosopher and theologian—in
1871, Darwin admitted that "I have never systematically thought much
on religion in relation to science," maintaining that "I do not feel that
I have thought deeply enough" about the matter to warrant making a
public pronouncement on it (Darwin 1929:141, 140).

However, Darwin did not start out as an agnostic. He was raised an orthodox Christian, and when it was time for him to undertake a university education—after finding medical studies at Edinburgh distasteful—his father suggested that he study for the clergy in the divinity school at Cambridge. Darwin "asked time for consideration, in order that he might satisfy himself that he could sign the Thirty-nine Articles with a clear conscience" (Huxley 1896a:264). (The Thirty-nine Articles were passages on religion in the Book of Common Prayer to which every proper Anglican cleric had to subscribe.) This condition proved no obstacle to him. "I did not then in the least," Darwin wrote, "doubt the strict and literal truth of every word in the Bible, I soon persuaded myself that our Creed must be fully accepted" (quoted in Ward 1943:43). "The logic of the book [Paley's *Evidences of Christianity*] and, as I may add, of his 'Natural Theology,'" Darwin later said, "gave me as much delight as did Euclid" (quoted in Huxley 1896a:265). And in a letter written to John Lubbock in 1859, just as *The Origin* was going through the press, he noted, "I do not think I hardly ever admired a book more than Paley's 'Natural Theology.' I could almost formerly have said it by heart" (Darwin 1959:II, 15).

The Weakening of His Religious Beliefs

Nevertheless, due in large part to his close observation and intense study of nature during the five years he spent aboard the *Beagle,* Darwin's Christian beliefs slowly fell away. Not that they were ever very powerful to begin with, for he wrote in his *Autobiography*, "I do not think that the religious sentiment was ever strongly developed in me" (Darwin 1929:149). Years later, again in his *Autobiography*, Darwin noted that "I had gradually come by this time, i.e., 1836 to 1839, to see that the Old Testament was no more to be trusted than the sacred books of the Hindoos," its stories fanciful, its miracles unacceptable (Darwin 1929:143). As a result he "gradually came to disbelieve in Christianity as a divine revelation" (Darwin, 1929:144). But since "disbelief crept over me at a very slow rate ... I felt no distress," he wrote, at separating himself from the religious orthodoxy of his youth (Darwin 1929:144).

By the time *The Origin of Species* was published, Darwin could write that "[t]he old argument from design in Nature, as given by Paley, which formerly seemed to me so conclusive, fails, now that the law of natural selection has been discovered" (Darwin 1929:144–145). Indeed, by then he was ready to affirm that "the more we know of the fixed laws of nature the more incredible do miracles become" (Darwin 1929:144).

When the *Beagle* landed on the coast of Brazil in 1836 and Darwin—for the first time in his life—found himself in the midst of a tropical rain forest, a feeling of exaltation came over him that he felt was akin to a religious experience. Many years later, though, reflecting on the effect this experience had had on him at the time, he remarked:

> In my Journal I wrote that whilst standing in the midst of the grandeur of a Brazilian forest, 'it is not possible to give an ade-quate idea of the higher feeling of wonder, admiration, and devotion which fill and elevate the mind,' I well remember my conviction that there is more in man than the mere breath of his body; but now [many years later] the grandest scenes would not cause any such convictions and feelings to rise in my mind. (Darwin 1929:148)

And to this passage he added that "the sense of sublimity," such as he had experienced in the rain forest, "can hardly be advanced as an argument for the existence of God" (Darwin 1929:148).

Still, Darwin was well aware that the *feeling* many people had that God *must* exist was not only widespread but firmly held. "At the present day," he wrote, "the most usual argument for the exis-tence of an intelligent God is drawn from the deep inward convic-tion and feelings which are experienced by most persons" (Darwin 1929:147). But while admitting that "[f]ormerly I was led by feel-ings such as those just referred to ... to the firm conviction of the existence of God and of the immortality of the soul," his mature judgment was that such inner feelings did not constitute reliable evi-dence of such beliefs (Darwin 1929:147–148).

Another argument to which Darwin alluded, which was some-times invoked by others in favor of God's existence, was the claim that all peoples believed in him. "This argument," Darwin countered, "would be a valid one if all men of all races had the same inward conviction of the existence of one God; but we know that this is very far from being the case. Therefore I cannot see that such inward convictions ... are of any weight as evidence of what really exists" (Darwin 1929:148).

Continuing Doubt on Theological Issues

As far as religious beliefs were concerned, Darwin was inclined to give greater credence to intellectual arguments rather than emotional ones. Thus he wrote:

> Another source of conviction in the existence of God, connected with the reason and not with the feelings, impresses me as having much more weight. This follows from the extreme difficulty or rather impossibility of conceiving this immense and wonderful universe, including man with his capacity of looking far backwards and far into futurity, as the result of blind chance or necessity. (Darwin 1929:149)

This conviction led Darwin into deeper theological waters and he added, "When thus reflecting, I feel compelled to look to a First Cause having an intelligent mind in some degree analogous to that of man; and I deserve to be called a Theist. This conclusion was strong in my mind about the time, as far as I can remember, when I wrote the *Origin of Species*" (Darwin 1929:149).

This attitude would appear to account for the fact that (as we have seen) in the last sentence of the book, as it appears in most editions, Darwin invoked the Creator. Yet as we have also seen, by this invocation Darwin claimed to have only meant to placate the orthodox. But can we really take Darwin at his word in this regard? To probe more deeply into the matter, we have to examine his writings further—not only *The Origin of Species* but also the *Essays* of 1842 and 1844 that preceded and presaged it.

In the first edition of *The Origin*, the much admired and oft-quoted last sentence of the book read in full:

There is grandeur in this view of life, with its several powers having been originally breathed into a few forms or into one; and that, whilst this planet has gone cycling on according to the fixed law of gravity, from so simple a beginning endless forms most beautiful and most wonderful have been, and are being, evolved. (Darwin 1970:459–460)

There was no mention at all of the Creator. But that was the *first* edition of *The Origin*. In the second edition, which was published just a few months later, Darwin made one small change in this passage. Between "having been originally breathed" and "into a few forms" he inserted three words: "by the Creator." Why did he make this slight but significant addition?

As we have seen in an 1863 letter to Joseph Hooker, Darwin wrote that in bringing the Creator into the picture, he had "truckled to public opinion" (Darwin 1999:278). A question naturally arises: was making this change—which Darwin later said he "regretted"— the result of complaints by certain individuals? Was he indeed bowing grudgingly to a public outcry at his failure to involve the Deity in the evolutionary process?

At the time he added those three words, Darwin was busily corresponding with a number of persons, including Charles Lyell and Asa Gray—both of whom, while distinguished scientists as well as friends, were also theists. Might *they* have urged him to introduce the Creator into the last sentence of *The Origin*, the grand summation of his transcendental book?

Let us see what the evidence has to say in this regard. *The Life and Letters of Charles Darwin,* compiled by Darwin's son Francis, contains many letters written to Darwin around the time he was preparing the second edition of *The Origin*. Included were several letters from Lyell and Gray, but no such plea was made by either man—nor, indeed, by anyone else who wrote to Darwin during this period.

Darwin Engages the Creator

What further sources of information might we turn to for more light on this matter? The most promising would appear to be the *Essays* of 1842 and 1844, which—as we noted—were precursors to *The*

Origin of Species. It is clear from these texts that at the time he wrote them Darwin believed in the existence of God, for in the concluding section of each *Essay* there were several explicit references to the "Creator."

In the *Essay* of 1842, Darwin wrote as follows: "It accords with what we know of the law impressed on matter by the Creator, that the creation and extinction of forms ... should be the effect of secondary means" (Darwin 1909:51). Now by this Darwin meant that organic evolution did not result from direct intervention by God, but rather that it came about by "secondary means"—that is, by the operation of laws that God had put in place at the very beginning of things and allowed to operate on their own. Here it seems that Darwin was embracing and making use of the traditional deist conception that God exists ... that at a certain point he performed an essential function, but that nowadays he needed to be kept at arm's length.

Following the passage just quoted, Darwin went on to say, "It is derogatory that the Creator of countless systems of worlds should have created each of the myriads of creeping parasites and worms which have swarmed each day of life on land and water" (Darwin 1909:51). What Darwin appears to have meant by this is that it would be demeaning of God to require him to have created, one by one, each of the billions of tiny creatures that existed on earth.

From here Darwin went on to assert that "however much we may deplore, that a group of animals should have been directly created to lay their eggs in bowels and flesh of other" animals, nevertheless "[f]rom death, famine, rapine, and the concealed war of nature we can see that the highest good, which we can conceive, the creation of the higher animals has directly come" (Darwin 1909:51–52).

Still, Darwin appeared to find it distasteful for a beneficent God to have to take part in so ruthless a process as the one that brought all this about. For Darwin it seemed more fitting for the dirty work of evolution to have been performed by an impersonal, mindless force like natural selection, thus sparing the Deity from direct participation. At the same time, though, Darwin seemed to have thought it presumptuous of human beings to have hit upon God's hidden evolutionary mechanism, and so he wrote, "Doubtless it at first transcends our human powers, to conceive laws capable of creating individual organisms, each characterized by the most exquisite workmanship and … adaptations" (Darwin 1909:52).

Indeed, he went on to say, "It accords better with … the lowness of our faculties to suppose each must require the fiat of a creator" (Darwin 1909:52). But just as Kepler exulted in the formulation of his laws of planetary motion, Darwin—though much more modestly—could scarcely refrain from taking pride in having discovered the mechanism capable of explaining all of organic evolution. To ward off any charge of immodesty, however, he skillfully turned the argument around and affirmed that, after all, the existence of such laws as accounted for evolution "should exalt our notion of the power of the omniscient Creator" (Darwin 1909:52). And then, following this statement and in essentially the same words as appeared in the last sentence of the first edition of *The Origin*, came the grand summation quoted above.

Note, however, that while Darwin invoked the Creator several times in earlier parts of the *Essay* of 1842, he failed to do so in the last sentence of the *Essay*. In this sentence as it appeared in print, life still had its powers breathed into it, but not by the Creator. Nonetheless it is quite clear that a mention of the Creator here would have accorded well with Darwin's thinking at the time. And even by 1859, while Darwin's regard for the Creator may have diminished, it had not been completely extinguished.

Thus it may have been a bit disingenuous of Darwin to suggest to Hooker that it was the pressure of public opinion which had forced him to use an expression that, in point of fact, he might readily have used on his own. Indeed, the very structure of the sentence—"with its powers having been breathed into it"—almost cries out for some *agent* to have done the breathing! And who could that agent be if not God? Moreover, had Darwin really regretted inserting "by the Creator" into the second edition of *The Origin*, he had every opportunity to delete it from the four succeeding editions of the book. But he never did.

In subsequent years Darwin's allusion to the Creator became even more tenuous. Writing in 1876, he noted of his belief in God—expressed diffidently enough in 1859—that "since that time … it has very gradually, with many fluctuations, become weaker. But then arises the doubt—can the mind of man, which has, as I fully believe, been developed from a mind as low as that possessed by the lowest animals, be trusted when it draws such grand conclusions?" (Darwin 1929:149).

It is not entirely clear what Darwin meant by this. What *is* clear is that he continued to find the question of God's existence a vexing one, and one that he never completely resolved. Moreover, with his accustomed modesty he presented himself as incapable—or at least uncomfortable—in trying to cope with the great issues. Thus he wrote, "The mystery of the beginning of all things is insoluble by us; and I for one must be content to remain an Agnostic" (Darwin 1958b:78).

Time and time again, Darwin expressed his uncertainty and ambivalence in the face of such ultimate questions. For example, answering a Dutch student who had written to him in 1873 inquiring about his religious views, Darwin replied:

> But I may say that the impossibility of conceiving that this grand and wonderful universe, with our conscious selves, arose through chance, seems to me the chief argument for the existence of God; but whether this is an argument of real value, I have never been able to decide. I am aware that if we admit a First Cause, the mind still craves to know whence it came, and how it arose.... I am, also, induced to defer to a certain extent to the judgment of the many able men who have fully believed in God; but here again I see how poor an argument this is. The safest conclusion seems to me that the whole subject is beyond the scope of man's intellect. (Darwin 1929:142)

Darwin's Continuing Ambivalence

This inability on Darwin's part to arrive at a firm conclusion in matters of religious belief, and his readiness to defer to the judgment of unnamed others whom he deemed more competent to decide the issue, was again expressed in a passage in *The Descent of Man* (1871). After discussing whether primitive peoples believed in true gods or only in bush spirits, Darwin stated that this question "is of course wholly distinct from that higher one, whether there exists a Creator and Ruler of the universe; and this has been answered in the affirmative by some of the highest intellects that have ever existed" (Darwin 1998:97).

These doubts and uncertainties, and Darwin's feelings of inadequacy in resolving them once and for all, surfaced repeatedly in his correspondence with the American botanist Asa Gray. While a convert to evolution, Gray nevertheless wished to retain teleology and design as somehow active elements in the process. In response to one of Gray's remarks on the subject, Darwin wrote to him in 1860 that "[w]ith respect to the teleological view of the question, this is always painful to me—I am bewildered—I had no intention to write atheistically. But I own that I cannot see, as plainly as others do, & as I sh'd wish to do, evidence of design and beneficence on all sides of us. There seems to me too much misery in the world" (Darwin 1993:224).

But then, in the very same letter, Darwin declared, "On the other hand I cannot anyhow be contented to view this wonderful universe & especially the nature of man, & to conclude that everything is the result of brute force. I am inclined to look at everything as resulting from designed laws, with the details, whether good or bad, left to the workings out of what we might call chance." Still, Darwin could not let it go at that, feeling compelled to add, "Not that this notion *at all* satisfies me…. But the more I think the more bewildered I become, as indeed I have probably shown by this letter" (Darwin 1929:224). Ambivalence and uncertainty about God and religion continued to reign in Darwin's mind to the end of his life.

In another letter to Asa Gray also written in 1860, speaking of the idea of "an Omnipresent & Omniscient Creator," Darwin wrote that "when I come to think over this I get into an uncomfortable puzzle something analogous with necessity & free-will or 'the Origin of evil,' or other subjects quite beyond the scope of the human intellect" (Darwin 1993:309).

What can we make of Darwin's repeated and heartfelt expressions of doubt and vacillation in the face of the great question of God's existence? Here we find yet another example of a man who, having made a major contribution—perhaps the greatest ever made—to the substitution of naturalistic for supernaturalistic explanations, still felt unable to completely free himself from the latter. The Darwin who began as a believing divinity student at Cambridge was transformed by degrees into the Darwin who could not comfortably accept the notion that the hand of God lay behind the modification of species. Yet at the same time, he could not totally reject this possibility. He had done a great deal in his decades of scientific work to make God's existence as a creator and a prime mover unnecessary and superfluous, but he never found himself able to disown God altogether.

Along with Kepler and Newton, Darwin affords a prime example of a scientist who was responsible for greatly extending naturalistic at the expense of supernaturalistic explanations. Yet there was a major difference between them. Kepler and Newton were unequivocal and unflagging in their religious fervor: they *knew* that God existed. With Darwin, however, serious doubts had begun to appear.

CHAPTER 15

The Twin Specters of Atheism and Materialism

The underlying philosophy of materialism is that the world consists of matter and only entities derived from matter. There is no room for the existence of "spirit"— for anything that is, and always has been, entirely immaterial and incorporeal and therefore empirically undetectable. The system of thought that espouses materialism was given its first formal expression by the early Greek philosopher Leucippus (fifth century B.C.) and his disciple Democritus (460–370 B.C.). Not only did they proclaim the fundamental nature of matter, they also identified its basic constituent units as *atoms*. The entire scheme of existence posited by Leucippus and Democritus has been succinctly summarized by the philosopher Keith Campbell.

> (1) Nothing exists but atoms and empty space. (2) Nothing happens by chance (for no reason at all); everything occurs for a reason and of necessity. This necessity is natural and mechanical; it excludes teleological necessitation. (3) Nothing can arise out of nothing; nothing that is can be destroyed. All changes are new combinations or separations of atoms. (4) The atoms are infinite in number and endlessly varied in form. They are all of the same stuff. They act on one another only by pressure or collision. (5) The variety of things is a consequence of the variety in number, size, shape, and arrangement of the atoms which compose them. (Campbell 1967:180)

A century or so later, the philosopher Epicurus (342–270 B.C.) came to Athens and founded a school in which a materialist view of the world was taught, with atoms again forming the basic building blocks of matter. According to the Epicurean theory, "[t]here are an infinite number of atoms falling through an infinite space.... [T]he

241

faster, heavier atoms occasionally strike the lighter ones obliquely, giving them a slight lateral velocity.... [T]he original lateral deviations result in more collisions ... and the establishment of vortexes. From these vortexes ordered arrangements of atoms arise" (Campbell 1967:181).

In this purely materialist philosophy, there was no room for God. Accordingly, materialism and atheism have always been closely linked. And so, to the devout believer, the two have continued to be regarded as twin specters—not only to be rejected, but to be vigorously opposed and even punished.

The Birth of Atheism and Reactions to It

Of course before there was *atheism*—the denial of the existence of God—there had to be *theism*, the affirmation of his existence. Atheism in this sense probably goes no further back than ancient India, following shortly after the rise of Buddhism. According to Max Müller, a specialist in Indian religions, "In the eyes of the Brahmans, Buddha was an atheist" because "some of the Buddhist schools of philosophy were certainly atheistical" (Max Müller 1879:294). And according to another Indian scholar, "Buddhism, in so far as it is a philosophic system, is radically averse to the idea of a Supreme Being—of a god, in the Western sense of the word" (Upton 1909:183).

Since it squarely contradicted what most members of Greek society believed, almost from the beginning atheism was denounced and its advocates severely punished. Anaxagoras (500–428 B.C.), though for thirty years a celebrated teacher in Athens who numbered among his students Pericles, Euripides, and possibly Socrates, was banished from that city for life after being charged with impiety and atheism. His offense was teaching that the sun was not a god at all but merely "a fiery ball, a glowing mass of stone" (Büchner 1891:56).

The most famous early example of such persecution was the case of Socrates, who was accused of atheism and condemned by Athenian judges to die by his own hand by drinking a potion of hemlock. According to Max Müller, though, this punishment was undeserved since Socrates "did not even deny the gods of Greece, but simply claimed the right to believe in something higher and more truly divine than Hephaistos and Aphrodite" (Max Müller 1879:294). "Plato advocated five years of imprisonment for atheists, who, if they did not recant at the end of that time, were to be put to death" (Cohen 1930:294). When things went wrong in Rome, the cry of the populace was "Away with the atheists! To the lions with Christians!" Indeed, "the Romans called the Jews and early Christians atheists because they did not pay the customary honors to the *sacra* of the established imperial cult" (Cohen 1930:292).

In his long poem *De Rerum Natura*, Lucretius—a follower of Epicurus's materialist philosophy—found no need for God, saying that "we seek those elements / From which alone all things created are, / And how accomplished by no tools of Gods" (quoted in Osborn 1929:92). Living in a more tolerant era than the one that followed it, Lucretius suffered no harsh consequences for his atheism. Had he lived a few centuries later, though, after the Roman Empire had become officially Christian, things might well have been more difficult for him. Still later the same philosophy of atomism that Lucretius had professed with impunity in the first century B.C. was denounced and castigated in the fourteenth century A.D. In Paris in 1348, Nicolaus de Autricuris "was compelled to make recantation of several doctrines, and among others the doctrine, that *in the processes of nature there is nothing to be found but the motion of the combination and separation of atoms*" (Upton 1909:176).

The Catholic Church was prepared to deal harshly with atheism, seeing it as a challenge to the very core of Christian faith. Indeed, so abhorrent was atheism to Thomas Aquinas that in his *Summa Theologica* he urged that "heretics [including atheists] ... be not only excommunicated but also put to death" (quoted in Edwards 1967a:174).

By and large, though, during medieval times no true atheists arose to unsettle orthodox Christians. As explained by Charles Upton in his article on atheism in Hastings's *Encyclopaedia of Religion and Ethics*:

> The influence of the Church, and the reverence for Aristotle's writings, as well as the absence of any vigorous interest in science, explain the fact that until the close of the Middle Ages

atheistic speculation was to a great extent in abeyance. It was
not till the Renaissance, when new scientific discoveries were
made, and freer principles of Biblical criticism began to be
applied, that atheism again raised its head. (Upton 1909:176)

But belief in God continued to be almost universally held and
deeply felt. Anyone who challenged it was regarded as a menace to
Christianity and thus had to be dealt with severely. Moreover, once
the accusation of atheism was leveled at someone, it became very
serious business for the accused. In 1593 Shakespeare's friend and
fellow dramatist Christopher Marlowe was accused of atheism and
would most likely have been hanged for the crime had he not died
in a tavern brawl (Bury 2007:65). In 1619 Lucilio Vanini, like
Giordano Bruno an itinerant savant and preacher, was convicted in
Toulouse of being a blasphemer and atheist and his tongue was torn
out before he was burned at the stake (Bury 2007:65). And in 1648,
when Puritan intolerance reached its apex under Oliver Cromwell,
an ordinance was passed proclaiming that anyone who denied the
Trinity, questioned Christ's divinity, or refused to accept the Bible as
divinely inspired could be put to death (Bury 2007:66). Even John
Locke, generally regarded as a champion of freedom of thought,
nonetheless argued that "[t]hose are not all to be tolerated who deny
the being of God. Promises, covenants and oaths, which are the
bonds of human society, can have no hold upon an atheist" (quoted
in Bury 2007:81). "It was not until 1813 that the English penal acts
making denial of the Trinity a crime were repealed, and that the
Unitarians and their property were made safe from apprehension by
the law" (Smith 1955:375).

Moreover, in the sixteenth and seventeenth centuries, the charge
of atheism was often made indiscriminately. Indeed, it was frequently leveled at one's opponents with little cause. Spinoza, for example,
was called an atheist "because his concept of God was wider than
that of Jehovah" (Upton 1909:174). Furthermore, some men were
called atheists "simply because they declined to accept any longer
the authority of Aristotle. Descartes himself had been accused of
atheism on this ground" (Upton 1909:177). Even men like Bacon,
Hobbes, and Gassendi, who (though professing a certain degree of
allegiance to materialism) were by no means atheists—in fact were

openly Christian—were at one time or another charged with atheism.

"Such was in fact the confusion of ideas during the seventeenth
century with regard to the true meaning of atheism," wrote Max
Müller, that as late as 1696 the Parliament of Edinburgh passed an
act "against the Atheistical opinion of the Deists," and men such as
Spinoza and Archbishop Tillotson—though they could no longer be
burned at the stake—were both branded indiscriminately as atheists
(Max Müller 1879:296). "Nor has even the eighteenth century been
quite free from similar blots," Max Müller went on to say. "Many
men were called atheists even then, not because they dreamt of
denying the existence of a God, but because they wished to purify
the idea of the Godhead from what seemed to them human exagger-
ation and human error" (Max Müller 1879:296).

The Development of Atheism in France

Not until the eighteenth century can the first true atheist be identified: Julien La Mettrie (1709–1751). Of La Mettrie's views there
can be no doubt. He was a mechanist and materialist in biology and
an atheist in philosophy. For "the traditional belief in an Intelligent
Creator" he substituted "the concept of an active, self-creating
nature" (Vartanian 1967a:381). His books—primarily *Man a
Machine*—got him exiled, first from France and then even from lib-
eral-minded Holland, until at last he found refuge in the court of
Frederick the Great in Prussia. That La Mettrie was an atheist (as
well as a materialist) was not completely clear cut. He himself
wrote, "For our peace of mind it is indifferent to know whether there
is a God or not, whether He created matter, or whether it is eternal"
(quoted in Upton 1909:177). At any rate, "on July 9, 1746, the
Parliament [sic] of Paris condemned [La Mettrie's] *The Natural History of the Soul* to be burned by the public hangman" (Leiber 1994:
3).

Although clearly it was in France that atheism first arose in
modern Europe, its "prehistory" is sometimes traced back to John
Locke (1632–1704) in England. Locke, as we have seen, was no
atheist but a devout theist, for even though "according to his basal
theory, all our ideas are derived from sensations or from reflexion

on sensations, he still held that the human mind is compelled to postulate an adequate creative cause for all material and psychical existences" (Upton 1909:174). But then, "when Locke's ideas were introduced into France in the 18th cent., his doctrine of the origin of all knowledge as sensation was consistently worked out, and led several thinkers to atheism.... [Thus] what was simply neutral materialism in London became quite positive atheism in Paris" (Upton 1909:177).

Among those French intellectuals of the latter half of the eighteenth century who were said to be atheists, the most prominent—although he himself made no such claim—was Denis Diderot (1713–1784), editor of the great French *Encyclopédie*. An accusation made against the *Encyclopédie* itself was that it was a vehicle for materialism. While it did not "officially" espouse such a philosophy, a number of its articles gave strong expression to materialist views. This was especially true of articles dealing with the mind-body problem, such as the ones on "Spinosists" and "Âme" (Wilson 1967:507).

Voltaire (1694–1778) is popularly thought of as an atheist because of his strident critique of Christianity, but this was decidedly not the case. Indeed, he proposed several arguments in favor of God's existence. His first argument was based on *necessity*: God was needed to account for the origin of things, whose beginnings would otherwise remain shrouded in obscurity. Later, though, he shifted his ground to that of *utility*. God, he held, was a great consolation to humanity in times of stress. Moreover, Voltaire felt that "to deprive the poor and uneducated of the consolation of superstitions would endanger society" (Martin 1962:174). From this second line of argument arose Voltaire's famous aphorism that if God had not existed, it would have been necessary to invent him. The general feeling prevailed—and Voltaire reflected it—that atheism robbed the world of the nurturing, supportive God to which it had grown accustomed.

The first forthright, unambiguous, and outspoken atheist of the eighteenth century was Baron d'Holbach (1723–1789), a Frenchman of German birth. Holbach combined the three principal elements of naturalism that were being welded together in advanced European thought: *empiricism, materialism,* and *determinism.* And it was the logical synthesis of these three principles that led Holbach irresistibly to atheism—a position he set forth most vigorously in his major work *The System of Nature*, published in 1770 (Upton 1909:177).

Holbach's work unabashedly rejected not only Christianity, but belief in God as well. Indeed, the book has been called "the bible of scientific materialism and dogmatic atheism," and it has been claimed that "[n]othing before or since has ever approached it in its open and unequivocal insistence" on those two philosophical tenets (Cushing 1914:38). It has even been asserted that "[n]o book of a philosophic or scientific character has ever caused such a sensation at the time of its publication, excepting perhaps Darwin's *Origin of Species*" (Cushing 1914:38). Yet today the book and its author are scarcely remembered.

Admiring the book's clarity and directness, Holbach's friend Diderot said of him, "[H]e will not be quoted on both sides of any question. His uncompromising atheism is the very heart and core of his system.... All supernatural ideas are to be abandoned. Experience and reason are ... made supreme, and henceforth refuse to share their throne or abdicate in favor of faith" (quoted in Cushing 1914:45).

Of God Holbach wrote, "[I]t is a being the metaphysicians have made the contriver, the Author of Nature. As man, in all his speculations, takes himself for the model, he no sooner imagined a spirit within himself, than giving it extent, he made it universal; then ascribed to it all those causes with which his ignorance prevents him from becoming acquainted" (Holbach 2006:92). Here we see, clearly foreshadowed, Tylor's and Spencer's view of how religious beliefs arose and developed.

The message of *The System of Nature* proved too strong for all but the most liberal and tough-minded of the *philosophes*. The Parlement of Paris condemned the book on August 18, 1770 (shortly after its publication) and ordered it burned by the public hangman (Cushing 1914:38). The fact that the book was pseudonymously published (under the name of Mirabeau, the French revolutionary) may have saved Holbach from imprisonment, or at least banishment, although perhaps it was Holbach's "intimate connexion with the brilliant coterie of bold thinkers and polished wits" of Paris that protected him (Unsigned 1911a:577). And his circle of friends did include a glittering array of the leading intellectuals of the age—men such as "Helvétius, D'Alembert, Diderot, Condillac, Turgot, Buffon, Grimm, Hume, Garrick, Sterne, and, for a time, Jean Jacques Rouseau" (Unsigned 1911a:577). Moreover, some of them may secretly have shared Holbach's views, as the following incident suggests.

> It is related of David Hume that, when dining once with a party of eighteen at the house of Baron d'Holbach, he expressed a doubt as to whether it was possible to find any person who would avow himself dogmatically an atheist. On which his host replied, "My dear sir, you are at this moment sitting at table with seventeen such persons." (Upton 1909:178)

The Response to Holbach's Atheism

So forcefully and unequivocally had Holbach argued the case for materialism and atheism in an environment of entrenched theism that it was not long before a dozen attempted refutations of his book appeared. Chief among them was one by Voltaire, who—outraged by *The System of Nature*—called it "un chaos, un grand mal moral, un ouvrages de ténèbres, un péché contre la nature, un système de le folie et de l'ignorance [a chaos, a great moral evil, a work of darkness, a transgression against nature, a system of folly and ignorance]" (quoted in Cushing 1914:39) and sought "to refute the philosophy of the *Système* in the article 'Dieu' in his *Dictionaire philosophique*" (Unsigned 1911a:577; see also Cushing 1914:40–41).

A more charitable reproof of Holbach's book came from the pen of Rousseau, who is said to have used Holbach as his model for a character—"the virtuous atheist Wolmar"—in his novel *Nouvelle Héloise* (Unsigned 1911a:577).

The System of Nature was feverishly read outside the borders of France as well. When it reached Germany, where the predominant idealist philosophy was being wedded to a newly emerging romanticism, the reaction to Holbach's book was intensely negative. Goethe, who was then a young student of twenty-one at the University of Strasbourg, described the horror that the book brought to his circle: "It came to us so gray, so Cimmerian, so corpse-like, that we could hardly endure its presence; we shuddered before it, as if it had been a specter" (quoted in Plekhanov 1940:167).

Opposition to Atheism in England

It is worth noting that although closely intertwined in the writings of La Mettrie and Holbach, materialism and atheism were not always tied to one another. The best example of a perceived disjunction between them is provided by Joseph Priestley. Priestley, it is true, described himself as "a materialist and a determinist" (Priestley 1965:17). And indeed his contribution to the establishment of the materialist position was considerable. As Keith Campbell described it in his survey of the history of materialism:

> The revolution in chemistry which was effected by Joseph Priestley in England and Antoine-Laurent Lavoisier in France in the 1770s and 1780s was of importance for the later development of materialism, for it established chemistry as a strictly physical science all of whose explanations appeal only to material substances and their natural interactions. (Campbell 1967: 183)

But Priestly was also a theist, and while a liberal Unitarian in theology, he still believed in the existence of God. In his *Disquisitions Relating to Matter and Spirit* (1777), he set out to demonstrate that materialism was theologically, scientifically, and metaphysically superior to the dualism expounded by Descartes and others (Passmore 1967:453). One of the arguments against materialism was that it was incompatible with a belief in immortality, an idea held dear by all. But Priestley insisted that the two were not incompatible. There was more to matter than met the eye, he proclaimed. "Most of the objections that have been made to the possibility of the powers of sensation and thought belonging to matter," he held, "are entirely founded on a mistaken notion of matter as being necessarily inert and impenetrable" (Priestley 1965:119). In fact, according to Priestley, matter was suffused with the qualities of life. Despite his rejection of atheism, however, Priestley's views were anathema to the orthodox. John Wesley, the founder of Methodism, called Priestley "one of the most dangerous enemies of Christianity" (quoted in Passmore 1965:17).

As we have seen, the stigma attached to atheism was not only strong but of long standing. Hume had noted that "custom has given it [the term 'atheist'] an abusive connotation" (quoted in Huxley 1908:187). And the "specter" of atheism, as Goethe called it, not only disconcerted and appalled the clergy—to say nothing of simple, devout parishioners—but also threw consternation into the ranks of university officials. As an undergraduate at Oxford, the poet Percy Shelley (1792–1822) published a pamphlet entitled *The Necessity of Atheism* in which he wrote, "God is hypothesis, and as such, stands in need of proof: the *onus probandi* rests on the theist.… God is represented as infinite, eternal, incomprehensible; he is contained under every predicate *in non* that the logic of ignorance could fabricate. Even his worshippers allow that it is impossible to form any idea of him" (quoted in Smith 1955:346). This was more than the officials at Oxford were prepared to tolerate and Shelley was promptly expelled from the university.

Atheism continued to be regarded with opprobrium in England and those who professed it were subjected to legal penalties. Although repeatedly elected to Parliament, Charles Bradlaugh (1833–1891)—an outspoken English atheist—was denied his seat in the House of Commons more than once because of his beliefs. Furthermore, "[u]ntil the passing of the Evidence Amendment Act of 1869, unbelievers in Great Britain were considered incompetent to give evidence in a court of law," since their being unable to affirm anything as being true "so help me God" was thought to make their testimony "unreliable" (Edwards 1967a:175).

Materialism Comes in for Reproach

But it was not only the apparent belittling and repudiation of God that disquieted and perturbed orthodox Christians. It was materialism—the broader philosophy that so often accompanied atheism—that also troubled them. For example, fear of materialism was one of the main reasons given for opposing evolution, many people being convinced that its acceptance would signal the serious weakening of spiritual Christianity. In an effort to reassure the faithful on this score, Charles Lyell (1797–1875)—himself a theist—tried hard to muster an effective response: "[S]o far from having a materialistic tendency, the supposed introduction into the earth at successive geological periods ... [of such things as] the intelligence of the higher mammalia bordering on reason, ... presents us with a picture of the ever-increasing dominion of mind over matter" (Lyell 1863:506).

Materialism, as John Tyndall observed, had long been "maligned by philosophers and theologians" alike (1871: 415). And a distaste for this philosophy was all but universal among the upper classes in nineteenth century England, who regarded it as harsh and crass, so much so that even the champions of evolution (and of the vigorous naturalism that accompanied it) thought it best to deny their materialism—or if not deny it outright, then at least to downplay it or clothe it in subtle trappings.

Darwin's way of dealing with materialism was to avoid any straightforward discussion of it. In one of his notebooks, meant only for his own eyes, he gave himself the following stage directions on how to handle the question of materialism, should it arise: "To avoid stating how far I believe in Materialism, say only that emotions, instincts[,] degrees of talent, which are hereditary are so because brain of child resembles parent stock" (quoted in Bowlby 1991:213). Darwin also avoided the issue by making no attempt to provide his theory of evolution with any sort of philosophical underpinnings. Moreover (as we saw in the previous chapter) he never completely turned his back on the concept of God. Thus he could not have been expected to give full-throated allegiance to materialism.

A certain dodging of the sting of being labeled a materialist can also be seen here and there in the writings of three leading British scientific thinkers of the nineteenth century—Thomas Henry Huxley (1825–1895), John Tyndall (1820–1893), and Herbert Spencer (1820–1903). Their intellectual contortions in this regard were a clear reflection of the opprobrium with which materialism was still regarded.

Huxley: Apostle of Agnosticism

Perhaps from his close reading of David Hume, Thomas Henry Huxley was a skeptic from an early date. And this skepticism led him to develop his philosophical stance of agnosticism. In fact, he placed on record a detailed account of just how he arrived at agnosticism, a term that he himself had coined.

> When I reached intellectual maturity and began to ask myself whether I was an atheist, a theist, or a pantheist; a materialist or an idealist; a Christian or a freethinker; I found that the more I learned and reflected, the less ready was the answer; until, at last, I came to the conclusion that I had neither art nor part with any of these denominations except the last. The one thing in which most of these good people were agreed was the one thing in which I differed from them. They were quite sure they had attained a certain "gnosis,"—had, more or less successfully, solved the problem of existence; while I was quite sure I had not, and had a pretty strong conviction that the problem was insoluble. (Huxley 1896b:237–238)

But then Huxley found himself in circumstances that led to a clarification and subsequent solidification of his views.

> This was my situation when I had the good fortune to find a place among the members of that remarkable confraternity of antagonists, long since deceased, but of green and pious memory, the Metaphysical Society. Every variety of philosophical and theological opinion was represented there, and expressed itself with entire openness; most of my colleagues were -*ists* of one sort or another; and however kind and friendly they might be, I, the man without a rag of a label to cover himself with, could not fail to have some of the uneasy feelings which must have beset the historical fox when, after leaving the trap in which his tail remained, he presented himself to his normally elongated companions. So I took thought, and invented what I conceived to be the appropriate title of "agnostic." (Huxley 1896b:239)

Huxley's agnosticism showed itself as he confronted many issues, most prominently when he was discussing the question of questions—

the existence of God. In his typically pungent and picturesque way, he wrote, "Of all the senseless babble I have ever had occasion to read, the demonstrations of these philosophers who undertake to tell us all about the nature of God would be the worst, if they were not surpassed by the still greater absurdities of the philosophers who try to prove that there is no God" (Huxley 1897:245).

As it turned out, Huxley's philosophy was a complex amalgam of affirmation and denial. He was unsparingly critical of Christianity and spoke not only unequivocally but almost gleefully of "the critical process which has shattered the foundations of orthodox Christian doctrine" (Huxley 1896b:251), a demolition in which he himself played a leading role.

On the other hand, Huxley's agnosticism surfaced when he said, "I neither deny nor affirm the immortality of man. I see no reason for believing in it, but, on the other hand, I have no means of disproving it" (quoted in Gould 1999:41). Still, when an Anglican clergyman declared that "[i]t is, and it ought to be, an unpleasant thing for a man to have to say plainly that he does not believe in Jesus Christ," Huxley thundered back, "A thousand times no! It ought not to be unpleasant to say that which one honestly disbelieves" (Huxley 1896b:240, 241).

Ironically, Frederic Harrison, who had abandoned traditional religion himself, was led to accuse Huxley of making a religion out of his agnosticism—much as Auguste Comte had done when, toward the end of his life, he transformed positivism into the Religion of Humanity. "Agnosticism is a stage in the evolution of religion, an entirely negative stage," Harrison asserted (quoted in Huxley 1896b:249). But Huxley bristled at this accusation, affirming that agnosticism had not "the least pretension of being a religious philosophy" (Huxley 1896b:250). And he went on to say that "[a]gnosticism, in fact, is not a creed, but a method, the essence of which lies in the rigorous application of a single principle. That principle is of great antiquity; it is as old as Socrates; as old as the writer who said, 'Try all things, hold fast by that which is good'" (Huxley 1896b:245). "As to agnosticism being a distinctive faith," he added, "I have already shown that it cannot possibly be anything of this kind, unless perfect faith in logic is distinctive of agnostics; which, after all, it may be" (Huxley 1896b:250).

Huxley then proceeded to make what he considered to be a clear distinction between religion and theology, stating wryly, "If ... Mr. Harrison, like most people, mean by 'religion' theology, then, in my judgment, agnosticism can be said to be a stage in its evolution, only as death may be said to be the final stage in the evolution of life" (Huxley 1896b:250).

However, if "religion" meant a general broad outlook on the world not specifically tied to a belief in—and a worship of—supernatural beings, then he was willing to countenance having his philosophy called religious. "[A] deep sense of religion" he noted, is "compatible with the entire absence of theology" (quoted in Gould 1999:61).

But did Huxley's agnosticism not, in fact, mask a consistent and thoroughgoing naturalism that bordered closely on materialism? V. I. Lenin thought so, declaring that "in Huxley, agnosticism serves as a fig-leaf for materialism" (quoted in Passmore 1968:40). And George Plekhanov went a step further, declaring that "[i]t would be correct to say that agnosticism is ... simply cowardly materialism attempting to observe good form" (Plekhanov 1967:192n). In practice, moreover, it has been observed that "agnosticism is apt to result in an attitude towards religion which is hardly distinguishable from a passive and unagressive atheism" (Unsigned 1910c:828). And indeed the label "agnostic" is often applied to themselves by those who find its underlying and concealed atheism too harsh and stark to be openly proclaimed.

Huxley and Tyndall: Uneasy Materialists

In terms of his actual scientific work, Huxley was not only naturalistic but materialistic. One of his best known articles was entitled "On the Physical Basis of Life" (1868), and in it he expounded on his belief that life was not some vague spiritual and amorphous essence, but "matter in motion."

Here, though, we must take account of the extraordinary prejudice in the English society of Huxley's day against materialism and all that it implied. And it was this decided abhorrence of materialism that led him—almost forced him—to write, against the thrust of the entire body of his work, such statements as "I am utterly incapable of conceiving the existence of matter if there is no mind in which to picture that existence" (Huxley 1897:245). And, again sounding perilously like Bishop Berkeley, he declared, "[I]f I were obliged to choose between absolute materialism and absolute idealism, I should feel compelled to accept the latter alternative"—no doubt with fingers crossed behind his back as he spoke (Huxley 1908:279)!

The next noted materialist who engaged in awkward gyrations in order to deny or obscure his fundamental view of nature was the physicist John Tyndall. To be sure, Tyndall remained unswervingly in the camp of science against the religious orthodoxy of his day. His presidential address to the Belfast meeting of the British Association for the Advancement of Science stands, in fact, as one of the celebrated milestones of scientific pronouncements of the nineteenth century. In that speech Tyndall made it clear that when it came to understanding and interpreting nature, religion must consider itself subservient to science: "All religious theories, schemes and systems," he wrote, "which embrace notions of cosmogony, or which otherwise reach into the domain of science, must, in so far as they do this, submit to the control of science, and relinquish all thought of controlling it" (Tyndall 1874:61). In fact, he was determined that "we shall wrest from theology the entire domain of cosmological theory" (quoted in Brooke 2003:203).

Reducing the issue to earthly matters, Tyndall affirmed his belief in a mechanistic view of life, seeing it as emerging from a material substratum. In keeping with this belief, he remarked, "[B]ut I must go still further, and affirm that in the eye of science *the animal body* is just as much the product of molecular forces as the stalk and ear of corn, or as the crystal of salt or sugar." And later he added, "You see I am not mincing matters, but avowing nakedly what many scientific thinkers more or less distinctly believe" (Tyndall 1871:117, 118).

However, Tyndall introduced a subtle qualification regarding the potentialities that he thought lay hidden within matter itself.

> Believing as I do in the continuity of Nature, I cannot stop abruptly where our microscopes cease to be of use. Here the vision of the mind authoritatively supplements the vision of the eye. By an intel-

lectual necessity I cross the boundary of experimental evidence, and discern in that Matter which we, in our ignorance of its latent powers, have hitherto covered with opprobrium, the promise and potency of all terrestrial Life. (Tyndall 1874:155)

Similarly, on another occasion Tyndall wrote, "Divorced from matter, where is life to be found? Whatever our *faith* may say, our *knowledge* shows them to be indissolubly linked" (quoted in Büchner 1891:54). Yet Tyndall was unable to stay with a thorough-going materialism. In the final analysis, he could not quite see how unaided matter could give rise to life and how life could give rise to its highest manifestation, thought.

Take your dead hydrogen atoms, your dead oxygen atoms, your dead carbon atoms, your dead nitrogen atoms, your dead phospho-rous atoms, and all the other atoms, dead as grains of shot, of which the brain is formed. Imagine them separate and sensation-less, observe them running together and forming all imaginable combinations. This, as a purely mechanical process, is *seeable* by the mind. But can you see, or dream, or in any way imagine, how out of that mechanical act, and from those individually dead atoms, sensation, thought, and emotion are to arise? Are you likely to extract Homer out of the rattling of dice? Or the Differential Calculus out of the clash of billiard-balls? (Tyndall 1874:32)

Still, the *Iliad* and the *Odyssey* had been written and the differ-ential calculus had been devised. And thus, Tyndall reasoned, hav-ing the potential to give rise to great works of intellect and emotion, matter must "at bottom, [be] essentially mystical and transcenden-tal" (Tyndall 1871:415)!

Tyndall's attitude toward materialism was strangely similar to that of the German biologist Ernst Haeckel, who did not believe in the existence of free and independent "spirit" but who nevertheless held that matter had—tucked away inside it—some ill-defined spir-itual component that could somehow spring to life once it (matter) was organized in a particular way.

Tyndall's materialism was thus not unalloyed. It was fused at its deepest level with an ill-defined metaphysical substratum—not quite spirit, but not altogether matter. This view of things, in

Tyndall's eyes, left room for the wellsprings of religion. Thus at times, in words that must have surprised many of his listeners, he spoke of "that deep-set feeling which, since the earliest dawn of history, and probably for ages prior to all history, incorporated itself in the Religions of the world." Then, addressing his scientific colleagues directly, he said, "You who have escaped from these religions into the high-and-dry light of the intellect may deride them, but in so doing ... fail to touch the immovable basis of the religious sentiment in the nature of man" (Tyndall 1874:60).

Once again, then, we see a man who—while advancing the cause of science and considered one of its leading spokesmen—nonetheless retained within his core of fundamental ideas a small but undeniable residue of supernatural thinking. Materialism may have been the chain mail that Tyndall wore when battling against organized religion, but stuff of a different kind could be dimly discerned between its links.

Herbert Spencer: Equivocating Materialist

No one writing in the nineteenth century did more to interpret the world—indeed the universe—in naturalistic terms than Herbert Spencer. Yet in Spencer too we find an inability or a disinclination to embrace materialism unstintingly.

As a prolegomena to the nine volumes of his *Synthetic Philosophy* that were to follow, Spencer—as we have seen—wrote a book entitled *First Principles* (1862), in the first pages of which he began by distinguishing between two aspects of the universe, the Knowable and the Unknowable. Clearly his interest, sympathy, and allegiance lay with the Knowable—those things that could be empirically perceived and naturalistically explained. And the nine volumes that came after *First Principles* elaborated in great detail, and with the tools of science sharply honed and vigorously applied, the origin and evolution of virtually all aspects of knowable nature. However, Spencer also left room in his philosophy for what he termed the Unknowable, a domain that lay beyond human comprehension. Although Spencer's interest and association clearly lay with the Knowable, it was the Unknowable that drew a good deal more attention—and fire—than Spencer ever anticipated.

In later editions of *First Principles*, Spencer alluded to the many criticisms that had been made of this section of his book (Spencer 1937:103). The major one was this: "[I]t is illegitimate to assert of the Ultimate Reality lying behind Appearances, that it is unknown and *Unknowable*. The statement that it is *Unknowable* is said to assume knowledge greater than we can have: alike as putting an arbitrary limit to possible human faculty, and as asserting something concerning that of which we are said to know nothing: a contradiction" (Spencer 1937:103). Indeed, in the first hundred pages or so of *First Principles,* Spencer tried to clear the metaphysical decks so he could get on to what he really wanted to discuss, telling his reader, "The subjects on which we are about to enter [the Knowable] are independent of the subjects thus far discussed [the Unknowable]; and he may reject any or all of that which has gone before, leaving himself free to accept any or all of that which is now to come" (Spencer 1937:105).

But despite Spencer's attempt to downplay the role of the Unknowable in his system of thought, it caused great uneasiness among his followers. Indeed, it raised such great misgivings that this amorphous and impenetrable Unknowable threatened to derail Spencer's naturalistic enterprise. The American sociologist Lester Ward, for example, thought that this portion of *First Principles*, "if published at all, should have been placed at the end as a sort of appendix or curious metaphysical by-product" (Ward 1909:8).

The primary difficulty that some readers experienced with the Unknowable was Spencer's characterization of it. One critic remarked wryly that Spencer's treatment of it "said too much: it asserted (*a*) that it exists; (*b*) that it is infinite; (*c*) that it is absolute; (*d*) that it is impersonal; (*e*) that it is inscrutable; (*f*) that it is unconditioned; (*g*) that it is indestructible. By the time the end of the dissertation is reached the reader feels that the Unknowable is an old familiar acquaintance" (Hearnshaw 1933:66–67).

Basically, the fundamental flaw in Spencer's conception of the Unknowable was that it was pure metaphysics, leaving the student of nature incapable of investigating it. After all, if there is no way of grasping the Unknowable, how do we even know that there really is *something there not to know*?

Those who talk about the Unknowable—there were others besides Spencer who did so—posit, in effect, a realm of existence impenetrable to human cognition. But *positing* or *stipulating* something is no proof that it actually exists. What it does, by designating something as *unknowable*, is to set it conveniently beyond the possibility of refutation by empirical means.

Considered in its most characteristic form, Spencer's operating philosophy—the way in which he envisioned the phenomena of the universe and proposed to deal with them—was a naturalistic one. In keeping with this philosophy, he affirmed that "the deepest truths we can reach, are simply statements of the widest uniformities in our experiences of the relations of Matter, Motion, and Force" (Spencer 1937:497).

"[W]hat we are conscious of as properties of matter, even down to its weight and resistance," he had said, "are but subjective affections produced by objective agencies." So far, so good, but then he added the words "which are unknown and unknowable" (quoted in Case 1911:227). So while the universe consisted basically of matter rather than "spirit," we could never really get to know "matter" in any profound way.

The Vexing Question of the Unknowable

This mode of thinking was by no means unique to Spencer, however. It afflicted a surprising number of scientists of the day. Thus the physicist and philosopher Peter Guthrie Tait proclaimed that "we do not know and are probably incapable of discovering what matter is" (quoted in Stebbing 1958:271). And in almost the same words, the biologist J. Arthur Thomson asserted some years later that "[w]e do not know what matter really is" (Thomson 1911:160). The physicist John Tyndall—whose metaphysical tendencies we have just explored—held similar views. Beyond the tangible phenomena that science deals with, he said, "the real mystery of the universe lies unresolved." And he was pessimistic about its ever being resolved, for "as far as we are concerned, [it] is incapable of solution." He was convinced of this because, he said, "we cannot get behind the curtain, which is reality" (quoted in Copleston 1967:129, 130).

What lay behind or beneath the knowable, then, sounded—in the words of these men—suspiciously like the *noumena* of Immanuel Kant. Somehow it was more real, more fundamental, than mere appearances but at the same time lay forever beyond our ability to perceive or comprehend.

But we are not quite through with this issue. Whether there is an "ultimate reality" underlying the perceptible material world is an intriguing question calling for further scrutiny.

It is not easy to determine who first posited the existence of this fugitive, Unknowable, ultimate reality. It is said, however, that in the seventeenth century Pierre Gassendi, "[u]sing the arguments of the ancient skeptics, tried to show that all that we can know is how things appear, not how they really are in themselves" (Popkin 1967:270). Thus while expressing a praiseworthy preference for the observable world rather than for an intuited one, Gassendi nonetheless *assumed* that there *was* an underlying reality beneath it all even though there seemed no way of getting at it. And while Gassendi merely assumed such a thing, others were inclined to openly assert and embrace it.

John Locke, for example, is known to have said that "the real essence of substance" is forever unknowable (quoted in Jeans 1947:155). And two centuries later—almost as a proud boast, in fact—the idealist astronomer Sir James Jeans declared that "the outstanding achievement of twentieth-century physics … is the general recognition that we are not yet in contact with ultimate reality" (Jeans 1947:150–151).

It is probably fair to say that idealists are most concerned with and drawn to the prospect of an "ultimate reality." Materialists, on the other hand, who tend to look indulgently on the quixotic quest for this will-o'-the-wisp, are themselves generally content with "proximate reality." George Henry Lewes, for instance, was "so far a positivist as to pronounce all inquiry into the ultimate nature of things fruitless" (Sully 1911:520). And in the opinion of the bluntspoken German physicist and materialist Ludwig Büchner, the Unknowable of the agnostics "is nothing more than the good old God of the theologians" (Handy 1967b:412–413).

Frederick Copleston, a Jesuit historian of philosophy, summed up the matter neatly when he wrote, "One would have thought that if the phenomenal world is once equated with 'reality,' there is not good reason for supposing that there is any unknowable beyond it. What is the reason for supposing that there is a secret which always remains a secret?" (Copleston 1967:131). Or as Bertrand Russell put it even more succinctly, "What is absolutely and essentially unknowable cannot even be known to exist, and there is no point in supposing that it does" (Russell 1997:117). And to quote Copleston once more, Spencer's Unknowable "is not itself converted into a reality by being spelt with a capital letter" (Copleston 1967:130).

Finally, to urge the existence of the Unknowable is implicitly to adopt an epistemology that transcends empiricism. This conclusion strikes me as ineluctable, for if one believes that in order to exist something has to be empirically detectible, then if—by fiat—something is declared to be *imperceptible*, how can an empiricist suppose it to exist?

This form of reasoning may be convincing to someone firmly in the grasp of science, but it is not so likely to be persuasive to theists—or even to their secular successors, the literary humanists. That this is no mere surmise can be demonstrated by quoting the words of someone known to be a prime example of such a person, the noted English professor and writer Joseph Wood Krutch. Years after reading Spencer's *First Principles*, Krutch came to the conclusion that "[m]uch of the Unknowable is so much more important than most of the Knowable that even guesses about it are more interesting ... than positive knowledge about the [Knowable].... To this day I am more sympathetic toward those who recognize the two realms, the Knowable and the Unknowable, than to those who maintain that by hook or by crook—by induction or deduction, science or metaphysics, logic or revelation—everything is knowable. After all, it is with the Unknowable, not with the Knowable, that literature is primarily concerned" (Krutch 1962: 22).

Krutch the literary humanist might have long since laid aside his original Christian vestments, but he still stood wrapped in a cloak of metaphysical impermeability. Thus if we are to pigeonhole his philosophy, it belongs in the murky past rather than in the resplendent future of human comprehension. Nevertheless his brand of obscurantism continues to charm the type of mind that finds itself transfixed by the inscrutable.

Spencer: A Materialist in Spite of Himself

Nonetheless let us return to Herbert Spencer and his evasive materialism. In his *Autobiography* Spencer avowed that the first part of *First Principles* had been written expressly to counter the charge of materialism that he expected to have hurled at the second part of the book—as well as at the nine volumes that were to follow it (Spencer 1924:II, 75). But his efforts to evade that charge proved unavailing. Henry George, for instance, wrote that "[t]hough Mr. Spencer objects to the characterization, I can only describe this philosophy as materialistic, since it accounts for the world and all it contains, including the human ego, by the interactions of matter and motion, without reference to any such thing as intelligence, purpose or will, except as derived from them" (George 1965:115).

Indeed, much as he tried, Spencer never succeeded in dispelling the notion that his was—resolutely—a philosophy of materialism. In a letter to a friend, written in 1891, he complained that "[a]s to the charge of materialism it has been thrown at me continually for the last thirty years and when one man has been answered another man somewhere else presently throws it again." (Unpublished letter from Herbert Spencer to John Fiske dated May 20, 1891. Henry E. Huntington Library, Catalog no. HM 13750.)

But need Spencer really have objected so repeatedly and so strenuously to being considered a materialist? Looked at in broadest perspective, it seems unwarranted and unnecessary to dispute this charge. For all practical purposes, Spencer *was* a materialist. Moreover, a telling defense of Spencer's materialism came from an unexpected quarter—his occasional adversary William James.

> I remember a worthy spiritualist professor who always referred to materialism as the "mud-philosophy," and deemed it thereby refuted. To such spiritualism as this there is an easy answer, and Mr. Spencer makes it effectively. In some well-written pages at the end of the first volume of his [*Principles of*] *Psychology* he shows us that a "matter" so infinitely subtle, and performing motions as inconceivably quick and fine as those which modern science postulates in her explanations, has no trace of grossness left. (James 1955:70–71)

And James went on to bolster the logic of his argument with a touch of poignancy and grace.

> To an abstract objection an abstract rejoinder suffices; and so far as one's opposition to materialism springs from one's disdain of matter as something "crass," Mr. Spencer cuts the ground from under one. Matter is indeed infinitely and incredibly refined. To any one who has ever looked on the face of a dead child or parent the mere fact that matter could have taken for a time that precious form, ought to make matter sacred ever after. It makes no difference what the principle of life may be, material or immaterial. That beloved incarnation was among matter's possibilities. (James 1955:71)

Ironically, Spencer was also subjected to the charge opposed to materialism and atheism: that his Unknowable contained the kernel of religious belief. Those making such a charge cited passages like the following from Spencer's writings: "But one truth must grow ever clearer—the truth that there is an Inscrutable Existence everywhere manifested, to which he can neither find nor conceive either beginning or end. Amid the mysteries which become the more mysterious the more they are thought about, there will remain the one absolute certainty, that he is ever in presence of an Infinite and Eternal Energy, from which all things proceed" (Spencer 1896b:175). And there was also the fact that in speaking of this elusive force or energy, Spencer had declared, "[T]here is as much warrant for calling it spiritual as for calling it material" (Spencer 1900:350). And he went so far as to say, much as Huxley had, that "were we compelled to choose between the alternatives of translating mental phenomena into physical phenomena, or of translating physical phenomena into mental phenomena, the latter alternative would seem the more acceptable of the two" (Spencer 1899:I, 159).

The philosopher George Santayana maintained that Spencer was thereby throwing a "sop to religion," and that with the Unknowable he "was in fact silently reconciling religion with science behind his back and without suspecting it." In fact, Santayana felt that in "the recognition of a universal substance far removed from the imagination … there lies a quite positive religion" (Santayana 1923:19). However, if this was indeed religion, most theologians wanted no part of it. James

McCosh, a Protestant minister and president of Princeton University, dismissed the alleged religious pretensions of the Unknowable.

> I do not know what religious profit Mr. Spencer may derive from meditating on this Unknown…. But of this I am sure, that if people generally should be led to embrace this creed, it would come to mean that men need not trouble themselves about religion, in the darkness of which no object can be seen to revere or to love. I am sure that if we banish religion to this Siberia, it will be to make it perish in the cold. To consign it thus is to bury it in the grave from which it will not send forth even a ghost to trouble anyone. (McCosh 1875:142)

Augustus Hopkins Strong, another theologian of the period, also dismissed the possibility that Spencer's Unknowable might be God in disguise, declaring, "What practical difference is there between saying that there is no God, and saying there is no God apprehensible to us, no God that we can distinguish from the sum total of things, no God that certainly exists apart from our subjective ideas of Him?" (Strong 1888:53).

Curiously enough, another of Spencer's one-time adversaries, the positivist Frederic Harrison, came to Spencer's defense in this debate, insisting that it was very wide of the mark to try to use Spencer's pronouncements about the Unknowable as evidence that his philosophy was in any way a religion.

> But let no one suppose that this ["Infinite and Eternal Energy"] is merely a new name for the Great First Cause of so many theologies and metaphysics. In spite of the capital letters, and the use of theological terms as old as Isaiah and Athanasius [e.g., "from which all things proceed"], Mr. Spencer's Energy has no analogy with God. It is Eternal, Infinite, and Incomprehensible; but still it is not He, but It. It remains always Energy, Force, nothing anthropomorphic…. None of the positive attributes which have ever been predicated of God can be used of this Energy. Neither goodness, nor wisdom, nor justice, nor consciousness, nor will, nor life, can be ascribed, even by analogy, to this Force. (Harrison 1885:40)

Ultimately there are two contrasting and opposing views of the world. One view regards it as perceptible and describes and interprets it through the eyes of science; the other sees it as basically intangible and impalpable. In this dichotomy Santayana stood squarely with the materialistic Spencer.

> When I rub my eyes and look at things candidly, it seems evident to me that this world is the sort of world described by Herbert Spencer, not the sort of world described by Hegel or Bergson. At heart these finer philosophers, like Plato, are not seeking to describe the world of our daily plodding and commerce, but to supply a visionary interpretation of it, a refuge from it in some contrasted spiritual assurance, where the sharp facts vanish into a clarified drama or a pleasant trance. Far be it from me to deride the imagination, poetic or dialectical; but after all it is a great advantage for a system of philosophy to be substantially true. (Santayana 1923:4)

British Materialism Encapsulated

In summary we can say of Huxley, Tyndall, and Spencer that while they made profound contributions to their respective sciences, they nonetheless were unable to step away and completely leave behind them attitudes that derived from an earlier era of human thought. Huxley's agnosticism was an intellectual badge—one might even say a mask—that belied his unequivocal and positive efforts on behalf of an uncompromising materialism. Tyndall's professed materialism was staunchly proclaimed and acted upon when facing the claims of theologians, and failed him only when he found himself unable to see how mind—and the lofty thoughts it generated—could have arisen out of brute matter. And Spencer's Unknowable was an unnecessary intrusion into his philosophy that needlessly clouded what was otherwise a broad-ranging and illuminating naturalism and materialism.

Thus once again we find in the writings of these three stalwarts the familiar instance of advances in science rarely coming unalloyed, but showing traces—in the minds of those who made them—of ways of thinking more characteristic of the age that preceded them than of the one that was to follow.

German Materialism

At about the same time, it should be noted, we find in the writings of several German thinkers a more consistent and thoroughgoing materialism and atheism. While Germany had long been known as the warm hearth of idealism—absolute or otherwise—less conspicuously it also had been, during the first half of the nineteenth century, incubating materialist ideas. After all, during that time Germany was the country where major scientific advances were being made, and so it was not unexpected that the material foundation of scientific theory and practice should have begun to influence German philosophy in significant ways as well.

German materialism can be said to begin with Ludwig Feuerbach (1804–1872) and we will deal with him in a moment. First, though, some background is required to understand what was happening in German intellectual circles at that time.

Georg Friedrich Hegel dominated German philosophy for the first three decades of the nineteenth century. After his death in 1831, though, a group of radical German students became disenchanted with Hegel's extreme metaphysical idealism and began to look elsewhere for an alternative philosophy that suited them better. These students became known as the "Young Hegelians" and, for a time, Karl Marx and Friedrich Engels were among them.

In casting about for a different philosophy to embrace, the Young Hegelians initially turned to French materialism. In writing about this period of intellectual ferment, Marx said, "[T]he French Enlightenment of the eighteenth century, in particular, French *materialism,* was not only a struggle against the existing political institutions and the existing religion and theology, it was just as much an open struggle against *metaphysics* of the seventeenth century, in particular that of Descartes, Malbranche, Spinoza and Leibnitz" (Marx and Engels 2002:168). And in the 1830s some German students were drawn in this direction.

But the Young Hegelians did not find French materialism entirely to their liking and soon began to look at the homegrown variety of materialism being offered to them by Feuerbach, to whom they turned for intellectual guidance. It was Feuerbach, according to Marx, who launched the "first decisive attack" on Hegel's "drunken speculations," opposing them with his own "sober philosophy" (Marx and Engels 2002:168)

Feuerbach commenced his academic career studying theology under Hegel but after two years decided to give it up. "Theology," he explained to a friend, "I can bring myself to study no more. I long to take nature to my heart, that nature before whose depth the faint-hearted theologian shrinks" (quoted in Sturt 1910:302). And he went on to complete his education by pursuing natural science.

Beginning in 1830 Feuerbach published a series of books highly critical of Christian dogma, arguing (as Freud was to do years later) that God was merely a *projection* of humanity itself into the infinite and thus constituted a figure endowed with familiar human qualities. God, then, was clearly a human invention and—when regarded in this light—an illusion as well. "There is no God," Feuerbach proclaimed, "it is clear as the sun and as evident as the day that there is no God, and still more that there can be none" (quoted in Unsigned 1910c:827). "God is nothing else than man: he is, so to speak, the outward projection of man's inward nature" (quoted in Sturt 1910:302).

Feuerbach had therefore traded his early Hegelian idealism for stark, unvarnished materialism. His most celebrated work, *Das Wesen des Christentums* (1841), was translated into English in 1853 by Marian Evans—later to be known as George Eliot—and appeared under the title *The Essence of Christianity*. It was this book that gave Marx and Engels their first solid taste of materialism and they feasted on it. In sketching the history of German philosophy, Engels wrote:

> Then came Feuerbach's *Essence of Christianity*. With one blow it pulverized the contradiction [between Hegelian idealism and eighteenth century Anglo-French materialism], in that without circumlocution it placed materialism on the throne again. Nature exists independently of all philosophy. It is the foundation upon which we human beings, ourselves products of nature, have grown up. Nothing exists outside nature and man, and the higher beings our religious fantasies have created are only the fantastic reflections of our own essence. (Engels 1941:18)

Marx too heaped praise on Feuerbach. "Feuerbach's great achievement," he wrote, "is ... the establishment of *true materialism* and *real science*" (quoted in Garaudy 1967:85). Indeed, Marx wrote to Feuerbach in 1844, "I am glad to have the opportunity of assuring you of the great respect ... I feel for you. You have provided ... a philosophic basis for socialism" (quoted in Wheen 2001:55).

But in time Marx, who was—above everything else—a revolutionary, changed his mind and became convinced that "radical philosophers shouldn't spend their lives atop a lofty pillar like some ancient Greek anchorite; they must come down and engage with the here and now" (Wheen 2001:54). Marx now found Feuerbach's philosophy to be "a studiously cerebral materialism, unrelated to the social and economic conditions of his time or place" (Wheen 2001:54). So it was that Marx came to regard Feuerbach's way of thinking of the world as being "confined on the one hand to mere contemplation of it, and on the other to mere feeling" (quoted in Wheen 2001:94). It was this attitude that gave rise to Marx's oft-quoted remark: "The philosophers have only *interpreted* the world ...; the point is to *change* it" (quoted in Wheen 2001:54–55).

Nonetheless Marx continued to feel a debt of gratitude to Feuerbach, whom he regarded as "the man who had turned Hegel upside down" (Wheen 2001:93). Feuerbach's materialism still bore traces of his earlier Hegelianism. It was a materialism that granted a certain degree of autonomy to consciousness and was thus touched with a bit of the old idealism. Though (as we have just seen) Engels thought that Feuerbach had "placed materialism on the throne," at the same time he felt that Feuerbach's philosophy "stopped halfway; the lower half of him was materialist, the upper half idealist" (quoted in White 1967:192).

While Feuerbach's influence in Germany had begun to wane by 1850, materialism received a new impetus through the publication in 1855 of two important books—Carl Vogt's *Superstition and Science* and Ludwig Büchner's *Force and Matter*. The latter work was immensely popular, going through fifteen German and four English editions. However, it was also very controversial, costing Büchner his professorship at the University of Tübingen.

One of Büchner's aims was "to protest against the romantic idealism of his predecessors and the theological interpretations of the universe" (Unsigned 1910d:719). More specifically, he argued that "the brain is the organ of thought, and that these two—brain and thought—stood in such an immediate and necessary connection that neither could exist without the other" (quoted in Hocking 1939:97). "The simple solution of the mind-body problem," Büchner wrote, "lies in the fact that not only *physical* but also *psychical* energies inhere in matter, and that the latter always become manifest wherever the necessary conditions are found, or that, wherever matter is arranged in a certain manner" (Büchner 1891:52).

Furthermore, he maintained, "The words 'mind,' 'spirit,' 'thought,' 'sensibility,' 'volition,' and 'life' do not designate any entities; rather, they designate properties, or actions that living matter manifests" (Büchner 1891:412). Büchner also declared that "there is no God, no final cause, no immortality, no freedom, no substance of the soul" (Case 1911:226).

The most famous German materialist of the nineteenth century—aside from Marx and Engels—was the renowned biologist Ernst Haeckel, who formulated the familiar proposition that ontogeny recapitulates phylogeny. To Descartes's notion of *dualism*—that is, the idea that there were two separate and distinct entities in nature, mind and matter—Haeckel counterpoised the philosophy of *monism*. According to this view, the universe did not consist of dual constituents (mind and matter) but was made up of a single substance, *matter*. However, seeming to feel the need to file down the sharp edges of his materialism and atheism, Haeckel wrote in his *Confessions of Faith*, "The True, the Beautiful, and the Good, thus are the three august Divine Ones before which we bow the knee in adoration" (quoted in Lodge 1905:80).

We cannot close this discussion of Ernst Haeckel without noting that he too took a stand with regard to the Unknowable. "Haeckel held that the thing-in-itself lying behind knowable phenomena is unknown. He suggested that we need not trouble about this situation; we have no means for investigating the thing-in-itself, and are not even certain it exists" (Handy 1967a:400). Nevertheless the very fact that Haeckel even entertained the possibility that the "thing-in-itself" just *might* exist shows the powerful hold the old Kantian idea of the *noumenon* still had on German philosophy, even in the late nineteenth century.

While making significant advances in German thought during the latter half of that century, materialism was nonetheless also experiencing some setbacks. The influence of metaphysics on biology (which fostered an adherence to vitalism) was still strong. Rudolph Virchow and Emil du Bois-Reymond, staunch materialists in their earlier years, abjured this point of view in their later ones (Haeckel 1992:93–95).

Summary

This chapter has surveyed some of the philosophical issues whose clash highlighted the nineteenth century. The twentieth century saw a muting of the assertion of atheism, the opprobrium still attached to it leading non-theistic scientists to understate their disbelief in God. Instead they emphasized the contributions of science to a rendering of the notion of God increasingly tenuous and therefore less necessary. Science was making "spirit" appear much less tenable as the ultimate stuff of the universe, and as a result materialism was becoming the dominant philosophy, progressively more acceptable and widespread. In his Herbert Spencer lecture delivered at Oxford in 1930, the distinguished biologist Peter Chalmers Mitchell summarized the prevailing view when he said simply, "Materialism has proved itself the best working hypotheses of science" (Mitchell 1930:24). And an increasing majority of scientists was inclined to agree.

CHAPTER 16

Vitalism versus Mechanism in the Interpretation of Life

Since well back in the animistic stage of human thought, it had been accepted without question that the human body was animated by an immaterial essence—the soul. Without the soul, it was firmly believed, there could be no bodily movement and scarcely any signs of life. And in the soul's complete and permanent absence, death was bound to occur. This simple, almost primordial belief was elevated to a formal doctrine by classical Greek philosophers, especially Plato and Aristotle, for whom—as they made abundantly clear in their writings—the soul was the central operating principle guiding human life. Some centuries later Galen (130–200), the leading physician of the Greco-Roman world, "adopted an essentially Platonic view of the soul," recognizing the three divisions of it that Plato had proposed (Gilbert 1967:262). One can state with assurance, then, that in classical antiquity the doctrine that came to be known as *vitalism*—that a spiritual essence was necessary for the body to function—was the reigning philosophy of life.

Not until the late sixteenth and early seventeenth centuries did the question of what quickens the human body become a subject of serious inquiry, not just by philosophers but by scholars and scientists as well. This questioning of ancient beliefs occurred only when a novel way of regarding the activities of the body—*mechanism*—entered the picture. This new view represented a challenge to the older established notion that mechanical processes, while of course recognized as present and important, were insufficient to activate the body. The view had long been held, as I noted, that a non-material entity—the soul—was required to make it go. With the rise of the new doctrine of mechanism, which placed much greater emphasis on the purely physical functions of the body, the battle was

joined. Vitalists and mechanists formally emerged, aligned themselves on opposite sides, and vigorously debated the issue.

The Mechanistic Views of René Descartes

During the very early stages of this debate, the leading figure on the
mechanist side—though in a qualified way—was René Descartes
(1569–1650). Indeed, Descartes is often called the father of mechanistic biology. He declared that the body had two clearly distinguishable aspects, one material and the other immaterial. He was,
therefore, not a pure mechanist (few if any at the time actually
were). Descartes was in fact a *dualist:* body and mind existed side
by side but were essentially independent of each other. Indeed, he
"insisted that there could be no possible connection between mind
and matter…. They were two entirely distinct kinds of entity, the
essence of matter being extension in space, and that of mind being
thought" (reference lost). The two ran on parallel tracks but never
met.

Well, not entirely: there *was* a point of contact between them.
Descartes believed that the soul, which he regarded as unique to
human beings, was lodged in the pineal gland deep inside the brain
and interacted with the body by means of a valve.

In carrying out many of its functions, the body (Descartes
claimed) could operate entirely on its own, without relying on the
mind or soul in any way. Indeed, he proposed that a functioning
machine—much like the one he thought the body to be—could be
built and powered by means of running water, with no other motive
force. This hypothetical machine, he thought, could on its own carry
on such biological functions as digestion, respiration, and growth,
as well as maintaining the beating of the heart (Tyndall 1874:212).

Harvey and the Circulation of the Blood

In formulating this mechanistic concept, Descartes was bolstered by
his knowledge of some of the research then being conducted by
William Harvey (1578–1657), who in 1628 had discovered the circulation of the blood. Before Harvey it was generally supposed that
the blood flowed back and forth in the veins without coursing in any

particular direction. Harvey was able to show, however, that its flow through the arteries went only in one direction. By observations and experiments, he established the fact that not only did the blood circulate throughout the body, but that the heart acted as a pump, propelling it through the arteries. This discovery was, of course, a blow for the cause of mechanism. It was "a demonstration that ordinary principles of hydraulic engineering could be successfully applied to explain a vital function of the human body" (Wooldridge 1966:6–7).

However, as we have seen before, a great advance in widening the scope of naturalistic interpretations was often accompanied—in the thinking of the very individual who made it—by a retention of older supernatural beliefs, beliefs that in this case were reminiscent of Galen's in Greco-Roman times. For Galen "it was the spirits in the blood which were … regarded as the cause of the blood's motion, the heart serving mainly as the organ preparing the vital spirits" (Mason 1962:224). That belief had remained unchallenged until Harvey showed that "spirits" were no longer needed to account for the blood's flow.

Nevertheless Harvey continued to believe that such spirits did exist. They were, in fact, one and the same with the soul. Along with the earlier Spanish physician and theologian Miguel de Servet (Servetus [1511–1553]), Harvey held that "[t]he soul itself is the blood" (Mason 1962:224). However, even though the soul continued to be thought of as an actual entity, it was relieved of the duty of circulating itself throughout the body. That function had now been shown to be under the control of a specific organ, the heart (Mason 1962:224).

The Contributions of Vesalius

In citing early writers who contributed to the advance of mechanistic thinking, the work of the Flemish anatomist Andreas Vesalius (1514–1564) should not go unmentioned. It has been said that "[t]he testing of ideas by observation and experiment … was begun in anatomy by Vesalius" (Brunton 1911:794). A student at the University of Padua when it possessed the leading medical school in Europe, Vesalius graduated in 1536 and the very next day was appointed professor of anatomy at that university.

"At once he abandoned the tradition whereby the professor read appropriate texts from Galen while a demonstrator dissected a corpse as a sort of animated ... demonstration" (Longmore 1971: 11). "Not long ago," Vesalius himself wrote, "I would not have dared to turn aside a hair's breadth from Galen," but now, having dissected cadavers and been guided by what he saw rather than by what Galen had stated, he was ready to challenge the Greco-Roman master on many points of human anatomy (quoted in Longmore 1971:12). Vesalius's great book *De Humani Corporis Fabrica* (1543) was indeed a landmark in "the triumph ... of observation over authority" (Longmore 1971:9) and succeeded in overthrowing a number of Galen's precepts and principles, which for over a thousand years had impeded a factual understanding of the body. The noted historian of science Charles Singer wrote of this work by Vesalius that "at one stroke [it] placed the investigation of the structure of the human body in the position of a science in the modern acceptance of the term" (Singer 1955:132).

Although mechanism was beginning to make serious inroads into traditional conceptions of the nature of life, an underlying and pervasive vitalism continued to dominate the thinking of most biologists. The "spirit" of which vitalists—and even mechanists—so often spoke was none other than the familiar soul substance of classical antiquity and, as we have seen, of even more remote times. Enlarged and embroidered though it was, the "spirit" alluded to by more recent vitalists continued to be essentially the same immaterial, incorporeal essence that had long been thought to animate the otherwise material body. The soul of Tylor's "animism," though now wearing gaudier raiments, could not disguise its ancient visage.

The Early German Vitalists

Throughout the seventeenth and eighteenth centuries, the issue of vitalism versus mechanism was increasingly debated by both biologists and philosophers. During much of this time, the vitalists remained in control of the field, their case being argued vigorously by numerous powerful voices. To counter the views of the early atomists, who were largely materialists and saw the world as being built of hard, material atoms, the German philosopher Gottfried

Leibniz (1646–1716) proposed an essentially opposite doctrine. He held that the world was built not of atoms at all, but of *monads*— small, immaterial entities endowed with a vital force of their own. As Stephen Mason observed, unlike the Newtonian world, "which was composed of units ... atoms, that were material, inert, and all alike, the world of Leibniz was composed of ... monads, which were active forces, purely spiritual and infinitely graded one from the other so that no two were alike" (Mason 1962:354).

To be sure, Leibniz was a philosopher rather than a scientist, but there were also biologists who shared his opinion about the nature of life. Among them Georg Stahl (1660–1734) is generally regarded as being the first to give standing to vitalism as a formal doctrine, bestowing upon it the name that clearly reflected its ultimate derivation—*animism*.

Stahl believed that "the animal organism was formed, governed, and preserved by an immaterial principle, or soul" and he "conceived of it as essentially a rational and spiritual substance distinct from matter." Immaterial it might be, but Stahl nevertheless assigned it "the ability to control the organism by an unconscious mode of activity" (Vartanian 1967b:4).

The next biologist of note to enter the lists on the vitalist side was Lorenz Oken (1779–1855), who was part naturalist and part mystic philosopher. Among other things Oken argued that "all life is cast in the mold of mathematical symbols. Zero is nothingness and the infinite at the same time.... Metaphysically, zero is God" (Boeschenstein 1967:535).

Oken exemplified the recurring combination of objective scientist and metaphysical speculator. On the positive side, he made significant advances in embryology and the study of protozoa, but at the same time he wrote *Elements of Physiophilosophy*, a treatise on pantheism. For him "all that exists is embedded in and permeated by an everlasting stream of vitality," thus combining pantheism and vitalism in one philosophical package (Boeschenstein 1967:535).

Oken also espoused a bizarre kind of evolution in which the lower animals had somehow contributed their most salient characteristics to the human species. "Mollusks gave man prudence and caution; courage and nobility came from the insects; and the fish brought him the dowry of memory" (Boeschenstein 1967:535).

Next in the history of this issue came Johannes Müller (1801–1858), a prominent nineteenth century physiologist who also was a firm believer in vitalism. "There is in living organic matter," he wrote, "a principle constantly in action, the operations of which are in accordance with rational plan, so that the individual parts which it creates in the body are adapted to the design of the whole; and this it is which distinguishes organism" (quoted in Haldane 1929:61).

Finally, on the vitalist side of the debate, we may cite the German chemist Justus von Liebig (1803–1873), best known for formulating the important ecological principle known as Liebig's Law of the Minimum. While this law was a solid contribution to science, Liebig was also a vitalist who "regarded the vital principle as a source of energy which could be exhausted, but could apparently, renew itself spontaneously and from no known source" (Haldane 1929:63).

These early German vitalists had peculiarities unique to their own theories, the details of which need not be explored here. It was their underlying shared belief that physico-chemical processes alone were insufficient to explain life, and thus had to be supplemented by the active presence of an immaterial spiritual essence (a "life force"), that needs to be emphasized. This underlying belief in a metaphysical vital principle—"nature philosophy" as it came to be called—dominated biological thinking well into the nineteenth century (Mason 1962:355). In his *Lehrbuch der Naturphilosophie*, Lorenz Oken had given the watchword to this view when he wrote, "The philosophy of Nature is the science of the eternal transformation of God into the world" (quoted in Lovejoy 1936:320).

La Mettrie, Priestley, and Other Mechanists

But the adoption of vitalism was not unanimous. A few thinkers during this time espoused a mechanistic view of life.

Outstanding among these thinkers was Julien La Mettrie (1709–1751). La Mettrie was a physician whose studies led him to conclude that psychic phenomena were the result of changes in the nervous system, especially in the brain, and nothing else. His findings were first presented in *Histoire naturelle de l'âme*, which appeared in 1745. But so great was the outcry caused by its publication that La Mettrie was forced to leave France and take refuge in Leiden, where he developed his doctrines still more boldly and completely and published them in *L'Homme machine* (1747). Again he was forced to flee, seeking refuge this time at the court of the liberal monarch Frederick the Great. La Mettrie's principal contention, repeated in various of his writings, was that thought is a property of organized neural tissue, needing no other source (Leiber 1994:8).

It should be pointed out that a belief in the human soul was so universal and deep seated at the time that even in the work of an outspoken mechanist like La Mettrie, its existence was taken for granted. At least, though—in conformity with La Mettrie's basically mechanistic philosophy—the soul was not thought of as ethereal and vaporous, but as tangible and substantial. Instead of existing prior to matter and being entirely divorced from it, the soul (according to La Mettrie) emanated directly *from* matter. Matter capable of giving rise to the soul was lodged inside the human brain and organized in a special way. The intellectual activity of the soul, La Mettrie argued, depended "on the structure and functions of the central nervous system in general, and on the brain in particular" (Vartanian 1967a:380). Still, the salient feature that emerged from La Mettrie's study of life was its uncompromising mechanism. Upon his death Frederick the Great pronounced a eulogy over him in which he noted that La Mettrie "found only mechanism where others had supposed an essence superior to matter" (quoted in Leiber 1994:2).

A further blow on mechanism's behalf was struck by the Swiss physiologist Albrecht von Haller (1708–1777), who made a significant contribution to the understanding of the nervous system. Prior to Haller it was supposed that nerves were hollow tubes through which flowed a mysterious "spirit" fluid that somehow activated the muscles. But then in the mid-1700s, through a series of carefully designed experiments, Haller showed the true nature and function of nervous tissue (Asimov 1964:116; Leiber 1994:8).

Another eighteenth century advocate of mechanism and materialism—the two conceptions tended to go hand in hand—was Joseph Priestley (1733–1804), the English scientist best known for his discovery of oxygen. Priestley was opposed to the philosophy of dualism because he thought it failed to explain how mind and body could interact (Passmore 1967:454). Mind, Priestley argued, was not a separate, independent, immaterial entity; rather, it was a product of the highly structured matter that constituted the brain. Thought, then, was simply the result of brain function (Passmore 1967:453). Thus Priestley would most likely have agreed with the French physician Pierre Cabanis's (1757–1808) famous phrase that "the brain secretes thought as the liver secretes bile" (quoted in Hocking 1939:97).

However, Priestley assigned to matter some very special properties. It was not—in his view—a completely inert and lifeless substance, incapable on its own of manifesting the powers of mind. Instead he believed that matter contained or consisted of "centers of force," and because of these centers was capable of exercising thought.

Despite the efforts of men like La Mettrie and Priestley, vitalism very largely ruled biology throughout the first half of the nineteenth century. Indeed, according to J. S. Haldane, "In the writings of … the most eminent physiologists, medical men, chemists, and biologists up to near the middle of the last [nineteenth] century we find vitalism of some kind to be an accepted doctrine" (Haldane 1929:60).

While this was largely true, an important step on behalf of mechanism took place in 1828 when Friedrich Wöhler (1800–1882), working in his laboratory, was able to synthesize the organic compound urea. Hitherto it had been assumed that the formation of such compounds by the animal body required the operation of a distinct vital principle. With Wöhler's experiment, though, this supposition was shattered, for it demonstrated conclusively that an organic compound could be created in the laboratory by purely chemical means, no "vital force" being required (Hoagland 1960:22; Needham 1955:237).

Darwinian Evolution Bolsters Mechanism

With the arrival of the theory of organic evolution shortly after the middle of the nineteenth century, a sea change of enormous proportions in biological thinking began to take place. Since Darwin himself shunned controversy and avoided openly championing the mechanistic side of this quasi-philosophical debate, it fell to others to do so.

Chief among these men was the self-styled "Darwin's bulldog," Thomas Henry Huxley. The vitalists' argument had always run pretty much along these lines: since living organisms are composed of chemical elements; and since these elements are, initially, inert and inanimate; then some kind of spark, some spiritual essence—such as Aristotle's *entelechy*—must exist and be infused into these elements in order to imbue them with life. Huxley's sharp rejoinder to this argument, which appeared in his essary "On the Physical Basis of Life," was that no metaphysical entity was involved or required in order to explain the attributes of life. Accordingly, he wrote:

> Carbon, hydrogen, and nitrogen are all lifeless bodies. Of these, carbon and oxygen unite in certain proportions and under certain conditions, to give rise to carbonic acid; hydrogen and oxygen produce water; nitrogen and other elements give rise to nitrogenous salts. These new compounds, like the elementary bodies of which they are composed, are lifeless. But when they are brought together, under certain conditions, they give rise to the still more complex body, protoplasm, and this protoplasm exhibits the phenomena of life. (Huxley 1909:111)

Huxley scoffed at the vitalists' contention, asking scornfully, "What better philosophical status has vitality than aquosity?" (Huxley 1909:113). Nevertheless, well aware that this was not only a biological question but a charged religious issue, he wryly warned his sympathetic readers, "I bid you beware that, in accepting these conclusions, you are placing your feet on the first rung of a ladder which, in most people's estimation, is the reverse of Jacob's, and leads to the antipodes of heaven" (Huxley 1909:113).

Darwin's other major champion, Herbert Spencer, also took part in this debate. After tracing the pedigree of vitalism back to the early history of human thought, and specifically to the primordial conception of the soul, he observed, "This indwelling second self [which became, in time], more and more conceived as the real self which uses the body for its purposes, is, with the advance of intelligence, still further divested of its definite characters; and, coming in medieval days to be spoken of as 'animal spirits' ends in later days in being called a vital principle" (Spencer 1898:114–115).

Spencer then pointed out the poverty of vitalism, even as a concept, regarding it with hardly less derision than had Huxley: "[T]he alleged vital principle exists in the minds of those who allege it only as a verbal form, not as an idea; since it is impossible to bring together in consciousness the terms required to constitute an idea. It is not even 'a figment of imagination,' for that implies something imaginable, but the supposed vital principle cannot even be imagined" (Spencer 1898:117).

In a chapter entitled "The Dynamic Element in Life," inserted into the second edition of *The Principles of Biology,* Spencer subjected the basic nature of life to close examination. There, within the narrow compass of four pages, he presented one of the most acute and penetrating critiques of vitalism ever penned (Spencer 1898: 114–117).

The Relationship Between Life and Matter

At this point let me interject a subject already touched on briefly but deserving fuller treatment: the relationship between life and matter. Dividing philosophers into two distinct camps—the materialists and the idealists—as we have done so far, presents too sharp and simple a contrast. It fails to take account of the niceties and subtleties involved in their spirited exchanges about life and matter. This clash of ideas was not always between a delicate idealism on the one hand and a tough, flinty materialism on the other. There was sometimes a middle ground between the two.

In 1675 Ralph Cudworth (1617–1688) had given a name to this middle ground: *hylozoism.* The conception to which he applied this term was much more complex than traditional materialism. Hylozoism, however, was nothing new. In one form or another, it had been espoused by Greek philosophers like Thales and Anaximenes. Although the notion was expressed in a variety of ways, essentially it amounted to this. Matter and life or spirit were not separate and independent entities at all. Rather, in some ill-defined way, "spirit," the essence of life, was an *inherent property* of matter. It was thought that matter had always had within it the quality of life. This quality may have lain dormant for ages, but it was simply waiting for the opportunity to spring forth and manifest itself. (Since this way of looking at nature emphasized the supposed existence of life and mind everywhere, it was sometimes called "panpsychism.")

In a way hylozoism provided a ready answer to dualism. It did so by holding that matter and spirit were not categorically and qualitatively distinct, as the dualists held. Logically the two might be distinguishable, but in point of fact they were fused into an indissoluble whole. Hylozoism could thus be thought of as an early form of *monism*. Whereas dualism held that matter and spirit were parallel but separate entities, with life having come into existence only when spirit was somehow infused into matter by God, hylozoism contended that—from the very start—life and matter had been closely intertwined ... indissolubly linked.

Cudworth, coiner of the term, regarded hylozoism as a disguised form of atheism, feeling that its advocates ascribed to matter "a certain living and energetic nature" that allowed it to bring forth life spontaneously, without requiring a divine infusion (Sorley 1965:91). This view was exemplified by the French mathematician and astronomer Pierre de Maupertuis (1698–1759) who believed that "all material particles are in some degree invested with the psychical properties of the higher organisms.... By this assumption of the investment of non-living matter with the properties of living matter, he was in a position to readily derive the latter from the former and to directly unite the animate and inanimate worlds" (Osborn 1929:168).

Because it was often seen as "the view that matter is 'intrinsically' active," hylozoism ran counter to "the view of philosophers, like Plato and Berkeley, who asserted that matter is 'essentially' inert or passive" (Edwards 1967b:23). The fact is that a number of those who championed hylozoism were, in effect, raising matter to a loftier status than it had enjoyed at the hands of orthodox materialists, for whom it was completely lifeless and inert.

Among those espousing this higher form of materialism was the American philosopher and "panpsychist" Josiah Royce (1855–1916), who wrote, "Where we see inorganic Nature seemingly dead, there is, in fact, conscious life, just as surely as there is any Being present in

Nature at all" (quoted in Edwards 1967b:22). But the most effusive expression of this enriched form of materialism came from the pen of the German philosopher and physician Ludwig Büchner (1824–1899). To the charge that matter was a lifeless, empty thing, Büchner replied with unrestrained eloquence and passion.

> Matter is not dead, inanimate or lifeless, but ... is in motion everywhere and is full of most active life. It is not shapeless; but ... form as well as motion, is its necessary and inseparable attribute. Nor is it crude, ... but is so infinitely delicate that all conception of it fails us. It is not worthless, but is the common mother and generatrix of all that exists or is coming into existence, and is thus of the highest importance. It is not senseless, spiritless or thoughtless, but is full of the most delicate sensibility and capable of the highest evolution of thought in the living creatures that proceed therefrom stage by stage. Neither is it unconscious, but in its gradual earthly process of evolution and development it evolves all imaginable stages of consciousness from the lowest to the highest. (Büchner 1891:55)

It should be stressed, however, that hylozoism was not the same thing as the view of matter held by, say, Thomas Henry Huxley. For Huxley matter was indeed dead and inert and had been so for eons. Nevertheless it provided the building blocks that, *once assembled in a very special way,* were able to give rise to the properties of life. Hylozoism, as we noted, held that in some peculiar way life was *already present* in matter, waiting only for the right moment to issue forth in perceptible form.

Looked at in broad perspective, hylozoism can be seen as a *transitional stage* from the time when an airy idealism dominated Western thought to a time when a hard-edged materialism rose to challenge it. Under hylozoism, spirit no longer stood serenely alone in the world, but now existed in close association with matter ... permeating it, in fact. Hylozoism can even be thought of as affording a certain measure of *protection* to spirit, enfolding the fragile creature in a tight embrace. And in an age grown increasingly materialist, spirit was ever more in need of such protection!

In time, though, hylozoism gave way to an unequivocal, thoroughgoing, monistic materialism. Typifying this change we can cite the remark of Friedrich Engels (1820–1895) that "our conscious-ness and thinking, however suprasensuous they may seem, are the product of a material, bodily organ, the brain. Matter is not a prod-uct of mind, but mind itself is merely the highest product of matter" (Engels 1941:25). Similarly, the noted British neuroscientist Sir Charles Sherrington (1857–1952) declared that "though there is matter which exists apart from mind, we know of no instance when mind exists apart from matter" (Sherrington 1952:2).

To sum up, the conclusion to which we are irresistibly drawn is that matter existed before mind, and mind arose only when matter became organized in a particular way. To the best of our knowledge, this development was very rare and very recent. In a cosmic sense, then, mind is subordinate to matter and derivative from it. Furthermore, the emergence of life and mind out of raw matter—a momentous event though it was—occurred entirely according to natural law, requiring no divine guidance or intervention to bring it about.

The Mind-Body Problem

Closely related to the issue of matter and spirit—but not quite the same thing—was what philosophers call the mind-body problem. One side of the debate held fast to *psychophysical parallelism,* a view advanced by such men as Spinoza and Kant. "According to their opinion," explained Joseph Needham, "there was no causal connection between mind and body, but both are the shadow thrown by some underlying reality, just as two shadows are often seen thrown by the same object when two lights exist on the other side of it" (Needham 1955:259).

This view, according to which mind and body are completely inde-pendent, held sway for a time but in later years began to be seriously questioned. The physicist John Tyndall, for instance, affirmed that "the growth of the body is mechanical, and that thought, as exercised by us, has its correlates in the physics of the brain" (Tyndall 1871:120). Here Tyndall was asserting more than just a simple correlation between the two, for he held that "for every fact of consciousness, whether in the domain of sense, or of emotion, a definite molecular condition of motion or structure is set up in the brain" (Tyndall 1871:118–119).

Thomas Henry Huxley, as we have seen, had staunchly maintained that life was nothing more than complexly organized matter in motion. "And if this is so," he argued, "it must be true, in the same sense and to the same extent, that the thoughts to which I am now giving utterance, and your thoughts regarding them, are the expression of molecular changes in that matter of life which is the source of our other vital phenomena" (Huxley 1909:114).

In summary, the strongest statement of materialistic, mechanistic psychology that can be made—and one that accords well with the prevailing view of cognitive scientists—is this: no thought enters the human mind without there being some neurochemical movement in the brain immediately preceding it. That is to say, no thought can be entertained for which there is not a corresponding activity in the physical organization of the brain. Ideas cannot interact with each other *purely on the level of thought.* There must, at the same time, be some material counterpart to this interaction for it to occur.

Vitalism versus Mechanism Resumed

After this long digression, let us return to the nineteenth century debate between vitalism and mechanism. So powerful were the voices being raised against vitalism in the latter half of that century that in 1881 the physiologist Burdon Sanderson confidently proclaimed it "the epoch of the death of 'vitalism'" (quoted in Lodge 1914:73). But Sanderson's assertion of vitalism's demise proved a bit premature. As J. S. Haldane (1929:65) noted, "Vitalism was by no means dead at the end of the last century." In fact, the early twentieth century saw its continued espousal by several eminent men of science.

Chief among these men was the German biologist and philosopher Hans Driesch (1867–1941). Driesch believed that physics and chemistry, essential as they were to life, were insufficient to explain its processes. A "vital principle" he argued, must also be involved. And to designate this immaterial life force he resurrected Aristotle's old term *entelechy*, which Driesch defined as "an autonomous, mindlike, nonspatial entity that exercises control over the course of organic processes" (Beckner 1967:255)

Driesch felt strongly that a purposive, directing principle in life—in short, "teleology"—was also involved (Henderson 1917: 85). "[S]omething ... seems to show," he argued, *that nature is nature for a certain purpose*. But I confess at the same time that I am absolutely unable to consider this purpose in any other than a purely anthropomorphic manner" (quoted in Henderson 1958: 296n).

Thinly veiled, then, in Driesch's idea of a propulsive life force was something very nearly akin to the Christian God. Indeed, the underlying religious basis of much of vitalism is as indisputable as it is transparent. And as I have argued before, the supernatural, metaphysical essence deemed to be animating human life—deriving ultimately if not immediately from an omnipotent God—can be traced without a break back through the biblical Deity to its original source in the venerable and familiar concept of the soul!

Almost in direct opposition to Driesch's tenets stood the work of the German-born American biologist Jacques Loeb (1859–1924). Loeb's most notable contribution to the struggle between vitalism and mechanism was his book *The Mechanical Conception of Life*, published in 1912. Loeb did notable work in the laboratory and in one of his best known experiments "studied the responses of insects and other lower animals to such external influences as light, chemicals, and electrical stimuli. These responses, he contended, were forced or automatic reactions of the organism as a whole. He called them 'tropisms,' extending a term which had previously been applied to the forced movements of plants. Tropisms are wholly mechanical modes of response and can be interpreted quantitatively so as to make superfluous any teleological or vitalistic notions" (Goudge 1967a:503).

Henri Bergson Defends Vitalism

The twentieth century saw renewed attempts to defend the theory of vitalism against mounting evidence against it. Now, though, the arguments became more subtle, as in the case of the French philosopher Henri Bergson (1859–1941). While on the one hand Bergson spoke of "the stumbling-blocks of ... vitalistic theories" (Bergson 1998:42), he nonetheless indicated his discontent with mechanism.

Indeed, he stated his belief that "the assertion that pure mechanism is insufficient" to explain life "assumes great authority when made by such scientists as Driesch" (Bergson 1998:42n).

Instead of openly espousing vitalism, however, Bergson spoke of "consciousness in general ... which must be coextensive with universal life" (Bergson 1998:186). This "consciousness," he thought, was somehow prior to and independent of life in its actual manifestations. "Consciousness" was an intangible and elusive element, "distinct from the organism it animates" (Bergson 1998:270).

Resorting to metaphor in an effort to convey his meaning more dramatically, Bergson declared that "it is consciousness, or rather supra-consciousness, that is at the origin of life. Consciousness—or supra-consciousness—is the name for the rocket whose extinguished fragments fall back as matter," matter "into which this vital principle had 'insinuated itself'" (Bergson 1998:261; Goudge 1967b:293). The conclusion seems inescapable that if Bergson's belief in this "consciousness" as an active principle that had been impressed into matter to make it come alive was not actually "vitalism," it came perilously close!

The Inexorable Advance of Mechanism

Despite such excursions by philosophers—and even biologists—into metaphysics, the advance of the mechanistic view of life remained steady and inexorable, eventually becoming irresistible. As long as the exact nature of certain physiological processes was not well understood, of course, it was still possible—and assuredly tempting—for thinkers so inclined to introduce some kind of mysterious essence into the picture. This nebulous "life force" appealed to certain biologists as a way of extricating themselves from a particular difficulty that remained to be overcome. But when experimentation became firmly established as the prime method of biological research, one by one unexplained physiological processes began to yield to mechanistic solutions. And with the continued accumulation of such successes, the tenability of vitalism was seriously eroded. Thus those dark recesses of biology within which vitalistic explanations were occasionally proposed shrank almost to the vanishing point.

Clearly the increasing reliance by biologists on experimentation put vitalists at a severe disadvantage. After all, what experiments could *they* perform—or even envision—that could reveal, for all to see, the presence of some unspecifiable, immaterial, and impalpable essence? How could the vitalists subject to scientific scrutiny this incorporeal, insubstantial principle in which they so fervently believed? How were they to grasp it with their forceps? How could they place it under the microscope? It was hard even to *imagine* an experiment that could prove the existence of a life principle since it was—virtually by fiat—unobservable by empirical means. And empiricism had increasingly become the only epistemology that science would admit as a means of gaining reliable knowledge of the world. As doggedly as its proponents adhered to it as an explanation of life, vitalism in the end had proved to be a blind alley and a dead end.

Looked at in broad perspective, vitalism can be seen as a meta-physical, theological, religious conception. It sought to maintain the primacy of "spirit" in a realm where it was being irresistibly driven out by materialistic science. It was part of a set of supernatural beliefs that vitalist biologists, far from having invented, had merely *inherited* from the past and stubbornly clung to. They had simply carried over into their interpretations ancient ways of looking at nature. They had embraced a mode of thinking into which they had been born and reared, and in which they continued to be steeped. It was as simple as that. Even as these men endeavored—"scientifical-ly," so they thought—to work out the problems of biology, their underlying metaphysical views colored (indeed warped) their sci-ence. Vitalism was in fact *pseudo*-science that its practitioners brought to bear in pursuit of a desperate attempt to understand life by invoking something categorically distinct from matter.

Eventually the doctrine of vitalism fell away because the entities and forces that it postulated, lacking anything demonstrable or ver-ifiable, lay beyond empirical observation. And as science came rig-orously to demand of any explanation that it be of a substantial nature, related to physical experience, anything that lacked this abil-ity succumbed in the battle of ideas.

Its demise, however, was gradual, and in this way exemplified a recurring theme of this book: that advances in science are rarely abrupt, complete, and unalloyed. And it was often the case that the individuals who made such advances continued to entertain a vestige of supernatural beliefs. The great discoveries made by these men did not succeed in extinguishing in them—let alone among their lay followers—all traces of such beliefs. Victories of mechanism over vitalism were won but rearguard actions remained to be fought, and they were often stubborn and protracted.

To exemplify this pattern of scientific advance, which can be labeled *sawtoothed* as opposed to *rectilinear*, I will introduce here the views of two scientists who worked during the early decades of the twentieth century. Their writings embody the ambivalence that I have just noted. While accepting mechanistic interpretations of life up to a point, they could not altogether free themselves of the feeling that mechanism was not enough. Something intangible and elusive, they felt, was needed to complete the picture of how life actually worked. The first of these men to be discussed here was the British physicist Sir Oliver Lodge (1851–1940), whom we have met before (Chapter 5).

The Rearguard Actions of Lodge and Haldane

From the time of Johannes Müller, wrote Lodge, "[I]t has become fundamental in our science not to regard any vital process as understood at all unless it can be brought into relation with physical standards, and the methods of physiology have been based exclusively on this principle" (Lodge 1914:74). Accordingly, he continued, "To attribute the rise of sap to vital force would be absurd, it would be giving up the problem and stating nothing at all. The way in which osmosis acts to produce the remarkable and surprising effect is discoverable and has been discovered" (Lodge 1914:76). So far, so good. Indeed, to the charge leveled by some critics that he was a vitalist, Lodge retorted, "I am not a vitalist if vitalism means an appeal to an undefined 'vital force' (an objectionable term I have never thought of using) as against the laws of Chemistry and Physics" (Lodge 1914:75).

However, Lodge went on to qualify these remarks. First, he wanted to make it clear that "Biology is an independent science, and it is served, not dominated, by Chemistry and Physics" (Lodge 1914:80). Furthermore, while Lodge affirmed his belief that "[t]here is plenty of physics and chemistry and mechanics about every vital action, ... for a complete understanding of it something beyond physics and chemistry is needed" (Lodge 1914:78). And what would this "something" be? "I will risk the assertion," Lodge continued, "that Life introduces something incalculable and purposeful amid the laws of physics ... [something which] thus distinctly supplements those laws" (Lodge 1914:78–79). All forms of life, then, he believed, "are animated by something which does not belong to the realm of physics and chemistry, but lies outside their province" (Lodge 1912:79). Here apparently was a vitalism not openly espoused or expressed, perhaps, but smuggled in through a side door.

The next British scientist to be considered is J. S. Haldane (1860–1936), father of the more materialistic J. B. S. Haldane and regarded in his day as the leading biologist in England. In his book *The Sciences and Philosophy* (1929), Haldane started out—as had Lodge—by declaring that "in every direction there is ... the clearest evidence in favour of a physico-chemical determinative, and consequent mechanistic interpretation, of conscious behavior" (Haldane 1929:125). "Actual experience," he noted, "shows that there is no end to the further light which experimental investigation of the physical and chemical environment may throw on any physiological phenomena" (Haldane 1929:71). And again Haldane declared that "[t]he more deeply we probe into the conditions which determine any physiological phenomena, the more clearly does it appear that it is dependent on what are generally interpreted as physical and chemical conditions" (Haldane 1929:66–67).

Forthright as Haldane's adherence to mechanism appears at this point, it turned out to be less than wholehearted and unqualified. Thus while he wrote that "Vitalism is ... a quite unsatisfactory hypothesis, both ultimately and from the standpoint of scientific advance," he nonetheless added that "the mechanistic theory of life is equally unsatisfactory" (Haldane 1929:71).

In an attempt to justify this modification of his earlier views, for example, Haldane had argued that it was impossible to explain the process of bone formation along purely mechanistic lines. However, almost as if to refute this contention, the biochemist Joseph Needham (1900–1995) wrote, "Yet the *Biochemical Journal* for 1924 contains an account of Robison's discovery of an enzyme in calcifying bone which transmutes phosphorus in combination with sugar into phosphorus in combination with calcium for bone" (Needham 1955:246).

Haldane had once expressed his disagreement with the opinion of the South African philosopher Jan Christian Smuts (1870–1950), who claimed that "while the spiritual or psychical factor is a real element in the universe, it is a comparatively recent arrival in the evolutionary career of things; ... the universe existed untold millions of years before its arrival" (quoted in Haldane 1929:130). According to Smuts, although the spiritual was not present from the very beginning of things, at some point it had arisen out of the nonspiritual. But for Haldane this contention was nonsense. He believed that the spiritual (whatever that was) had existed from the remotest time. It was not the case, then, that for eons the world had lain completely material and inert, since, "[in] actual fact," Haldane insisted, "what is taken [by Smuts] for a non-spiritual world is only part of the spiritual world" (Haldane 1929:132). "Spirituality," he declared, had *always* existed.

At the very end of his book, Haldane finally laid his cards on the table, pointing to "the real evidence that this universe is nothing but a spiritual universe and [that] the manifestation of God [is] present within and all around us" (Haldane 1929:323). If not outright, classical vitalism, this was at the very least neo-vitalism. And if so, it was certainly a frail philosophical reed. In view of the progress that mechanistic explanations of life had already made, and of the enormous strides it was destined to take, we may consider well justified Joseph Needham's admonition to those with a theological bias in these matters that "it may be doubted whether, even from a narrow apologetic point of view, it was wise to nail the colours of religion to the precarious mast of neo-vitalism" (Needham 1955:239).

Teleology and Vitalism

A closely associated aspect of vitalism was *teleology*, the belief that life was suffused with *purpose*. It was universally recognized, of course, that much of an *individual's* behavior is purposeful: people have intentions and act on them. But something beyond this was meant by those who expounded teleology, men like C. Lloyd

Morgan (1852–1936) who contended that in their behavior people were responding not only to their own will but to a will *outside* of themselves—to put it plainly, to the will of God.

Of such a metaphysical doctrine, the biologist William Beck has observed:

> Many vitalists are *finalists*, holding the teleological view that the universe is purposeful, evolution has a goal, and that all life has been a means to some end, persuasions which are clearly on the fringes of theology.... Actually, no one denies that there is a purpose. Anything going anywhere has direction but need this be called purposiveness? (Beck 1961:195)

The Triumph of Mechanism Becomes Complete

By the mid-1930s even the celebrated astronomer Sir James Jeans, who liked to think of God as a Great Mathematician who had calculated and engineered the precise clockwork of the universe, was nonetheless ready to accept an entirely mechanistic explanation of life's processes. In this vein he wrote:

> To-day one phenomenon after another which was at one time attributed to "vital force" is being traced to the action of the ordinary processes of physics and chemistry.... [I]t is becoming increasingly likely that what specially distinguishes the matter of living bodies is the presence not of a "vital force," but of the quite commonplace element of carbon, always in conjunction with other atoms with which it forms exceptionally large molecules. (Jeans 1947:9)

The present status of the issue of vitalism versus mechanism can be epitomized as follows. If in 1925 Joseph Needham could say that "at the present day the triumph of mechanistic biology is undoubted and it has no serious rivals" Needham (1955:250), today the case is all the more conclusive. Writing most recently, the noted physicist Freeman Dyson observed that "during the last fifty years, biologists have made enormous progress in understanding the basic processes of life," adding that these "processes are chemical reactions.... The chemistry of living cells is the essence of life" (Dyson 2004:55).

In *A Short History of Biology*, Isaac Asimov summarized the results of the vitalism-mechanism struggle. With the advances in biochemistry, especially in the twentieth century, he wrote, "[T]he heart went out of the vitalist position. Individual biologists might still speak diluted forms of vitalism in theory (and some do even today) but none seriously act upon it. It is generally accepted that life follows the laws that govern the inanimate world, that there is no problem in biology that is innately beyond solution in the laboratory.... The mechanistic view is supreme" (Asimov 1964:97).

The last word in this matter should go, appropriately enough, to James Watson, one of two men—Francis Crick being the other—who in recent decades have done more than anyone else to drive the final nail into vitalism's coffin. When Watson began to study biology, he tells us, "a small minority of scientists still thought life depended upon a vital force emanating from an all-powerful god. But like most of my teachers, I disdained the very idea of vitalism. If such a vital force were calling the shots in nature's game, there was little hope life would ever be understood through the methods of science" (Watson 2003:36). However, with Watson and Crick's discoveries of DNA and RNA and their interrelation in the famous "double helix," a tremendous step forward was taken in the scientific understanding of the elemental functioning of life. Watson himself wrote that "[t]he discovery of the double helix sounded the death knell for vitalism. Serious scientists, even those religiously inclined, realized that a complete understanding of life would not require the revelation of new laws of nature. Life was just a matter of physics and chemistry" (Watson 2003:61).

Summing up the culmination of a long scientific voyage, Watson remarked that the double helix "brought the Enlightenment's revolution in materialistic thinking into the cell. The intellectual journey that had begun with Copernicus displacing humans from the center of the universe and continued with Darwin's insistence that humans are merely modified monkeys had finally focused in on the very essence of life. And there was nothing special about it. The double helix is an elegant structure, but its message is downright prosaic: life is simply a matter of chemistry" (Watson 2003:xii–xiii).

Thus after centuries (indeed millennia) during which it dominated interpretations of life, vitalism has withdrawn from center stage into a small, dark corner of biology—if it has not been extinguished altogether. Continuing its relentless advance, naturalism has again registered a resounding victory over supernaturalism.

CHAPTER 17

Accounting for the Origin of Life

All societies are curious about the origin of life (especially human life) and virtually all have myths to account for it. The Christian myth, as we have seen, is recounted in the Book of Genesis. On the fifth day of creation—according to Genesis—after the land and the sea had been brought forth, God said, "Let the waters bring forth abundantly the moving creature that hath life, and fowl that may fly above the earth in the open firmament of heaven" (Genesis 1:20). And so the first forms of life were created.

As long as the biblical theory of creation was accepted as the true and definitive account of how life on earth began, there was no need for believers in Christianity to trouble themselves further about the matter. However, there came a time in the sixteenth century—if not earlier—when the biblical account was no longer accepted by everyone. Deeming this story to strain rationality, critical minds began to cast about for alternative explanations of how life began.

A theory that came readily to mind was the doctrine of spontaneous generation. Though problematic in itself, it at least required no divine intervention. The notion had a long pedigree, going back at least to the time of Aristotle, and was subscribed to by such later thinkers as Descartes and Newton. According to this theory, all sorts of strange transformations were thought possible: "[F]rom the ooze of rivers could come eels and from the entrails of dead bulls, bees; worms from mud, and maggots from dead meat" (Beck 1961:101).

Spontaneous Generation as an Alternative to Creation

For a time spontaneous generation was regarded as "the only reasonable alternative to a belief in supernatural creation" (Beck 1961:106). But then doubts began to be cast on the possibility of such an occurrence. The first significant challenge to the doctrine came from the Italian naturalist Abbé Lazzaro Spallanzani (1729–1799), who by means of a series of experiments showed that while a broth—if left standing in the open air—eventually developed bacteria, when boiled in a container sealed from the air, spontaneous generation never occurred (Beck 1961:102).

But Spallanzani's experiments were not widely credited. Not until the experiments of Louis Pasteur (1822–1893) a century later was the possibility of spontaneous generation convincingly refuted. In a public lecture in Paris in 1864, Pasteur declared triumphantly, "Never will the doctrine of spontaneous generation recover from the mortal blow of this simple experiment" (quoted in Beck 1961:104).

Pasteur had demonstrated beyond a doubt that life could not arise from dead matter. It had to come from life. But while this was in one sense a triumph for science, it reopened the question of how life could have arisen in the first place.

According to Alexander Oparin (1894–1980), who was to become a major figure in the study of the origin of life, "A period of disillusionment and pessimism set in [after spontaneous generation had been disproved], which survived from the last years of the nineteenth century well into the twentieth" (Oparin 1957:73). Indeed, with spontaneous generation ruled out, how life had originated remained for many an unfathomable mystery.

For Charles Darwin, who had done so much to elucidate the development of life once it had come into existence, the explanation of how it arose initially seemed an intractable—perhaps even an insoluble—problem. Writing to the botanist Joseph Hooker in 1863, he virtually threw up his hands: "It is mere rubbish thinking at present of the origin of life; one might as well think of the origin of matter" (quoted in Ward 1943:339).

However, for religiously orthodox biologists at the time, the origin of life posed no problem. Thus a botanist named William Harvey wrote to Darwin that the "Divine Creator" could, "without seed," summon up "from the dust of the ground a new organism, by the power of his omnipotent word" (quoted in Browne 2002:175).

Naturalistic Views of the Origin of Life

Then there was Herbert Spencer, who in almost every respect was a champion of naturalism and who had in fact contributed very substantially to biological and social science. Despite this, though, he seemed as nonplussed as Darwin by the question of life's origin. While ready to accept the fact that at some point life must have arisen from inanimate matter—from non-life—he "confessed that Life as a principle of activity is unknown and unknowable," and again he spoke of "life, the ultimate nature of which is incomprehensible" (Spencer 1898:122; Duncan 1908:II, 119).

The redoubtable Thomas Henry Huxley, however, was not ready to give up on the problem so easily. Indeed, he took the occasion of his presidential address to the British Association for the Advancement of Science in 1870 to speculate about the inorganic raw materials out of which the first constituents of life had arisen.

> If it were given to me to look beyond the abyss of geologically recorded time to the still more remote period when the earth was passing through physical and chemical conditions, which it can no more see again.... I should expect to be a witness of the evolution of living protoplasm from not living matter. I should expect to see it appear under forms of great simplicity endowed like existing Fungi, with the power of determining the formation of new protoplasm from such matter as ammonium carbonates, oxalates and tartrates, alkaline and earthy phosphates, and water, without the aid of light. (quoted in Oparin 1957:73–74)

Doubts About Unraveling Life's Origin

Perhaps these very words reanimated Darwin's interest in the subject, for in 1872 he wrote to Alfred Russel Wallace:

> On the whole it seems to me probable that Archebiosis [the term being used for the theory that life had originally arisen from non-living matter] is true. I should like to live to see Archebiosis proved true, for it would be a discovery of transcendent importance. (quoted in Oparin 1957:75)

But the pessimism and disillusionment spoken of by Oparin persisted for decades. Lawrence J. Henderson (1878–1942), a leading
biologist of the early twentieth century and a man firmly in the
mechanist camp, confessed his bafflement at the problem, asserting
in 1913 that "the origin of life itself remains shrouded in mystery"
(Henderson 1958:288). And four years later he still maintained that
"any theory about the origin of life is nothing but an unfounded
guess" (Henderson 1917:89). Henderson's gloomy assessment of
attempts to solve this problem was that "a half century has greatly
diminished the number of substantial biologists who really look forward to its scientific explanation" (Henderson 1958:309). In fact, he
went so far as to assert that even "assuming a gradual evolution of
the organic from inorganic, biochemists are more than ever unable
to perceive how such a process is possible" (Henderson 1958:310n).

Henderson was even ready to lay aside his accustomed mechanistic views and proclaim, with barely suppressed emotion, that "if
life has originated by an evolutionary process from dead matter, that
is surely the crowning and most wonderful instance of teleology in
the whole universe" (Henderson 1958:210).

Alexander Oparin Appears on the Scene

Into this barren and unpromising landscape of conjecture regarding the
origin of life there stepped the Russian biochemist Alexander Oparin.
In his groundbreaking book *The Origin of Life on Earth* (1936), an
expansion of an earlier work published in 1924, Oparin rejected the
idea that life was "something spiritual, the essential nature of which is
inaccessible to experimental study," arguing instead that "life, like
everything else in the world, is material in nature and an explanation
of it does not call for the acknowledgement of anything supernatural"
(Oparin 1957:347). He was prepared to affirm that "primaeval living
things arose by stages as a result of a prolonged evolution of organic
substances, as a particular stage in the general historical development
of matter" (Oparin 1957:78). And in *The Origin of Life on Earth*, he
advanced bold conjectures about how the first steps—essential to the
synthesis of life—might have occurred.

Oparin described the environment in which this process could
have begun. Basically, he said, there were conditions that *could* have

been present at the very beginning of life and conditions that could *not* have been present. Among the latter was the presence of already existing life. As Oparin explained this curious stipulation, "Only in the absence of organisms could life develop. Organic substances arising on the surface of the Earth at present would not be able to undergo prolonged evolution. After a comparatively short time they would be annihilated, devoured by the multitude of organisms, well equipped for the struggle for existence" (Oparin 1957:78–79).

A second condition that could not have existed on the primitive earth for early life to have arisen and taken root was the presence of oxygen, for that active gas would have oxidized (and therefore destroyed) any incipient form of life. However, in this respect the primitive earth provided a favorable environment. Atmospheric oxygen, which is largely the product of the transpiration of plants, was simply not present on the primitive earth—there being at the time, of course, no plants. As the biologist William Beck emphasized, "[C]hemical attack by oxygen could not have occurred to the first organism because the earth's atmosphere at the time contained no oxygen" (Beck 1961:264).

The *positive* conditions that had to be present for life to arise were of three sorts: (a) the chemical substratum that provided the new materials—the building blocks—out of which the precursors of life were to be constructed; (b) the processes and forces—such as electrical storms—involved in the synthesis of organic substances; and (c) a suitable medium in which these processes could take place. The latter was not hard to find on the early earth. It was the seas that formed after the earth had cooled to the point where water vapor (at first ubiquitous) could condense into water and spread over the earth's surface. The oceans thus created, which contained many organic molecules in solution, are sometimes referred to as the "Oparin Sea." It was an apt designation, being named after the man who first proposed the seas as the primeval hearth for the early development of life. J. B. S. Haldane—who, like Oparin, pioneered the scientific study of the origin of life—equated the upper layers of this ocean with a "hot thin soup" (quoted in Luria 1973:115).

At the time of the initial publication of Oparin's book in 1924, the outlook for understanding the origin of life on earth was—as we have seen—bleak. "It appeared as if it was a forbidden subject in the world of science," Oparin observed. Indeed, he recalled that "the problem was generally felt unsolvable in principle using objective research methods. It was felt that it belonged more to the sphere of faith than knowledge, and that, for this reason, serious scientists should not waste their time and efforts on hopeless attempts to solve the problem" (quoted in Lahav 1999:45).

Undaunted by what the scientific community regarded as a very dim prospect, Oparin mounted a frontal attack on the problem. He proposed that the prebiotic atmosphere of the earth had little or no free oxygen, the oxygen initially there having been reduced by hydrogen and other chemical elements, and concluded that "[u]nder the hypothesized reducing conditions, the synthesis of organic molecules ... would be feasible" (Lahav 1999:44).

Haldane's Primitive Ocean

Around this time the English biochemist and geneticist J. B. S. Haldane (1892–1964), independently of Oparin, "proposed that the primordial sea served as a vast chemical laboratory powered by solar energy. The early atmosphere was oxygen-free, and the combination of dissolved carbon dioxide and ammonia with UV radiation ... gave rise to a host of organic compounds in the upper layer of the primordial sea" (Lahav 1999:45).

By the beginning of the 1950s, there was a fairly good understanding of the conditions of the primitive earth, conditions that formed the substratum out of which the first primordial forms of life had emerged. Carbon, oxygen, nitrogen, and hydrogen, indispensable constituents of life, were all there and—because of their chemical activity—had combined with each other or with other elements, as in the case of nitrogen (N_2), carbon dioxide (CO_2), and methane (CH_4). Moreover, as Francis Crick pointed out, "[T]he primitive ocean did not consist merely of water and a few simple salts but had accumulated a fair variety of small organic molecules, formed from the molecules in the atmosphere and dissolved in the ocean by means of electrical discharges, ultraviolet light or other energy sources" (Crick 1981:77).

Thus in the early days of the prebiotic earth, there were already present a collection of simple compounds. "Such simple but highly reactive compounds, interacting with ammonia, would produce more complex carbon compounds, which in turn react to produce even more varied and complex organic compounds. There is thus imagined a long period of purely chemical evolution that produced an enormous variety of organic compounds in the primeval sea" (Lanham 1968:248).

The crux of the explanation of the origin of life, then, amounts to this: how simple inorganic molecules could have formed increasingly complex organic molecules that eventually developed the capacity to metabolize and replicate themselves, and thus be said to constitute living matter. What happened up to that point may be thought of as *chemical* evolution. From that point forward, what occurred can be considered *biological* evolution.

Before any experiments had been performed, the prevailing ideas of biologists about the origin of life were more or less conjectures based on a knowledge of chemical reactions and educated deductions about the conditions that prevailed during the early constitution of the earth. But optimism over the prospects of a major step forward was beginning to emerge. Thus, writing in 1930, the British biologist Peter Chalmers Mitchell said, "It cannot yet be claimed that the aritificial synthesis of living matter is on the eve of accomplishment. But, step by step, the advance is being made" (Mitchell 1930:16). Experimental evidence bearing on the problem was still lacking, but all that was about to change dramatically.

Stanley Miller's Landmark Experiment

A major advance in the search for conditions that might have produced the first steps in the synthesis of life took place in the laboratory of Harold Urey in 1953. It was a landmark experiment carried out by one of Urey's graduate students, Stanley Miller. The setting for this experiment had been provided by some of Oparin's speculations. As described by the chemist Hudson Hoagland, "Based upon considered geological evidence, he [Oparin] suggested that in very remote times the earth's atmosphere lacked free oxygen but was rich in methane (Ch_4), ammonia (NH_3), and water vapor (H_2O). He postulated that electric discharges in the form of lightning might produce a synthesis of amino acids, the building blocks of proteins" (Hoagland 1960:22).

Stanley Miller's experiment consisted of passing an electrical current through a mixture of four gases—methane (CH_4), ammonia (NH_3), hydrogen (H_2), and water vapor (H_2O). These four gases were enclosed in a vessel that formed part of a closed system. The system included a "flask of water which was boiled to promote circulation of the gases and which served to trap any volatile water-soluble products which were formed and protect them from dismemberment by the electric spark" (Crick 1981:77). This spark, which discharged continuously during the course of the experiment, was meant to simulate a lightning strike in the primitive earth's atmosphere.

After about a week, the experiment was stopped and the liquid in the flask examined. The organic molecules that had formed were found to contain twenty-five amino acids, principally glycine and alanine, two of the amino acids in animal protein. As Noam Lahav (1999:48) expressed it, "[T]his experiment was immediately recognized as an important breakthrough in the study of the origin of life." It had shown that given the gases supposed to have been present on the early earth, a powerful energy source—such as a lightning strike—could have produced several of the basic building blocks of life.

Of course life was not actually produced in this experiment. The products yielded by Miller's experiment were far from being able to metabolize and could not reproduce themselves. However, the experiment represented a major step in understanding how some of the elemental building blocks of life could have been assembled from simpler constituents, under the conditions present on the primitive earth. It made the next step in the evolution of life seem much less mysterious, perhaps even likely. A great gap had been narrowed, if not bridged, and another blow had been struck for the mechanistic explanation of the origin of life. No longer was a divine spark required to set the process in motion. Now the only spark required seemed to be the perfectly natural one of a lightning strike.

Teilhard's Futile Resistance

To be sure, a few educated individuals remained who clung to a more orthodox religious view of the matter. Pierre Teilhard de

Chardin, for example, a paleontologist but at the same time a Catholic priest, declared that "[t]he most important thing," as one contemplates the question of how life had arisen, "is that at the first appearance of life we encounter a phenomenon that is linked with the total evolution of the earth." And that phenomenon, according to Teilhard, was the fact that "[t]he 'juvenile earth' contained a *quantum of consciousness*; and this quantum passed completely into the biosphere" (Teilhard de Chardin 1969:26). But in doing so consciousness apparently "exhausted" and "devitalized" itself since, while "terrestrial matter is capable of sustaining and nourishing life" (i.e., life that is already here), it "cannot give rise to new life." For that "scientists would have to make a new earth" (Teilhard de Chardin 1969:26). However, in light of what biochemists have since accomplished, they may not have to go quite that far!

And what *have* they accomplished? Laboratory research has succeeded in giving rise to proto-cells that produce protein but are not yet able to replicate themselves, or reproduce only for a few generations and then die, or reproduce only part of themselves. But this is already a notable step forward, as Pier Luigi Luisi—a professor of macromolecular chemistry and himself a leading figure in this research—has written.

> [A]ll these may and probably are intermediates experimented with by nature to arrive at the final destination, the fully-fledged biological cell. Thus, the realization in the laboratory of these partially living cells may be of fundamental importance to understand the real essence of cellular life, as well as the historical evolutionary pathway by which the final target may have been reached. (Luisi 2006:265)

In concluding this chapter, we again give the last word to a biologist, Francis Crick, who sees these developments as signaling a triumph of mechanism and naturalism over vitalism and supernaturalism. "Reproducible experiments demonstrating that a rudimentary living system can evolve from a purely nonliving one should strengthen our feeling of unity with nature in the broadest sense, meaning with atoms and molecules of which all materials on earth are made" (Crick 1981:162).

CHAPTER 18

Evolution and Emergence

To an overwhelming degree, the doctrine of evolution advanced the cause of naturalism in understanding the living world and how it came to be. A few biologists and philosophers, though, seized on one aspect of evolution in order to reintroduce a bit of metaphysics back into the explanation of nature. They did so by means of the concept of *emergent evolution*. This concept highlighted the fact that at various stages during the course of evolution, qualitatively new features—previously absent and unknown—seemed to make their appearance suddenly and abruptly. The novelty thus brought about by these apparent "saltations" seemed so totally new and unpredictable to some observers as to require—they argued—something supernatural to give rise to them. Here, then, was a place where the deity might be invoked as a veritable *deus ex machina*.

Lloyd Morgan and Emergence

The person most closely associated with the view that something about emergent evolution transcended the purely natural was the psychologist C. Lloyd Morgan (1852–1936). For the most part, it should be noted, Morgan pictured emergent evolution in a straightforward, objective way, describing it as conforming to natural law with no metaphysical elements or overtones. "What I seek to emphasize," he wrote, "is that emergence is for me a scientific proposition" (Morgan 1929:29). But he also said that evolution "appears to present, from time to time, something new. Under what I here call emergent evolution stress is laid on this incoming of the new" (Morgan 1923:1).

An emergent, as Morgan saw it, seemed to have the following characteristics: (a) it was something genuinely novel, distinct from anything that had gone before; (b) it was qualitatively—not just quantitatively—different from what preceded it; (c) its existence involved more than just a simple rearrangement of previously existing parts; and (d) it was unpredictable on the basis of a knowledge of the properties of its constituent elements (Goudge 1967c:475, 1967d:393; Morgan 1923, 1929).

So far, so good. But Morgan felt compelled to seek some driving force to account for this qualitative newness that he felt was distinctive of emergent evolution. These novel qualities must be impelled, he thought, by something above and beyond the ordinary processes and forces of nature. And to identify this underlying or overriding mechanism, he reached into the realm of metaphysics. "For better or worse," he wrote, "I acknowledge God as the Nisus through which Activity emergents emerge, and the whole course of emergent evolution is directed. Such is my philosophic creed" (Morgan 1923:36).

For professional biologists with a more mechanistic view of the phenomena of their field, there was in Morgan's pronouncements an unacceptable departure from strict science. Thus, summarizing the case Morgan seemed to be making, Peter Chalmers Mitchell wrote:

> Lloyd Morgan expanded "emergence" into a general principle and described the path of evolution as being interrupted at intervals by sudden jumps in which new qualities "emerged." In his Gifford Lecture, he seemed to produce a vitalistic rabbit out of his bag at each of these jumps, and discover in them evidence of purpose and direction. If I am right in this interpretation, then "emergent evolution" is simply another instance of vitalism. (Mitchell 1930:29)

Morgan was by no means an idealist. He readily acknowledged the existence of a real world, "a physical world existent in its own right quite independently of any human … mind." But, he added, "for me, [this world] leads upward towards God … [a]s directive Activity on whom the manner of going in all natural events ultimately depends" (Morgan 1923:61).

Samuel Alexander, Jan Smuts, and Emergence

Emergent evolution was said by its proponents to have given rise to successive levels of phenomena. According to Morgan, there were four such levels: physical events, organic life, mind, and spirit or

God (Goudge 1967c:475). Samuel Alexander (1859–1938), who like Morgan espoused emergent evolution, believed that it had produced five levels: space-time, matter, life, mind, and—just as with Morgan—deity (Goudge 1967c:475). Explaining this evolution beyond mind, Alexander said that there was "a further quality of existence beyond mind, which is related as mind is to life or life to matter. That quality I call deity, and the being which possesses it is God" (quoted in Russell 1997:212).

A third proponent of emergent evolution was the South African philosopher Jan Christian Smuts (1870–1950). Like Morgan and Alexander before him, Smuts believed in the existence of God. But more clearly than they did, he saw God not as primordial creator of the universe and everything in it, but as an *emergent himself*—the final and most ethereal of a succession of levels of evolution that went back deep into geological time. In poetic prose he emphasized the absence of the Deity during earlier stages of the world's evolution.

> Where was the Spirit when the warm Silurian seas covered the face of the earth, and the lower types of fishes and marine creatures still formed the crest of the evolutionary wave? Or going still further back, where was the spirit when in the pre-Cambrian system of the globe the first convulsive movement threw up the early mountains which have now entirely disappeared from the face of the earth ...? (quoted in Haldane 1929:130)

The answer, Smuts implied, was *nowhere*. Spirit had come into being only after the geological evolution of the world was well under way. But whenever it was that God had arisen, he had played a role in all subsequent forms of development.

Lecomte du Nouy and Emergence

This view of evolution as involving (indeed requiring) a guiding spirit of some sort continued to appeal to a certain segment of biologists—for example, Alexis Carrell. But this line of thinking was petering out. One of the last advocates of an emergent evolution strongly tinged with metaphysics was the French biologist and philosopher Lecomte du Noüy, whose books defending this view enjoyed considerable popularity in the 1940s and 1950s. Indeed, they were warmly embraced by those seeking some kind of scientific buttressing for their underlying religious views. Indicative of this was a blurb on the back cover of du Noüy's *The Road to Reason* that quoted from a religious journal, *The Living Church,* which stated enthusiastically, "We predict that the book will become an important milestone along the road to man's adventure Godward."

In the book itself, du Noüy argued that "anti-chance," on which he said science was forced to rely when it could not provide a convincing explanation, was an admission of its inadequacy. "Modern science," he said, "can only supply relative answers" that too often referred processes not fully understood to *chance*. Such explanations, though, were stretched too thin and at some point science was "forced to call upon 'anti-chance,' which one might well call God" (du Noüy 1948:195, see also 221).

Lecomte du Noüy then went on to present the following argument. "Certain scientists simply say that the reason we cannot foresee new properties [of the sort that arise in emergence] lies in our incomplete knowledge of the constitutive elements" (du Noüy 1948:152). And if that is the case, he continued, then if it "were some day possible" to deduce the occurrence of water merely from a complete knowledge of hydrogen and oxygen alone, "the theory of emergence would be disproved" (du Noüy 1948:152). But, he contended, the theory of emergence as he interpreted it "affirms that the properties of water are not implicitly contained in those of oxygen and hydrogen" (du Noüy 1948:152). And thus they could never be deduced from even the most intimate knowledge of hydrogen and oxygen. Similarly, he asserted, "Neither can the properties of life be inferred even from a complete knowledge of the proteins or their constituent atoms" (du Noüy 1948:152).

Emergence Without Metaphysics

Here, however, a critical distinction must be made between *inferred* and *derived*. It may never be possible to "infer" (in any strict logical sense) the properties of liquid water from the properties of the gases hydrogen and oxygen, regardless of how well known the latter come to be. But we can be sure that the properties of water *derive from* the properties of hydrogen and oxygen when brought together under specifiable conditions. Nothing *external* to hydrogen and oxygen—other than, say, an electric spark—has to be introduced into the process to make water possible. To put it bluntly, the emergence of water does not require the intercession of God. Similarly, although we may not be able to "infer" life from its protein constituents, we can still assert that the latter *derives* from the former and does so without the need for divine intervention.

Without any metaphysical trappings, emergence—whether under that name or not—had long been recognized by scientists. Sir Humphrey Davy (1778–1829), for example, discovered that common salt was made up of a soft metal (sodium) and a green gas (chlorine). When the two elements were brought together, a new substance—table salt—was produced. Nothing "metaphysical" had to be invoked to account for the formation of salt. It was simply *what happened* to sodium and chlorine under certain conditions.

It was the philosopher-scientist George Henry Lewes (1817–1878) who in 1874 first coined the term "emergent evolution." Lewes made a distinction between two types of evolutionary change that he called *resultant* and *emergent*. *Resultant* changes were those that did not involve any sort of fundamental novelty in the process of coming into being. The outcome of a resultant change was thus not something totally new, but was in some sense additive, and predictable from the characteristics of the elements immediately antecedent to it.

An *emergent*, on the other hand, resulted from a change that brought about a discontinuity (a sharp break) from what had preceded it, and produced a new substance or state that could not have been predicted simply from a knowledge—even a deep knowledge—of the nature or properties of the elements from whose conjunction it had emerged (Kaminsky 1967:453). As portrayed by Lewes, then, emergent evolution was a solid scientific concept. No metaphysical element had been smuggled into it to account for the process. That bit of sleight of hand was introduced only later.

In a way, in formulating the concept of emergence, Lewes had been anticipated by John Stuart Mill. In his *System of Logic,* Mill had called attention to the fact that some effects were the simple additive results of several causes and could clearly be foreseen as following from that addition. "But in the other description of cases," he wrote, "the agencies which are brought together cease entirely, and a totally different set of phenomena arise" (Mill 1886:244). In this case, he added, "a concurrence of causes takes place which calls into action new laws bearing no analogy to any that we can trace in the separate operation of the causes" (Mill 1886:245).

Emergent changes were hardly problematic when they involved only a simple transformation. In his essay "On the Physical Basis of Life," Thomas Henry Huxley illustrated this by using the familiar example of water: "When hydrogen and oxygen are mixed in a certain proportion, and an electric spark is passed through them, they disappear, and a quantity of water, equal in weight to the sum of their weights, appears in their place" (Huxley 1909:111). There was nothing mysterious or metaphysical about *that*. But the plot thickened when—he went on to argue—living matter could similarly be said to have arisen from non-living matter. "If the properties of water may be properly said to result from the nature and disposition of its component molecules," he argued, "I can find no intelligible ground for refusing to say that the properties of protoplasm result from the nature and disposition of its molecules" (Huxley 1909: 113).

Naturally this assertion contradicted the vitalist contention that something categorically new and different and beyond the natural order of things—a divine spark, if you will—must have been involved at the moment when the organic first arose out of the inorganic ... when life arose from non-life.

The origin of life was of course a transcendental, qualitative step in the evolution of nature. But it was not a single, simple step; the very first step—whatever it was—had to be followed by many others. The development of life consisted, in fact, of a succession of small steps, culminating in a major transformation. And it was the tracing of these steps, especially identifying the *mechanism* behind their transformation (natural selection), that was Darwin's great contribution to the science of life. To be sure, in all his work Darwin laid great emphasis on the *continuity* of the process of evolution. He argued against saltations or breaks in the process, believing that they came too close to suggesting special creation. "Natural selection," he wrote in *The Origin of Species*, "will banish the belief in the continued creation of new organic beings, or in any great and sudden modification of their structure" (quoted in Goudge 1967c: 474)

Thus Darwin's contributions were all on the side of pointing out the continuity of life forms rather than focusing on any discontinuities. And looked upon at close range, Darwin was right. One generation of animals was derivable from the previous generation with but the smallest modifications. However, examined over the course of millions of years, it was possible to discern in certain life forms striking differences from one era to another. Over the grand sweep of time, we see the rise of categorically new forms of life—eukariotic from prokaryotic forms, multicellular organisms from unicellular ones, vertebrates from invertebrates, amphibians from fishes, reptiles from amphibians, and mammals from reptiles.

Actually, in the evolutionary process itself both continuity *and* discontinuity can be discerned. Moreover, even stasis, the virtual absence of change, can be observed here and there in the fossil record. Thus we have so-called "living fossils" like the tuatara and the lungfish. It was the marked contrast between such stagnated species—showing little or no change over millions of years—contrasted with rapid spurts of change, as among the *Hominoidea*, that led Stephen Jay Gould and Niles Eldredge to formulate the concept of *punctuated equilibra.* This view of evolution describes it as following an alternating course: periods of rapid growth followed by periods of stagnation. Although Gould and Eldredge do not invoke emergent evolution, they do highlight sudden episodes of rapid evolution—almost of discontinuity—rather than the slow and steady drumbeat of evolutionary change that Darwin liked to emphasize.

Returning to the distinction first made by George Henry Lewes, we can see organic evolution as being both resultant and emergent—*resultant* when we focus on the tiny changes taking places over the generations, *emergent* when we look at the process over long stretches of time, as when we see reptiles emerging from amphibians or mammals from reptiles. When we examine the characteristics of each, the properties of one group are not quite predictable or *deducible* from a knowledge of the properties of the previous one, but yet they are perfectly *derivable* from them. No *deus ex machina* comes knocking at the door, asking to be let in.

Whether we look at it as a short-term, flashpoint phenomenon or a long-term contrast of the two ends of a continuum, emergence is nonetheless a valid, objective, and edifying concept. It is a straightforward phenomenon with nothing metaphysical about it. The effort of C. Lloyd Morgan, Samuel Alexander, and Lecomte du Noüy to smuggle into it a supernatural element is unwarranted and invalid.

Let me end this discussion by quoting Ernest Nagel's concise encapsulation of the matter: "'[E]mergent evolution' ... asserts that novel forms of organization appear in time, new traits are exhibited, and types of activities are manifested which did not previously exist, and which cannot be understood in terms of what had preceded them." And undermining any claim of metaphysical spontaneity being involved in the process, Nagel added, "[T]he doctrine of emergence ... [is] fully compatible with determinism" (Nagel 1969: 337).

CHAPTER 19

The Diminishing Role of God in History

Just as occurred in the realm of nature, we can discern in the realm of human history a steady trend in which the supernatural interpretation of events gradually yielded to a naturalistic one.

If early Christianity can be said to have had a philosophy of history at all, it was a philosophy derived directly from the Bible. Implicit in Scripture, this philosophy was made explicit and further elaborated by the early Church fathers. Christianity itself, of course, had begun as a messianic movement in which the oppression of the Jewish people by the legions of the Roman Empire was so complete that no realistic hope existed of being able to overthrow it. Accordingly, the message imparted by Jesus to his followers was that a person's ultimate reward was to be sought not here on earth, but in the hereafter. This early Christian philosophy of history has been summarized by a present-day historian.

> [M]en are the vehicles through which history occurs but history has a direction and a purpose decided by a force beyond man. This Christian concept of history also contained the idea of fulfillment. The purpose of history would one day be realized in the salvation of mankind at the Last Judgment. History is thus a teleological process with a purpose and an end. (Winschuttle 1997:14)

This initial philosophy was given fuller form by Augustine, who saw Christian history as "moving along a line with a clear beginning, marked by the Creation, a middle, and an end. The birth and death of Christ denoted the central event, and the salvation of all believers at the termination signified the completion of the process" (Gilderhaus 1996:22). Augustine further divided this trajectory into six stages, corresponding to the six days of cre-

313

ation. The first one spanned the period from Adam to Noah, the second from Noah to Abraham, and so on until the sixth—which began with the birth of Jesus and extended to the end of the world. In propounding his philosophy of history, Augustine thus instilled in Christians an outlook that "turned away from the world that now is and fixed on the world to come" (Haskins 1966:229). For the Christian faithful of the Middle Ages, then, "anticipation of the future held more significance than their perceptions of the past" (Gilderhaus 1996:20).

God's Intercession in History

Still, Christians needed some way to interpret life on earth, here and now. And the course of human history, difficult as it might be to discern, was proposed as the unfolding of a master plan. And of this master plan God was not only the architect, but also a major participant. He concerned himself intimately with the affairs of the world and actively intervened in them when he found it necessary to do so.

Moreover, this intervention often involved deflecting the normal course of events. Thus in seeking to explain the unexpected defeat of King Alfonso I in the Battle of Fraga after twenty-nine successive victories, the author of the *Chronicle of San Juan de la Peña*—the official fourteenth century history of the Crown of Aragon—was convinced that it must be in punishment for the fact that, unable to pay his troops from his own coffers, Alfonso "turned his hand against sanctuaries, churches, and monasteries. He robbed them of their treasure and sold and made levies against their properties and possessions," thus offending God and bringing upon himself divine retribution (Nelson 1991:29).

Often, though, divine intervention involved more than merely turning the tide of battle. It sometimes saw the commission of wondrous and unnatural acts—that is, miracles. Outright violations of nature though they might be, in an age of unswerving Christian faith these miracles were unblinkingly accepted. In these remarkable instances of the direct intercession of God's hand, wrote Gibbon, "[T]he lame walked, the blind saw, the sick were healed, the dead raised, demons were expelled, and the laws of Nature were frequently suspended" (quoted in Clive 1989:57).

Indeed, political leaders were at times regarded as instruments of God. When Charles VIII of France entered Florence at the head of his armies in 1494, Savonarola—the city's principal political figure—was convinced that Charles was the direct agent of Providence, come to punish the Florentines for their lives of sin (Robinson 1965:361). And "[e]verything goes to show," reported Plekhanov (1940:12n), "that Cromwell also regarded himself as such an instrument.... He always called his actions the fruits of the will of God."

The fullest portrayal of world history as the workings of the Deity was Bishop Bossuet's *Discours sur l'histoire universelle* (1681). Bossuet was convinced that "[h]igh up in His Heaven God holds the reins of all kingdoms. He has every heart in His hand. Sometimes He restrains passions, sometimes He leaves them free, and thus agitates all mankind. By this means God carries out His redoubtable judgments according to ever infallible rules. He it is who prepares results through the most distant causes, and who strikes vast blows, whose repercussion is so widespread. Thus it is that God reigns over all nations" (quoted in Renier 1950:264).

But, said Bossuet, it was not always necessary for the Lord to intervene directly. By a limited number of judicious examples, he could teach the lesson that his will would prevail and must be respected.

> God does not every day declare his will by prophets, concerning the kings and monarchies, which He sets up or pulls down. But having done it so many times in these great empires we have been speaking of, He shows by those famous instances, how He acts in all others. (quoted in Lowith 1949:141)

Such was the position of a Catholic theologian. Calvinists, on the other hand, might argue that *their* God was even more firmly and fully in control of the course of events, since that Deity found it unnecessary to engage in even occasional interventions. After all, had not Calvin asserted that all human actions were *already* divinely predetermined? "By predestination we mean," wrote Calvin, "the eternal decree of God, by which he within himself has ordained what it behoves shall happen to each man" (quoted in Plekhanov 1940:12n).

The overriding role of God in history continued to be accepted and expressed not only by theologians, but also by historians and philosophers. According to the early American cleric and historian Increase Mather (1639–1723), "[A]s to all events which come to pass in the world, he that [sitteth] upon the Throne hath an hand therein" (quoted in Cohen 1980:11). Two hundred years later another American historian, George Burton Adams (1851–1925), continuing to invoke God as a major force in the course of events, saw "the whole of human history as ... the sure unfolding of a foreordained plan" (Adams 1909:221).

German Idealists' Notion of God

German idealist philosophers, whose God was sometimes slightly obscured beneath the diaphanous veil of "Spirit" or "the Absolute," continued to see history as manifesting a divine plan. Immanuel Kant, for one, declared that "[t]he History of the Human Species as a whole may be regarded as the unraveling of a hidden Plan of Nature" (quoted in Pollard 1968:86). And here "Nature" was clearly the proxy through which God works his ways.

Hegel was a little more straightforward in identifying the force giving impetus to the great movements of history. He spoke frequently of "Spirit" and the "Absolute Idea" but made it clear that at bottom both were manifestations of God. In typically vague and mystical prose, he wrote that "the history of the world ... is ... the justification of God in history.... [W]hat has happened and is happening every day, is not only not 'without God,' but is essentially his work" (Hegel 1969:90).

Schelling too saw history as "a continuous revelation of the Absolute gradually accomplishing itself" and held that "[h]istory is an epic composed in the mind of God." In fact, history was simply "God's march through the world" (quoted in Beard 1972:318). Even more specifically, Christianity for Schelling was "the centre and key of all history" (quoted in Nordau 1910:63).

However, about the same time that the German philosophers of history were expounding their metaphysical, crypto-religious views of how history played itself out, the men of the French Enlightenment were putting forth a very different kind of interpretation.

Voltaire, for one, took exception to history refracted through a theological prism. Bossuet's magisterial presentation of history, Voltaire declared, "had mistaken a pious retelling of Hebrew tales for the history of the world" (Gay 1969:391).

Deists' Conception of God

The last third of the eighteenth century—the period known as the Enlightenment—witnessed a strengthening of the secular interpretation of history. Deism was now manifesting a stronger presence. As an alternative to theism, it challenged the traditional manner of looking at how human events had unfolded. As we have just seen, theologians like Bishop Bossuet held that God intervened immediately and directly in worldly affairs, temporarily setting aside his own laws (if need be) and thereby causing wonderful—or terrible—things to happen if he so desired.

The pages of the Bible, which told of God's exploits, were liberally sprinkled with miracles. The earlier writing of history, reflecting the Bible's influence, likewise had its share of miraculous events. However, the history that began to be written in the seventeenth and especially the eighteenth centuries changed all that. No longer did God exercise a direct involvement in human affairs. Much as he might regret or deplore a particular outcome, he did not become involved in it himself. He could not (or at least *would not*), historians now felt, interfere to save a righteous monarch from being overthrown or a pious host from being slaughtered on the battlefield.

As the times became more rational and skeptical, historians began to challenge the benevolence—if not the very existence—of a God who, for example, permitted the terrible excesses of the French Revolution. Nonetheless there were still staunch believers who felt that even those excesses were manifestations of God's unfathomable will. The poet Samuel Taylor Coleridge, for example, admonished the historian that in his "just contempt and detestation of the crimes and follies of the Revolutionists, he suffers himself to forget that the revolution itself is a process of the Divine Providence, and that as the folly of men is the wisdom of

God, so are their iniquities instruments of His goodness" (quoted in Acton 1985:527n). Thus the fruits of God's inscrutability, no matter how appalling they might seem, could somehow still be justified.

Social Scientists' View of History

Nevertheless such a dogged acceptance of God's actions, whatever they might be, was becoming more and more of an anachronism. Already in the Renaissance, as pointed out by the historian Peter Gay, "Humanists ... had begun to liberate history writing from its subservience to theology, dependence on miracles, and apocalyptic expectations" (Gay 1969:372). Indeed, something that could be called social science, with a more hardheaded, skeptical, and secular approach to the past, was beginning to emerge. Thus we see such notions expounded as far back as 1566 by Jean Bodin in his *Method for the Easy Comprehension of History*. In the opening pages of that work, Bodin explicitly disavowed theological interpretations of history. "Such interpretations are not valid, in his view, because history ... is a discipline which has nothing in common with the study of God" (Huppert 1970:93).

One hundred fifty years later, we find a similar treatment of history in Giambattista Vico's *The New Science* (1725). While Vico's avowed purpose in writing this book was to describe the working out in history of the will of divine providence, it produced much the opposite effect. According to the sociologist Floyd House, Vico "held that God directs the course of human affairs through natural causes rather than by miraculous intervention in particular cases. His inquiry into the operation of divine providence, therefore, assumes the form of an inquiry into the natural sequence of events, and thus Vico's point of view makes possible a secular interpretation of history" (House 1936:108).

For the next two centuries, the sharply varying interpretations of history—the religious and the secular—continued to vie for supremacy. As late as 1874, the Scottish philosopher and theologian Robert Flint proclaimed grandly, "The ultimate and greatest triumph of historical philosophy will really be neither more nor less than the full proof of Providence, the discovery by the processes of scientific method of a divine plan which unifies and harmonizes the apparent chaos of human actions" (quoted in Nordau 1910:22).

But "the processes of scientific method" turned out to point in just the opposite direction. In the middle of the nineteenth century, a profound change in human thinking began to take shape, a change ushered in largely by the arrival of the theory of evolution. Darwin's *The Origin of Species* stirred not only biologists but scholars in virtually all other fields of learning. For a mind unclouded by theological preconceptions, the implications of the grand idea of evolution were irresistible. If evolution could explain the origin and development of biological organisms—without the need of supernatural agents or forces—could it not do the same for the succession of events that constituted human history?

Professional Historians Assume Center Stage

As the historian Carl Becker described this sea change, "Much serious, minutely critical investigation into the origins of institutions seemed to show that all things human might be fully accounted for without recourse to God or the Transcendental Ideas" (Becker 1958: 274). The latter half of the nineteenth century saw the steady advance of this interpretation of history. I know of no better example of this change in the philosophy of history than the following passage from the works of the historian Hubert Bancroft.

> At first, man and his universe appear to be regulated by arbitrary volitions, by a multitude of individual [i.e., polytheistic gods]; each governs absolutely his own actions; every phenomenon of nature is but the expression of some single will. As these phenomena, one after another, become stripped of their mystery, there stands revealed not a god, but a law; seasons come and go, and never fail; sunshine follows rain, not because a pacified deity smiles, but because the rain clouds have fallen and the sun cannot help shining. Proximate events first are thus made godless, then the whole host of deities is driven farther and farther back. Finally the actions of man himself are found to be subject to laws. Left to his own will, he wills to do like things under like conditions. (Bancroft 1883:80)

By the end of the nineteenth century, while God had not been entirely driven from the temple of history, he was playing a muted and subordinate role. He might be invoked in the preface to a historical work as being the ultimate source of human existence, but as an explanatory device in accounting for a particular sequence of events, he was kept pretty much at arm's length. Lord Acton, though a lifelong Catholic, gave the following advice to his professional colleagues: "Historians have not to point out everywhere the hand of Providence, but to find out all the natural causes of things. Enough will always remain that cannot be so explained" (quoted in Butterfield 1960b:138n).

By the twentieth century, the feeling prevailed among historians that, as Edward Cheyney phrased it, "the belief that God has a plan for the progress of a nation or of the world, and that his plan can be discovered by any one historian and used for the explanation of events, belongs in the field of religion, not of history" (Cheyney 1927:162). And the British historian A. L. Rowse appeared to express the definitive judgment of his profession when he affirmed that in the interpretation of history, "[t]he idea of God has been rendered superfluous" (Rowse 1963:81).

Superfluous but not altogether extinct. As we have noted over and over again in other fields, the supernatural—though waging a rearguard action and even, here and there, in full retreat—doggedly fights on. In the field of human history, no better example of this continued struggle can be cited than the lonely voice of Arnold Toynbee, whose *A Study of History* was immensely popular not so many years ago. For Toynbee the pageant of history was more than the individual stirrings of mere mortals. Far grander than that, "It was a tale told by God, unfolding itself from the Creation through the Fall and Redemption to the Last Judgment" (Toynbee 1949:79). Yet without question this voice stands out today for its marked contrast with the views of the vast majority of professional historians.

CHAPTER 20

Free Will versus Determinism

O f the many issues dividing science and religion, that of free will versus determinism is one of the most basic. Science seeks to extend the rule of law—of cause and effect—to every domain of phenomena on the supposition that no part of nature is exempt from it. Many religions, on the other hand, eliminate cause-and-effect from certain aspects of human behavior. And even when they do not exclude it altogether, they severely restrict its sphere of operation. The view of religion—at any rate of the Christian religion—is that when making a choice between two or more ways of acting, individuals do so in large part by *exercising their free will*. This can only mean acting *independently of*—that is, unaffected by—*antecedent conditions*. A person's choice, then, is spontaneous, unconstrained, and therefore (from a scientific point of view) unaccountable.

Clearly such a view is directly at odds with how science looks at behavior. A scientist would argue that since the workings of cause and effect underlay the development of the cosmos, from the Big Bang onward, why should they suddenly be suspended when—during the last second of geological time—human beings arrived on the scene?

Upholders of Free Will

Notwithstanding this objection, the doctrine of free will is still immensely popular, pervasive, and enduring. It is, in fact, cherished by the multitude. Going back in the history of philosophy, one can find free will embraced and defended—not unexpectedly—by Plato. It was, after all, much easier for a bred-in-the-bone idealist like Plato to argue for free will than for a materialist like Democritus. For if the will is regarded as something that one exercises entirely independently of matter, what is there left to determine a person's volition?

The doctrine of free will has been upheld not only by philosophers like Plato, but by very practical men who were anything *but* idealists. Samuel Johnson, for example, who thought he had demolished Berkeley's idealism when he gave a stone a vigorous kick, was nevertheless a believer in free will. With his customary self-assurance, Johnson once told the faithful Boswell, "Sir, ... we *know* our will is free, and *there's* an end on't" (Boswell 1952:161). Besides Dr. Johnson, innumerable others of almost every philosophical stripe have doggedly clung to the notion of free will. William James (1842–1910), for one, stated flatly, "I believe in free will myself," referring on another occasion to "our intuitive belief in free will" (James 1880:442). In fact, free will is the doctrine of choice among literary humanists, artists, and many others—including even, or perhaps especially, the man in the street.

However, that an adherence to a consistent and thoroughgoing materialism, empiricism, and determinism would lead one to reject the notion of free will was recognized as far back as the early Greek atomists. By the Middle Ages, though, during which Catholic dogma dominated Western thought, free will was not only embraced but enthroned. Indeed, it was considered one of the precious gifts that God had bestowed on humanity.

The Rising Advocacy of Determinism

With the coming of the Renaissance and the burgeoning of scientific thought, advocates of determinism began to re-emerge and marshal their arguments against free will. Anthony Collins (1676–1729), one of the early deists, denied the existence of free will outright, and it was a reading of Collins's book *Philosophical Inquiry Concerning Human Liberty and Necessity* (1714) that led Joseph Priestley (1733–1804), the discoverer of oxygen and—along with Lavoisier—the father of modern chemistry, to deny free will as well (Passmore 1967:454). "[E]very volition of choice," he wrote, "is constantly regulated and determined by what precedes it" (Priestley 1965:57). And carrying this thought to its logical conclusion, he proclaimed that "how little soever the bulk of mankind may be apprehensive of it or staggered by it, according to the established laws of nature no event could have been otherwise than it has been" (Priestley 1965:58).

But Priestley's opposition to the doctrine, unlike that of most other of its opponents, had a religious basis. "The doctrine of free will," he asserted, "is theologically objectionable because it cannot be reconciled with the existence of an all-seeing [and all-powerful] Providence" whose omnipotence could readily allow it to override human freedom any time it wished to (Passmore 1967:454). Furthermore, Priestley was ready to affirm, "[M]y conduct through life is determined by the Being who made me and placed me in the circumstances in which I first found myself" (Priestley 1965:60).

Holbach Champions Determinism

Religious beliefs, though, were decidedly *not* behind the objections to free will advanced by Baron d'Holbach (1723–1789), the most out-spoken materialist and atheist among the circle of French *philosophes*. Holbach argued his case as follows. "You will say that I feel free. This is an illusion, which may be compared to that of the fly in the fable, who, lighting upon the pole of a heavy carriage, applauded himself for directing its course. Man, who thinks himself free, is a fly who imagines he has power to move the universe, while he is himself unknowingly carried along by it" (quoted in Edwards 1961:120).

Less metaphorically, Holbach described the process of choice in these terms. A person's action, he said, "is the result of the impulse he receives either from the motive, from the object, or from the idea, which has modified his brain, or disposed his will. When he does not act according to this impulse, it is because there comes some new cause, some new motive, some new idea, which modifies his brain in a different manner, gives him a new impulse, determines his will in another way" (Holbach 2006:169).

"Our volitions," wrote Holbach, putting his finger on the crucial point, "are never in our power. You think yourself free, because you do what you will, but are you free to will or not to will, to desire or not to desire?" Holbach thus anticipated Schopenhauer's oft-quoted remark: "A man can surely do what he wills to do, but he cannot determine what he wills" (quoted in Edwards 1961:121; see also Planck 1981:201).

Persuasive as Holbach's argument may have seemed to some, it remained unconvincing to Goethe (1749–1832) and his circle, who found Holbach's *System of Nature*—in which such views were espoused—"so black, so Cimerian" and countered that despite what Holbach argued with so much force, "we nevertheless felt within us something that appeared like perfect freedom of will" (quoted in Mason 1962:349).

Goethe's contemporary Immanuel Kant (1724–1804) treated the question of free will versus determinism in a more nuanced way that, according to Thomas Henry Huxley (1825–1895), went as follows.

> Kant's mode of dealing with the doctrine of necessity is very singular. That the phenomena of the mind follow fixed relations of cause and effect is, to him, as unquestionable as it is to Hume. But then there is the *Ding an sich*, the *Noumenon*, or Kantian equivalent for the substance of the soul. This, being out of the phenomenal world, is subject to none of the laws of phenomena, and is consequently as absolutely free, and as completely powerless, as a mathematical point, *in vacuo,* would be. Hence volition is uncaused, as far as it belongs to the noumenon; but, necessary, so far as it takes effect in the phenomenal world. (Huxley 1908:226)

This, I would say, is a rather neat example of having your cake and eating it too!

Huxley and Lewes Argue for Determinism

Huxley himself, unlike Kant, was a full-throated champion of determinism and was convinced that "[w]hatever it is that leads us to seek for a cause for every event in the case of phenomena of the external world, compels us, with equal cogency, to seek it in that of the mind" (Huxley 1908:214). Still, Huxley recognized that the *illusion* of free will was so strong in human beings as to lead them to advance it as an argument in its favor. "The last asylum of the hard-pressed advocate of the doctrine of uncaused volition," he wrote, " is usually, that, argue as you like, he has a profound and ineradicable consciousness of what he calls the freedom of his will" (Huxley 1908:219).

We might note here in passing that Charles Darwin, who was loath to take on broad philosophical issues—feeling himself unsteady in such matters—wrote to Asa Gray in 1860, "I am in the same sort of muddle (as I have said before) as all the world seems to be with respect to free will" (Darwin 1994:267–268).

George Henry Lewes (1817–1878), who like Huxley was unabashed at tackling such questions, had a good deal to say on the subject of free will versus determinism. First, he began by asserting emphatically that "[a]ll the massive evidence to be derived from human conduct, and from our practical interpretation of such conduct, points to the conclusion that actions, sensations, emotions, and thoughts are subject to causal determination no less rigorously than the movements of the planets or the fluctuations of the waves" (Lewes 1879:102). Then, bringing the argument down to cases, he argued that to believe in free will made the will something entirely divorced from the functioning brain, a supposition he considered inadmissible. As he put it, "To suppose that when several conflicting motives arise there is no corresponding struggle among neural groups, and that when a choice is made there is not corresponding neural arrangement, is to assume that Will is not the function of the organism, but an independent entity" (Lewes 1879:104).

Nor would Lewes countenance the existence of the will as an immaterial, incorporeal, insubstantial entity, existing on its own outside the individual. "Free will," he said, "must be explained in terms of the entire organism and to its relationship to the environment." Indeed, "every element in Sentience is represented by a corresponding element in cerebral re-arrangement" (Lewes 1879:103, 453). However, "[no] sooner do we quit the metaphysical for the biological point of view, and regard Volition as a function of the organism, than the asserted freedom is seen to fall within the limits of determinism as a particular case of the general law of causation" (Lewes 1879:102–103).

Social Science Sides wih Determinism

Not only the biological and psychological sciences, however, had a stake in this issue. The social sciences and history did as well. Speaking on their behalf, John Stuart Mill (1806–1873) saw the matter clearly and by implication made the case for determinism.

Among the impediments to the general acknowledgement, by
thoughtful minds, of the subjection of historical facts to scientific laws, the most fundamental continues to be that which is
grounded in the doctrine of Free Will, or, in other words, on the
denial that the law of invariable Causation holds true of human
volitions; for if it does not, the course of history, being the result
of human volition, cannot be a subject of scientific laws, since
the volitions on which it depends can neither be foreseen nor
reduced to any canon of regularity even after they have
occurred. (Mill 1930:607)

This was the issue as painted by Mill himself, who favored the
idea of a science of history. Among those of Mill's contemporaries
who sought in the facts of history the pattern of its trajectory were
men such as Herbert Spencer and E. B. Tylor, who like Mill were
firmly on the side of determinism but still recognized the high
degree of aversion to it by others. "To many educated minds," wrote
Tylor, "there seems something presumptuous and repulsive in the
view that the history of mankind is part and parcel of the history of
nature, that our thoughts, wills, and actions accord with laws as definite as those which govern the motion of waves, the combination of
acids and bases, and the growth of plants and animals" (Tylor
1871:I, 2).

Again, in the opening pages of *Primitive Culture,* Tylor wrote
that "the popular notion of free human will involves not only freedom to act in accordance with motives, but also a power of breaking loose from continuity and acting without cause—a combination
which may be roughly illustrated by the simile of a balance sometimes acting in the usual way, but also possessed of the faculty of
turning by itself without or against weights. This view of an anomalous action of the will, ... it need hardly be said is incompatible
with scientific argument" (Tylor 1871:I, 2–3).

Humanists Defend Free Will

However, the American psychologist and philosopher William
James (a contemporary of Tylor) seemed at times to throw up his
hands when it came to taking sides on this issue: "For ourselves, we

can hand the free will controversy over to metaphysics. Psychology will never grow refined enough to discover, in the case of any individual's decision, a discrepancy between her scientific calculations and the fact" (James 1963:390).

This issue has continued to command the liveliest general interest. It is, of course, one of the issues on which artists and writers—humanists for the most part—have found themselves almost unanimously arrayed against the determinism proclaimed and defended by science. This opposition is nicely illustrated in Dostoevsky's *Notes From the Underground* (1864) in which the hero intentionally adopts antisocial behavior as a way of expressing what he believes to be his freedom of action. "I say, gentlemen, hadn't we better kick over the whole show and scatter rationalism to the winds, simply to send those logarithms to the devil, and to enable us to live once more at our sweet foolish will?" (Dostoevsky 1945:145). And to further emphasize the point, the protagonist of the story later says, "[T]he whole work of man really seems to consist in nothing but proving to himself every minute that he is a man and not a piano-key" (Dostoevsky 1945:149).

Still, a few writers seem to have made a more realistic assessment of things, as when Robert Browning included a line (line 51) in his poem "Andrea del Sarto" that reads, "So free we seem, so fettered fast we are!"

Quantum Uncertainty Seized Upon

The twentieth century brought with it a new weapon, eagerly seized upon by proponents of free will in their continuing struggle against determinism. This alleged weapon was the discovery, in the newly developing field of quantum physics, that the behavior of atoms and subatomic particles was not readily predictable. Phrasing the matter somewhat loosely—and indeed inappropriately—Bertrand Russell wrote, "[W]e do not know why some atoms of radioactive substances break down while others do not.... So far as quantum theory can say at present, atoms might as well be possessed of free will, limited, however, to one of several possible choices" (Russell 1954:38).

According to Max Planck, when Heisenberg's uncertainty principle was first enunciated, "[I]t was almost immediately interpreted, even among physicists themselves, as definitely effecting an over-throw of the causation principle" (Planck 1981:32). Those among them who were already strongly inclined to believe in free will eagerly seized upon this uncertainty as buttressing their position. They argued that what occurred among elementary particles of matter mirrored what they fancied took place in the human brain when a decision was to be made.

Werner Heisenberg (1901–1976) had shown that since the very act of observing elementary particles interfered with their behavior, one could never simultaneously ascertain with exactitude both the *position* and the *velocity* of these particles. This limitation he had labeled—reasonably enough—the uncertainty principle. However, the physicist-astronomer Sir Arthur Eddington (1882–1944) soon began referring to it unjustifiably as the "principle of indeterminacy," proclaiming that "the indeterminacy of quantum physics solved the traditional philosophical problem of free will versus determinism in favor of free will" (Nerlich 1967:460). Along with a number of his fellow physicists, Eddington—who was a metaphysical idealist—was only too happy to accommodate the supposed import of these new findings into his philosophy.

Eddington's fellow astronomer-physicist Sir James Jeans (1877–1946) held very similar opinions in this regard. He feared that a thoroughly mechanistic, deterministic view of life "left no room for the operation of choice and free-will, [and thus] ... removed all basis for morality" (Jeans 1947:211). And like Eddington, he seized on quantum mechanics as providing a way out of the rigidly deterministic world of classical physics. In the uncertainties of subatomic particles, he thought that he had found a model for the uncertainties of human behavior. Heartened by this prospect, he wrote optimistically:

> [F]or aught we know, or for aught that the new science can say to the contrary, the gods which play the part of fate to the atoms of our brains may be our own minds. Through these atoms our minds may perchance affect the motions of our bodies and so the state of the world around us. To-day science can no longer shut the door on this possibility; she has no longer any unanswerable arguments to bring against our innate conviction of free-will. (Jeans 1947:36)

Such pronouncements by Eddington and Jeans, however, were something in the nature of grasping at straws. Indeed, the position that they advocated was openly challenged by Heisenberg himself. Well aware that his uncertainty principle "is often used as an argument in favor of free will and divine intervention," he nevertheless held that such usage was invalid and that "the question whether natural laws determine events completely or only statistically has no direct bearing on the question of free will" (Heisenberg 1972:91).

One way in which religious advocates of free will have sought to battle science on this issue is by trying to undermine the doctrine of determinism as it applies to human conduct. The freedom to act, unfettered by overriding determinants, is considered by them to somehow bring us closer to God. Thus if indeterminism can be shown to reign in the domain of quantum physics, that must surely be counted a victory for their side of the argument and a validation of the human connection with the divine.

Laplace and Universal Determinism

The story of this battle may be said to have begun with the great French mathematician and astronomer Pierre-Simon de Laplace (1749–1827). Laplace was a staunch believer in universal determinism. In his *Philosophical Essay on Probability* (1814), he envisioned a "supreme intelligence capable of grasping both the position at any time of every particle in the universe and all the forces acting upon it" (Harré 1967:392). For such an intelligence, Laplace reasoned, "nothing would be uncertain and the future, as the past, would be present to its eyes. The human mind offers, in the perfection which it has been able to give to astronomy, a feeble idea of this intelligence" (Laplace 2007:4).

Nor was it only in astronomy that such strict determinism reigned. "The curve described by a simple molecule of air or vapor," Laplace affirmed, "is regulated in a manner just as certain as the planetary orbit; the only difference between them is that which comes from our ignorance" (quoted in Harré 1967:392). And Laplace's statement of universal determinism has been considered the master formulation of it ever since. To be sure, human beings cannot know in detail all the factors and forces involved in every sublunar event, and it was precisely to deal with such situations that Laplace developed the theory of probability. He proposed to apply this branch of mathematics to cases in which only partial knowledge was available and only an approximation to exactitude could be attained.

Does Quantum Physics Undermine Laplace?

As long as classical physics reigned supreme, no one seriously challenged Laplace's presentation of the matter. However, when the field of atomic physics rose to prominence after 1900, things began to change. Bertrand Russell summarized the situation as follows. "According to quantum mechanics, it cannot be known what an atom will do in given circumstances; there are a definite set of alternatives open to it, and it chooses sometimes one, sometimes another. We know in what proportion of cases one choice will be made, in what proportion a second, or third, and so on. But we do not know any law determining the choice in an individual instance" (Russell 1997:152).

Again, the use of the word "choice" here seems ill advised, since only sentient beings can exercise choice, but otherwise this is a fair statement of the problem. This lack of assurance of how an atom will move was later (as we have seen) formalized by Werner Heisenberg as the uncertainty principle.

Theists—physicists and non-physicists alike—happily found in Heisenberg's uncertainy principle evidence of what they alleged to be the failure of determinism at both the atomic and subatomic levels. They interpreted this principle as denying that Laplace's supreme intelligence could predict the exact behavior of every particle of matter. And if it could not, they loudly proclaimed, that sounded the death knell for a universal determinism.

Had they thought the matter through, however, they would have realized that such a belief led them into theological quicksand. They might have asked themselves, for example, whether their God—whom they deemed omniscient—could make an exact prediction about an atom's behavior. And if he *could*, could then Laplace's proposed supreme intelligence not do the same? After all, Laplace attributed to this intelligence—by fiat—the same God-like powers that the founders of Christianity had attributed to *their* Deity.

And if to stymie Laplace, the theists affirmed that because of the uncertainty principle, *no one*—earthly or celestial—could make such a determination, then what happened to their God's omniscience? Thus, for a theist, jumping too eagerly on the indeterminacy bandwagon was fraught with peril.

Arguments Against Indeterminacy

Let us, however, put theology aside and pursue the argument on strictly scientific grounds. In the first place, as the philosopher Susan Stebbing noted, "It is unfortunate that this unpredictability [on the part of the electron] has often been expressed by saying that the electron is 'free to choose' where it will jump. Such language is wholly inappropriate and has led to much confusion in discussions concerning the bearing of recent developments in physics upon the problem of free will" (Stebbing 1958:178).

Now it should be pointed out that quantum physics is by no means entirely a black box of unknowns. It possesses, in fact, a number of discovered regularities. True, these regularities have come to be expressed in terms of *probabilities* rather than *certainties*, as was possible in classical physics. We can tell to the fraction of a minute when the moon will begin to obscure the face of the sun, but only with a certain degree of probability can we say that electron x will jump to orbit y.

The two sides of the argument—probability versus determinism—can be summarized as follows. The proponents of an overriding, ineluctable indeterminacy will say that the widespread use of probability in quantum physics is proof that causality is not a universal scientific principle, but breaks down at the subatomic level. In rebuttal, though, the determinist will argue that while it may be true "in principle" that we may never be able to devise an experiment that will *prove* determinism to hold at the subatomic level, this fails to prove that determinism *does not exist* at that level.

The issue revolves around this question: are the regularities manifested by large collections of atoms or electrons simply the aggregate behavior of masses of particles, about which nothing more can be said, or are these regularities the summation and expression of the regular behaviors of the *individual particles* that make up the aggregate, whether we can ascertain the behavior of each one of them or not?

It is theoretically impossible *for us* (as ordinary human beings) to simultaneously ascertain *both* the position *and* the velocity of an electron. The reason for this limitation is that the very act of observing an electron by "photographing" it—that is, by shooting a stream of photons at it—affects either its position or its velocity, or both. However, what if Laplace's supreme intelligence could observe an electron *without* interfering with it? Since by *stipulation* we can assign whatever capabilities we want to this hypothetical intelligence, why should *it* be bound by *our* limitations? Why couldn't it surmount or transcend them if we assign it that power? Why couldn't it be able to determine *both* the position *and* the velocity of an electron simultaneously? After all, Heisenberg's principle as formulated by him (contra Eddington) is the *uncertainty* principle, not the principle of *indeterminacy.*

Let us look more deeply into *why* we cannot know an electron's exact position and velocity at the same time. First, as formulated by the philosopher Susan Stebbing:

> [A]n electron must be illuminated if we wish to see where it is. But an electron has dimensions very much smaller than a light wave of the shortest visible light. Hence, in the sense in which one of the minute infusoria may be "seen" through a microscope, an electron cannot be seen. This "unseeability" of an electron is not the result of any defect in the construction of microscopes, which might "ideally"—to use Eddington's word—be overcome. It is the result of the corpuscular structure of light. Hence, it is not in principle remediable. It is obviously impossible to see a body that is smaller than the wave length of the light by which it is illuminated. (Stebbing 1958:179)

"But that is only the word of a philosopher," an indeterminist might quibble. "I would like to hear it from a more authoritative source." All right, then, let us listen to what the Nobel Prize winning physicist Steven Weinberg has to say on the subject.

> In order to make an accurate measurement of [an electron's] position it is necessary to use light of short wavelength.... But

> light of short wavelength consists of photons with correspond-
> ingly high momentum, and, when photons of high momentum
> are used to observe an electron, the electron necessarily recoils
> from the impact .... Thus the more accurately we try to measure
> the position of an electron, the less we know after the measure-
> ment about the electron's momentum. (Weinberg 1992:72–73)

To cite another authoritative observation, here is what Albert Einstein said in his analysis of the problem: "The indeterminism which belongs to quantum physics is a subjective indeterminism. It must be related to something, else indeterminism has no meaning, and here it is related to our own inability to follow the course of individual atoms [or electrons] and forecast their activities" (quoted in Planck 1981:202). And finally, to quote Weinberg again, "Even in quantum mechanics there is still a sense in which the behavior of any physical system is completely determined by its initial condi-tions and the laws of nature" (Weinberg 1992:37).

A brief but incisive summary of the uncertainty principle and its significance was given by the anthropologist Philip Bagby: "This is not, as some hopeful idealists have claimed, a statement about the fundamental character of elementary particles and therefore of nature, but a statement about the limitations of precise observation in the physical sciences" (Bagby 1959:60).

Further Arguments for Causation

We can give the problem another look ourselves by posing a ques-tion: is the indeterminist really ready to affirm that when an elec-tron jumps from one orbit to another, it does so absolutely sponta-neously ("freely") and that nothing whatsoever is acting on it to *make* it jump that way? Isn't it at least as plausible to say that—even though in theory we will never be able to discover what they are—nevertheless causal factors are at work here, impelling the electron to behave as it does? Doesn't it make more sense to suppose that causality is operating here, just as it is in the macroscopic world, but that it is doing so just below the threshold of detection? Or one can put the matter this way. If the law of causation has been found to hold in the case of all manner of phenomena of everyday experience, as well as in the movement of the stars and galaxies, are we really justified in jettisoning it when it is found to be—not absent, but simply not *demonstrable*—in one tiny, elusive, virtually inaccessible domain of nature?

We can approach the problem in still another way. When we toss a coin, we are uncertain as to which way it will land, heads or tails. But does this mean that the coin's fall is not strictly determined? Not at all. It is simply that ordinarily it is too difficult to know and take account of all the factors involved in determining the coin's fall for us to be able to predict in advance whether it will land heads or tails. Suppose, though, that we could *control* all the forces at work on each individual toss of the coin; could we then predict the outcome of each toss? The answer is that we could. In an experiment carried out in England with a specially built coin-tossing machine that imparted to every toss of a coin the same amount of force, in just the same way, the result in a trial experiment of one hundred tosses was ninety-eight heads and two tails. Then, after slightly adjusting a lever in the device, the experiment was repeated, and this time tails came up ninety-nine times and heads once (Horzelski 1945:111). Within the narrow margins of experimental error, this has all the earmarks of strict determinism!

Individual versus Aggregate Regularities

The matter can be looked at in the following way. We have a case where the *aggregate* behavior of certain events is known to be highly regular—enough so that we can say it is *determined*. Moreover, we know that the behavior of the *individual* events making up the aggregate is *likewise* determined. Clearly, then, the regularity of the aggregate's behavior *results from* the combined regularities of the individual behaviors that comprise it. Isn't it reasonable, therefore, to suppose that whenever we have a case of regular aggregate behavior, but where the individual behaviors that compose it cannot be tracked precisely, those individual behaviors *also* are determined?

Applying this argument to quantum mechanics, if in the aggregate electrons show a definite pattern in jumping from one orbit to another (as they do), may not individual jumps be the result of some underlying determinism? Bertrand Russell looked at the matter in a similar way: "I do not believe that there is any alchemy by which [the theory of probability] can produce regularity in large numbers out of pure caprice in each single case" (Russell 1997:160–161; for a similar argument, see Stebbing 1958:194). Or as Russell also held, "[W]e shall have to suppose that the statistical laws of atomic behavior are derivative from hitherto undiscovered laws of individual behavior" (Russell 1997:161). With the same expectation in mind, Russell had earlier said, "No one can deny that laws may [yet] be discovered which will show why an atom chooses one possibility on one occasion and another on another" (Russell 1997:153).

Free Will and Brain Function

At times the argument in favor of free will based on quantum uncertainties takes a more subtle form, running somewhat as follows. Even if one concedes that in some ultimate sense determinism reigns on the subatomic level, it is still impossible in practice to predict the exact pathway that any given elementary particle will take. Is it not entirely possible, then, that the random movement of atoms inside the human brain might—in their cascading effect—end up influencing a person's thought and conduct in some unpredictable way? And if so, does that not signal the demise of strict determinism of human affairs? Does it not, in fact, enthrone free will?

Not so fast, there! The determinist is ready to counter this argument in the following way. Even the smallest neurological structure of the human brain, the state of which channels one's thinking and behavior in one direction or another, is highly organized and extremely complex. Every neurological structure consists of countless numbers of molecules, each one composed of an even greater number of atoms. Each atom is thus but an extremely tiny part of the assemblage of organized particles that constitutes a neuron or a dendrite. The chances that the particular pathway a *single atom* (let alone a single electron!) happened to take would alter the overt behavior of an individual are therefore vanishingly small.

Just for a moment, though, let us play devil's advocate and concede that an atom's—or even an electron's—random movement *might* affect the choice that a person makes in a given situation.

What then? Is that what its proponents are ready to embrace as free will? To be sure, the likelihood of such an effect is next to nil, but let us suppose it to occur. And let us say that a supporter of the doctrine accepts this as an example of free will. If so, he has hoisted himself on his own petard! For what we are faced with here is *still* determinism! After all, this is not a case of *behavior without a cause.* It is simply that the cause—the determinant—of a person's behavior turns out to be, in this case, *the capricious movement of a single atom*! And just because something may be *capricious* in its action does not mean it is *undetermined*.

Would the apostle of free will really be satisfied with this finding? Who would be willing to say that in this case a person's true being, his unique personality, had exercised a free choice and was thus manifesting itself? In fact, it is quite the opposite. One's "personal" choice has here been, in effect, *abdicated*—turned over to something extraneous, even alien to his personality. The accidental movement of a tiny particle of matter inside the brain, operating at the quantum level and entirely independent of the psyche, the personality, has played a decisive role in directing behavior. Again I ask, is this state of affairs really something that proponents of "free will" are prepared to accept as exemplifying the freedom their philosophy dearly espouses?

Let us pursue this aspect of the problem a bit further. The Harvard physiologist George Wald once wrote, "All the processes I know of in living organisms are multimolecular. Usually they involve millions if not billions of molecules. Any process of that nature has a regularity that comes out of its statistics, a regularity that would disappear the moment that one went over from processes involving large numbers of molecules" to those involving one or just a few (Wald 1965:34).

Here, though, Wald is pursuing the argument up the wrong street. What he *should* have concluded is that since "undetermined" events occur only at the level of the electron or the single atom, and since the brain is organized into neurons and dendrites composed of *millions of molecules*, anything as insignificant as the jump of an electron from one orbit to another would be so infinitesimal an event in the total configuration of brain function that the chances of it affecting a person's choice, his "willing," are absurdly small.

Is Determinism Incompatible with Moral Responsibility?

Turning to yet another aspect of the problem, there is a practical—rather than a theoretical—argument that is sometimes raised against the reign of determinism in human affairs. It is this: what happens to moral responsibility and right conduct if the will is not free? The British philosopher Sir Isaiah Berlin worried that if "social determinism" is true, and "if we begin to take it seriously, then, indeed the changes ... in our notions, our attitudes toward one another, our views of history, of society and of everything else will be too profound to be even adumbrated. The concepts of praise and blame, innocence and guilt, and individual responsibility," which Berlin believes are the foundation of social morality, "would collapse or disappear" (Berlin 1954:75).

But Sir Isaiah's fears were groundless. An analysis of the issue makes it clear that the notion that right conduct depends on the will's being free is completely erroneous. I know of no better refutation of Berlin's argument than that put forward more than a century ago by the British historian George Grote, whose monumental *History of Greece* was one of the classics of nineteenth century scholarship.

> The very reason for giving notice that we intend to punish certain acts, and for inflicting punishment if the acts be committed, is that we trust in the efficacy of the threat and the punishment as deterring motives. If the volition of agents is not influenced by motives, the whole machinery of law becomes unavailing, and punishment a purposeless infliction of pain. In fact it is on that very ground that the madman is exempted from punishment; his volition being presumed to be not capable of being acted on by the deterring motive of legal sanction. The *free* agent, thus understood, is one who can neither feel himself accountable, nor be rendered accountable to or by others. It is only the necessary agent (the person whose volitions are determined by motives, ...) that can be held really accountable, can feel himself to be so. (quoted in Fiske 1903:I, 97)

Determinism and the Advance of Naturalism

The whole issue of determinism versus free will is a thread that runs deep through the controversy between naturalism and supernaturalism. Accordingly, it has cropped up again and again in the pages of this book. Here let me simply add that much as we may be impressed by the idiosyncratic and the unexpected that at times crop up in people's conduct, we are in fact surrounded by—and thus tend to take for granted—a degree of order and regularity in human behavior that simply would not exist but for the recurring, insistent, and systematic workings of cause and effect. As the psychologist B. F. Skinner summed it up, "[S]cience insists that action is initiated by forces impinging upon the individual, and that caprice is only another name for behavior for which we have not yet found a cause" (Skinner 1955–56:52–53).

The contrast between naturalism and supernaturalism is never more sharply highlighted than by the issue of determinism versus free will. The task of science is to explain things, to account for them. And accounting for something is finding that set of causal elements that brought it about, and to do so as simply and directly as possible without introducing complicating and unnecessary factors, such as hypothesized supernatural agents.

The philosophy of free will clearly eschews or renounces a rigorous and thoroughgoing attempt to account for human actions. For specific causal elements determining human behavior it substitutes a virtually inexpressible and unaccountable spontaneity, thus retaining the comforting illusion of untrammeled personal freedom. Despite the fact that adherents of the doctrine often try to make it appear to be a gift from God, ironically a belief in free will *abjures* the will of God—or of anything else—as a causal element in shaping human conduct. If we did what God wished, we would be acting *according to his dictates*—a far cry from exercising our own free choice. Proclaiming the freedom of the will is thus a *retreat* from both natural and supernatural causation into … nothing!

CHAPTER 21

The Doctrine of the Two Magesteria

One possible way to resolve the conflict between science and religion is to declare a truce between the two and divide the disputed territory between them. The main difficulty with this approach, of course, is to determine just where to place the dividing line and have both sides respect it. The most obvious problem here is that one side might declare the other guilty of claiming a larger share of the terrain than it is entitled to.

Leaving such difficulties aside for the moment, a recent proponent of this solution to the struggle between religion and science is the paleontologist Stephen Jay Gould. Gould saw the distinction to be drawn as one involving what he called "magesteria," a magesterium being—in theological language—a domain or realm. He proposed that we recognize two magesteria, one of science and the other of religion. In establishing a bipartite division between them, Gould specified the characteristics of each magesterium: "[T]he ... magesterium of science covers the empirical realm: what is the universe made of (fact) and why does it work this way (theory). The magesterium of religion extends over questions of ultimate meaning and moral value" (Gould 1999:6).

Furthermore, Gould proposed that these two magesteria should be "non-overlapping," that there should be a clear distinction between them with no disputed middle ground. He labeled this principle of divided territory "non-overlapping magesteria." To further define the difference between them, he seized upon a distinction first made by the philosopher David Hume between *is* and *ought*. Propositions about the nature of *reality* ("is") fall squarely within the domain of science, while propositions about the nature of *morality* ("ought") fall within the province of religion. In this way Gould sought to dispose of what he called "the mythical model of warfare between science and religion" (Gould 1999:123).

Enforcing the Dividing Line

As long as religion adheres to moral injunctions—"thou shalt's" and "thou shalt not's"—and remains securely within its designated province, Gould felt that it would be living up to its end of the bargain. It would provide a clear example of a magesterium that was not overstepping the boundary and thus not overlapping with its counterpart. And Gould seemed to offer himself as a fair and impartial arbiter between the two, remarking that "[i]f religion can no longer dictate the nature of factual conclusions residing properly with the magesterium of science, then scientists cannot claim higher insight into moral truth from any superior knowledge of the world's empirical constitution" (Gould 1999:9–10).

Being a scientist, Gould's chief concern was that persons speaking in the name of religion should not trespass on the domain of science (Gould 1999:5). In this way he hoped to end the long-standing war between the two—a war that had been declared in the nineteenth century by John William Draper in his famous work *History of the Conflict Between Religion and Science* (1874). Draper had asked, "Then has it in truth come to this, that Christianity and Science are recognized by their respective adherents as being absolutely incompatible; [that] they cannot exist together; [that] one must yield to the other; [that] mankind must make its choice—it cannot have both?" (quoted in Gould 1999:119). To these weighty questions, Draper's answer was a resounding yes, it has come to that. Gould, however, denied the necessity of such a conflict as Draper declared existed, and hoped by means of his proposed solution to bring it to an end.

Other Exponents of the Doctrine

To be sure, Gould was not the first to offer this resolution to the issue. One of his many predecessors in this regard was the philosopher Alfred North Whitehead. Writing in the early years of the twentieth century, Whitehead summarized the problem: "It seems as though, during the last half-century, the results of science and the beliefs of religion had come into a position of frank disagreement, from which there can be no escape, except by abandoning either the clear teaching of science, or the clear teaching of religion" (Whitehead 1963:206).

Whitehead, however, rejected such an irrevocable dichotomy, suggesting instead that "there are wider truths and finer perspectives within which a reconciliation of a deeper religion and a more subtle science will be found" (Whitehead 1963:210). The "finer perspective" to which he alluded turned out to be simply this: "Science is concerned with the general conditions which are observed to regulate physical phenomena, whereas religion is wholly wrapped up in the contemplation of moral and aesthetic values" (Whitehead 1963:210).

Many decades later another paleontologist, George Gaylord Simpson (at one time Gould's mentor), expressed much the same sentiment: "Speaking now for myself," said Simpson, "I see no excuse for warfare between religion and science. Each has its own sphere, and friction arises when either one is invaded by the other" (Simpson 1982:17). And elsewhere he also said, "I take it as now self-evident ... that evolution and true religion are compatible.... [T]he place and need for true religion are still very much with us" (Simpson 1949:5). He never did say, though, just what "true" religion is. Similarly, the biologist J. Arthur Thomson had written years earlier that "Science and Religion are incommensurable.... [T]here is [thus] no true antithesis between them" (Thomson 1911:192).

More recently the physicist Freeman Dyson likewise embraced the notion of non-overlapping magesteria. "Science and religion," said Dyson, "are two windows through which we can look at the world around us," adding that "[r]eligion and science can live harmoniously together in the human soul so long as each respects the other's autonomy" (Dyson 2004:4, 11).

It is not without significance that scientists who call for a formal partition between science and religion, and even a reconciliation of the two, are usually those who have had a religious upbringing and thus have an allegiance to both sides. Religion was (so to speak) something these scientists brought to the table, and thus they had a vested interest in seeing that it played a prominent role in the negotiations. On the other hand, it is rare to find a scientist with a secular upbringing arguing for the same kind of resolution. Thus the Nobel Prize winning physicist Richard Feynman said flatly, "I do believe there is a conflict between science and religion" (Feynman 1998:35).

Some theologians like Millar Burrows, professor of biblical theology at Yale Divinity School, also spoke in favor of recognizing two separate domains. "Theology and history [in this context, science]," he wrote, "are not inveterate foes, locked in a struggle from which only one of them can come out alive. They are two mutually supplementary ways of seeking truth, each with its own field and its own methods of inquiry" (Burrows 1958:44).

Difficulties in Gaining Adherence to the Doctrine

So much for general pronouncements in favor of non-overlapping magesteria. What about its implementation? First, how do practicing theists look at the matter? Remember Gould's contention that as long as ministers of the gospel stick to moral injunctions, science has no quarrel with them. But as soon as they enunciate factual propositions, they enter the realm of science, which is prepared to examine and reject any proposition that runs counter to how the world—looked at empirically—actually works.

Pronouncements from the pulpit about matters of morals and right conduct (says Gould) are assertions that science should be ready to concede to religion, since science is not in the business of telling people what to believe or how to behave. However, it is not so likely that denials of the existence of supernatural entities—for which science has found no evidence—will be accepted by ministers of God. After all, for them belief in supernatural beings capable of affecting (or even controlling) human affairs lies at the very core of religion. Would religious leaders, stripped by geologists and cosmologists of their creator God, who was no longer allowed to play any role in the origin and evolution of the earth and its creatures, be satisfied with that state of affairs? It seems most unlikely for, as Whitehead noted, "Every great religious teacher has revolted against the presentation of religion as a mere sanction of rules of conduct" (Whitehead 1963:217).

No, it seems more likely that those firmly in the camp of religion would push hard to move the dividing line to *increase* the size of their magesterium—or, at the very least, to keep it from shrinking. Some writers, ostensibly in the camp of science, even appear ready to grant more terrain to religion than would most of their scientific colleagues. The distinguished historian of science George Sarton, for example, firmly believed that "[t]here is no conflict between science and religion," and furthermore he was convinced that "[t]here shall never be a dearth of religion" since "science and religion complete one another, each helps to purify and exalt the other, each needs the other for its own perfection" (Sarton 1955:13, 12, 13). Since Sarton harbored the view that "[m]odern science is no longer antagonistic to religion," he felt comfortable in asserting, "We can believe in God" (Sarton 1955:11).

Sarton's pronouncements, however, sound suspiciously like the view to which Gould strenuously objected when he wrote, "This *syncretic* school continues to embrace the oldest fallacy of all as a central premise: the claim that science and religion should fuse to one big happy family, or rather one big pod of peas, where the facts of science reinforce and validate the precepts of religion, and where God shows his hand (and mind) in the workings of nature" (Gould 1999:212).

As anxious as Gould seems to have been to keep the two magesteria not only distinct but co-equal, at times he seems to come down strongly on the side of science. Thus at one point he argues that "the spectacular growth and success of science has turned the tables for modern versions of syncretism. Now the conclusions of science must be accepted a priori, and religious interpretations must be finessed and adjusted to match unimpeachable results from the magesterium of natural knowledge" (Gould 1999:213).

On the other hand, Gould also wrote, quite surprisingly, "The Big Bang happened, and we must now find God at this tumultuous origin" (Gould 1999:213). What Gould meant to say here was that if God is allowed to play any creative role at all, it would have to be moved from the time of biblical creation—as represented in the Book of Genesis—back fourteen billion years to the point at which the Big Bang started it all. Everything that happened in between would be securely accounted for by the solid naturalistic explanations of astronomers and astrophysicists, with no need for God's intervention.

Gould Professes Agnosticism

Yet if one is to take Gould's words at face value, he still retains the Deity as the cause of the tremendous inauguration of the physical universe. But does Gould really want to be in that position? After all, he does say that he is not a theist. "I am not a believer," he tells us, "I am an agnostic in the wise sense of T. H. Huxley, who coined the word in identifying such open-minded skepticism as the only rational position because, truly, one cannot know" (Gould 1999:8–9).

But one cannot know *what*? How agnostic can one really be without seeming indecisive? There is a very broad spectrum of nature about which we can claim—with complete confidence—a great deal of precise and positive knowledge. Yet Gould seems at times to align himself with a group of "agnostic scientists who welcome and celebrate the rapprochement" between religion and science, despite the fact that at other times he declares that this point of view "fills me with dismay" (Gould 1997:61). Once again he reaffirms that he is not "a believer or a religious man" but then proceeds to declare that religion has "always fascinated me" (Gould 1997:61). And then, growing a bit mawkish, he adds, "I believe with all my heart, in a respectful, even loving concordat between our magesteria" (Gould 1997:61).

Now, in assigning various beliefs to one magesterium or another, let us examine where Gould would place certain elements and see if these assignments can be reasonably sustained. Gould contends that moral questions of "ought" rightfully belong in the province of religion because, he asserts, they do not belong in the magesterium of science (Gould 1999:66). In fact, he seems to feel that in confronting such issues as the problem of immortality, science finds itself at a loss to take a decided position since, according to him, "in attempting to think of these questions, the human intellect flounders at once out of its depth"—a rather strange admission for a scientist of Gould's caliber to make (Gould 1999:41).

Anthropology Expands Science's Magesterium

Gould may be correct that the claims of religion cannot be analyzed by *his* magesterium (paleontology), but that does not mean that they cannot be analyzed by *mine* (anthropology). Each science has its own "magesterium" and anthropology, as it happens, feels quite competent to grapple with questions of religious beliefs.

The early chapters of this book showed how, for more than a century, anthropologists traced in extended and convincing detail how supernatural beliefs arose and were elaborated—first to include a great variety of bush spirits, and finally to create and embrace powerful and exalted gods. In point of fact, then, anthropologists have labored assiduously to trace the *natural* evolution of *supernatural* beings.

Moreover, anthropologists have also shown how "meaning" and "moral values" were not ideas implanted in the human mind by the Deity, but were worked out by primitive societies as each one strove to create and maintain a viable and enduring social system. Initially these social arrangements for the regulation and integration of society's members were essentially secular in nature. Only at later stages did they become overlaid with supernatural sanctions as rulers and priests (facing larger, more diverse, and more unruly populations) sought through the strictures of divine commandments to make social controls more stringent and effective.

We see, then, that scientists—especially social scientists—are ready to enlarge their magesterium at the expense of that which Gould and other traditionalists would assign to religion. Increaingly, the whole range of ideas entertained by the human mind (social scientists would argue) fall legitimately and fruitfully within their purview—into their *magesterium*. And here they are submitted to the most searching analysis.

The Clergy Resists Encroachment on Its Magesterium

But how will clergymen and theologians react to this invasion of "their" magesterium? Will they be ready to accept, for example, anthropology's contention that the soul is a purely human construct and not a divine implantation at all? Are they prepared to acknowledge that no space probe has ever found the slightest shred of evidence for the existence of something identifiable as heaven? And most challenging of all, will any minister of God accept anthropology's interpretation that Christianity was simply one particular manifestation of a general religious phenomenon—the rise of prophetic nativistic movements under conditions of political oppression?

In the nineteenth century, Cardinal John Henry Newman asserted that if the whole of existence were to be divided into two parts—two *magesteria*—science (which he called "Physical Theology") could in no way properly transgress onto the field of religion. Declared he, "What does Physical Theology tell us of duty and conscience? Of a particular providence and, coming at length to Christianity, what does it teach us … of … death, judgment, heaven and hell," the very essence of Christianity? No, he concluded, science "cannot tell us anything of Christianity" (quoted in Brooke 2003:204). And it would not be out of place here to add that the First Vatican Council (1869–70) proclaimed, "Let him be anathema … [w]ho shall say that no miracles can be wrought, or that they can never be known with certainty" (quoted in Gould 1999:119).

Most theologians would heartily concur with Newman's assertion and would be ready to defend at all cost what they consider to be their sacred ground. Thus Stephen Jay Gould's advocacy of an irenic scene of "non-overlapping magesteria" seems to me little more than a pious hope. When it comes to dividing up the things of heaven and earth, a peaceful accord between religion and science appears most unlikely. Indeed, a continued turf war, protracted and intense, seems inescapable.

The Shrinking Magesterium of Religion

But one thing is overwhelmingly evident. The battle lines in this great struggle have not remained static. Over the last four hundred years, there has been a dramatic, relentless, and irresistible shift in the size of the territory claimed by one of the magesteria. More and more areas of knowledge have been taken over by science and incorporated into its domain. Correspondingly, the sphere that religion has traditionally deemed its own has shrunk—as those theologians with a broader vision of the world have themselves acknowledged. Religious beliefs may seem to Gould to lie outside the range of scientific explanation, but if so that is *his* limitation, not a limitation of science … not of anthropology.

Religion as a human invention, as a cultural phenomenon, lies squarely within the realm of what anthropologists study and attempt to explain. The thrust of this volume has been to show that the inexorable march of human understanding has seen the diminution of the role played by the supernatural in accounting for the phenomena that surround us. Supernaturalism was once humanity's best—indeed virtually its only—way to explain what it experienced and could not readily comprehend. During the last few centuries, though, this view has yielded (if only grudgingly) to a robust and expanding philosophy of naturalism.

A few clear-eyed and strong-minded theologians have, on occasion, come to recognize the truth of this assertion. Regarding the biblical account of Eve, for example, the Reverend E. C. Mesenger—a scholar at the Catholic University of Louvain—conceded that "the narrative contains figurative elements." Then, putting the issue into broader perspective, he wrote that the Church's initial attempts to defend literal biblical accounts have "the appearance of a losing battle, and of rearguard action, in which successive positions are defended to the last, only to be abandoned under the pressure of necessity." And, Mesenger continued, "A different attitude is surely desirable" (quoted in Greene 1960:258–259). It seems almost superfluous to add that in this endeavor—that is to say, in bringing about the abandonment of discredited traditional beliefs—science is only too happy to assist.

CHAPTER 22

The Scientists Speak Up: The Theists

The battle between the believers and the non-believers continued into the twentieth century. And it was not only theologians and clergymen who were the strongest voices in the
camp of the believers. The former could marshal a substantial number of philosophers interested in science as well as a fair sprinkling
of scientists themselves. Some philosophers were ready to harness
the epistemology associated with science and put it to work in the
service of religion. Notable among them was William James, who
wrote, "Let empiricism once become associated with religion, as
hitherto, through some strange misunderstanding, it has been associated with irreligion, and I believe that a new era of religion as well
as of philosophy will be ready to begin" (James 1996:314).

The British physicist Sir Oliver Lodge, whom we have met several times before, took a different tack. While upholding the incon-
testability of the laws of physics, he still thought that *life* and *purpose* had brought a categorically new element into the equation: "I
will risk the assertion," he declared, "that Life introduces something
incalculable and purposeful amid the laws of physics; it thus distinctly supplements those laws, though it leaves them otherwise precisely as they were and obeys them all" (Lodge 1914:78–79).

The Pronouncements of Alfred North Whitehead

The distinguished philosopher Alfred North Whitehead saw religious
beliefs as far more than a happenstance in human history. He perceived
them as stemming from something deep within the human psyche as it
quested for a certifiable supernatural reality. "Religion," he wrote, "is
the reaction of human nature in its search for God" (Whitehead
1963:217). But beyond the mere identification of a God, there was to be

349

a prayerful subjugation to him, so that "[t]he immediate reaction of human nature to the religious vision is worship" (Whitehead 1963:218).

Whitehead went on to characterize religion, although in rather nebulous and equivocal terms, as being genuine and meriting pursuit—but at the same time, when all is said and done, elusive.

> Religion is the vision of something which stands beyond, behind, and within the passing flux of immediate things; something which is real, and yet waiting to be realized; something which is a remote possibility, and yet the greatest of present facts; something that gives meaning to all that passes, and yet eludes apprehension; something whose possession is the final good, and yet is beyond all reach; something which is the ultimate ideal, and the hopeless quest. (Whitehead 1963:218)

Well aware of the effect that scientific advances were having on religion, Whitehead—unlike many others who were uneasy at this effect—was convinced that science had redounded to the benefit of religion. Thus he held that "[t]he progress of science must result in the unceasing codification of religious thought, to the great advantage of religion" (Whitehead 1963:215).

Whitehead, though, was a purist and bridled at the pragmatic tendency to accord religion a proper place in society only for its instrumental value. Perhaps with William James's pragmatism in mind, he wrote, "The non-religious motive which has entered into modern religious thought is the desire for a comfortable organisation of modern society. Religion has been presented as valuable for the ordering of life. Its claims have been rested upon its function as a sanction to right conduct. Although the purpose of right conduct quickly degenerates into the formation of pleasing social relations." The result of all this, he thought, was "a subtle degradation of religious ideas" (Whitehead 1963:217).

The Astronomer-Idealists Jeans and Eddington

Next to be considered here are the "twin" British astronomer-physicists, Sir James Jeans and Sir Arthur Eddington, whom we have already encountered as staunch advocates of free will and idealism.

Although their professional work was concerned with physics, it is probably fair to say that their heart was more with *meta*physics.

Jeans, as we have seen, was an idealist who found the arguments put forward by Bishop Berkeley particularly appealing and persuasive. He quoted with approval Berkeley's assertion that the "bodies which compose the mighty frame of the world, have not any substance without the mind.... So long as they are not actually perceived by me, or do not exist in my mind, or that of any other created spirit, they must either have no existence at all, or else subsist in the mind of some Eternal Spirit" (Jeans 1947:171). And everyone knew, of course, who *that* was. Jeans went on to assert,"[W]e may think of the laws to which phenomena conform ... [as] the laws of nature, as the laws of thought of a universal mind," whose identity again could readily be guessed (Jeans 1947:175).

According to Jeans, the universe was basically thought, and since thought must exist in *some* mind, what better candidate for that distinction than the mind of God? Now in addition to being a physicist and an astronomer, Jeans was also a mathematician and believed that "the final truth about a phenomenon resides in the mathematical description of it" (Jeans 1947:176)—and not only its description, but its origin as well. After examining several other possibilities of cosmic origins, Jeans concluded, "[W]e have already considered with disfavour the possibility of the universe having been planned by a biologist or an engineer; [however] from the intrinsic evidence of his creation, the Great Architect of the Universe now begins to appear as a pure mathematician" (Jeans 1947:165). In her brilliant book *Philosophy and the Physicists*, Susan Stebbing remarked wryly of this supposition, "Jeans makes no effort to explain how it is that the Great Mathematician should have turned aside from his mathematical activities and condescended to create the world" (Stebbing 1958:27).

Although God may have been a celestial mathematician, Jeans could hardly have been expected to know just how he had gone about his work of creation since he had done so beyond where even the most gifted astronomer could observe him. As Jeans put it, "Primitive cosmologies pictured a creator working in space and time, forging sun, moon, and stars out of already existent raw material. Modern scientific theory compels us to think of the creator as working outside time and space" (Jeans 1947:182).

Sir Arthur Eddington expressed views rather similar to those of Jeans. His "Universal Mind or Logos" is not readily distinguishable from Jeans's "Eternal Spirit," although perhaps it was not quite so good at making calculations. The existence of this Universal Mind, thought Eddington, was "a fairly plausible inference from the present state of scientific theory" (quoted in Stebbing 1958:20). Here Eddington was referring to the quantum theory, which (as we have seen) had such a profound philosophical impact on physical science. In Eddington's words, "On the scientific side, a new situation has arisen. It is a consequence of the advent of the quantum theory that *physics is no longer pledged to a scheme of deterministic laws*" (quoted in Stebbing 1958:141). As we saw in Chapter 20, those scientists predisposed to a belief in free will—and thus theistically inclined—had always been uncomfortable with the strict determinism of classical physics, and eagerly seized on the challenge to determinism that quantum theory seemed to pose.

The American Physicists Robert Andrews Millikan and Irving Langmuir

Essentially similar views about science and religion were held by the American physicist Robert Andrews Millikan. Like Jeans and Eddington—although perhaps more orthodox and less veiled in his supernaturalism—Millikan was a theist who made his feelings quite clear: "Personally, I believe that essential religion is one of the world's supreme needs" (Millikan 1941:53). Indeed, he considered the world to be "incurably religious." Why? "Because everyone who reflects at all must have conceptions about the world which go beyond the field of science" (Millikan 1927:86). Nor did Millikan find any inconsistency between being a scientist and cleaving to religious beliefs. "The fact that the most outstanding scientists," he wrote, "have frequently been men who were identified with religious organizations constitutes at least presumptive evidence that there is no essential conflict between the two fields; indeed, it is definite proof that there is no conflict" (Millikan 1927:5).

As a result of this rapprochement between the two, Millikan contended, "Modern science, of the real sort, is slowly learning to

walk humbly with its God, and in learning that lesson it is contribut-
ing something to religion" (Millikan 1927:94–95). And how did
Millikan envision God? Through the advances in physical science,
most notably the formulation of the laws of gravitation and celestial
mechanics, *"mankind began to know a God not of caprice and
whim, such as were all the gods of the ancient world, but a God who
works through law"* (Millikan 1927:39). The idea that God rules
through law rather than caprice, Millikan declared, "has laid the
foundations for a new and stupendous advance in man's conception
of God, for a sublimer view of the world, and man's place and destiny in it" (Millikan 1941:44). "Stupendous" he might have labeled
it but "new" it hardly was, having been proposed—as we have
seen—by Jean Buridan seven hundred years earlier, and by many
others in the years that followed.

Prompted by the analogy that Millikan's conception of God
seemed to suggest, the anthropologist Leslie White remarked that
his portrayal of the Deity as a god of laws made him appear as "a
super-scientist working in his cosmic laboratory, his experiments to
perform" (White 1987:353).

Another noted American physicist of the time, Irving Langmuir,
saw in quantum physics (as did Jeans and Eddington) a welcome
way out of the iron grip of determinism. First he cited the championing of determinism by Laplace and repeated by André-Marie
Ampère, who held—as had his predecessor—that if a Super Intelligence "were given the positions and velocities of all the atoms
in the universe, it should be possible theoretically to determine the
whole future history of the universe" (Langmuir 1943:260). But
then, joining the chorus of so many other latter-day physicists,
Langmuir expressed the view that "[t]he net result of the modern
principles of physics has been to wipe out almost completely the
dogma of causation" (Langmuir 1943:267). As we saw in Chapter
20, however, not all physicists concur in that opinion.

Stephen Hawking and Freeman Dyson Express
Their Views

Next we turn to the views of Stephen Hawking, whose book *A Brief
History of Time* proved so enormously popular. On the question of

the existence and nature of God, however, one is not always sure just where Hawking stands. True enough, he did say in an oft-quoted passage:

> However, if we do discover a complete theory [of the universe], it should in time be understandable in broad principle by everyone, not just a few scientists. Then we shall all, philosophers, scientists, and just ordinary people, be able to take part in the discussion of the question of why it is that we and the universe exist. If we find the answer to that, it would be the ultimate triumph of human reason—for then we would know the mind of God. (Hawking 1998:191)

Hawking, though, likes to tantalize us regarding what he actually believes about God. He seems to flirt with—indeed almost to embrace—the idea of God's reality, but then appears to back away from it. Thus after saying that the laws of nature "do not tell us what the universe should have looked like when it started," since "it would still be up to God to wind up the clockwork and choose how to start it off," he proceeds to pose a different possibility: "So long as the universe had a beginning, we could suppose it had a creator. But if the universe is completely self-contained, having no boundary or edge, it would have neither beginning nor end: it would simply be. What place, then, for a creator?" (Hawking 1998:146).

But then again Hawking says, "At the big bang ... all the laws would have broken down, so God would still have had complete freedom to choose what happened and how the universe began" (Hawking 1998:189). In effect, then, for Hawking God would have constituted his own deus ex machina!

Dennis Brian has pointed out that Hawking might have been influenced in his way of conceptualizing God by reading Einstein's statement: "It would be perfectly consistent with all we know to say that there was a [Supreme] Being who was responsible for the laws of physics. However, I think it could be misleading to call such a Being 'God,' because this term is normally understood to have personal connotations which are not present in the laws of physics" (quoted in Brian 2005:193). Was Hawking using "God" in the very loose sense in which Einstein did, thus avoiding being labeled a theist in the conventional sense? In the next chapter, we shall see how Einstein himself dealt with this issue.

Freeman Dyson is another contemporary physicist who, seeing no conflict between religion and science, is quite comfortable embracing them both. "[S]peaking as a physicist," he tells us, "scientific materialism and religious transcendentalism are neither incompatible nor mutually exclusive. We have learned that nature is weird stuff. It is weird enough, so that it does not limit God's freedom to make it do what he pleases" (Dyson 2004:8). Yet despite his use of the term, Dyson's views could hardly be called "religious transcendentalism" when he tells us that while "[m]any first-rate scientists are Christians, Moslems, Buddhists, or Jews" and "many are Marxists … [or] militant atheists," still "many are like me, loosely attached to Christian beliefs by birth and habit but not committed to any particular dogma" (Dyson 2004:5). One wonders, though, if the Transcendentalists of yesteryear would have been willing to admit Dyson into their midst as one of theirs.

The Biologists Have Their Say: Miller, Ayala, and Collins

We have just examined the views of a few physicists who are believers of one stripe or another. Now let us consider some biologists who, while definitely siding with evolution against creationism, nevertheless hold explicit religious convictions. First we can cite J. Arthur Thomson, who stated unequivocally that "there can be no radical antithesis between the scientific description of Man as the outcome of a process of natural evolution and the religious interpretation of Man as the Child of God" (Thomson 1925:238).

More recently Kenneth Miller, a staunch Darwinist, affirmed that "Darwin lifted the curtain that allowed us to see the world as it really is. And to any person of faith, this should mean that Charles Darwin ultimately brought us closer to an understanding of God." "What kind of God do I believe in?" he then asked, and replied that "[t]he answer is in the words" to be found in the last sentence of *The Origin of Species*, in which Darwin refers to those early organisms into which life was "breathed by the Creator." "I believe in Darwin's God," Miller concludes (Miller 1999:286). Miller was thus evidently unaware of Darwin's 1863 letter to Joseph Hooker in which he regretted having used the word "Creator" in this passage and confessed that by doing so he had knuckled under to orthodox opinion!

Another evolutionary biologist who deserves mention here is Francisco Ayala. Ayala is a good example of a scientist who concurs with Stephen Jay Gould's idea that by adopting the notion of "non-overlapping magesteria," science and religion can be assigned to separate and distinct compartments, the traditional competition between them thus being avoided. That at least seems to be the conclusion to be drawn from Ayala's assertion that "scientific conclusions and religious beliefs concern different sorts of issues, belong to different realms of knowledge, [and thus] they do not stand in contradiction" (Ayala 2007:175). Accordingly, he thinks it "possible to believe that God created the world while also accepting that the planets, mountains, plants, and animals came about, after the initial creation, by natural processes" (Ayala 2007:175).

Once again Ayala echoes Gould since he argues that "[s]cientific knowledge cannot contradict religious belief, because science has nothing definitive to say for or against religious inspiration, religious realities, or religious values," and that "[m]atters of value and meaning are outside science's scope" (Ayala, 2007:175, 178). In accepting Gould's assertion in this regard, it is probably not irrelevant to point out that before becoming a professional biologist, Ayala was a Jesuit priest.

Another biologist—the noted paleontologist George Gaylord Simpson (1902–1984)—also a stalwart champion of evolution, was nonetheless somewhat equivocal on the possible role of God in the creation of things. "Surely the world we live in is full of mystery," he wrote. "We do not know how or by what it was created. Scientific study can neither deny or affirm a concept of creation by a literally ineffable someone or something, nor can a scientist object to calling the creator god, uncapitalized and undescribable" (Simpson 1982: 17).

Francis Collins, a geneticist who for a time headed the Human Genome Project, tells us that initially he was a non-believer. However, "[i]n my early teens I had had occasional moments of the experience of longing for something outside myself.... Nevertheless, my sense of the spiritual was very undeveloped" (Collins 2006:15). Reflecting back upon his beliefs, however, he came to realize that—although he was unfamiliar with the term at that time—he was actually an agnostic. But then his views about religion and God underwent a further transformation, his "conversion" coming about in the following way.

> There are all kinds of agnostics; some arrive at this position after intense analysis of the evidence, but many others simply find it to be a comfortable position that allows them to avoid considering arguments they find discomforting on either side. I was definitely in the latter category. (Collins 2006:15–16)

Then, going more deeply into why he abandoned his agnosticism and became a believer, Collins remarks in his book *The Language of God*:

> It ... became clear to me that science, despite its unquestioned powers in unraveling the mysteries of the natural world, would get me no further in resolving the question of God. If God exists, then he must be outside the natural world, and therefore the tools of science are not the right ones to learn about Him. Instead, ... the evidence of God's existence would have to come from other directions, and the ultimate decision would be based on faith, not proof. (Collins 2006:30)

This is a very illuminating statement. Collins tells us—in effect—that he discovered that empiricism, the method of arriving at scientific knowledge he had used so successfully in gaining positive knowledge of one particular realm of nature, failed to yield any knowledge of God. God simply lay beyond anything that could be empirically ascertained. Collins was therefore forced to lay aside science, to go *outside* of science to *faith*, which does not require the standards of proof that are necessary for science. Only then was he able to find anything that he could identify as God.

It is instructive to note the contrast between Collins and other scientists who are believers. The latter often say that it was by probing deeply into the interstices of nature that they were led to find God at the very core. Collins, however, makes no such claim; indeed, he denies it. Not until he had set aside the canons of evidence that he required in pursuing his science of genetics was he able to discover God.

Robert Hazen Repeats an Old Argument

Finally, another recent biological scientist may be cited who, while maintaining his belief in God, took the now-familiar position that his God was one who had created all things and assigned them their laws but had henceforth allowed them to operate on their own— finding it unnecessary to intercede in their natural unfolding. I refer to Robert Hazen, professor of earth sciences at George Mason University, who in his recent book *Genesis: The Scientific Quest for Life's Origin* wrote as follows.

> Isn't it more satisfying to believe in a God who created the whole shebang from the outset—a God of natural laws who stepped back and doesn't meddle in our affairs? In the beginning God set the entire magnificent fabric of the universe into motion. Atoms and stars and cells and consciousness emerged inexorably, as did the intellect to discover laws of nature through a natural process of self-awareness and discovery. In such a universe, scientific study provides a glimpse of creator as well as creation. (Hazen 2005:80)

How familiar this litany has now become!

It is time now to end this recitation and try to interpret the remarks of those scientists quoted above who unhesitatingly identify themselves as theists. Does their status as scientists add weight to their contention that God exists? Does the acceptance of religion become more validated and justified thereby? Not in my estimation. Susan Stebbing spoke cogently when she said, "Every scientist turned philosopher tends to find support in his special studies for the metaphysical theory which *on other grounds* he finds attractive" (Stebbing 1958:283).

Exactly! Before becoming physicists, Jeans and Eddington and others like them had lived a good two decades, during which they had imbibed and embraced a view of the universe not of their own making. Nevertheless it was one that went a long way toward molding their thinking about the large questions of existence, and which endured into their mature years. (For a similar argument, see Stebbing 1958:283.)

We have seen that Freeman Dyson was "loosely attached to Christian beliefs by birth and habit," and Robert Millikan once remarked, "I have myself belonged to two churches" (Millikan 1941:53). Kenneth Miller, a Roman Catholic, spoke of taking communion as a boy and Francisco Ayala was a Jesuit priest. Would it surprise anyone if similar upbringings and allegiances were to be found in the backgrounds of other scientists who proclaim themselves theists? One cannot, then, count as solid evidence for the existence of God that a scientist—even a distinguished one—should continue to cling to the faith of his formative years.

CHAPTER 23

The Scientists Speak Up:
The Non-Theists

It is time to consider the views of those modern-day scientists who either denied the existence of God outright, or at least leaned in that direction. Their pronouncements thus tend to serve as a counterpoise to those of the theists whom we have just cited.

Ernst Mach

We begin with the Austrian physicist and philosopher Ernst Mach (1838–1916), one of the founders of the logical positivist movement who saw it "as an antidote to the metaphysics of Immanuel Kant" (Weinberg 1992:175). Mach was a super-empiricist. Nothing that did not come directly or indirectly through the senses—including God—could be granted the status of actually existing. For him "the world consists only of our sensations" (quoted in Alexander 1967:116). But though this philosophical stance debarred God from being real, it also debarred atoms! Even after the existence of atoms was generally accepted by physicists, Mach and his followers "regarded this as a departure from the proper procedure of science because these atoms could not be observed with any technique that was imaginable" (Weinberg 1992:176). Indeed, as Steven Weinberg noted, "Mach himself never made his peace with the existence of atoms. As late as 1910, after atomism had been accepted by nearly everyone else, Mach wrote in a running debate with Planck that 'if belief in the reality of atoms is so crucial, then I renounce the physical way of thinking. I will not be a professional physicist, and I hand back my scientific reputation'" (Weinberg 1992:177).

Mach's view that "all the basic concepts of mechanics must ultimately be derived from, and related to, sense experience"

(Alexander 1967:116) was an empiricism pushed to the limit—a philosophy sometimes called "sensationalism"—and it laid him open, according to Lenin and other Marxists, to the charge of idealism, thus making him (in their view) an enemy of materialism. Materialism, they insisted, placed its emphasis on the existence of an external world rather than on *observations* of that world.

Empiricism—the way of looking at the world that led directly to materialism—had been given clear and forceful expression by Baron d'Holbach, who argued that nothing could be accepted as factual that could not be perceived through the senses. And Mach chose to emphasize empiricism as the only source of genuine knowledge. True enough. But the materialists argued that this emphasis on empiricism posed the danger of sliding back into idealism. After all (the materialists affirmed), sense impressions were impressions of *something*. And that "something" existed independently of, and prior to, its being perceived. Thus, it was claimed, one was more justified in considering the perceived object as more fundamental—more "real" in some sense—than the mechanics of perceiving it. As Max Planck noted, "[W]e do not construct the external world to suit our own ends in the pursuit of science, but that *vice versa* the external world forces itself upon our recognition with its own elemental power," adding that this "is a point which ought to be categorically asserted again and again in these positivistic times" (Planck 1981:198).

Max Planck

Having introduced Planck into our discussion, let us examine his views in more detail, since they are particularly revealing in that they are not all of a piece. Max Planck (1858–1947), though raised in the tradition of classical physics, nevertheless lived well into the era of quantum mechanics. Indeed, he contributed significantly to its development. *Planck's constant* is, in fact, an extremely important number that figures in a variety of quantum calculations.

We need to consider where Planck stood in relation to the principle of causation. He was well aware that this principle was being called into question in the 1920s and 1930s. "Some ... physicists declare categorically," he said, "that the development of the quantum theory has led to the overthrow of the principle of causation as an axiom in scientific research" (Planck 1981:29). Here he was thinking particularly of men like James Jeans and Arthur Eddington, the latter having stated categorically that "so far as we have yet gone in our probing of the material universe, we find no evidence of determinism" (quoted in Stebbing 1958:188).

But Planck was not ready to accept this conclusion. In his book *Where Is Physics Going?* (1933), he repeatedly declared his allegiance to strict causation, stating his conviction that "natural phenomena invariably occur according to the rigid sequence of cause and effect" (Planck 1981:107) and affirming that "I have not been able to find the slightest reason, up to now, which would force us to give up the assumption of a strictly law-governed universe" (Planck 1981:100).

In fact, Planck declared, "[S]cientific thought is identical with causal thought, so much so that the last goal of every science is the full and complete application of the causal principle to the object of research" (Planck 1981:158). But, one may ask, what about statistical laws, expressed in terms of probabilities? "In point of fact," Planck held, "statistical laws are dependent upon the assumption of the strict law of causality functioning in each particular case" (Planck 1981:145). Consequently, "in studying the happenings of nature, we strive to eliminate the contingent and accidental and to come finally to what is essential and necessary" (Planck 1981:198). In the face of challenges to this point of view from some quantum physicists, he remained optimistic: "I firmly believe, in company with most physicists, that the quantum hypothesis will eventually find its exact expression in certain equations which will be a more exact formulation of the law of causality" (Planck 1981:143).

Thus Max Planck showed himself a champion of determinism— *in physics*. But a curious reversion happened when he came to discuss causation *in human affairs*. The determinism that he seemed to espouse so staunchly in the physical world suddenly disintegrated! Accordingly, we find him asserting that "the freedom of the ego here and now, and its independence of the causal chain, is a truth that comes from the immediate dictate of the human consciousness" (Planck 1981:163). Then, indicating just where this idea had come from, Planck went on to argue, "The law of causation is the guiding rule of science; but the Categorical Imperative—that is to say, the dictate of duty—is the guiding rule of life" (Planck 1981:167).

So! Here was the old German idealism, as embodied in Immanuel Kant's "categorical imperative," insinuating itself into the mind of an empirical physicist. As we saw in Chapter 20, while quite ready to espouse determinism in the realm of *phenomena*, Kant denied it when it came to *noumena*, the elusive abode of immaterial entities like the mind. Here strict causation no longer held and freedom reigned. But there was a substantial contradiction in this. At the same time that the categorical imperative was thought to exist in the domain of the *noumena*, it was nonetheless said to be an innate moral sense of obligation that impelled people to behave properly here and now. It was this traditional Prussian "dictate of duty" that Planck, like a good German, accepted and embraced.

What Planck failed to grasp—as Kant had failed to before him—was that "the dictate of duty," no matter what realm it was assigned to, was *still* determinism. The only difference was that it could best be seen as operating on a different level—the *cultural* level—in which it had originated and out of which it had become embedded in the human psyche. Thus to its greater effect it seemed for all the world not to be an external constraint, but to be acting from within.

This supposed exception to the law of causation opened the way, in Planck's view, for religion to assert itself as independent of science and therefore in no way subordinate to it. As he explained:

> Religion belongs to that realm that is inviolable before the law of causation and therefore closed to science. The scientist as such must recognize the value of religion as such, no matter what may be its form, so long as it does not make the mistake of opposing its own dogmas to the fundamental law upon which scientific research is based, namely the sequence of cause and effect in all external phenomena. (Planck 1981:168)

Planck expounded further on the alleged inviolability of religion in the face of science: "There can never be any real opposition between religion and science; for the one is the complement of the other. Every serious and reflective person realizes, I think, that the religious element in his nature must be recognized and cultivated if all the powers of the human soul are to act together in perfect balance and harmony" (Planck 1981:168–169).

What can we make of Planck's attempt to isolate religion and thus maintain its invulnerability from assault by science? It seems to me that this is yet another case of a scientist standing squarely behind the approaches, discoveries, and conclusions of science *as long as* he is dealing strictly with phenomena within his field of study. But as soon as Planck leaves the realm of science and moves into the field of religion, a field in which he has no special knowledge or qualification and one heavily charged with its own set of beliefs and values, he forsakes his scientific standing and finds himself a mere layman. Here, then, his views are no more authoritative than those of the common man.

Albert Einstein

Next among the scientists whose views on religion we propose to examine is Albert Einstein. Without question the most famous scientist of the twentieth century, Einstein was repeatedly asked to give his views about God and religion. He often spoke on the subject, and because of his prestige, those who were theistically inclined hopefully searched his every word for evidence indicating that the great man could be included in their ranks. Accordingly, they eagerly embraced such statements as "I maintain that the cosmic religious feeling is the strongest and noblest motive for scientific research" and, again, "A contemporary has said, not unjustly, that in this materialistic age of ours the serious scientific workers are the only profoundly religious people" (Einstein 1954:49).

Contemplating the grandeur and mystery of the cosmos, Einstein observed, "To sense that behind anything that can be experienced there is something that our mind cannot grasp and whose beauty and sublimity reaches us only indirectly and as a feeble reflection, that is religiousness. In this sense I am religious" (quoted in Brian 2005:183). And once, when asked directly if he was deeply religious, Einstein replied, "Yes, you can call it that. Try and penetrate with our limited means the secrets of nature and you will find that, behind all the discernable concatenations, there remains something subtle, intangible and inexplicable. Veneration for this force beyond anything we can comprehend is my religion. To that extent I am, in point of fact, religious" (quoted in Brian 2005:178).

Elaborating on this view, Einstein declared that

> whoever has undergone the intense experience of successful advances made in this domain [science], is moved by profound reverence for the rationality made manifest in existence. By way of the understanding he achieves in far-reaching emancipation from the shackles of personal hopes and desires, and thereby attains that humble attitude of mind towards the grandeur of reason incarnate in existence, and which, in its profoundest depths, is inaccessible to man. This attitude, however, appears to me to be religious, in the highest sense of the word. And so it seems to me that science not only purifies the religious impulse of the dross of its anthropomorphism but also contributes to a religious spiritualization of our understanding of life. (Einstein 1993:27)

But Einstein took pains to make clear that his conception of "religion" was not at all what a Christian or a Jew took religion to be. When a rabbi who was preparing a lecture on the religious implications of the theory of relativity wrote to Einstein in 1939 asking him some questions on the subject, Einstein answered, "The religious feeling engendered by experiencing the logical comprehensibility of profound interrelations is of a somewhat different sort from the feeling that one usually calls religious. It is more a feeling of awe at the scheme that is manifested in the material universe. It does not lead us to take the step of fashioning a god-like being in our own image—a personage who makes demands of us and who takes an interest in us as individuals" (quoted in Dukas and Hoffmann 1979:69–70).

An anthropomorphic God was a concept that Einstein never found believable. Therefore "[t]he idea of a personal God," he wrote, "is quite alien to me and seems even naïve" (quoted in Calaprice 2000:217). And the notion of life after death seemed equally unacceptable. "I do not believe in immortality of the individual," he affirmed (quoted in Dukas and Hoffman 1979:39). Elaborating on this opinion, he wrote, "Neither can I believe that the individual survives the death of his body, although feeble souls harbor such thoughts through fear or ridiculous egotism" (quoted in Seldes 1996:134).

Similarly, Einstein felt that human conduct was not a sphere for divine involvement, saying, "I cannot imagine a God who rewards and punishes the object of his creation, whose purposes are modeled after our own—a God, in short, who is but a reflection of human frailty" (quoted in Seldes 1996:134). Ethics he thus considered to be "an exclusively human concern with no supernatural authority behind it" (quoted in Dukas and Hoffman 1979:39).

Indeed, Einstein resented being portrayed as a believer in the conventional sense. In 1954, responding to a correspondent who had read about his supposed theological pronouncements, Einstein replied, "It was, of course, a lie what you read about my religious convictions, a lie which is being systematically repeated. I do not believe in a personal God and I have never denied this but have expressed it clearly. If something is in me which can be called religious then it is the unbounded admiration for the structure of the world so far as our science can reveal it" (quoted in Dukas and Hoffmann 1979:43)

When it came to specifying those attributes that he thought a God would have and in which he could believe, Einstein found it easier to say what attributes he would *not* have. His "cosmic religion," Einstein said, "can give rise to no definite notion of a God and no theology" (Einstein 1954:48). "I cannot imagine," he remarked, "a God who rewards and punishes the objects of his creation, whose purposes are modelled after our own—a God, in short, who is but a reflection of human frailty" (Einstein 1940:72). Expanding on this point and speaking apparently of the Paleolithic—when the chief sources of human apprehension were such things as hunger, wild beasts, sickness, and death—Einstein said, "Since at this stage of existence understanding of causal connections is usually poorly developed, the human mind creates illusory beings more or less analogous to himself on whose wills and actions these fearful happenings depend" (Einstein 1954:46). In this manner does Einstein account for the anthropomorphic deities of the Judeo-Christian and other religions. As one of his biographers put it, "Whenever he [Einstein] said or wrote 'God,' he never meant a supernatural being who reigned in heaven, took interest in the fate of mankind, and answered prayers" (Brian 2005:173).

Einstein made it clear that his commitment to science and its tenets made it impossible for him to entertain a belief in a capricious, willful God: "The man who is thoroughly convinced of the universal operation of the law of causation cannot for a moment entertain the idea of a being who interferes in the course of events.... A God who rewards and punishes is inconceivable to him" (Einstein 1954:48).

When he spoke of his allegiance to science rather than God, Einstein was on more familiar and more secure ground. "The more a man is imbued with the ordered regularity of all events the firmer becomes his conviction that there is no room left by the side of this ordered regularity for causes of a different nature. For him neither the rule of human nor the rule of divine will exist as an independent cause of natural events" (Einstein 1954:56–57). And if Einstein had any "faith" at all, it was "faith in the possibility that the regulations valid for the world of existence are rational, that is, comprehensible to reason. I cannot conceive of a genuine scientist without that profound faith" (Einstein 1993:24).

The orderliness and regularity that Einstein sought and found in the universe that he studied was predicated on a belief in the operation of a cosmic determinism. "[T]he scientist is possessed," he said, "by the sense of universal causation. The future, to him, is every whit as necessary and determined as the past" (Einstein 1954:50). This staunchly held belief brought him into conflict with the subatomic physics that was coming to dominate physical science in the 1920s and 1930s. Heisenberg spoke of "Einstein's refusal to accept the statistical character of the new quantum mechanics" (Heisenberg 1972:104). He was, Stebbing observed, "desperately seeking to find some way of reintroducing a completely deterministic scheme of law into modern physics" (Stebbing 1958:210). His most famous remark about the situation, so often quoted, was couched wryly in religious terms: "I shall never believe that God plays dice with the universe." And he likewise opposed the inclination of not a few quantum physicists to transfer the supposed indeterminacy of electrons to the will in human behavior, declaring, "I do not at all believe in human freedom in the philosophical sense. Everybody acts not only under external compulsion but also in accordance with inner necessity" (quoted in Morris 1984:77).

Julian Huxley

Let us turn now to the views of other scientists who found no basis in science for accepting the premises of traditional religion, beginning with the biologist Julian Huxley. Like his grandfather Thomas Henry Huxley, Julian was an evolutionary biologist; and like him as well, Julian was hostile toward organized religion. However, the younger Huxley sought to salvage the term "religion" in some sterilized and secular sense by entitling one of his books *Religion Without Revelation* (1957). Despite the title, in its pages traditional religion—as well as God himself—took a severe pummeling. Explaining the book's title, Huxley wrote, "I have called this book *Religion Without Revelation* in order to express at the outset my conviction that religion of the highest and fullest character can co-exist with a complete absence of belief in revelation" (Huxley 1957:13).

Referring to the long-standing conflict between religion and science, Huxley characterized it as "between two dominant types of cultural entity—the god hypothesis organised on the basis of mythical thinking, and the naturalistic hypothesis, organised on the basis of scientific method" (1957:58). Huxley made it clear that in this competition he stood fully behind naturalism. And he left no doubt that the principal aim of the naturalism he espoused was "to expel gods from positions of effective control, from direct operative contact with more and more aspects of nature, to push them into an ever further remoteness behind or beyond phenomena" (Huxley 1957:58).

In his attitude toward God, Julian Huxley was more inclined than his grandfather to question the Deity's very existence. "A personal God, be he Jehovah, or Allah, or Apollo, or Amen-Ra, or without name but simply God, I *know* nothing of. What is more, I am not merely agnostic on the subject. It seems to me quite clear that the idea of personality in God or in any supernatural being or beings has been put there by man" (Huxley 1957:18). And indeed, in his contribution to the volume *I Believe*—which contains the personal testaments of two dozen famous persons—Huxley stated flatly, "I do not believe in the existence of a god or gods" (Huxley 1940:133).

And why it was that man created God he readily explained as follows: "Gods, like scientific hypotheses, are attempts to understand the cosmos and explain or at least interpret the facts of experience"

(Huxley 1957:52–53). Thus gods "are … unscientific in essence, and in the long run anti-scientific in their effects" (Huxley 1957:53).

Huxley was convinced that "[t]he time is ripe for the dethronement of gods from their dominant position in our interpretation of destiny, in favour of a naturalistic type of belief system. The supernatural is being swept out of the universe in the flood of new knowledge of what is natural" (Huxley 1957:62). Sanguine in this belief, Huxley was ready to assert that "God is beginning to resemble not a ruler, but the last fading smile of a cosmic Cheshire Cat" (Huxley 1957:59).

Rather than simply dismissing him out of hand and giving him no further thought, however, Huxley believed that God should be made the subject of scientific scrutiny, like any other cultural phenomenon. "Gods are among the empirical facts of cultural history. Like other empirical facts, they can be investigated by the method of science—dispassionate observation and analysis" about their origin and evolution (Huxley 1957:49).

So far Huxley's book must be judged a forthright statement of a thoroughgoing naturalism by a distinguished biologist. But as so often happens, we find—inexplicably mixed in with the naturalism—a kernel or two of something that is jarringly discordant with everything else in the book. Thus Huxley says, "As to the existence of another world or another life at all, there I am simply agnostic: I do not know"—although he does admit, "I find extreme difficulties, in the light of physiological and psychological knowledge, in understanding how a soul could exist apart from a body" (Huxley 1957: 18). Not "extreme difficulties" in understanding how a soul *could exist at all*, mind you, but only how it could exist "apart from a body"!

And finally, Huxley tells us, "[T]here is the so-called evidence for spiritualism. I have seen some of this, and read a good deal on the subject; there seems to be a good *prima facie* case for the existence of such 'super-normal' phenomena as clairvoyance and telepathy" (Huxley 1957:19). What satisfaction this observation would have given Alfred Russel Wallace after having been ridiculed by Julian's grandfather on this very subject! We can leave this statement by the younger Huxley without further comment, merely with a bewildered shaking of the head.

But it would be unfair to Julian Huxley to leave him so deflated. Rather, let us remember him as having stated categorically, "History shows an increasingly successful extension of the naturalistic approach to more and more fields of experience, coupled with a progressive failure and restriction of supernaturalistic interpretation" (Huxley 1957:51).

Hudson Hoagland, Richard Feynman, and Steven Weinberg

We turn next to the chemist Hudson Hoagland, who maintained that "[t]he scientist cannot accept supernatural revelation as a way to knowledge" (Hoagland 1960:21). Indeed, Hoagland could hardly accept the claims of theists that religion provided them with a means of discovering the truth because, he said, "naturalistic interpretations of religious phenomena in anthropological and psychological terms preclude for many of us the type of faith enjoyed by others" (Hoagland 1960:20).

Developing this view more fully, Hoagland wrote:

> As a result of experiences with the elusiveness of truth in limited fields in which much is known and where technics are highly developed, the scientist is skeptical of conclusions arrived at by methods devoid of control and independent of his criteria of evidence. Thus logical proofs of the existence of a beneficent personal God are to most scientists meaningless because they cannot accept the assumptions upon which the logic operates. The historical bases of divine revelation are devoid of the evidential qualities essential for observation. (Hoagland 1960:19)

Accordingly, Hoagland was led to this observation: "It seems probable that, for better or for worse, agnosticism may increase in the future rather than diminish. If this is so, a frank facing of the situation is in order" (Hoagland 1960:24).

The Nobel Prize winning physicist Richard Feynman (1918–1988) was much interested in the question of the existence of God, as he was in many other things. But unlike so many of his colleagues—Freeman Dyson, for example—he did not try to reconcile religion and science and did not try to harmonize the two under the overarching tent of Stephen Jay Gould's Two Magisteria, but declared without equivocation, "I do believe that there is a conflict between science and religion" (Feynman 1998:35). And although he noted that "I know many scientists who believe in God," he nevertheless affirmed that "more than half of the scientists do not believe in their father's God, or in God in a conventional sense" (Feynman 1998:35).

Feynman seemed to dispute the argument, sometimes raised in favor of religion, that having religious convictions made people more moral. On this score he said of his "atheistic scientific colleagues," with whom he was "on the same side," that he did not think they were "particularly different from the religious ones" (Feynman 1998:46). He thus felt that "moral feelings ... apply to the believers as well as the disbelievers" (Feynman 1998:40–41).

Turning to another Nobel Prize winning physicist, Steven Weinberg, let us see where he stands in confronting questions of God and religion. It is clear that Weinberg is far from wishing to call in God when dealing with the major issues of physics. Thus he says, "It seems to me to be a profoundly important discovery that we can get very far in explaining the world without invoking divine intervention" (Weinberg 1992:248). Of the compassionate, caring God who many believers think runs the universe, Weinberg finds no trace. He agrees that "it is hardly possible not to wonder whether we will find any answer to our deepest questions" in "the workings of an interested God" but concludes, "I think that we will not." And he buttresses this conclusion by saying, "All our experience throughout the history of science has tended in the opposite direction, toward a chilling impersonality in the laws of nature" (Weinberg 1992:245).

Weinberg takes note of the fact that persons who at all costs are intent on clinging to the concept of—or even just the term—"God" broaden the definition to embrace virtually every manifestation of the cosmos. He dismisses this attempt, though, by saying, "Scientists and others sometimes used the word 'God' to mean something so abstract and unengaged that He is hardly to be distinguished from the laws of nature" (Weinberg 1992:244–245). Clearly Weinberg has little sympathy with those who advocate a kind of super-pantheism: "One hears it said that 'God is the ultimate' or ...

'God is the universe.' Of course, like any other word, the word 'God' can be given any meaning we like. If you want to say that 'God is energy' then you can find God in a lump of coal" (Weinberg 1992:244).

Finally, Weinberg rejects Stephen Jay Gould's proposed harmonious reconciliation of religion and science under the broad tent of the Two Magisteria. Realistically—and ironically—he says it is the true theist who is most likely to reject it: "On most things," he wrote, "I tend to agree with Gould, but here I think he goes too far; the meaning of religion is defined by what religious people actually believe, and the great majority of the world's religious people would be surprised to learn that religion has nothing to do with factual reality" (Weinberg 1992:249).

The Biologists Speak Again

To end this catalog of opinions by scientists on the issue of God and the supernatural, I would like to quote again from the biologists. J. B. S. Haldane disagreed sharply with his illustrious father when he asserted, "There is no supernatural, and nothing metaphysical. Our minds are real, but there was matter before there was mind" (Haldane 1940:111). And Francis Crick summarized the views of most of his colleagues when he wrote, "[T]he remarkable thing about Western civilization, looked at in the broad sense, is that while the residue of many of these [religious] beliefs are still held by many people, most modern scientists do not subscribe to any of them" (Crick 1981:163).

And if this is the view of most biologists, it is even more the prevailing opinion of anthropologists—who, tracing the whole history of supernatural beliefs from their very beginnings to the present day, are in the best position of all scientists to understand how such beliefs arose and how they came to be what they are.

CHAPTER 24

Trends in Belief to the End of the Nineteenth Century

In the preceding chapters, we surveyed the kinds of answers given over the course of untold centuries to the questions that arose in inquisitive minds as they strove to comprehend the world around them. At first these answers were couched largely in terms of the actions of spirit beings who were thought to be much like humans themselves. These spirits differed primarily in being endowed with greater power, which they exercised largely in a malevolent way. The spirits also differed—and this was a critical distinction—in being undetectable to the senses.

Only in the last two thousand years or so have human beings begun to understand the actual workings of nature. A way of thinking emerged that permitted a new interpretation of the external world. This new way was the method of *science*. It embodied not only causal thinking—already inherited from our Paleolithic forebears—but added to it an insistence on *verification,* the checking of hypotheses against empirical observations. This method of thinking, and the ways of acting that it entailed, proved extraordinarily successful. It yielded answers that were demonstrably superior to those that people had previously accepted without question. Slowly but steadily science began to supplant the reigning philosophy: *naturalism* began to displace *supernaturalism.*

The two systems of thought, being in many ways opposites, became competitors. Since the answers that they provided were often contradictory, they could not both be true. And so the two theories clashed. A struggle between them ensued that continues to this day, coloring the whole history of thought. The pages of this book are in large measure a catalog of these struggles—struggles that have been intense and prolonged. The tide of battle, though at times swinging back and forth, has moved predominantly—and overall inexorably—in one direction.

The advance of science has thus been checkered. Individuals who have made singular contributions to it have at the same time often retained a stubborn allegiance to ideas that preceded science and ran counter to it. Anomalous as this might seem, it is in fact the normal way in which scientific advance has proceeded. Forward movement has often been accompanied by a resolute clinging to the old ways. Still, looked at broadly, naturalism has continued to make steady inroads into the domain that once was the sole possession of the supernatural.

In this chapter I propose to follow the course of this trajectory during the nineteenth century. Although it was in the seventeenth century that scientific discoveries and inventions had their first great impact on Western thought, it was the nineteenth century that saw the most profound and dramatic changes take place. But rather than trying to survey an entire array of thinkers of this period, two men may be singled out as representing or reflecting the cross-currents that were sweeping over the intellectual landscape during the nineteenth century. These men were John Stuart Mill and William James.

The Religious Views of John Stuart Mill

Mill had been given a thoroughly secular upbringing by his father, the Scottish economist and philosopher James Mill, who already had grave misgivings about traditional Christian teachings. The younger Mill said of his father that "[h]e found it impossible to believe that a world so full of evil was the work of an Author combining infinite power with perfect goodness and righteousness" (Mill 2007:54). And the elder Mill imparted to his son the same skeptical view of religion toward which he himself had been gravitating. "I am thus one of the very few examples, in this country," Mill wrote in his *Autobiography*, "of one who has not thrown off religious belief, but never had it: I grew up in a negative state with regard to it" (Mill 2007:59).

It should not be assumed, however, that Mill had never contemplated religious questions. He had. But he found traditional Christian answers to such questions wanting in logic and explanatory power. For example, he reasoned that "the question, 'Who made me?' cannot be answered, because … any answer only throws the difficulty a step further back, since the question immediately presents itself, Who made God?" (Mill 2007:58).

Looking back over the course of his life, Mill later reflected on "[t]he great advance in liberty of discussion, which is one of the most important differences between the present time and that of my childhood" (Mill 2007:60). In this observation Mill was not alone. Charles Darwin was struck by the same trend, noting in his own *Autobiography* that "[n]othing is more remarkable than the spread of skepticism or rationalism during the latter half of my life" (Darwin 1958b:79).

Though this opinion was generally a muted one, a few bold individuals dared to express it openly. Francis Galton, for example, "could declare that science was a valid alternative to all forms of religion" (Browne 2002:250). And George Romanes, after having given up his Roman Catholicism, remarked that "[t]here can no longer be any more doubt that the existence of God is wholly unnecessary to explain any of the phenomena of the universe" (Romanes 1878:64).

But again such opinions were not, as a rule, public utterances. For the most part, they were expressed guardedly and privately, leading Mill to observe, "The world would be astonished if it knew how great a proportion of its brightest ornaments—of those most distinguished even in popular estimation for wisdom and virtue—are complete skeptics in religion" (Mill 2007:62).

Nonetheless, as we saw in Chapter 11, while Mill demanded that his God be a strictly law-abiding deity—no longer dealing in the kinds of miracles that once had awed and humbled primitive Christians—he was still unable to free himself from a belief in God altogether. The universe, he felt, needed an Author, a Creator, and only a God such as the omnipotent one envisioned by the Bible—and not some set of cold and impersonal natural forces—seemed to him up to the task.

Yet to anyone capable of looking closely, the handwriting was on the wall. Even dedicated theists did not shrink from admitting the trend and warning their listeners against it. Henry Sidgwick, professor of philosophy at Cambridge (whom we met before as a staunch opponent of Darwinian evolution), declared, "I feel convinced that

English religious society is going through a great crisis now. And it will probably become impossible soon to conceal from anybody the extent to which rationalist views are held and the extent of their deviation from traditional [Christian] opinions" (quoted in Blum 2006:40).

Still, not every true believer considered the trend to be so obvious or so ominous. The liberal Christian scholar Friederich Max Müller was actually optimistic about it. Said he, "[T]he history of religion ... has been shown to exhibit a constant growth and development, its very life consisting in a discarding of decayed elements, which is necessary in order to maintain all the better whatever is still sound and vigorous" (Max Müller 1879:248).

Nevertheless the nineteenth century was best exemplified by the relentless march of science in the face of opposition by organized religion. Even those questions that to the most progressive minds seemed beyond the capacity of science to resolve, ultimately proved not to be so intractable after all. The renowned British physicist John Tyndall told the story of the Emperor Napoleon, who one night—during his campaign in Egypt—turned to the scientists who had accompanied him, pointed to the stars so crisply visible in the desert sky, and asked, "Who, gentlemen, made all these?" "That question," Tyndall declared, "still remains unanswered, and science makes no attempt to answer it" (quoted in Edwards 1967a:185). The fact is, of course, that we now know a great deal about how the stars were formed. Indeed, the spectacular advance made in cosmogony during the twentieth century ranks as one of the greatest intellectual triumphs in the history of thought.

The Religious Ambivalence of William James

At the point where the nineteenth century turns into the twentieth, it might be well to pause and assess the status of religious belief among the leading intellectuals of the day. And as indicated earlier, William James may be taken as holding—in some rough way—the various metaphysical beliefs that were then jostling each other for acceptance. James lived in a period during which science was flexing its muscles. Indeed, it was riding the crest of an enormous popularity based mostly on the triumph of evolution, but also on the impressive advances being made in the field of physical science. And in several of his pronouncements, James actually struck hammer blows for the cause of science in opposition to the soft-edged tenets of established religion. In his essay "The Will to Believe" (1897), he wrote:

> When one turns to the magnificent edifice of the physical sciences, and sees how it was reared; what thousands of disinterested moral lives of men lie buried in its mere foundations; ... wrought into its very stones and mortar; how absolutely impersonal it stands in its vast augustness,—then how besotted and contemptible seems every little sentimentalist who comes blowing voluntary smoke-wreaths, and pretending to decide things from out of his private dream! Can we wonder if those bred in the rugged and manly school of science should feel like spewing such subjectivism out of their mouths? (quoted in Thomson 1911:215–216).

While James recognized that a man might be a scientist and at the same time hold close to his heart supernatural beliefs, he was firm in his conviction that science itself could not be legitimately used to bolster religion. As he put it, "Though the scientist may individually nourish a religion, and be a theist in his irresponsible hours, the days are over when it could be said that for Science herself the heavens declare the glory of God and the firmament showeth his handiwork" (James 1994:534–535).

To be sure, none of this meant that James himself had forsaken God. Far from it. However, although at times he called himself a Christian, James nonetheless harbored a rather un-Christian conception of the Deity. For one thing he insisted that his God had to be a God in modern garb, tailored to the demands of science. As with John Stuart Mill and the deists before him, James's God had limited powers and exercised them sparingly and with restraint: "The God whom science recognizes must be a God of universal laws exclusively," he affirmed (James 1994:536–537).

But lawful and orderly as God's universe might be, there were regions of it that James felt were still impalpable and mysterious and lay outside the realm of empirical understanding. In the shadowy corners of this universe, he made room for the spiritualist will-o'-the-wisp that he so fruitlessly pursued for some twenty years. Justifying his infatuation with the inexplicable, he wrote that "[a] man's religious faith (whatever more special items of doctrine it may involve) means for me essentially his faith in the existence of an unseen order of some kind in which the riddles of the natural order may be found explained" (James 1992:495). Amorphous and elusive as it might be, for James this obscure region of the cosmos was nonetheless real. And he staunchly held that there was "no philosophical excuse for calling the unseen or mystical world unreal. God is the natural appellation, for us Christians at least, for the supreme reality, so I will call this higher part of the universe by the name of God" (James 1994:561). However, he regarded this readiness in himself to find divinity in the cosmos as something more deeply rooted than simply the result of a searching intelligence. Thus he wrote, "I only translate into schematic language what I may call the instinctive belief of mankind: God is real" (James 1994:561).

In *The Varieties of Religious Experience*, James had written that for him God is a God "who cannot accommodate his processes to the convenience of individuals" (1994:536–537). Yet this statement put him squarely at odds with the God of his fully developed pragmatism. According to this latter view, "[T]hat which produces effects within another reality must be termed a reality itself." Then on the next page he reaffirmed, "God is real since he produces real effects" (James 1994:560, 561). Finally, giving full play to his pragmatic philosophy, James wrote, "We cannot reject any hypothesis if consequences useful to life flow from it" (quoted in Russell 1945:817). Applying this point of view to matters of religion, James asserted boldly, "On pragmatic principles, if the hypothesis of God works satisfactorily in the widest sense of the word, it is true" (quoted in Blum 2006:308). It would appear presumptuous, then, for God to assume that the faithful would continue to believe in him simply as a matter of course. In line with James's pragmatic demands, God would have to demonstrate and justify his claim to existence by repeatedly performing useful acts. Thus it was clear that if these pragmatic requirements were strictly enforced, God would have to continuously prove himself a friend and helper to mankind.

It is perhaps worth noting here that in matters of religious belief, James's pragmatism may almost be said to be a direct descendant of the views of Voltaire. As we have seen, Voltaire looked at belief in God in a very practical light. Initially he believed that God was *necessary*, his existence being required to account for the origin of the world and all it contained. Later, though, he changed the basis of his belief. God now was seen as *useful,* providing welcome solace and support to the believing masses. It would appear, then, that if God were prepared at least to be useful, James (like Voltaire) was perfectly willing to accept his reality—whatever empirically minded thinkers might say to the contrary.

Like many other high intellects of his day, James was an amalgam of naturalism and supernaturalism. By and large naturalism predominated in his general outlook, but now and then, here and there, supernaturalism obtruded itself through the crevices in his thinking.

Galton's Survey of English Scientists

We have just had a kaleidoscopic look at the shifting views of God and religion of one man, William James. It would be enlightening, though, to have a broader picture of what the leading lights of the late nineteenth century thought about religious issues. And as it happens, in the 1870s Francis Galton—whose well-known study *Hereditary Genius* (1869) had just appeared—undertook a somewhat similar study, probing the lives, careers, and beliefs of the leading British scientists of the day.

Describing this study, which was published as *English Men of Science* (1874), Galton wrote, "My data are the autobiographical replies to a very long series of printed questions addressed severally to ... 180 men," questions that among other things inquired about their religious beliefs (Galton 1874:16). Curiously enough, Galton failed to ask his subjects directly whether they believed in God. Nevertheless, after tabulating the replies to his questions, he was able to present a wide spectrum view of the religious beliefs that these men entertained.

Most of the men in Galton's study, it would seem, were theists. Summing up his findings, he noted, "It appears that out of every ten scientific men, seven call themselves members of the established Churches of England, Scotland, and ... Ireland" (Galton 1874:126).

In spite of the religious affiliations of most of them, Galton felt confident in asserting of English scientists in general that, being "exacting of evidence and questioners of authority, they sturdily object to much that others accept easily" (Galton 1874:127).

Still and all, many of these scientists spoke openly of their allegiance to religion, one of them offering the view that "there is no real antagonism between revealed religion and the study of nature" (quoted in Galton 1874:136). Another put it more emphatically: "I have no more doubt about the plenary inspiration of Scripture than I have about the simplest axioms of mathematics" (quoted in Galton 1974:131).

One believer, though, admitted that his faith had been hard won. "The most pernicious influence to which I was subjected," he recalled, "was that arising from J. Stuart Mill. It took me a long time to work through the sensationalist empirical philosophy, and to come out at the other side" (quoted in Galton 1874:139).

Another scientist had had just the opposite experience, having to overcome the early influence of religion. "I lay to early theological teaching," he said, "so much hindrance in the quest of the most precious of our possessions—truth" (quoted in Galton 1874:141). One respondent, however, reported a much easier path to non-belief. Said he, "I gave up common religious belief, almost independently from my own reflection" (quoted in Galton 1874:130).

Finally one British scientist, using words reminiscent of those employed by John Stuart Mill in a passage quoted earlier, serenely proclaimed, "I was not taught creed or dogma, and had therefore the great advantage of not having to fight my way out of darkness into light" (quoted in Galton 1874:137).

Leuba's Survey of American Scientists

To the best of my knowledge, no similar survey of religious opinions was attempted for another forty years. Then in 1916 James Leuba, professor of psychology at Bryn Mawr College, conducted a careful study of the religious beliefs of American scientists. The study was based on a sample of one thousand scientists selected at random from the fields of physical science, biological science, sociology, and psychology. The individuals included in the survey were in turn subdivided into two categories, the greater scientists and the lesser ones—their placement into one or the other of these categories being determined by their professional colleagues.

In summary form the results of Leuba's survey were as follows. For all scientists taken together, adding "doubters" and "agnostics" to those who categorically denied belief in God, 58.2 percent of American scientists were non-believers (Leuba 1916:250). When the religious views of the greater and lesser scientists were compared, the comparison showed that 68.4 percent of the greater scientists did not believe in God, as opposed to 51.8 percent of the lesser scientists, who were likewise non-believers (Leuba 1916:250).

Leuba also compared the degree of belief found among the four kinds of scientists included in his sample. The results showed that biologists were less likely than physical scientists to believe in God, while sociologists (and psychologists) believed in God even less. This difference, it seemed to Leuba, was significant enough to call for an explanation, and he offered the following one.

> When the student of physical laws has come to accept determinism in the physical world, he may and often does keep for the less generally understood biological and sociological phenomena the traditional belief in divine intervention. The biologist and the sociologist, however, better acquainted with the natural causes of these phenomena than their brothers in the physical sciences, find it just as impossible to admit God's action in the biological and sociological domains as in the physical. (Leuba 1916:265)

This explanation brings to mind one offered by Leslie White in accounting for the order in which the various sciences had arisen historically. According to White, in what he phrased almost as a law, "*Science emerges first and matures fastest in fields where the determinants of human behavior are weakest and most remote; conversely, science appears latest and matures slowest in those portions of our experience where the most intimate and powerful determinants of our behavior are found*" (White 2005:69).

Although in certain respect these two interpretations are at odds with each other, the underlying thesis of both provides the basis for formulating still another generalization: social scientists, being more aware of how supernatural ideas arose in the human mind, are less likely to believe that they were put there by divine implantation. Physical scientists, on the other hand, whose professional concern is not with supernatural ideas and how they arose, are corresponding- ly less likely to see these ideas for what they are—purely human inventions. At the same time, greater scientists, generally having a fuller and deeper understanding of all domains of nature than their lesser colleagues, are less inclined to view any phenomenon as depending for its existence on the actions of supernatural beings.

But let us return once more to William James. At one point James engaged in correspondence with James Leuba regarding the basis of one's religious ideas. Having been asked by Leuba to explain the basis of his own belief in God, James replied, "Call this, if you like, my mystical *germ*. It creates the rank and file of the believers. As it withstands in my case, so it will withstand in most cases, all purely atheistic criticism" (quoted in Dennett 2006:84).

Curiously enough, with that statement James seemed to antici- pate a position proposed a century later (which we will examine in the last chapter) that there might be something like a *genetic basis*—indeed, even a "God gene"—predisposing human beings to believe in a deity. But whether such a belief was merely a *projection* emanating from within the human mind, or whether it was a *recog- nition* of an entity actually existing in the external world, as far as James and countless millions were concerned, God was still a pres- ence to be reckoned with.

CHAPTER 25

Secularism and Religion Continue to Compete

So much for the nineteenth century. The twentieth century saw a continuation of the struggle between science and religion for dominance in the realm of great ideas. The conflict was perhaps not as bitter as in the preceding century. The strict believers, however, remained as entrenched in their views and as dogmatic in their assertion of them. For example, in a 1904 address to his congregation, the Bishop of Newport (England) declared that "[i]f the formulas of modern science contradict the science of Catholic dogma, it is the former that have to be altered, not the latter" (quoted in Lodge 1905:68–69).

Needless to say, few clergymen today—or even then—would speak in such uncompromising terms. To a large extent, religion had been forced to reconcile itself to science and accommodate itself to scientific findings—not the other way around. Speaking to this point, Bertrand Russell affirmed that "[s]uccessive scientific discoveries have caused Christians to abandon one after another of the beliefs which the Middle Ages regarded as integral parts of their faith" (Russell 1997:172). The sea change in human thinking that began in astronomy took place in other sciences as well. "We have seen," added Russell, "that, in the period since Copernicus, whenever science and theology have disagreed, science has proved victorious" (Russell 1997:244). And in the face of a steady series of reverses, the upholders of religion began to adopt new strategies in an effort to bolster their Christian doctrines against the claims of an emboldened secularism. Instead of trying to defend every fortified position it once held, "religion, by surrendering the outworks [as, for example, a belief in the strict historicity of Adam and Eve] has sought to preserve the citadel intact" (Russell 1997:17). These successive theological retreats have meant that the struggle between science and religion has narrowed in scope and abated in intensity.

The one area where vigorous open combat between naturalism and supernaturalism has continued to this day is over the issue of evolution versus special creation. To be sure, many Christians (including most notably the Pope!) have come to terms with evolution, accepting its reality. But there remains a staunch core of believers who refuse to accept evolution and who continue to fight it relentlessly. For instance, in an interview with *Newsweek* magazine editor Jon Meacham entitled "The God Debate," Rick Warren—pastor of Saddleback Church in California, the fourth largest congregation in the United States—said at one point, "If you're asking me do I believe in evolution, the answer is no, I believe that God, at a moment, created man" (Meacham 2007:60).

Not only has creation versus evolution been the subject of endless harangues from the pulpit, it has led to protracted litigation—beginning in 1925 with the famous Scopes trial in Dayton, Tennessee. Although the forces of creationism technically won that case, they have lost a significant number of subsequent ones. Despite their best efforts, creationists have been unable to prevent evolution from being taught in public schools throughout the country. In view of these reverses, creationists started to copy the ways of science, seeking "equal time" in the schools for the teaching of what they presented to school boards as "creation science."

Intelligent Design

However, having suffered a series of legal defeats in trying to pass off "creation science" as science, creationists decided to try a different tack. They dusted off the venerable "argument from design" and attempted to have it pass muster as genuine science.

The argument from design is familiar to anyone acquainted with the eighteenth century theologian William Paley (1743–1805), especially with his last book *Moral Theology* (1802). However, the argument did not originate with Paley, having been advanced as early as 1691 by the naturalist John Ray. Nonetheless it was Paley who elaborated it and with whom it is most closely associated.

By the time Paley was writing, the day had passed when the Bible and divine revelation were enough to satisfy searching minds about the existence of God. Belief in him had to be buttressed with a series of arguments. And Paley strove to provide the argument from design as being a powerful one. The familiar example he chose to present was that of finding a watch on the ground and wondering how it came to be. How do we know, he asked, that the watch did not just happen to exist like, say, a stone? His answer was "what we discover ... [is] that its several parts are framed and put together for a purpose" (quoted in Sprague 1967:20)—that purpose being, of course, to tell time. And the capacity to envision and create a mechanism that would carry out that purpose (Paley held) required the active participation of an "intelligent designer," in this case the watchmaker.

Transferring this analogy to the relationship between man and God, Paley began by saying that "[f]or my part I take my stand on human anatomy" (quoted in Unsigned 1911d:629), elaborating the argument as follows: "The bones and muscles of human beings, the fitting together of joints and the adaptation of muscles are mechanisms which imply most forcefully a designing intelligence" (Sprague 1967:20). And no one needed to be told that the "designing intelligence" in this case could be none other than God.

Modern-day creationists appropriated this argument, but in order for it to circumvent the legal challenge that it was clearly a religious doctrine, they carefully tried to conceal the identity of the intelligent designer. They simply presented "intelligent design" as proving that an impersonal and purposeless process like natural selection simply could not account for the finely wrought and purpose-driven mechanism that is man. Something above and beyond an unthinking, lifeless process, they insisted, was required for human beings to have arisen from the dust of the earth.

The creationists, as already mentioned, were careful not to identify this purposive force with "God" in order to avoid giving their argument the clear stamp of "religion." Had this association between "intelligent design" and the Christian God been admitted, it would clearly have been illegal to propose teaching this doctrine in public schools, running afoul of the constitutional ban on mixing church and state. Still and all, it was obvious to anyone but a dolt that only God had the power and purpose to be that unnamed designer. Hence when the argument was brought to trial in the case of Katzmiller versus the Dover (Pennsylvania) School Board, presiding judge John E. Jones III had little trouble seeing through the subterfuge. In a 169-page decision, he ruled that Intelligent Design—an obvious form of creationism—was not science at all but a religious doctrine masquerading as science. Any attempt, therefore, to teach it in a public school would violate the law and thus would be prohibited.

In this landmark case, the law found on the side of science. But the decision cannot be considered as settling the issue once and for all. After all, there are other jurisdictions in which a similar case might be brought. And had the presiding judge been of a different mindset, the outcome might well have been different. Though in the Dover case the opponents of evolution suffered a major setback, they did not give up the struggle. They continue to wage the war, quietly planning new strategies and tactics to use in contesting the issue.

It is interesting to note in passing that the Roman Catholic Church, commonly thought to adhere to the most conservative theological principles in Christendom, actually *accepts* organic evolution. The Catholic historian of philosophy Frederick Copleston, for example, wrote that "[e]ven those who question the sufficiency of the evidence to prove the evolution of the human body from some other species [and Copleston makes it clear he is not one of them] commonly recognize that the first chapters of *Genesis* were not intended to solve scientific problems, and that the matter is one which has to be settled according to the available empirical evidence" (Copleston 1967:123–124).

The most convincing evidence of the modern-day Catholic Church's acceptance of evolution is to be found in the radical change that over the course of time has taken place in papal pronouncements on the subject. As we saw in Chapter 13, Pius IX— shortly after the appearance of Darwin's theory of evolution— declared it to be "repugnant at once to history, to the tradition of all people, to exact science, to observed facts, and even to Reason herself" (quoted in White 1899:I, 75n). But almost a century later, Pope Pius XII affirmed the Church's acceptance of evolution

(Gould 1999:80). Then John Paul II, in an address to the Pontifical Academy of Science on October 22, 1996, declared that the Bible was not to be regarded as a scientific document, but rather as a collection of religious teachings. He pointed out that "[n]ew scientific knowledge has led us to realize that the theory of evolution is no longer a mere hypothesis. It is indeed remarkable that this theory has been progressively accepted by researchers, following a series of discoveries in various fields of knowledge" (quoted in Ayala 2007:164–165).

Catholic doctrine today will countenance the physical evolution of the body, but holds that man became fully human *only* after God had implanted within him his immortal soul (Gould 1999:80). In this regard it would be illuminating to ask a Catholic theologian—or better still, the Pope himself—in which hominid species God chose to implant the first soul: *Australopithecus afarensis?* ... *Homo habilis?* ... *Homo erectus?* ... or not until *Homo sapiens?*

The Anthropic Principle

I mentioned earlier that creationists and other strict believers in God are quietly planning a new approach in their struggles with science. Given the ever-growing robustness of scientific explanations of cosmic phenomena, certain theists have been led to adopt subtler and more sophisticated arguments to justify their beliefs. The old appeals to faith, revelation, and Scripture having lost a substantial amount of their former potency, newer arguments have had to be devised. The latest one—although it too, like intelligent design, is actually centuries old—is the so-called *anthropic principle*. Even though it is not the sort of doctrine that simple creationists have readily seized upon, the anthropic principle is one to which certain theists have recently turned to support their beliefs. Basically, the argument is this: since giving rise to the human species was undoubtedly God's culminating accomplishment, all the prerequisites for it were carefully put in place by him beforehand as he strove to achieve his ultimate end.

Unfurled under its new name in 1973 by the cosmologist Brandon Carter (Shotwell 2003:47), the anthropic principle came to have a variety of different meanings. Some of them have at least a semblance to being quasi-scientific. One of them, though—easily the most prominent and certainly the one most germane to our discussion—is decidedly teleological, and as such basically religious.

Reduced to its essentials, the anthropic principle amounts to this. It took very special conditions for intelligent life, specifically human beings, to be able to arise in the universe. But intelligent life *did* arise and therefore the universe must have been designed in such a way as to make this *possible*—and not only to make it possible, but to actually have it *happen*. A more formal way of stating the argument is to say "How can the universe possibly have given rise to the unique and exquisite combination of physical conditions it had to have for human life to evolve, except for the existence of some great cosmic power which had the emergence of human life in mind as its goal from the very start?" (Stenger 2003:43).

Stripping away the disguise with which the argument is carefully clothed, Stephen Jay Gould summarized the anthropic principle succinctly—and skeptically—when he wrote, "Since human life couldn't exist if the laws of nature were even a tad different, then the laws must be as they are because a creating God desired our presence" (Gould 1999:219).

Clearly, then, the underlying premise of the anthropic principle is that the universe developed as it did *in order that* conditions should be produced permitting the human race to arise. The principle thus embodies the premise that it was *intended*—in some cosmic sense—for the universe to give rise to mankind. Now *intention*, as we have argued before, is a manifestation of *purpose*. And purpose is a function only of highly organized nervous tissue. But what hard evidence is there that such nervous tissue existed in the universe until human beings appeared on the scene? And only someone with a decidedly religious cast of mind could believe that *intent* and *purpose* were to be found in the universe apart from and prior to the arrival of the hominid species. Thus if the anthropic principle (in the form just described) was first proposed by a scientist, it must have been one seeking to bolster his religious conviction that man's emergence was part of God's plan.

Despite the cogency of the above argument against the anthropic principle, several prominent scientists have openly embraced it. The geneticist Francis Collins, for instance, has claimed that "for those willing to consider a theistic perspective [as he is], the Anthropic Principle certainly provides an interesting argument in favor of a Creator" (Collins 2006:78). And not only does he suggest that others might adopt it, he is quite ready to do so himself. Accordingly, he says, "There is only one universe, and this is it. The precise tuning of all the physical constants and physical laws to make intelligent life possible is not an accident, but reflects the action of the one who created the universe in the first place" (Collins 2006:76).

Most surprising of all (in my estimation) is to find the renowned astrophysicist Stephen Hawking expressing the view that "it would be very difficult to explain why the universe would have begun in just this way except as the act of a God who intended to create beings like us" (quoted in Keller 2008:130).

However, to those not already committed to a belief in God, the anthropic principle—well before it had been dignified with an impressive-sounding name—had proved unconvincing. In his book *Force and Matter* (1855), the German physicist Ludwig Büchner scoffed at the idea underlying the principle, arguing that

> [i]f, as must be assumed according to the teleological idea of the world, a personal creative power, guided by definite aims, meant to create worlds as dwelling places for intelligent thinking beings worshipping his omnipotence, why should there be these huge, vacant and useless tracts of space, in which but here and there isolated suns and earths swim as almost imperceptible dots ...?
> (Büchner 1891:110)

Another perspective on the issue was that of Charles Darwin. Having read somewhere the claim that the day's length had been fixed by God to provide enough sleeping time for man, Darwin wrote in his notebook, "[L]ength of days adapted to duration of sleep of man!!! Whole universe so adapted!!! and not man to Planets—instance of arrogance!!!" (quoted in Graber 2006:14). Victor Scheffer, a modern-day biologist, put it this way: "To say that the universe was created to engender life is like saying that a marine snail was created that its empty shell might shelter a hermit crab" (Scheffer 2000:43).

Mark Twain, always ready to deflate human pretensions, used his short story "Was the World Made for Man?" as an instrument to lampoon the anthropic principle. Many animals, he said, from the pterodactyl to the oyster ("the most conceited animal there is, except man"), were convinced that everything preceding their appearance on earth was meticulously calculated to ensure their arrival.

The anthropic principle, then, as Darwin and Twain clearly saw, is a high presumption and a great conceit. Bertrand Russell also saw it in the same light when he wrote, "The Copernican revolution will not have done its work until it has taught men more modesty than is to be found among those who think Man sufficient evidence of Cosmic Purpose" (Russell 1997:222). And even more tellingly, one might advance the argument that if all the while it *was* almighty God's purpose and intent to bring forth the human race, why did it take him fourteen billion years to do so?

We may have inflicted some heavy blows on the anthropic principle already, but we are not through with it just yet. Criticism of it turns out to have a respectable antiquity that is worth adding to what we have already quoted. While the principle received its current name only three decades ago, it was enunciated at least as early as 1686. In that year, in his book *Conversations on the Plurality of Worlds*, the French natural philosopher Bernard de Fontenelle (1657–1757) held that "God must have designed the universe with us in mind. If Earth were slightly closer to the Sun, we would bake, and if it were slightly farther away, we would freeze" (quoted in Kaiser 2007:524).

An even more questionable belief in the truth of the anthropic principle was that of the German philosopher and mathematician Christian Wolff (1679–1754), who wrote:

> We see that God has created the sun to keep the changeable conditions on the earth in such an order that living creatures, men and beasts, may inhabit its surface. Since men are the most reasonable of creatures, and able to infer God's invisible being from the contemplation of the world, the sun in so far forth contributes to the primary purpose of creation: without it the race of man could not be preserved or continued. (quoted in James 1994:535n–536n)

Wolff went on to say, "Therefore since God so planned the world that men and beasts should live upon it and find there everything required for their necessity and convenience, he also made water as one means whereby to make the earth into so excellent a dwelling" (quoted in James 1994:537n).

William James, who quoted these lines in *The Varieties of Religious Experience* (1902), regarded such statements by Wolff as "grotesque" and was even led to ask, in obvious irritation, "How was it ever conceivable ... that a man like Christian Wolff, in whose dry-as-dust head all the learning of the eighteenth century was concentrated should have preserved such a baby-like faith in the personal and human character of Nature ...?" (James 1994:53n). Were he alive today, one wonders what James would have said of the distinguished scientists who, two hundred fifty years after Wolff and though dressing up their remarks in more pretentious language, still hold essentially the same view.

It seems to me that the correct way of regarding the anthropic principle is as follows. For whatever reasons—not *intentions*, but *reasons*—the universe has the properties it does. It developed in such a way that at least in one tiny corner it became possible for intelligent life—human life—to evolve. And life evolved here because it *could*, not because it *had to*, or because it was *intended to*. Nothing more profound was involved; no cosmic purpose, no divine plan, lay behind it. And if someone insists that it was indeed an all-powerful God's will from the very beginning to give rise to the human species, we ask again, "Why did it take so long?"

Moreover, it should be pointed out that the evolution of *Homo sapiens* was far from being inexorable or guaranteed. In fact, it was far more contingent than it was foreordained. Had there not been a period of desiccation in southern Africa some six million years ago, forcing an arboreal ape to descend from the trees and begin adapting to terrestrial life, there would be no human race today.

The Continuing Clash of Science and Religion

Theists, then, have been trying for centuries to find small cracks through which to introduce God as an explanatory mechanism when science was successfully explaining more and more of the universe without him. Despite such dissimulations and contortions as the anthropic principle, the fundamental issue remains simply this. Only two basic kinds of answers exist to questions of why the world exists and works the way it does: *naturalistic* ones and *supernaturalistic* ones. And the fact is becoming ever harder to deny that naturalistic answers to the Great Questions of existence are—to any objective observers—the more penetrating and persuasive ones, and thus are gaining ever more ground.

The historian of science Gerald Holton has summed up the effects of this trend: "As science has pushed back the frontiers of the unknown, it has made untenable the position of theologians ... and has left fewer and fewer chores for the Deity in the everyday functions of the world" (Holton 1960:60). Put even more succinctly, Bertrand Russell noted that "every step in known human development has involved a diminution of religion" (Russell 1997:214).

Narrowing the issue between science and religion once again to the confrontation between creationism and evolution, the philosopher of science Michael Ruse has declared that "many of those on the science side of these debates think that Darwinism sounds the death knell to Christianity and other theistic systems" (Ruse 2003:333). If this statement seems to overstate the case, it at least can be said—and we repeat it here—that nowadays theologians find themselves compelled to reconcile and accommodate religion to the findings of science. No longer can they deny or ignore them, as they once did.

Today clerics and theologians alike must come to terms with science as best they can—or suffer the consequences. Indeed, some entire churches have attempted to do just that. In 1982, for example, the General Assembly of the United Presbyterian Church "adopted a resolution stating that 'Biblical scholars and theological schools ... find that the scientific theory of evolution does not conflict with their interpretation of the origins of life found in Biblical literature'" (Ayala 2007:165). It should be pointed out, though, that what the United Presbyterians were saying was *not* that they were bending scriptural interpretations to accord with scientific findings, but rather that the scientific facts happened not to conflict with biblical truth as currently understood. This I would say is acceding while appearing not to accede! And of course on the other side of the debate, science feels no need—to say nothing of an obligation—to trim its sails to conform to any religious doctrine.

Still, there have long been those who, while finding themselves predominantly in the camp of science, have nonetheless been unwilling to renounce or forsake their allegiance to religion. More than a century ago, the linguist and scholar Friedrich Max Müller remarked with evident disagreement and discomfort, "Every day, every week, every month, every quarter, the most widely read journals seem just now to vie with each other in telling us that the time for religion is past, that faith is a hallucination or an infantile disease, that the gods have at least been tossed out and exploded" (Max Müller 1879:218). Shortly thereafter William James echoed the sentiment: "There is a notion in the air about us that religion is probably only an anachronism, a case of 'survival,' an atavistic relapse into a mode of thought which humanity in its more enlightened examples has outgrown" (James 1994:534).

Such assessments and predictions—which Max Müller and James with their sarcasm tried to ridicule—proved in fact premature. Religion remains to this day a powerful voice in the debates about how the universe began, what attributes it manifests, and how it continues to run. If our survey of the development of human thought has revealed anything at all, it is that advances in science—incontestable and irresistible as they may be—have been met grudgingly and with resistance. When such advances have challenged some strongly held religious belief or seemed to threaten religious institutions, they have been vigorously opposed. Such institutions have been quick to recognize a formidable competitor when one appeared. And scientific victories, when achieved, were often only partial. The great irony has been that momentous scientific advances were often led by men who continued to hold fast to an underlying set of supernatural beliefs, at the same time that their inventions or discoveries were serving to undermine and eventually sweep away those same beliefs.

Sometimes we also find the anomaly that men who counted themselves firmly in the secular camp have nonetheless tried to give their philosophy a semblance of even-handedness by throwing a sop to religion. We have seen that in his waning years Auguste Comte tried to erect a secular superstructure closely patterned on that of the

Roman Catholic Church. More than a century later, the biologist Julian Huxley—whose grandfather had ridiculed Comte's attempt to do so—tried something of the same sort himself, although, to be sure, on a much more limited scale. First of all, the younger Huxley explicitly denied a belief in a personal God. Indeed, he predicted boldly, "It will soon be as impossible for an intelligent, educated man or woman to believe in a god as it is now to believe that the earth is flat" (Huxley 1957:62). Nevertheless this did not deter him from authoring a book entitled *Religion Without Revelation* (1957). And in his introduction to Teilhard de Chardin's *The Phenomenon of Man*, Huxley tried again to establish a kind of truce, even rapport, between science and religion.

> [I]t is no longer possible to maintain that science and religion must operate in thought-tight compartments or concern separate sectors of life. They are both relevant to the whole of human existence. The religiously-minded can no longer turn their backs upon the natural world, or seek escape from its imperfections in a supernatural world; nor can the materialistically-minded deny importance to spiritual experience and religious feeling. (Huxley 1961:26)

Michael Ruse, whom we quoted above as presenting the views of others on evolution and religion, gave voice to his own view as well: "My opinion," he says, "is that there is no absolute barrier to a committed Darwinian being a Christian, or indeed to adhering to any other of the major religions of the West." Then he asks, "Can a Darwinian be a Christian?" and answers resoundingly, "Absolutely!" (Ruse 2001:217). And the geneticist Francis Collins, whose views we have already discussed, holds that "there is nothing inherently in conflict between the idea of a creator God and what science has revealed" (Collins 2006:81).

But while there are those who sympathize with the aims of science and at the same time are not yet ready to abandon their religious beliefs, there are also those who steadfastly refuse to admit belief in God into their philosophy or show any sympathy for religion. Laplace, Holbach, and Büchner, for example, found it unwarranted to try to reconcile religion and science. They considered

them not only opposed but incompatible. The atheism of yesteryear—as represented by those men—found its modern equivalent in
the writings of Sigmund Freud and Bertrand Russell (to name but
two), who minced no words in proclaiming their complete and
uncompromising lack of faith. Russell even found a certain satisfaction in taunting the Almighty for what he considered his inferior
craftsmanship: "If I were granted omnipotence, and millions of
years to experiment in," he wrote, "I should not think Man much to
boast of as the final result of all my efforts" (Russell 1997:222). Not
content with that, he further chided a supposedly all-powerful and
benevolent God by insisting that "[a]n omnipotent Being, who created a world containing evil not due to sin[,] must Himself be at
least partially evil" (Russell 1997:194).

Philosophy Diminished

Theists and non-theists alike have long had an abiding interest in
what are often called the Great Questions of existence. Ancillary to
this question is another one: who can best answer those Great
Questions? Setting aside the sorts of answers traditionally given to
them by religious thinkers, to whom else would one turn to seek
answers to those questions? One obvious candidate for this distinction is the philosopher.

Philosophers long enjoyed an exalted place on the stage of
human understanding. Not only was the search for knowledge held
to be their proper function, the claim was even made that it was their
unique province. And over this domain men like Hume and Kant
and Leibniz presided majestically. Great truths (many thought) were
first discovered and enunciated by philosophers, and only then did
they trickle down to lesser minds.

With the rise of empirical science, though, all this began to
change. Important new truths were no longer being brought to light
by philosophers; now these truths began to emerge from the observations, experiments, and interpretations of scientists. Correspondingly, the discipline of philosophy began to diminish in its ambit and
stature. First it started to share the role of truth finder with science,
and then gradually it began to relinquish the role to that discipline.
As early as 1868, the physicist John Tyndall asserted prophetically

that "philosophy is forsaking its ancient metaphysical channels and pursuing those opened or indicated by scientific research" (Tyndall 1869:2).

As science broadened and deepened its quest for knowledge, those who pondered such matters as the constitution of the stars or the origin of life no longer felt the need to pose them to philosophers. Now the ones toward whom they directed such questions were astronomers and biologists. As time went on and the search for knowledge continued and expanded, the Great Questions were distributed more widely among an increasing number of scientific specialists. At the same time, the answers to such questions were becoming more precise, more convincing—and more naturalistic.

Once the undisputed Queen of Thought, philosophy was being relegated to the role of Handmaiden to Science. Instead of generating bold, new, all-encompassing theories, philosophy's role was increasingly reduced to *interpreting* the results that science was bringing forth. As the philosopher G. J. Warnock summarized the movement, after the demise of idealism in English philosophy, there then began "a persistent and quite proper tendency, as more and more aspects and departments of life and the world were made the subjects of systematic empirical study, to distinguish these as not within the philosopher's province" (Warnock 1958:52).

The developing school of logical positivism, which best exemplified this trend, held that "philosophers as such could have no concern at all with questions of fact" (Warnock 1958:56). Only that shrinking residue of ideas and concepts that did not involve purely empirical matters was to be retained by "philosophy" as its proper sphere. Ludwig Wittgenstein was led to declare, "The sole remaining task for philosophy is the analysis of language"—an observation that prompted the astrophysicist Stephen Hawking to remark, "What a comedown from the great tradition of philosophy from Aristotle to Kant!" (Hawking 1998: 191). In his *Tractatus Logico-Philosophicus* Wittgenstein went on to elaborate his views: "The object of philosophy is not a number of 'philosophical propositions,' but to make propositions clear" (quoted in Branch 1977:12). And this assertion was echoed by other philosophers of the early twentieth century. G. E. Moore, for one, believed that "the business of philosophy is clarification and not discovery; ... its concern is with meaning, not with truth" (quoted in Warnock 1958:29).

Today the dominant school of philosophy is analytic philosophy, which recognizes that science has taken over the role of understanding and explaining the cosmos—from the behavior of tiny electrons to that of enormous galaxies—and that the proper function of philosophy is not "the pursuit of truth" but "the pursuit of meaning" (Branch 1977:13).

Mathematics and the Interpretation of the Universe

Some philosophers, however, may not be so ready to abdicate their once-lofty role as explainers of the universe. The argument such men could advance is this. One of the recognized domains of philosophy is logic, and a major subdivision of logic is mathematics. It is mathematics, they contend, that allows us to formulate the relations among the various objects and forces of the universe. How insightful it is—they continue—to have determined (for example) that bodies attract each other inversely as the square of the distance between them. And this knowledge is essentially ... undeniably ... and supremely mathematical!

This contention, however, can be met with the counter-argument that mathematics did not *discover* that relationship, but merely *expressed* it. If that is the case, the question then becomes how well does mathematics express or reflect physical reality? Lord Kelvin—not known as a gifted mathematician—is said to have remarked that he could not understand something unless he could draw a picture of it. Physical representation, then, seemed to him a critical element in fixing an idea in the mind.

But that was then and this is now. The historian of science George Sarton—writing a half-century after Kelvin—observed that except for the simplest cases, drawing pictures of physical reality "has become utterly impossible.... Our pattern is made up of mathematical symbols connected to differential equations" (Sarton 1955:9). As a result, he concluded, "[t]he pattern of the material universe ... is no longer material. We are living in a universe of abstract thought" (Sarton 1955:9).

The physicist Werner Heisenberg, for his part, noted that "any attempt to unravel the dense skein of natural phenomena is dependent upon the discovery of mathematical forms" (Heisenberg 1972:8). And as we have seen, Sir James Jeans—an accomplished mathematician as well as a physicist and astronomer—happily proclaimed that "the final truth about a phenomenon resides in the mathematical description of it" (Jeans 1947:176). More recently this view was reaffirmed by yet another physicist, Freeman Dyson, who noted that "[t]he language of physics has moved steadily further into the domain of abstract mathematics. Instead of describing nature with mechanical models, physicists now describe it with infinite-dimensional spaces and other even more esoteric mathematical concepts" (Dyson 2004:55). Among the "esoteric mathematical concepts" Dyson alluded to are those dealing with dimensions beyond the three familiar ones of Length, Breadth, and Height, plus the one added by Einstein—Time.

To gain some notion of the shadowy world into which we were propelled by quantum physics, consider the following. Speaking of the seven-dimensional space that physicists have conjured up in discussing the meeting of two electrons, the physicist Erwin Schrödinger declared that while this conception has "quite a definite physical meaning, it cannot very well be said to 'exist'; hence a wave-motion in this space cannot be said to 'exist' either" (quoted in Jeans 1947:144). And more recently the physicist Richard Feynman noted that "[m]athematicians are only dealing with the structure of reasoning, and they do not really care what they are talking about. They do not even need to know what they are talking about" (quoted in Pickover 2008:135). Surely all this sounds even less tangible and more elusive than the immaterial, incorporeal human soul!

But it gets worse. Nowadays there is *string theory*, a highly abstract, highly mathematical family of theories that routinely posits the existence of at least *nine* dimensions. One observer writes, "According to string theory, all particles and forces arise from the vibration of tiny 'string-like' objects. For the theory to work, they have to vibrate in 10 dimensions, not the four familiar dimensions of space-time" (Ananthaswamy 2008:4). There is no question, then, that "the mathematics involved in string theory is quite remarkable by any standards. In subtleties and sophistication it vastly exceeds previous uses of mathematics in physical theory" (Atiyah 2005: 1082). And beyond string theory there is *super*string theory, an extreme version of which—if I recall correctly—posits the existence of no fewer than twenty-nine dimensions!

Can the human mind possibly *conceive*—let alone *comprehend*—something in nature that has ten dimensions, to say nothing of twenty-nine? Merely to satisfy the demands of some esoteric mathematical equation, are we obliged to accept the physical reality of a dozen or more dimensions beyond those we can conceive? Even Laplace's supreme intelligence would blanch at the prospect! The real question, though, is this: a large number of dimensions may be required to fulfill the demands of supremely abstruse mathematics, but do they correspond to anything we can actually say exists in the real world? It is going to be difficult to convince anyone besides a few dedicated string theorists that they do.

The dangers of the "overmathematization" of physics were pointed out at least a century ago by the physicist and philosopher Ernst Mach. According to him, "[A]n attempted mathematical demonstration can have no more rigor than a conclusion from observation. It can add nothing to observation and can tell us nothing about the world which sense experience cannot tell us" (quoted in Alexander 1967:116). Bertrand Russell, for his part, expressed the opinion that "[t]he appearance of deducing actual phenomena from mathematics is delusive" (Russell 1954:88). And Werner Heisenberg, whom we just quoted as pointing out the importance of mathematics for physics, nonetheless admitted that "[i]n the final analysis mathematical analysis is a mental game that we can play or not play as we choose" (Heisenberg 1972:90).

The brilliant English philosopher Susan Stebbing also had a warning to give in this regard. "The important, and in a way, too obvious and impressive, part played by mathematicians in physics must not blind us to the fact that the experimenter has to say the last words as well as the first" (Stebbing 1958:283). Moreover, Stebbing also characterized the difference between mathematicians and physicists in the following words.

> The pure mathematician is not at all concerned with the physical interpretation of his symbolic expressions. His procedure is as reasonable when there is no physical interpretation as when there is such an interpretation; his enjoyment of his work in mathematics

is equally independent of its physical application. The physicist, on
the contrary, is interested mainly in the interpretation, i.e., in the
experimental verification of the mathematical formulae provided
by the pure mathematician. (Stebbing 1958:26)

Even more pointedly the physicist Michael Atiyah noted the
danger of a mathematical "take-over" of physics, leading to the suspicion that formulations like string theory, while mathematically
elegant, may be "far removed, or even alien to, physical reality"
(Atiyah 2005:1081).

According to another biologist and philosopher of science,
Massimo Pigliucci, string theory "is a mathematically beautiful
construct that has the potential of unifying general relativity and
quantum mechanics. The problem is that—at the moment—it also is
entirely untestable empirically, which makes it an interesting philosophical position but not science" (Pigliucci 2006:22). Somewhat
more skeptical even is Lee Smolin, a theoretical physicist, who
affirms that "most of our reasoning about ... [string theories] is
based on conjectures that remain unproven after many years, at any
level of rigor. We do not even have a precise definition of the theory, either in terms of physical principles or mathematics. Nor do we
expect it in the foreseeable future" (Smolin 2006:13).

Thus string theory—to say nothing of *super*string theory—is a
highly abstract (indeed abstruse) mathematical concept. Since it has
not yet established empirical correlates, it must be judged as
remaining in the realm—not to say the *limbo*—of pure ideas. Thus
it would have greatly appealed to Plato as the quintessence of "idealism." Bishop Berkeley too would have warmed his hands over its
phantom flames. And it surely would have been found congenial by
the German idealists of the late eighteenth century.

Even so, it must be stressed that there is a way in which string
theory would *not* have fit with the thinking of Plato or Berkeley or
Hegel. For despite being so abstract as to press hard against the
bounds of human comprehension, string theory still remains within
the domain of *naturalism*. Whatever its shortcomings, it posits the
existence of no God and does not spill over into the spiritualized
realm of supernaturalism.

Grappling with the Great Questions

But more needs to be said about the Great Questions and who can best answer them. The views presented here so far may strike theologians as reflecting a certain timidity on the part of secularists when confronting broad philosophical issues. Religion is much bolder in dealing with such issues, the former might argue. Yes, they might continue, science has failed to grapple (for example) with the question "What is the meaning of existence?" Well, then, let us try to rectify this oversight by tackling that very question: what *is* the meaning of existence?

The best way to approach this question is by examining the premise underlying it. To begin with, implied by this questioner is a belief that it *has* an answer—that existence *does* have a meaning, one that is discernible and expressible. Probing the attitude lying behind the asker of such a question, we find the conviction that there must be some plan, some purpose, some design, behind the universe. It may not be readily apparent (the questioner might admit) but it is there just the same. And therefore we should bend every effort to ferret it out and lay it bare for all to see.

Continuing to probe into the matter, we can detect in the belief that there is such a master plan … a grand design … a further belief in the existence of a Master Planner, a Cosmic Mind—in short a *Deity*—capable of formulating and executing such a plan. But as we have argued before, purpose and intent—the elements underlying any conscious plan—are the attributes of a functioning *mind*. And mind, as we have emphasized, is the product of a complex organization of *nervous tissue*. Yet we have no tangible evidence that such a delicate organization of matter exists "out there" in cosmic space. The only place we know it to exist is here on earth, among ourselves. And once it is understood that the question "What is the meaning of existence?" *assumes* the reality of an entity for which we lack any substantiation, the question immediately deflates. We find, in effect, that "What is the meaning of existence?" itself has no meaning! And with that we need not trouble ourselves with it any further.

It was language that made culture possible. Language, then, is a tool of inestimable power, value, and versatility. But at the same time—as the General Semanticists never tire of telling us—language also makes it possible to formulate questions that are inherently unanswerable and thus, for those intent on asking them anyway, immensely troublesome. Such questions are merely verbal constructs, grammatically intelligible perhaps, but serving only to bemuse and bedevil those who seriously continue to ponder and pursue them.

Of course there are questions that *sound* legitimately scientific, but that are nevertheless by their very nature unanswerable. Returning to a question we raised earlier, almost rhetorically, why do bodies attract each other inversely as the *square* of the distance between them instead of, say, inversely as the *cube* of that distance? Why indeed should bodies attract each other *at all*? While a professional physicist loses very little sleep over such a question, a dedicated theist might not only ask it but be ready with a simple answer: "It was God's will that it be so." And if a skeptic should press the matter and ask, "Well, why should God have willed it so?" the theist might reply with a shrug of his shoulders and say that, as everyone knows, "God's will is inscrutable." And with that the conversation would come to an end, leaving us no closer to a satisfying answer.

Who Best Answers the Great Questions?

But isn't this an unhappy state of affairs? Are we still not left with the query "Who is best equipped to answer the Great Questions— questions that are both important and actually have an answer, which for untold centuries have vexed the human mind? Surely *someone* is best equipped to deal with such questions. But who?"

We have already expressed our unwillingness to consider mathematicians, or even mathematical physicists, as being the leading candidates to be asked these questions. And even before that, we noted that philosophers for the most part no longer feel comfortable addressing such questions. Indeed, by their own admission they have withdrawn from the competition, ceding their place to the scientists. All right, then, the question now becomes w*hich* scientists? Quite a number of them stand ready to contend for the part. Which among them is best equipped by virtue of their professional training and experience to deal with the Great Questions?

An obvious candidate to play the leading role in answering such questions is, again, the physical scientist, whom we perhaps disqualified too soon. The physicist, the astrophysicist, and the astronomer together comprise a powerful triumvirate. Even individually they are ready to stake a claim. After all, they are the scientists who concern themselves with the basic stuff of the universe—*matter*—as distributed throughout the limitless extent of space. Moreover, they deal with matter not just in its elemental state, but organized into highly subtle and complex forms. Isn't one of these scientists, then, the one who most authoritatively triangulates the most distant corners of the cosmos—where God ostensibly dwells? Isn't this scientist the one best suited to resolve the most profound questions that can be posed about the Almighty and his relation to the human race? The answer, in a word, is *no*!

In the professional activities of these physical scientists, God is simply not part of the subject matter of their research. He is not to be seen at the farthest reaches of a Hubble telescope, nor can he be discerned by a scanning electron microscope at its most powerful setting. No, the role we are discussing is better played by scientists who in the course of their professional research *do* concern themselves with the supernatural—even if only with *conceptions* of it conveyed to them by their informants. And it is to those scientists, who have written tomes on the subject, to whom we must turn.

The deepest understanding of why people believe in God or in other representatives of the supernatural comes not from the astronomer, nor from the biologist (for that matter), both of whom are far removed from the repository of supernatural lore. It comes instead from the dedicated student of those individuals whose ancestors *invented* supernatural beings in the first place. It comes from the anthropologist.

We have seen that the idea of a "high god," such as the God of Christianity, very likely did not arise in the human mind during the earliest stages of religious conjecture. Rather, it arose gradually through a process of evolution. The soul, conceived of as an immaterial essence, was the first supernatural notion entertained. Subsequently this notion was projected outward, ostensibly from human beings into the external world, where it gave rise to "bush spirits" in all their infinite variety. These beings in turn became magnified, transfigured, and empowered, an evolutionary transformation that culminated in their florescence into "high gods." Appearing first as multiple deities in a polytheistic pantheon, these gods in a limited number of cases—most notably in a corner of the Judeo-Christian world—evolved even further. Somewhere in ancient Israel, an unknown number of gods appeared to coalesce, as one of them finally triumphed over the rest. In a struggle whose details we lack, this victorious deity expelled his competitors from the pantheon and declared himself supreme, no longer to be challenged by his now-extinguished former rivals. "Thou shalt have no other gods before me," he demanded of his followers (Exodus 20:3).

The astronomer, *as such*, knows nothing of the theological evolution depicted above. Neither does the physicist nor the biologist. For anthropologists, though, the history of this development—conjectural as it may be in part—is grist for the mill and remains a major and legitimate focus of attention.

The anthropological study of religion, then, tells us immeasurably more about the origin, nature, attributes, and evolution of God than do the most powerful and penetrating instruments of the physical or biological sciences. But it tells us more than just about the development of religion in general. It also tells us about the specific circumstances that gave rise to particular elements of religious belief.

Stripped to its essential features, the concept of God—as anthropologists see it—is one that pictures him, first and foremost, as an explanatory mechanism. He was devised in order to account for a whole host of phenomena that human beings wanted to understand but that were otherwise inexplicable. How, for instance, could Paleolithic man have possibly known the cause of an earthquake when he was utterly ignorant of plate tectonics?

Not only full-fledged gods, but supernatural beings of all sorts supplied ready answers to all manner of insistent questions that puzzled primitive peoples. Being in no position to refute—or even challenge—supernatural answers to these questions, primitive peoples were disposed to believe and embrace supernatural explanations when they were put forward by some imaginative and persuasive storyteller. From our perspective, then, God (whether spelled with a capital "g" or a small one) was from the start a very human construct, a cultural product like so many others. He was distinctly human in form and attributes, only greatly magnified in power. Given his human roots, God can be considered not only a supernatural phenomenon but a *natural* one as well.

That is the way anthropologists regard religion—as something to be *studied* and *explained,* rather than *believed.* For anthropologists, then, religious beliefs constitute *phenomena*—"phenomena" being simply things and events viewed as the subject matter of science.

From this perspective God is the central figure in an elaborate tapestry of supernatural beliefs. And religion itself is not something utterly apart from the world of nature and culture. From William James's pragmatic point of view, God is unquestionably "real." From our perspective one might agree, but the crucial question then becomes is the locus of his reality in the mind or in the external world? Though clearly projected outward from the human mind, the supernatural has come to suffuse what primitive peoples perceive as the external world. Indeed, a great deal of primitive society is organized according to a framework that has many supernatural elements. One can even say that supernaturalism is the *warp* through which run the *weft* threads of social life.

Christianity and Its Origins

Leslie White, one of the leading anthropologists of the twentieth century and a scholar whom I have quoted on many occasions, had some acute observations to make about religion and society, especially as regards Christianity. "[R]eligion," said White, "is not to be regarded as a process sui generis, as a self-contained and self-determined process. Rather, it is an aspect, or a facet, of cultural systems as wholes. A religion is an expression, or a reflection, of a mode of life which is at bottom determined by the material, technological means of adjustment to and control over [the] terrestrial habitat." "A cultural system based upon a wild food technology," White went on to say, "could hardly have such concepts as 'Great God, our King,' or 'Christ, the royal Master.'" And he added that "[r]eligious expression, as a function of technology and social system, is well illustrated by our own Judeo-Christian tradition. A pastoral culture pictures the Lord as my Shepherd. In a cathedral building era God becomes an Architect, and is pictured as creating the world with square and compass. Commercialism introduces bookkeeping in heaven with a recording angel to set down the debits and credits of conduct" (White 1987:352).

But anthropology can go even further. It can give us a more penetrating insight into the rise of Christianity than is to be found in the writings of erudite biblical scholars. To such scholars—even those who do not necessarily regard Christ as the son of God—the emergence of Christianity appears as a unique event, totally unlike any other. And as such it is impossible to comprehend it except by the coincidence of an extraordinary set of circumstances, completely lacking in parallels. As it turns out, though, the origins of Christianity were given their most powerful illumination by a naturalistic anthropological explanation. Indeed, a full understanding of its origin did not come about until anthropologists had begun to study nativistic movements in various parts of the world. The result of such studies was the discovery of a striking pattern underlying them all.

What anthropologists found was that nativistic movements were socio-religious responses by a subject people to oppression by a superincumbent political authority. When an oppressed group felt there was a realistic chance to throw off the yoke of the oppressor, its response was generally a military uprising. Examples of this are the nativistic movement known as the Ghost Dance in the western United States, led by Jack Wovoka, and a similar uprising in Peru led by Juan Santos Atahualpa. However, when the dominant political power was deemed too strong to be overthrown, the leader of the nativistic movement taught his followers that their release from oppression would come not in this world, but in the next.

The rise of Christianity two thousand years ago was clearly an example of the latter. The Roman Empire was much too strong for the Jews living under its regime to believe they could throw it off. Jesus understood that perfectly well, and so his messianic message to his followers was that "my kingdom is not of this world" (John 18:36) and that it was in heaven where they would dwell in the presence of the Lord and enjoy the happiness and rewards denied them here on earth.

From a consideration of these facts, we can reach the following general conclusion. When an instance of a certain phenomenon can be shown to be an example of a broad regularity, the phenomenon can be said to be the expected outcome of certain specifiable antecedents. Such an instance—at least in its broad outlines—becomes explainable without recourse to anything outside the natural realm of circumstances. It can therefore be accounted for without recourse to anything supernatural, such as "divine intervention." The origin of Christianity, therefore, turns out to be far more understandable from a purely secular perspective than from a religious one. From the former it becomes almost predictable, while from the latter it stems ultimately from the will of God—which, we all know, is often capricious and always inscrutable.

CHAPTER 26

Current Status and Future Prospects

And now we come to the end of this survey of mankind's attempt to understand the cosmos and its place within it. Before concluding, though, it seems fitting to quickly recapitulate the evolution of human thinking about such matters. Starting with a revisiting of how it all started, let us take stock of where we are now and, finally, make some attempt to project current trends into the future.

Beginning with the concept of the soul, we saw how human beings began to populate the world around them with an ever-growing number and variety of supernatural beings modeled after the soul—and like it, incorporeal and immaterial. A proliferation and elaboration of such beings gave rise to a rich polytheism. And in one part of the world in particular, the number of deities in the pantheon progressively narrowed until only one was left standing. The Judeo-Christian God who thus triumphed over his competitors may have found himself alone, but his followers bestowed on him supreme knowledge and limitless power. And the God thus created continues his reign to this day.

However, beginning in ancient Greece, a categorically different way of explaining occurrences began to take shape. This radically new manner of thinking dispensed with gods altogether, declaring that what lay behind the behavior of the universe was not the actions of deities at all. Instead what governed the world and what stood beyond it was a series of faceless, impersonal forces. These forces, moreover, operated with such consistency and regularity that they warranted being called *laws*. No longer was it divine caprice that accounted for things as they were, but rather the laws of nature.

For the last four centuries or so, these two modes of interpretation—naturalism and supernaturalism—have vied with each other. Not only have they vied, they have clashed. Being based on categorically different premises and principles, they have come to radically different conclusions. And as each sought to gain ascendancy, they have waged an intense struggle. That struggle has, in large part, been the subject of this book.

Religion Accommodates to Science

Faced with the irresistible advances of science, however, twentieth century clergymen and theologians—the modern face of supernaturalism—have been forced to recognize and accommodate to these advances. In this process religious leaders have had to yield much of the ground that once was safely theirs. Moreover, the retreats they have been forced to make have often been artfully disguised. The once-solemn contentions that the stories presented in the Bible were (as Mark Twain liked to say) "the petrified truth" have had to be modified. Now the clergy began to claim that all along these stories were recognized as just parables or allegories.

And God, who at first showed his power by repeatedly and conspicuously intervening in world affairs, later came to be seen as voluntarily and gracefully stepping back and letting nature exercise these powers in his stead. The will of God thus became transformed into the laws of nature.

Eventually it began to be realized that a God who had initially laid down the laws by which nature now operated had essentially ceded his powers to her, and thereby made himself virtually *unnecessary* and *superfluous*. Shorn of his creative functions by the relentless progress of cosmology, geology, and biology, God appeared now to many as at best severely diminished. But not only were his powers sharply curtailed, in some quarters his very existence began to be questioned.

Indeed, to many who were not raised in the bosom of the church (either Catholic or Protestant) but had been exposed from childhood to the explanatory power of science, belief in God came to be regarded as a survival from a previous era—a relic of an earlier age when no better means of explanation was available. More than a century ago, the anthropologist E. B. Tylor gave voice to this changed perspective when he wrote, "As for ourselves, we have lived to see the time when men shrink from addressing even to Supreme Deity the old customary rain-prayers, for the rainfall is passing from the region of the supernatural, to join the tides and seasons in the realm of physical science" (Tylor 1871:II, 237).

And so with many of his functions relinquished, God remains "alive" today but with a greatly reduced role and altered functions. To those who still believe in him, God is now largely a comforter, a source of emotional strength and support, rather than a way to account for how the universe came to be or how it functions.

Contemporary Atheism

The opposite of theism is, of course, *atheism*, and it is time to examine the current status of atheism in the field of religious thought. As we noted earlier, during the twentieth century few philosophers or scientists openly professed their atheism. The opprobrium that continued to be heaped on atheists made free thinkers—especially those in the public eye—disinclined to voice their true feelings. In mid-century Homer Smith went so far as to state that "[n]ot one man in a thousand has either the strength of mind or the goodness of heart to be an atheist" (Smith 1955:346).

Scientists who did not believe in God generally avoided the social stigma attached to non-belief by stressing the positive contributions of science, avoiding thereby the negativity implied by "atheism." Their strategy—if indeed they had one—seemed to be to let the passage of time prove religion no longer necessary, and thus allow it simply to wither away and eventually disappear.

In the previous chapter, we presented the results of a survey conducted in 1916 by the psychologist James Leuba of the religious beliefs of American scientists. Here I would like to review a few scattered results of more recent surveys of religious opinions, not only of scientists but of the general public as well.

In 1998 Edward Larson and Jerry Witham surveyed members of the National Academy of Sciences, asking them about their religious beliefs. The results (in part) were as follows.

Percent believing in a personal god	7.0
Percent not believing in a personal god	72.2
Percent having doubt (agnostics)	20.8

Analyzing their results, Larson and Witham wrote, "We found the highest percentage of belief among NAS mathematicians (14.3% in God; 15.0% in immortality). Biological scientists had the lowest rate of belief (5.5% in God; 7.1% in immortality)" (quoted in Scheffer 2000:42). In 2003 Greg Graffin of Cornell University surveyed 149 prominent evolutionary biologists and found that 130 of them, or 87.2 percent, did not believe in God (Olson 2006:187).

The results of surveys of religious belief among the general public, though, were strikingly different. In 2006 the Baylor University Institute for Studies of Religion sampled 1,721 Americans and found that 91.8 percent said they believed in God (Grossman 2006:1). In February 2008 the Pew Forum on Religion and Public Life made a study of the "religious landscape" of the United States and determined that 16 percent of the population reported having no religious affiliation (McManus 2008:38). Needless to say, though, not all those individuals were necessarily atheists.

When we compare the degree of religious belief in the United States with that in Europe, we find marked differences. In recent years secularization has made rapid strides among European nations. A survey conducted in 2005 by a polling organization called Eurobarometer revealed that though decreasing, there was still a fairly high degree of belief in traditionally Catholic countries. For example:

Percent Believing in God

Portugal	81%
Poland	80%
Italy	74%
Ireland	73%

However, in countries where Catholicism had never gained a strong grip on religious thinking, belief in God was substantially lower.

Percent Believing in God

Sweden	23%
Denmark	31%
Netherlands	34%
Finland	41%

It is not without reason, then, that every so often this impressive trend has prompted the Vatican to issue a stern warning that secularism in Europe is advancing at an alarming rate!

Returning to the United States, we can say that atheism continues to be a distinctly minority opinion here—although evidently it is no longer viewed as the grim specter it once was. Summing up the import of the statistics presented above, it seems fair to say that in terms of religious opinions, the gulf between scientists who are nonbelievers and the rest of the population continues to be both wide and deep.

One reason that atheism is found unpalatable by so many persons is that the term itself focuses on the *negativity* of the concept. Thus dedicated believers could scornfully point to, and sympathize with, Einstein's assertion that "[m]ere unbelief is no philosophy at all" (quoted in Calaprice 2000:216). In the popular mind, an atheist is someone who vigorously denies the existence of God—is a "militant atheist"—but does not go beyond that. And the simple denial of something is nowhere near as intellectually appealing or satisfying as the affirmation of *something*. Denying the existence of God seems to leave an unfilled and uncomfortable *void*. If God is to be taken away, believers feel (correctly enough) that something else must replace him. While he reigned God served a useful function. There were things he did that needed to be done ... that believers in him *still* feel need to be done.

What does the atheist offer in place of God? The answer is a whole array of things. Alternatives to God, provided largely by science, are ready and waiting. What is popularly thought to be an atheist's void turns out not to be that at all. Atheists are intent on not leaving any intellectual niche unfilled. They are convinced that other ways of filling such niches exist. As we have seen, over the last few centuries, there has been a systematic replacement of supernatural explanations by naturalistic ones. And this steady replacement has occurred because, in the rigorous process of natural selection that affects ideas as well as organisms, naturalistic explanations have consistently proved themselves more successful than their supernatural rivals in dealing with important questions. This has been true whenever an objective, empirical test could be applied to decide between them.

The "Four Horsemen of the Apocalypse"

There has been a new development in the propounding of atheism. The first years of the twenty-first century have witnessed the publication of four books—each enjoying a wide audience—setting forth an unambiguous, unapologetic, and uncompromising atheism. The candor of these new volumes has gone some distance toward giving atheism a certain veneer of respectability. In fact, it has ushered in what is sometimes called the "New Atheism." The books in question are Richard Dawkins's *The God Delusion* (2006), Daniel Dennett's *Breaking the Spell* (2006), Sam Harris's *The End of Faith* (2004), and Christopher Hitchens's *God Is Not Great* (2007). The authors of these works are sometimes spoken of as the "Four Horsemen of the Apocalypse," although Dawkins has said he prefers to have himself and his cohorts called the "Four Horsemen of the *Counter*-Apocalypse."

The fact that all four books were published not by small radical presses, but by major publishing houses, indicates that their message—once deemed so distasteful to the general reader as to virtually preclude their respectable appearance—no longer causes shudders to run through the reading public. The frank assertion of atheism, which Goethe once found "so black, so Cimerian," is today accepted with apparent equanimity.

While each of the four books just cited has its own distinctive perspective and emphasis, their common thread is that good and sufficient reasons exist for *not* believing in God. Harris's and Hitchens's books stress the evil that has been done in the name of God and religion. They point to abundant historical evidence that religious rivalries and conflicts have brought untold suffering and misery to the world. Dawkins's and Dennett's books, on the other hand, seek (among other things) to discover why belief in God should exist at all.

Theorists who have proposed a non-supernatural origin for religion generally agree that it serves *some* purpose. Putting it in more biological terms, Dawkins and Dennett contend that since religion is so ancient, universal, and enduring, it must in some way be *adaptive*. That is to say, it must help the human species adjust to life conditions. Arguing along these lines, E. O. Wilson holds that "religions, like other human institutions, evolve so as to further the welfare of their practitioners" (Wilson 2006:561). And when a form of behavior is found to be adaptive, sociobiologists like Wilson often start looking for an *organic* basis to it ... that somehow it has become established in the genetic makeup of the species. In the terminology that sociobiologists are fond of using, religion has become "hardwired." Thus Wilson states unequivocally that "the mental processes of religious belief—consecration of personal and group identity, attention to charismatic leadership, mythopoeism, and others—represent programmed predispositions whose self-sufficient components were incorporated into the neural apparatus of the brain by thousands of generations of genetic evolution" (Wilson 1978:206).

Wilson's way of stating the case, however, goes further than either Dennett or Dawkins is prepared to follow. Dennett is willing to agree with the notion that "the apparent extravagances of religious practices can be accounted for in the austere terms of evolutionary biology" (Dennett 2006:93). However, while he himself flirts with—or at least is bemused by—the concept of a "God center" or even a "God gene" (Dennett 2006:82–83, 138–140), ultimately he is not prepared to embrace the idea of a genetic basis to religion. Thus he asserts that "we can already be quite sure there isn't going to be a 'God gene,' or even a 'spirituality' gene" (Dennett 2006:315). He is therefore ready to oppose Wilson and other sociobiologists—who in recent years have shown a flurry of interest in religion—remarking that "[t]he hypothesis that there is a (genetically) heritable 'spiritual sense' that boosts human genetic fitness is one of the less likely and less interesting of the evolutionary possibilities" (Dennett 2006:317).

Dawkins, for his part, offers a theory of the origin of religious belief. He writes that "[t]he general theory of religion as an accidental by-product—a misfiring of something useful—is the one I wish to advocate" (Dawkins 2006:188). Basically, his contention is that in early hominid history it was advantageous for the child's brain to be very receptive so it would readily accept the sound advice of its elders—especially its parents. But this also left the infantile brain open to "infection" by the "virus" of religion. Elaborating on this argument, Dawkins holds that "there will be a selective advantage to child brains that possess the rule of thumb: believe, without question, whatever your grown-ups tell you. Obey your parents, obey the tribal elders" (Dawkins 2006:174).

Conceivably all this might be true. However, Dawkins's theory would account only for the *ease of transmission* of religious beliefs from one generation to the next *once they were in existence.* But it would *not* account for the *origin* of religious ideas in the first place. *Why* did supernatural beliefs arise at all? Like Dennett, Dawkins is skeptical of there being anything like a "God gene," declaring that "if neuroscientists find a 'god centre' in the brain, Darwinian scientists like me will still want to understand the natural selection pressure that favored it" (Dawkins 2006:168–169). In other words, Dawkins still takes such a dim view of the value of religion as an adaptive mechanism that he demands proof that it conferred such a positive benefit on our Paleolithic forebears as to be favored by natural selection.

A "God Gene" Proposed

The idea of a "God gene" or a "God spot" is admittedly an intriguing concept that warrants closer attention. It was first proposed—or at least explored at length—by the geneticist Dean Hamer in his book *The God Gene.* The subtitle of the book, *How Faith Is Hardwired into Our Genes,* makes it clear from the outset just where Hamer stands on this issue. Central to the argument in favor of such an entity is an experiment cited by Hamer but carried out by Canadian psychologist Michael Persinger. Persinger, it turns out, conducted the experiment on himself.

> [U]sing transcranial magnetic stimulation to study the function of various brain regions, he stimulated his own temporal and parietal lobes. For the first time in his life he experienced God. He had hit the "God Spot." Based on this experiment and other lines of evidence, Persinger believes that the biological basis of all spiritual and mystical experiences is due to spontaneous firing of the temporoparietal region—highly focal microseizures without any obvious motor effects. (Hamer 2004:135)

All this led Hamer to conclude that "[o]ur genes can predispose us to believe" (Hamer 2004:215).

What can we make of these assertions? We must be ready to admit that it is possible for the human brain to be stimulated in such a way as to have a "spiritual experience" and to *feel* that it has established some sort of direct contact with God. But this experience remains at the level of *psychology*, not *cosmology*. The crucial question that we need to ask is this: is there an objective counterpart to the subjective impression undergone by the subject whose brain has been stimulated in this way? We may be ready to accept the subject's insistence that he or she has had a "religious experience," but is there actually something corresponding to that experience "out there" in the external world? Proof of the former is still far from proving the latter.

Let us look at the issue more broadly. A great debate is taking place between sociobiologists and cultural anthropologists about how much of human behavior is "hardwired" in the brain—that is, genetically programmed—and how much is entirely culturally determined. As a cultural anthropologist, I stand squarely on the cultural side of the argument. A form of behavior, even one directly adaptive to human survival, can still remain purely *cultural* in its determination as long as it carries out its intended function successfully. In fact, we can say that cultural adaptation generally acts in such a way as to preclude or forestall the necessity of having a useful form of behavior become biologically imbedded in the human genome. (This side of the argument also enjoys the philosophical advantage of being a clear-cut application of Occam's razor!)

Still, it needs to be stressed that this entire argument remains strictly *intrafamilial*. That is to say, the supporters of the two sides of this debate regard belief in God—and religion in general—as a human invention, not a divine revelation. The sociobiologist and the cultural anthropologist alike agree that the proper way to treat religious beliefs is to determine what it was in human experience that gave rise to them. Much as the two sides may differ in other ways, therefore, both are equally convinced that belief in the supernatural was not *implanted* into man, but was man-made and then *projected* outward from him. Thus if God can be said to exist at all, the locus of his reality remains in the mind and not in the external world.

Will Religion Be Entirely Superseded?

The trend toward non-belief, so strongly trumpeted by the "Four Horsemen," seems destined to continue and even to gather strength. How far will it go? Will there come a time when theism will be completely extinguished and atheism—or rather its positive face, completely secular science—unequivocally enthroned in its place? Many persons, including some scientists, have vigorously denied this possibility. Back in the nineteenth century, the English physicist John Tyndall—materialist though he largely was—wrote that "[n]o atheistic reasoning can, I hold, dislodge religion from the human heart. Logic cannot deprive us of life, and religion is life to the religious. As an experience of consciousness it is beyond the assaults of logic" (Tyndall 1903:308n).

The early American sociologist Lester F. Ward came to the same conclusion. The basis of it, for him, was the insoluble mysteries of the cosmos, encapsulated in a single word: the Unknowable. Following Herbert Spencer in this regard, Ward wrote that "there exists a something which the finite intelligence does not and cannot comprehend." And this Unknowable, he believed, was "the foundation of all religion, and, as it is for ever safe from all the encroachments of Science, it insures [sic] Religion a reign of perpetuity" (Ward 1883:I, 156).

For still other reasons, William James also granted religion an unending tenure. "Religion, occupying herself with personal destinies and keeping thus in contact with the only absolute realities which we know, must necessarily play an eternal part in human history" (James 1994:546).

Some physicists, such as Robert Andrews Millikan, felt that beginning around 1900 the newly discovered subtleties and intricacies in the behavior of subatomic particles that physics was revealing to the world had made scientists more *humble* in the presence of such perplexities, thus instilling in them a sense of *wonder* (Millikan 1927:27). This wonder became transmuted into *awe*, which in turn gave rise to *reverence*. In that way physicists had come close to an encounter with God and thus had gained a serene acceptance of his existence.

It was all well and good for Millikan, *as an individual*, to entertain and express such attitudes. But it is not the function of *science* as a discipline to harbor and nurture the feeling of mystery. On the contrary, its mission is to *dispel* it, and by so doing to *reduce* awe. Science may never succeed in eradicating such attitudes entirely, but nevertheless this eradication remains one of its goals. For a scientist like Millikan to argue otherwise is to betray an attitude that he no doubt brought with him into science, not one he absorbed or learned from it. Indeed, I would venture to guess that Millikan's belief in God was formed, if not at his mother's breast, at least at her knee. After all, belief in God is not (as we have argued) a genetic inheritance, but something acquired during life—imbibed, so to speak, from one's surrounding culture. Stated more bluntly, religious belief is a matter of *indoctrination* at an early age ... of *enculturation* rather than *revelation*.

A more realistic appreciation of the status of religion than Millikan's was that of William James, who wrote, "Though the scientist may individually nourish a religion, and be a theist in his irresponsible hours, the days are over when it could be said that for Science herself the heavens declare the Glory of God and the firmament showeth his handiwork" (James 1994:534–535).

The astronomer Jagjit Singh likewise saw the incompatibility of a thoroughgoing acceptance of science and a belief in a cosmos created and managed by God.

> It is impossible to understand a god in whom one did not believe already. This is why it is no longer possible to rationalize religion and find God in mathematical laws of the cosmos, as, for example, Kepler could in his day. In fact, the progress of science had already begun to make the rationalization of theological belief so increasingly difficult that a tortured Pascal could no longer experience God in the mathematical laws of the cosmos as Kepler did barely a generation earlier. (Singh 1970:390)

Do We Seek Truth or Solace?

As science strips away the reasons for holding onto religious beliefs, the question may be raised of whether we should feel forlorn and bereft, as George Romanes once did when he lost his Catholic faith. Not according to the philosopher Paul Edwards, who pointed to the enrichment in one's perspective to be gained from an espousal of an all-embracing secularism. "Even if the open windows of science at first make us shiver after the cozy indoor warmth of traditional … myths," wrote Edwards, "in the end the fresh air brings vigor, and the great spaces have a splendor of their own" (Edwards 1967a:188).

In one of his many columns in *Natural History* magazine, the paleontologist Stephen Jay Gould posed a momentous question: "As we strive to understand nature, do we seek truth or solace?" (Gould 1989:8). The very same question could be asked of the dedicated theologian or philosopher: what are *they* after in pursuing their professions? Along this line the anthropologist Leslie White used to say in class—much to the annoyance of his colleague, the philosopher William Frankena—that philosophy (to say nothing of religion) was, to a large extent, "intellectual thumb sucking."

The objective of science is clear enough. Its business is the pursuit of truth, leaving the solace that Gould inquired about to those who need it and who try to supply it. Moreover, Gould seemed to imply that solace was to be sought elsewhere than in science. As scientific understanding has successively widened and deepened, the believer has been forced to seek God—and the support and succor he is thought to provide—farther and farther away, in regions of the cosmos not yet intellectually colonized by science. For as Epicurus wisely noted many centuries ago, "The Gods dwell in the interspaces of our knowledge of the world (quoted in Büchner 1891: 116).

But those interspaces have grown fewer and farther away. Two thousand years ago, in speaking of the movement of the stars that every night could be seen falling from a great height and disappearing below the horizon, the Roman writer Seneca observed, "The day will come when, by study pursued through several ages, the things now concealed will appear with evidence; and posterity will be astonished that truths so clear had escaped us" (quoted in Laplace 2007:5–6).

And he was right. Ludwig Büchner summed up the long history of astronomical research as follows.

As far as the telescope reaches and as far as man is able to espy the laws of the heavens—and this has been done to the extent of billions and trillions of miles—he has met everywhere with the same law, the same simple, mechanical principles, the same mathematical formula, and the same phenomena that are subject to computation. But never has been found the slightest trace of an arbitrary finger ordaining the spheres of the heavens and appointing the courses of the earths, the suns, and the comets. (Büchner 1891:105)

Büchner then proceeded to quote the French astronomer Joseph Lalande, who put the same thought more bluntly: "I have searched through the heavens, and nowhere have I found a trace of God" (quoted in Büchner 1891:105–106).

A few pages later, Büchner noted that if God had been so disposed, he could have in a trice dispelled all the uncertainties about him: "Why did not the everlasting creative power write his name in starry letters in the heavens, and thus put an end to all those doubts that torture and trouble the human breast ...? How could God, if he existed, quietly witness all the sad results of this uncertainty about his own existence, seeing that he could so easily put an end to them?" (Büchner 1891:113).

Not only has astronomy found no trace of God, either among a billion galaxies or in the vastness of interstellar space, it has also brought about a diminution in the stature of the human observer as he scans the heavens. Laplace seemed almost to relish deflating human presumption when he wrote, "[M]an considered himself, for a long time, as the centre of the motion of the celestial bodies, and his pride was justly punished.... Man [now] appears, upon a small planet, almost imperceptible in the vast extent of the solar system, itself only an insensible point in the immensity of space" (quoted in Crowe 1994:373, 374).

That statement was uttered two hundred years ago. What has a student of the heavens to say today about the matter? Echoing Laplace's very words, the astrophysicist Neil deGrasse Tyson has remarked, "[W]hen I look upon the endless sky from an observatory on a mountaintop, I well up with an admiration for its splendor. But I do so knowing and accepting that if I propose a God beyond the horizon, ... the day will come when our sphere of knowledge will have grown so large that I will have no need of that hypothesis" (Tyson 2003:79).

Finally, surveying the progress in human understanding that has taken place over countless centuries and focusing on the stage to which this evolution has brought us, the historian Carl Becker once observed:

> As the time and space world is expanded ... the gods, withdrawing from the immediate affairs of men to the place where [the] absolute dwells, fade away into pale replicas of their former selves—into the Law of Nature, the Transcendent Idea, ... or whatever.... Philosophy in turn becomes Natural Philosophy, then Natural Science, then Science, and science, dispensing altogether with the assistance of the gods and their numerous philosophic progeny, presents for contemplation the bare record of how ... the outer world behaves, of what has occurred in past times, leaving man alone in an indifferent universe. (Becker 1938:28)

Returning to the question posed earlier by Gould, the answer I would give to it is this: it may take eons, but the day may yet come when the human race has grown accustomed to its own cosmic solitude and insignificance. And as it continues to explore the universe, it will be satisfied with truth and no longer feel the need to look for solace.

REFERENCES

Acton, H. B.
    1967   "Absolute, The." In *The Encyclopedia of Philosophy*, edited by Paul Edwards, Vol. 1, pp. 6–9. Macmillan Publishing Company, New York.

Acton, J. E. E. D., Lord
    1985   "The Study of History." In *Selected Writings of Lord Acton, Vol. 2: Essays in the Study and Writing of History*, edited by J. Rufus Fears, pp. 504–552. Liberty Classics, Indianapolis, IN. (Originally published in 1895)

Adams, George Burton
    1909   "History and the Philosophy of History." *American Historical Review*, Vol. 14, pp. 221–236.

Adamson, Robert
    1910   "Gassendi, Pierre." In *Encyclopaedia Britannica*, 11th edition, Vol. 11, pp. 503–504.

Alexander, Peter
    1967   "Mach, Ernst." In *The Encyclopedia of Philosophy*, edited by Paul Edwards, Vol. 5, pp. 115–119. Macmillan Publishing Company, New York.

Ananthaswamy, Anil
    2008   "How the Universe Turned Out This Way." *New Scientist*, January 5, pp. 4–5.

Applegate, Debby
    2006   *The Most Famous Man in America: The Biography of Henry Ward Beecher*. Doubleday & Company, New York.

Aquinas, St. Thomas
    1993   *The Philosophy of St. Thomas Aquinas*. Translated by Edward Bullough. Edited by G. A. Elrington. Barnes & Noble, New York.

Århem, Kaj
    1981   *Makuna Social Organization: A Study in Descent, Alliance, and*

the Formation of Corporate Groups in the North-Western Amazon. Academiae Upsaliensis, Stockholm.

Asimov, Isaac
  1964   *A Short History of Biology.* Natural History Press, Garden City, NY.

Atiyah, Michael
  2005   "Pulling the Strings." *Nature,* Vol. 438, December 22–29, pp. 1081–1083.

Ayala, Francisco J.
  2007   *Darwin's Gift to Science and Religion.* Joseph Henry Press, Washington, DC.

Bacon, Francis
  1994   *Novum Organum.* Translated and edited by Peter Urbach and John Gibson. Open Court, Chicago. (Originally published in 1620)

Bagby, Philip
  1959   *Culture and History: Prolegomena to the Comparative Study of Civilizations.* University of California Press, Berkeley.

Bancroft, Hubert H.
  1883   *The Works of Hubert Howe Bancroft, Vol. 2: The Native Races of the Pacific States.* A. L. Bancroft Company, Publishers, San Francisco.

Barnes, Harry Elmer
  1937   *An Intellectual and Cultural History of the Western World.* Cordon Company, New York.

Bartlett, Irving
  1967   "Channing, William Ellery." In *The Encyclopedia of Philosophy,* edited by Paul Edwards, Vol. 2, pp. 79–80. Macmillan Publishing Company, New York.

Beard, Charles A.
  1972   "That Noble Dream." In *The Varieties of History: From Voltaire to the Present,* revised edition, edited by Fritz Stern, pp. 315–328. World Publishing Company, New York. (First edition published in 1935)

Beck, William S.
1961   *Modern Science and the Nature of Life.* Doubleday & Company, Garden City, NY.

Becker, Carl L.
1938   "What Is Historiography?" *American Historical Review,* Vol. 44, pp. 20–28.
1958   *The Declaration of Independence: A Study in the History of Political Ideas.* Vintage Books, New York. (Originally published in 1922)

Beckner, Morton D.
1967   "Vitalism." In *The Encyclopedia of Philosophy,* edited by Paul Edwards, Vol. 8, pp. 253–256. Macmillan Publishing Company, New York.

Bergson, Henri
1998   *Creative Evolution.* Translated from the French by Arthur Mitchell. Dover Publications, Mineola, NY. (Originally published in 1911)

Berlin, Sir Isaiah
1954   *Historical Inevitability.* Oxford University Press, New York.

Blum, Deborah
2006   *Ghost Hunters: William James and the Search for Scientific Proof of Life After Death.* Penguin Press, New York.

Boeschenstein, Hermann
1967   "Oken, Lorenz." In *The Encyclopedia of Philosophy,* edited by Paul Edwards, Vol. 5, pp. 535–536. Macmillan Publishing Company, New York.

Boswell, James
1952   *The Works of James Boswell: The Life of Samuel Johnson.* Abridged and with an introduction by Bergen Evans. Black's Readers Service Company, Roslyn. NY.

Bowlby, John
1991   *Charles Darwin: A New Life.* W. W. Norton & Company, New York.

Branch, Taylor
1977   "New Frontiers in American Philosophy." *New York Times Magazine,* August 14, pp. 12–18, 22, 46–48, 62–66.

Brian, Dennis
    2005   *The Unexpected Einstein: The Real Man Behind the Icon.* John Wiley & Sons, New York.

Brooke, John Hedley
    2003   "Darwin and Victorian Christianity." In *The Cambridge Companion to Darwin*, edited by Jonathan Hodge and Gregory Radick, pp. 192–213. Cambridge University Press, Cambridge, UK.

Browne, Janet
    2002   *Charles Darwin: A Biography.* Vol. 2, *The Power of Place.* Princeton University Press, Princeton, NJ.

Brunton, Thomas Lauder
    1911   "Therapeutics." In *Encyclopaedia Britannica*, 11th edition, Vol. 26, pp. 793–803.

Büchner, Ludwig
    1891   *Force and Matter.* 4th English edition. Translated from the 15th German edition. Peter Eckler Publisher, New York. (First edition published in 1855)

Bunzel, Ruth
    1965   "The Nature of Katcinas." Reprinted in *Reader in Comparative Religion: An Anthropological Approach*, 2nd edition, edited by William A. Lessa and Evon Z. Vogt, pp. 442–444. Harper & Row Publishers, New York. (First edition published in 1958)

Burrow, J. W.
    1970   Editor's Introduction to *The Origin of Species* by Charles Darwin, pp. 11–48. Penguin Books, Harmondsworth, UK.

Burrows, Millar
    1958   *More Light on the Dead Sea Scrolls.* Viking Press, New York.

Bury, J. B.
    2007   *A History of Freedom of Thought.* International Debate Education Association, New York. (Originally published in 1912)

Butterfield, Herbert
    1960a   "The Scientific Revolution." Reprinted from *Scientific American*, September, pp. 1–9. W. H. Freeman & Company, San Francisco.

1960b   *Man on His Past: The Study of the History of Historical Scholarship.* Beacon Press, Boston.

Calaprice, Alice, editor
2000   *The Expanded Quotable Einstein.* Princeton University Press, Princeton, NJ.

Campbell, Keith
1967   "Materialism." In *The Encyclopedia of Philosophy*, edited by Paul Edwards, Vol 5, pp. 179–188. Macmillan Publishing Company, New York.

Cannon, Walter B.
1942   "Voodoo Death." *American Anthropologist*, Vol. 44, pp. 169–181.

Case, Thomas
1911   "Metaphysics." In *Encyclopaedia Britannica*, 11th edition, Vol. 18, pp. 224–253.

Chagnon, Napoleon A.
1997   *Yanomamö.* 5th edition. Harcourt Brace College Publishers, Fort Worth, TX. (First edition published in 1968)

Cheyne, Thomas Kelly
1910   "Cosmogony." In *Encyclopaedia Britannica*, 11th edition, Vol. 7, pp. 215–217.

Cheyney, Edward P.
1927   *Law in History and Other Essays.* Alfred A. Knopf, New York.

Clive, John
1989   *Not by Fact Alone: Essays on the Writing and Reading of History.* Houghton Mifflin Company, Boston.

Cohen, Lester H.
1980   *The Revolutionary Histories: Contemporary Narratives on the American Revolution.* Cornell University Press, Ithaca, NY.

Cohen, Morris R.
1930   "Atheism: History and Doctrine." In *Encyclopedia of the Social Sciences*, edited by Edwin R. A. Seligman and Alvin Johnson, Vol. 2, pp. 292–294. Macmillan Company, New York.

Collins, Francis S.
  2006 *The Language of God: A Scientist Presents Evidence for Belief.*
  Free Press, New York.

Copleston, Frederick, S. J.
  1967 *History of Philosophy, Vol. 8: Modern Philosophy—Bentham to Russell.* Doubleday & Company, Garden City, NY.

Cranston, Maurice
  1967 "Bacon, Francis." In *The Encyclopedia of Philosophy*, edited by Paul Edwards, Vol. 1, pp. 235–240. Macmillan Publishing Company, New York.

Crick, Francis
  1981 *Life Itself: Its Origin and Nature.* Simon & Schuster, New York.

Crowe, Michael J.
  1994 *Modern Theories of the Universe: From Herschel to Hubble.* Dover Publications, New York.

Cushing, Max Pearson
  1914 *Baron d'Holbach: A Study of Eighteenth Century Radicalism in France.* Hard Press, no place of publication indicated.

Dales, Richard C.
  1989 *The Scientific Achievement of the Middle Ages.* University of Pennsylvania Press, Philadelphia.

d'Alviella, Goblet
  1908 "Animism." In *Encyclopaedia of Religion and Ethics*, edited by James Hastings, Vol. 1, pp. 535–537. T. & T. Clark, Edinburgh, UK.

Danto, Arthur C.
  1967 "Naturalism." In *The Encyclopedia of Philosophy*, edited by Paul Edwards, Vol. 5, pp. 448–450. Macmillan Publishing Company, New York.

Darwin, Charles
  1890 *The Origin of Species.* 6th edition. John Murray, London. (First edition published in 1859)
  1909 *The Foundations of the The Origin of Species: Two Essays Written in 1842 and 1844.* Edited by his Son Francis Darwin. Cambridge University Press, Cambridge, UK.

1929   *Autobiography of Charles Darwin.* Edited by his Son Francis Darwin. Watts & Company, London. (Originally published in 1887)

1958a   *The Origin of Species.* 6th edition. Introduction by Julian Huxley. New American Library, New York. (First edition published in 1859)

1958b   *The Autobiography of Charles Darwin.* Edited by Nora Barlow. W. W. Norton & Company, New York. (Originally published in 1887)

1959   *The Life and Letters of Charles Darwin.* 2 vols. Edited by his Son Francis Darwin. Basic Books, New York. (Originally published in 1887)

1970   *The Origin of Species.* 1st edition. Edited by J. W. Burrow. Penguin Books, Harmondsworth, UK. (Originally published in 1859)

1993   *The Correspondence of Charles Darwin, Vol. 8, 1860.* Cambridge University Press, Cambridge, UK.

1994   *The Correspondence of Charles Darwin, Vol. 9, 1861.* Cambridge University Press, Cambridge, UK.

1998   *The Descent of Man.* 2nd edition. Introduction by H. James Birx. Prometheus Books, Amherst, NY. (First edition published in 1871)

1999   *The Correspondence of Charles Darwin, Vol. 11, 1863.* Cambridge University Press, Cambridge, UK.

Davies, Mansel
1947   *An Outline of the Development of Science.* Watts & Company, London.

Dawkins, Richard
2006   *The God Delusion.* Houghton Mifflin Company, Boston.

Dennett, Daniel C.
2006   *Breaking the Spell: Religion as a Natural Phenomenon.* Viking Press, New York.

Desmond, Adrian, and James Moore
1991   *Darwin: The Life of a Tormented Evolutionist.* W. W. Norton & Company, New York.

Dewey, John
1979   "The Influence of Darwin on Philosophy." Reprinted in *Darwin: A Norton Critical Edition,* 2nd edition, edited by Philip

Appleman, pp. 305–314. W. W. Norton & Company, New York. (First edition published in 1970)

Dilthey, Wilhem
1972 "Frederick and the Academy." In *Frederick the Great: A Profile*, edited by Peter Paret, pp. 177–197. Hill & Wang, New York.

Dostoevsky, Feodor
1945 *The Short Novels of Dostoevsky*. Translated from the Russian by Constance Garnett. Dial Press, New York.

Dreyer, J. L. E.
1953 *A History of Astronomy from Thales to Kepler*. 2nd edition. Dover Publications, New York. (First edition published in 1906)

du Noüy, Pierre Lecomte
1948 *The Road to Reason*. Translated from the French and edited by Mary Lecomte du Noüy. Longmans, Green, & Company, New York.

Dukas, Helen, and Banesh Hoffmann, editors
1979 *Albert Einstein, the Human Side: New Glimpses from His Archives*. Princeton University Press, Princeton, NJ.

Duncan, David
1908 *Life and Letters of Herbert Spencer*. 2 vols. D. Appleton & Company, New York.

Duncan, John Charles
1946 *Astronomy: A Textbook*. Harper & Brothers Publishers, New York.

Dupree, A. Hunter
1959 *Asa Gray: American Botanist, Friend of Darwin*. Johns Hopkins Press, Baltimore, MD.

Durkheim, Emile
1995 *The Elementary Forms of the Religious Life*. Translated from the French by Karen E. Fields. Free Press, New York. (Originally published in 1912)

Dyson, Freeman J.
2004 *Infinite in All Directions*. Harper-Collins, New York.

Eddington, Sir Arthur
  1948   *The Nature of the Physical World*. Cambridge University Press, Cambridge, UK. (Originally published in 1928)

Edwards, Paul
  1961   "Hard and Soft Determinism." In *Determinism and Freedom in the Age of Modern Science: A Philosophical Symposium*, edited by Sidney Hook, pp. 117–125. Collier Books, New York.
  1967a   "Atheism." In *The Encyclopedia of Philosophy*, edited by Paul Edwards, Vol. 1, pp. 174–189. Macmillan Publishing Company, New York.
  1967b   "Panpsychism." In *The Encyclopedia of Philosophy*, edited by Paul Edwards, Vol. 6, pp. 22–31. Macmillan Publishing Company, New York.

Einstein, Albert
  1940   Untitled statement in *I Believe* (no editor), pp. 69–75. George Allen & Unwin, London.
  1954   *Ideas and Opinions*. Translated from the German by Sonja Bargmann. Laurel-Leaf Library, New York.
  1993   "Science and Religion." In *Out of My Later Years: The Scientist, Philosopher, and Man Portrayed Through His Own Words*, pp. 19–28. Wings Books, New York. (Originally published in 1950)

Eldredge, Niles
  2005   *Darwin: Discovering the Tree of Life*. W. W. Norton & Company, New York.

Engels, Frederick
  1941   *Ludwig Feuerbach and the Outcome of Classical German Philosophy*. Translated from the German by Austin Lewis. International Publishers, New York. (Originally published in 1888)

Evans-Pritchard, E. E.
  1965   *Theories of Primitive Religion*. Clarendon Press, Oxford, UK.
  1974   *Nuer Religion*. Oxford University Press, New York. (Originally published in 1956)

Feynman, Richard
  1998   *The Meaning of It All: Thoughts of a Citizen Scientist*. Perseus Books, Reading, MA.

Fiske, John
　1903　*Outlines of Cosmic Philosophy*. 3 vols. Houghton Mifflin Company, Boston.

Francis, Keith A.
　2007　*Charles Darwin and The Origin of Species*. Greenwood Press, Westport, CT.

Frank, Jerome
　1945　*Fate and Freedom: A Philosophy for Free Americans*. Simon & Schuster, New York.

Freud, Sigmund
　1961　*The Future of an Illusion*. Translated from the German by James Strachey. W. W. Norton & Company, New York. (Originally published in 1927)

Galton, Francis
　1874　*English Men of Science*. Macmillan & Company, London.

Garaudy, Roger
　1967　*Karl Marx: The Evolution of His Thought*. Translated from the French by Nan Apothecker. Lawrence & Wishart, London.

Garvie, A. E.
　1918　"Polytheism." In *Encyclopaedia of Religion and Ethics*, edited by James Hastings, Vol. 10, pp. 112–114. T. & T. Clark, Edinburgh, UK.

Gay, Peter
　1969　*The Enlightenment: An Interpretation*. Vol. 2, *The Science of Freedom*. W. W. Norton & Company, New York.

George, Henry
　1965　*A Perplexed Philosopher*. Robert Schalkenbach Foundation, New York. (Originally published in 1892)

Gilbert, Neil W.
　1967　"Galen." In *The Encyclopedia of Philosophy*, edited by Paul Edwards, Vol. 3, pp. 261–262. Macmillan Publishing Company, New York.

Gilderhaus, Mark T.
　1996　*History and Historians: A Historiographical Introduction*. Prentice-Hall, Englewood Cliffs, NJ.

References 435

Goudge, T. A.

1967a   "Loeb, Jacques." In *The Encyclopedia of Philosophy*, edited by Paul Edwards, Vol. 4, pp. 503–504. Macmillan Publishing Company, New York.

1967b   "Bergson, Henri." In *The Encyclopedia of Philosophy*, edited by Paul Edwards, Vol. 1, pp. 287–295. Macmillan Publishing Company, New York.

1967c   "Emergent Evolution." In *The Encyclopedia of Philosophy*, edited by Paul Edwards, Vol. 2, pp. 474–477. Macmillan Publishing Company, New York.

1967d   "Morgan, C. Lloyd." In *The Encyclopedia of Philosophy*, edited by Paul Edwards, Vol. 5, pp. 392–393. Macmillan Publishing Company, New York.

Gould, Stephen Jay

1989   "Tires to Sandals." *Natural History*, April, pp. 12–15, 20.

1997   "Nonoverlapping Magesteria." *Natural History*, March, pp. 16, 18, 20–22, 61–62.

1999   *Rocks of Ages: Science and Religion in the Fullness of Life.* Ballantine Books, New York.

Graber, Robert Bates

2006   "Bye-Bye, BABY! A Culturalist's Response to Evolutionary Culture Theorists." *Social Evolution & History*, Vol. 6, pp. 3–28 (published in Moscow).

Gray, Louis H.

1911   "Cosmogony and Cosmology (Polynesian)." In *Encyclopaedia of Religion and Ethics*, edited by James Hastings, Vol. 4, pp. 174–175. T. & T. Clark, Edinburgh, UK.

Greene, John C.

1960   "Darwin and Religion." In *Science Ponders Religion*, edited by Harlow Shapley, pp. 254–276. Appleton-Century-Crofts, New York.

Grossman, Cathy Lynn

2006   "View of God Can Reveal Your Values and Politics." *USA Today*, September 12, pp. 1–2.

Haeckel, Ernst

1992   *The Riddle of the Universe.* Translated from the German by Joseph McCabe. Introduction by H. James Birx. Prometheus Books, Buffalo, NY. (Originally published in 1899)

Haldane, J. B. S.
  1940   Untitled statement in *I Believe* (no editor), pp. 109–112. George Allen & Unwin, London.

Haldane, J. S.
  1929   *The Sciences and Philosophy*. Doubleday, Doran & Company, Garden City, NY.

Hallam, Henry
  1897   "The Middle Ages as a Period of Intellectual Darkness." In *A Library of the World's Best Literature*, edited by Charles Dudley Warner, Vol. 17, pp. 6857–6860. International Society, New York.

Hamer, Dean
  2004   *The God Gene: How Faith Is Hardwired into Our Genes*. Random House, New York.

Hamilton, Edith
  1960   *Mythology*. Warner Books, New York.

Handy, Rollo
  1967a   "Haeckel, Ernst Heinrich." In *The Encyclopedia of Philosophy*, edited by Paul Edwards, Vol. 3, pp. 399–402. Macmillan Publishing Company, New York.

  1967b   "Büchner, Ludwig." In *The Encyclopedia of Philosophy*, edited by Paul Edwards, Vol. 1, pp. 411–413. Macmillan Publishing Company, New York.

Hanson, Norwood Russell
  1967   "Copernicus, Nicolas." In *The Encyclopedia of Philosophy*, edited by Paul Edwards, Vol. 2, pp. 219–222. Macmillan Publishing Company, New York.

Harner, Michael J.
  1962   "Jívaro Souls." *American Anthropologist*, Vol. 64, pp. 258–272.
  1972   *The Jívaro: People of the Sacred Waterfalls*. Natural History Press, Garden City, NY.

Harré, Rom
  1967   "Laplace, Pierre Simon de." In *The Encyclopedia of Philosophy*, edited by Paul Edwards. Vol. 4, pp. 391–393. Macmillan Publishing Company, New York.

Harris, R. Laird
    1975   "Sheol." In *Wycliffe Bible Dictionary*, pp. 1572–1573. Hendrickson Publishers, Peabody, MA.

Harris, Sam
    2004   *The End of Faith: Religion, Terror, and the Future of Reason.* W. W. Norton & Company, New York.

Harrison, Frederic
    1884   "The Ghost of Religion." *The Nineteenth Century*, n.s., Vol. 15, pp. 494–506.
    1885   "The Ghost of Religion." In *The Nature and Reality of Religion: A Controversy Between Frederic Harrison and Herbert Spencer*, pp. 30–58. D. Appleton & Company, New York.

Harvey, Graham
    2005   *Animism: Respecting the Living World.* Columbia University Press, New York.

Haskins, Charles Homer
    1966   *The Renaissance of the Twelfth Century.* World Publishing Company, Cleveland. (Originally published in 1927)

Hawking, Stephen
    1998   *A Brief History of Time.* Updated edition. Bantam Books, New York. (First edition published in 1988)

Hazen, Robert M.
    2005   *Genesis: The Scientific Quest for Life's Origin.* Joseph Henry Press, Washington, DC.

Hearnshaw, F. J. C.
    1933   "Herbert Spencer and the Individualists." In *The Social and Political Ideas of Some Representative Thinkers of the Victorian Age*, edited by F. J. C. Hearnshaw, pp. 53–83. George H. Harrap & Company, London.

Hegel, Georg Friedrich
    1969   "The Philosophy of History." Reprinted in *Ideas of History, Vol. 1: Speculative Approaches to History*, edited by Ronald H. Nash, pp. 89–106. E. P. Dutton & Company, New York.

Heisenberg, Werner
    1972   *Physics and Beyond: Encounters and Conversations.*

Translated from the German by Arnold J. Pomerans. Harper & Row Publishers, New York.

Henderson, Lawrence J.
>1917   *The Order of Nature: An Essay*. Harvard University Press, Cambridge, MA.

>1958   *The Fitness of the Environment: An Inquiry into the Biological Significance of the Properties of Matter*. Beacon Press, Boston. (Originally published in 1913)

Henry, Jules
>1941   *Jungle People: A Kaingáng Tribe of the Highlands of Brazil*. J. J. Augustin Publishers, New York.

Hepburn, Ronald W.
>1967   "Nature, Philosophical Ideas of." In *The Encyclopedia of Philosophy*, edited by Paul Edwards, Vol. 5, pp. 454–458. Macmillan Publishing Company, New York.

Hitchens, Christopher
>2007   *God Is Not Great: How Religion Poisons Everything*. Twelve/Hachette Book Group USA, New York.

Hoagland, Hudson
>1960   "Some Reflections on Science and Religion." In *Science Ponders Religion*, edited by Harlow Shapley, pp. 17–31. Appleton-Century-Crofts, New York.

Hobbes, Thomas
>1997   *Leviathan*. Simon & Schuster, New York. (Originally published in 1651)

Hocking, William Ernest
>1939   *Types of Philosophy*. Revised edition. Charles Scribner's Sons, New York. (First edition published in 1929)

d'Holbach, Baron
>2006   *The System of Nature*. Translated from the French. Introduction by Robert D. Richardson, Jr. BiblioBazaar, Charleston, SC. (Originally published in 1770)

Holmberg, Allan R.
>1969   *Nomads of the Long Bow: The Siriono of Eastern Bolivia*. Natural History Press, Garden City, NY.

Holton, Gerald
    1960   "Notes on the Religious Orientation of Scientists." In *Science Ponders Religion*, edited by Harlow Shapley, pp. 52–64. Appleton-Century-Crofts, New York.

Horzelski, J.
    1945   "Causality or Indeterminism?" *Nature*, Vol. 155, January 27, p. 111.

House, Floyd N.
    1936   *The Development of Sociology*. McGraw-Hill Book Company, New York.

Hubert, René
    1931   "Comte, Auguste." *Encyclopedia of the Social Sciences*, edited by Edwin R. A. Seligman and Alvin Johnson, Vol. 4, pp. 151–153. Macmillan Company, New York.

Hull, David L.
    2003   "Darwin's Science and Victorian Philosophy of Science." In *The Cambridge Companion to Darwin*, edited by Jonathan Hodge and Gregory Radick, pp. 168–191. Cambridge University Press, Cambridge, UK.

Hume, David
    1927   *Hume Selections*. Edited by Charles W. Hendel, Jr. Charles Scribner's Sons, New York.

Huppert, George
    1970   *The Idea of Perfect History: Historical Erudition and Historical Philosophy in Renaissance France*. University of Illinois Press, Urbana.

Huxley, Julian
    1940   Untitled statement in *I Believe* (no editor), pp. 131–140. George Allen & Unwin, London.
    1957   *Religion Without Revelation*. New American Library, New York.
    1961   Introduction to *The Phenomenon of Man* by Pierre Teilhard de Chardin, pp. 11–28. Harper & Row Publishers, New York.

Huxley, Leonard
    1900   *Life and Letters of Thomas Henry Huxley*. 2 vols. D. Appleton & Company, New York.

Huxley, Thomas Henry
    1896a   *Darwiniana: Essays.* D. Appleton & Company, New York.
    1896b   *Science and Christian Tradition: Essays.* D. Appleton & Company, New York.
    1897   *Methods and Results: Essays.* D. Appleton & Company, New York.
    1908   *Hume: With Helps to the Study of Berkeley.* Macmillan & Company, London.
    1909   *Autobiography and Selected Essays.* Edited by Ada L. F. Snell. Houghton Mifflin Company, Boston.

Im Thurn, Everard P.
    1883   *Among the Indians of Guiana.* Kegan Paul, Trench, & Company, London.

James, William
    1880   "Great Men, Great Thoughts, and the Environment." *Atlantic Monthly*, Vol. 46, pp. 441–459.
    1955   "Some Metaphysical Problems Practically Considered." In *Pragmatism and Four Essays from the Meaning of Truth*, pp. 63–86. World Publishing Company, Cleveland.
    1963   *Psychology.* Fawcett Publications, Greenwich, CT. (One-volume abridgement of *The Principles of Psychology* originally published in 1890)
    1992   "The Will to Believe." In *William James: Writings 1878–1899.* Library of America, New York.
    1994   *The Varieties of Religious Experience: A Study in Human Nature.* Modern Library, New York. (Originally published in 1902)
    1996   *A Pluralistic Universe.* University of Nebraska Press, Lincoln. (Originally published in 1909)
    2008   *Memories and Studies.* Arc Manor, Rockville, MD. (Originally published in 1911)

Jeans, Sir James
    1947   *The Mysterious Universe.* Macmillan Publishing Company, New York. (Originally published in 1930)
    1961   *The Growth of Physical Science.* Fawcett Publications, Greenwich, CT. (Originally published in 1947)

Joyce, G. C.
 1911 "Deism." In *Encyclopaedia of Religion and Ethics*, edited by James Hastings, Vol. 4, pp. 533–543. T. & T. Clark, Edinburgh, UK.

Kaiser, David
 2007 "The Other Evolution Wars." *American Scientist*, Vol. 95, pp. 518–525.

Kaminsky, Alice R.
 1967 "Lewes, George Henry." In *The Encyclopedia of Philosophy*, edited by Paul Edwards, Vol. 4, pp. 451–454. Macmillan Publishing Company, New York.

Keller, Albert Galloway
 1911 *Homeric Society: A Sociological Study of the Iliad and Odyssey*. Longmans, Green & Company, London.

Keller, Timothy
 2008 *The Reason for God: Belief in an Age of Skepticism*. E. P. Dutton & Company, New York.

Kerferd, G. B.
 1967 "Aristotle." In *The Encyclopedia of Philosophy*, edited by Paul Edwards, Vol. 1, pp. 151–162. Macmillan Publishing Company, New York.

Killen, R. Allan
 1975 "Hell." In *Wycliffe Bible Dictionary*. Hendrickson Publishers, New York.

Kramer, Edna
 1974 *The Nature and Growth of Modern Mathematics*. 2 vols. Fawcett Publications, Greenwood, CT.

Krutch, Joseph Wood
 1962 *More Lives Than One*. William Sloane Associates, New York.

Kurtz, Paul
 1967 "American Philosophy." In *The Encyclopedia of Philosophy*, edited by Paul Edwards, Vol. 1, pp. 83–93. Macmillan Publishing Company, New York.

Lahav, Noam
    1999   *Biogenesis: Theories of Life's Origin*. Oxford University Press, New York.

Laird, John
    1936   *Recent Philosophy*. Thornton Butterworth, London.

Lang, Andrew
    1898   *The Making of Religion*. Longmans, Green & Company, London.

Langmuir, Irving
    1943   "Science, Common Sense and Decency." *Nature*, Vol. 151, March 6, pp. 266–270.

Lanham, Url
    1968   *Origins of Modern Biology*. Columbia University Press, New York.

de Laplace, Pierre-Simon
    2007   *Philosophical Essay on Probabilities*. Translated from the French by F. W. Truscott and F. L. Emory. Cosimo Classics, New York. (Originally published in 1901)

Leiber, Justin
    1994   Introduction to *Man A Machine* and *Man A Plant* by Julien Offray de La Mettrie. Translated from the French by Richard A. Watson and Maya Rybalka, pp. 1–15. Hackett Publishing Company, Indianapolis, IN.

Lenin, V. I.
    1943   "Dialectical Materialism and Empiriocriticism." In *Selected Works* by V. I. Lenin, Vol. 11, pp. 87–409. International Publishers, New York.

Leuba, James H.
    1916   *The Belief in God and Immortality*. Sherman, French & Company, Boston.

Levy, H. [Hyman]
    1938   *The Universe of Science*. Watts & Company, London.

Lewes, George Henry
    1879   *Problems of Life and Mind*. Third Series, Problem the First: *The Study of Psychology*. Trübner & Company, London.

Lindley, David
2004 *Degrees Kelvin: A Tale of Genius, Invention, and Tragedy.* Joseph Henry Press, Washington, DC.

Lodge, Sir Oliver
1905 *Life and Matter: A Criticism of Professor Haeckel's "Riddle of the Universe."* G. P. Putnam's Sons, New York.
1908 Introduction to *Ecce Homo: A Study of the Life and Work of Jesus Christ* by J. R. Seeley, pp. vii–xv. J. M. Dent, London.
1912 *Man and the Universe.* Methuen & Company, London.
1914 "Continuity." Presidential Address to the British Association. G. P. Putnam's Sons, New York.

Longmore, Donald
1971 *The Heart.* McGraw-Hill Book Company, New York.

Losee, John
1993 *A Historical Introduction to the Philosophy of Science.* 3rd edition. Oxford University Press, Oxford, UK. (First edition published in 1972)

Lovejoy, Arthur O.
1936 *The Great Chain of Being: A Study of the History of an Idea.* Harvard University Press, Cambridge, MA.
1959 "The Argument for Organic Evolution Before *The Origin of Species*, 1830–1858." In *Forerunners of Darwin, 1745–1859*, edited by Bentley Glass, Owsei Temkin, and William L. Straus, Jr., pp. 356–414. Johns Hopkins Press, Baltimore, MD.

Lowie, Robert H.
1911 "Cosmology and Cosmogony (Mexico and South America)." In *Encyclopaedia of Religion and Ethics*, edited by James Hastings, Vol. 4, pp. 168–174. T. & T. Clark, Edinburgh, UK.

Lowith, Karl
1949 *Meaning in History.* University of Chicago Press, Chicago.

Lubbock, Sir John (Lord Avebury)
1870 *The Origin of Civilisation and the Primitive Condition of Man: Mental and Social Conditions of Savages.* D. Appleton & Company, New York.

Lucretius
 2005 *De Rerum Natura: The Poem on Nature*. Translated and with an introduction by C. H. Sisson. Fyfield Books, Exeter, UK.

Luisi, Pier Luigi
 2006 *The Emergence of Life: From Chemical Origins to Synthetic Biology*. Cambridge University Press, Cambridge, UK.

Luria, S. E.
 1973 *Life: The Unfinished Experiment*. Charles Scribner's Sons, New York.

Lyell, Sir Charles
 1863 *The Geological Evidences of the Antiquity of Man*. J. W. Childs, Philadelphia.

MacCulloch, J. A.
 1920 "State of the Dead (Primitive and Savage)." In *Encyclopaedia of Religion and Ethics*, edited by James Hastings, Vol. 11, pp. 817–828. T. & T. Clark, Edinburgh, UK.

Mach, Ernst
 1943 *Popular Scientific Lectures*. Open Court Publishing Company, LaSalle, IL. (Originally published in 1895)

MacIntyre, Alasdair
 1967 "Pantheism." In *The Encyclopedia of Philosophy*, edited by Paul Edwards, Vol. 6, pp. 31–35. Macmillan Publishing Company, New York.

Marchant, James
 1916 *Alfred Russel Wallace: Letters and Reminiscences*. 2 vols. Cassel & Company, London.

Marett, Robert R.
 1909 *The Threshold of Religion*. Methuen & Company, London.
 1914 *The Threshold of Religion*. 2nd edition. Macmillan Company, New York. (First edition published in 1909)

Martin, Kingsley
 1962 *French Liberal Thought in the Eighteenth Century: A Study of Political Ideas from Bayle to Condorcet*. Phoenix House, London. (Originally published in 1929)

Marx, Karl, and Frederick Engels
 2002 *The Holy Family*. Translated from the German. University Press of the Pacific, Honolulu, HI. (Originally published in 1845)

Mason, Stephen F.
 1962 *A History of the Sciences*. Revised edition. Macmillan Publishing Company, New York. (First edition published in 1956)

Max Müller, Friedrich
 1879 *Lectures on the Origin and Growth of Religion*. Charles Scribner's Sons, New York.

Maybury-Lewis, David
 1971 *Akwẽ-Shavante Society*. Clarendon Press, Oxford, UK.

McCosh, James
 1875 *Christianity and Positivism*. Robert Carter & Brothers, New York.

McManus, Sean
 2008 "If God Is Dead, Who Gets His House?" *New York*, April 28, pp. 36–39, 105.

Meacham, Jon
 2007 "The God Debate: Interview with Rick Warren and Sam Harris." *Newsweek*, April 9, pp. 58–63.

Mill, John Stuart
 1886 *A System of Logic*. 8th edition. Longmans, Green & Company, London. (First edition published in 1843)
 1930 *A System of Logic*. 8th edition. Longmans, Green & Company, London. (First edition published in 1843)
 1998 *Three Essays on Religion*. Prometheus Books, Amherst, NY. (Originally published in 1874)
 2007 *Autobiography*. ReadHowYouWant Classics Library, no place of publication indicated.

Miller, Kenneth R.
 1999 *Finding Darwin's God: A Scientist's Search for Common Ground Between God and Evolution*. HarperCollins Publishers, New York.
 2008 *Only a Theory: Evolution and the Battle for America's Soul*. Viking Press, New York.

Millikan, Robert Andrews
    1927   *Evolution in Science and Religion*. Yale University Press, New
            Haven, CT.
    1941   Untitled statement of belief in *Living Philosophies* (no editor),
            pp. 37–53. World Publishing Company, Cleveland. (Originally
            published in 1930)

Milner, Richard
    1994   *Charles Darwin: Evolution of a Naturalist*. Facts on File, New
            York.

Mitchell, Peter Chalmers
    1910   "Evolution." In *Encyclopaedia Britannica*, 11th edition, Vol.
            10, pp. 22–37.
    1930   "Materialism and Vitalism in Biology." *The Herbert Spencer
            Lecture for 1930*. Clarendon Press, Oxford, UK.

Moore, Patrick
    1987   *Astronomers' Stars*. W. W. Norton & Company, New York.

Moran, Michael
    1967   "New England Transcendentalism." In *The Encyclopedia of
            Philosophy*, edited by Paul Edwards, Vol. 5, pp. 479–480.
            Macmillan Publishing Company, New York.

Morgan, C. Lloyd
    1923   *Emergent Evolution*. Henry Holt & Company, New York.
    1929   "The Case for Emergent Evolution." *Journal of Philosophical
            Studies*, Vol. 4, No. 21, pp. 23–38.

Morley, Viscount (John)
    1910   "Comte, Auguste." In *Encyclopaedia Britannica*, 11th edition,
            Vol. 6, pp. 814–822.

Morris, Richard
    1984   *Dismantling the Universe: The Nature of Scientific Discovery*.
            Simon & Schuster, New York.

Mossner, Ernest Campbell
    1967   "Toland, John." In *The Encyclopedia of Philosophy*, edited by
            Paul Edwards, Vol. 8, pp. 141–143. Macmillan Publishing
            Company, New York.

Nagel, Ernest
    1969   "Determinism in History." Reprinted in *Ideas of History, Vol. 2:*

    The Critical Philosophy of History, edited by Ronald H. Nash, pp. 319–350. E. P. Dutton & Company, New York.

Needham, Joseph
  1955 "Mechanistic Biology and the Religious Consciousness." In *Science, Religion & Reality*, edited by Joseph Needham, pp. 223–261. George Braziller, New York. (Originally published in 1925)

Nelson, Lynn H., editor
  1991 *Chronicle of San Juan de la Peña: A Fourteenth-Century History of the Crown of Aragon*. Translated from the Spanish by Lynn H. Nelson. University of Pennsylvania Press, Philadelphia. (Originally published in 1931)

Nerlich, G. C.
  1967 "Eddington, Arthur Stanley." In *The Encyclopedia of Philosophy*, edited by Paul Edwards, Vol. 2, pp. 458–460. Macmillan Publishing Company, New York.

Newcomb, Simon
  1932 *Simon Newcomb's Astronomy for Everybody*. Revised by Robert H. Baker. New Home Library, New York. (First edition published in 1902)

Newton, Isaac
  1934 *Principia Mathematica*. Edited by F. Cajori. Book III. University of California Press, Berkeley. (Originally published in 1687)

Nimuendajú, Curt
  1942 *The Šerente*. Translated from the Portuguese (manuscript) by Robert H. Lowie. Publications of the Frederick Webb Hodge Anniversary Publication Fund, Vol. 4, Los Angeles.

Nordau, Max
  1910 *The Interpretation of History*. Translated from the German by M. A. Hamilton. Moffat, Yard & Company, New York.

Norris, Ray
  2008 "Emu Dreaming." *Australian Science*, May, pp. 16–19.

Olson, Steve
  2006 "Faces of the New Atheism." *Wired*, November, p. 187.

Oparin, A. I.
  1957 *The Origin of Life on Earth.* 3rd edition. Translated from the Russian by Ann Synge. Academic Press, New York. (First edition published in 1936)

Osborn, Henry Fairfield
  1929 *From the Greeks to Darwin: The Development of the Evolution Idea Through Twenty-Four Centuries.* 2nd edition. Charles Scribner's Sons, New York. (First edition published in 1894)

Padover, Saul K.
  1978 *Karl Marx: An Intimate Biography.* Abridged edition. New American Library, New York.

Paine, Thomas
  2006 *The Age of Reason.* The Echo Library, Teddington, UK. (Originally published in three parts in 1794, 1795, and 1807)

Parrington, Vernon Louis
  1930 *Main Currents in American Thought, Vol. 3: 1860–1920, The Beginnings of Critical Realism in America.* Harcourt, Brace & Company, New York.

Passmore, John A.
  1965 Editor's Introduction to *Priestley's Writings on Philosophy, Science, and Politics,* pp. 7–37. Collier Books, New York.
  1967 "Priestley, Joseph." In *The Encyclopedia of Philosophy,* edited by Paul Edwards, Vol. 6, pp. 451–455. Macmillan Publishing Company, New York.
  1968 *A Hundred Years of Philosophy.* Penguin Books, Harmondsworth, UK.

Peckham, Morse
  1959 "Darwinism and Darwinisticism." *Victorian Studies,* Vol. 3, pp. 19–40.

Peirce, Charles
  1955 *Philosophical Writings of Peirce.* Edited by Justus Buchler. Dover Publications, New York.

Peters, R. S.
  1967 "Hobbes, Thomas." In *The Encyclopedia of Philosophy,* edited by Paul Edwards, Vol. 4, pp. 30–46. Macmillan Publishing Company, New York.

Pickover, Clifford A.
  2008   *Archimedes to Hawking: Laws of Science and the Great Minds Behind Them*. Oxford University Press, New York.

Pigliucci, Massimo
  2006   "Is Physics Turning into Philosophy?" *Skeptical Inquirer*, May/June, p. 22.

Planck, Max
  1981   *Where Is Science Going?* Ox Bow Press, Woodbridge, CT. (Originally published in 1933)

Plekhanov, George
  1940   *The Role of the Individual in History*. Translated from the Russian. International Publishers, New York. (Originally published in 1898)
  1967   *Essays in the History of Materialism*. Translated from the Russian by Ralph Fox. Howard Fertig, New York. (Originally published in 1896)

Pollard, S.
  1968   *The Idea of Progress: History and Society*. Watts & Company, London.

Popkin, Richard H.
  1967   "Gassendi, Pierre." In *The Encyclopedia of Philosophy*, edited by Paul Edwards, Vol. 3, pp. 269–273. Macmillan Publishing Company, New York.

Priestley, Joseph
  1965   *Priestley's Writings on Philosophy, Science, and Politics*. Edited by John A. Passmore. Collier Books, New York.

Quammen, David
  2006   *The Reluctant Mr. Darwin: An Intimate Portrait of Charles Darwin and the Making of His Theory of Evolution*. W. W. Norton & Company, New York.

Radin, Paul
  1985   *Primitive Man as Philosopher*. Dover Publications, New York. (Originally published in 1927)

Randall, John Herman
  1979   "The Changing Impact of Darwin on Philosophy." Reprinted in *Darwin: A Norton Critical Edition*, 2nd edition, edited by

Philip Appleman, pp. 314–325. W. W. Norton & Company, New York. (First edition published in 1970)

Renier, G. J.
1950   *History: Its Purpose and Method.* Beacon Press, Boston.

Renouf, P. Le Page
1880   *Origin and Growth of Religion as Illustrated by the Religion of Ancient Egypt.* Charles Scribner's Sons, New York.

Robinson, James Harvey
1965   *The New History: Essays Illustrating the Modern Historical Outlook.* Free Press, New York. (Originally published in 1912)

Romanes, George John ("Physicus")
1878   *A Candid Examination of Theism.* Trübner & Company, London.

Rowse, A. L.
1963   *The Use of History.* Revised edition. Collier Books, New York. (First edition published in 1946)

Rubel, Maximillien, and Margaret Manale
1976   *Marx Without Myth: A Chronological Study of His Life and Work.* Harper & Row Publishers, New York.

Ruse, Michael
2001   *Can a Darwinian be a Christian?* Cambridge University Press, New York.
2003   "Belief in God in a Darwinian Age." In *The Cambridge Companion to Darwin,* edited by Jonathan Hodge and Gregory Radick, pp. 333–354. Cambridge University Press, Cambridge, UK.
2005   *The Evolution-Creation Struggle.* Harvard University Press, Cambridge, MA.

Russell, Bertrand
1945   *The History of Western Philosophy.* Simon & Schuster, New York.
1954   *The Analysis of Matter.* Dover Publications, New York. (Originally published in 1927)
1997   *Religion and Science.* Oxford University Press, New York. (Originally published in 1935)

Saleeby, C. W.
  1906   *Evolution the Master-Key*. Harper & Brothers, London.

Santayana, George
  1923   "The Unknowable." Herbert Spencer Lecture for 1923. Clarendon Press, Oxford, UK.

Sarton, George
  1955   Introductory Essay to *Science, Religion & Reality* edited by Joseph Needham, pp. 3–22. George Braziller, New York. (Originally published in 1925)

Schmidt, Father Wilhelm
  1965   "The Nature, Attributes and Worship of the Primitive High God." Reprinted in *Reader in Comparative Religion: An Anthropological Approach*, 2nd edition, edited by William A. Lessa and Evon Z. Vogt, pp. 21–33. Harper & Row Publishers, New York. (First edition published in 1958)

Scheffer, Victor B.
  2000   *A Biologist Looks at Religion*. Bamboo Press, Seattle, WA.

Sedgwick, Adam
  1979   "Objections to Mr. Darwin's Theory of the Origin of Species." Reprinted in *Darwin: A Norton Critical Edition*, 2nd edition, edited by Philip Appleman, pp. 220–222. W. W. Norton & Company, New York. (First edition published in 1970)

Seldes, George
  1996   *The Great Thoughts*. Ballantine Books, New York.

Seyffert, Oskar
  1995   *The Dictionary of Classical Mythology, Religion, Literature, and Art*. Grammercy Books, New York.

Shaw, George Bernard
  1977   Preface to *Back to Methuselah*. Penguin Books, Harmondsworth, UK. (Originally published in 1921)

Sherrington, Sir Charles
  1952   Introduction to *The Physical Basis of Mind,* edited by Peter Laslett, pp. 1–4. Basil Blackwell, Oxford, UK.

Shotwell, David A.
  2003   "From the Anthropic Principle to the Supernatural." In *Science*

and Religion: Are They Compatible? edited by Paul Kurtz, pp. 47–49. Prometheus Books, Amherst, NY.

Simpson, George Gaylord
  1949   *The Meaning of Evolution: A Study of the History of Life and Its Significance for Man.* Yale University Press, New Haven, CT.
  1982   Prologue to *The Book of Darwin*, edited by George Gaylord Simpson, pp. 13–17. Washington Square Press, New York.

Singer, Charles
  1955   "Historical Relations of Religion and Science." In *Science, Religion & Reality*, edited by Joseph Needham, pp. 91–152. George Braziller, New York. (Originally published in 1925)

Singh, Jagit
  1970   *Great Ideas and Theories of Modern Cosmology.* Revised edition. Dover Publications, New York. (First edition published in 1961)

Skinner, B. F.
  1955/6 "Freedom and the Control of Men." *American Scholar*, Vol. 25, pp. 47–65.

Smith, Edwin W., and Andrew Murray Dale
  1968   *The Ila-Speaking Peoples of Northern Rhodesia.* 2 vols. University Books, New Hyde Park, NY. (Originally published in 1920)

Smith, Homer W.
  1955   *Man and His Gods.* Little, Brown & Company, Boston.

Smolin, Lee
  2006   "A Crisis in Fundamental Physics." *Update: New York Academy of Sciences Magazine*, January/February, pp. 10–14.

Sorley, W. C.
  1961   "Philosophers." In *The Cambridge History of English Literature*, edited by Sir A. W. Ward and A. R. Waller, Vol. 14, *The Nineteenth Century*, Part III, pp. 1–49. Cambridge University Press, Cambridge, UK.
  1965   *A History of British Philosophy to 1900.* Cambridge University Press, Cambridge, UK.

Spence, Lewis
  1911   "Cosmogony and Cosmology (North America)." In

Encyclopaedia of Religion and Ethics, edited by James Hastings, Vol. 4, pp. 126–128. T. & T. Clark, Edinburgh, UK.

Spencer, Herbert
1852   "A Theory of Population Deduced from the General Law of Animal Fertility." *The Westminster Review*, Vol. 57, pp. 468–501.
1862   *First Principles*. Williams & Norgate, London.
1877   "Mr. Tylor's Review of *The Principles of Sociology*." *Mind*, No. 2, pp. 415–419.
1896a *The Principles of Psychology*. 2 vols. Revised edition. D. Appleton & Company, New York. (First edition published in 1870–72)
1896b *The Principles of Sociology*, Vol. 3. D. Appleton & Company, New York.
1898   *The Principles of Biology*, Vol. 1. 2nd edition. D. Appleton & Company, New York. (First edition published in 1864)
1899   *The Principles of Psychology*. 2 vols. 3rd edition. D. Appleton & Company, New York. (First edition published in 1870–72)
1900   "Professor Ward on 'Naturalism and Agnosticism.'" *Popular Science Monthly*, Vol. 56, pp. 349–357.
1901   *The Principles of Sociology*, Vol. 1. Revised edition. D. Appleton & Company, New York. (First edition published in 1876)
1924   *An Autobiography*. 2 vols. Watts & Company, London. (Originally published in 1904)
1937   *First Principles*. 6th edition. Watts & Company, London. (First edition published in 1862)

Sprague, Elmer
1967   "Paley, William." In *The Encyclopedia of Philosophy*, edited by Paul Edwards, Vol. 6, pp. 19–20. Macmillan Publishing Company, New York

Stebbing, L. Susan
1958   *Philosophy and the Physicists*. Dover Publications, New York. (Originally published in 1937)

Stenger, Victor J.
2003   "Anthropic Design: Does the Cosmos Show Evidence of Purpose?" In *Science and Religion: Are They Compatible?* edited by Paul Kurtz, pp. 41–46. Prometheus Books, Amherst, NY.

Strathern, Paul
1997   *The Big Idea: Newton and Gravity.* Doubleday & Company, New York.

Strong, Augustus Hopkins
1888   *Philosophy and Religion.* A. C. Armstrong & Son, New York.

Sturt, Henry
1910   "Feuerbach, Ludwig Andreas." In *Encyclopaedia Britannica,* 11th edition, Vol. 10, pp. 302–303.

Sully, James
1911   "Lewes, George Henry." *Encyclopaedia Britannica,* 11th edition, Vol. 16, pp. 520–521.

Swanson, Guy E.
1964   *The Birth of the Gods: The Origin of Primitive Beliefs.* University of Michigan Press, Ann Arbor.

Teilhard de Chardin, Pierre
1961   *The Phenomenon of Man.* Translated from the French by Bernard Wall. Introduction by Julian Huxley. Harper & Row Publishers, New York.
1969   *Human Energy.* Translated from the French by J. M. Cohen. Harcourt Brace Jovanovich, New York.

Thomson, J. Arthur
1911   *Introduction to Science.* Henry Holt & Company, New York.
1917   "Darwin's Predecessor." In *Evolution in Modern Thought* (no editor), pp. 1–22. Boni & Liveright, New York.
1925   *Concerning Evolution.* Yale University Press, New Haven, CT.

Torrey, Norman L.
1967   "Voltaire, François-Marie Arouet de." In *The Encyclopedia of Philosophy,* edited by Paul Edwards, Vol. 8, pp. 262–270. Macmillan Publishing Company, New York.

Toynbee, Arnold J.
1949   *The Prospects of Western Civilization.* Columbia University Press, New York.

Tuckwell, Rev. William
1908   *Reminiscences of Oxford.* 2nd edition. E. P. Dutton & Company, New York. (First edition published in 1901)

Turnbull, Colin M.
  1961   *The Forest People*. Simon & Schuster, New York.

Tylor, Edward B.
  1871   *Primitive Culture*. 2 vols. John Murray, London.
  1877   "Mr. Spencer's Principles of Sociology." *Mind*, No. 6, pp. 141–156.
  1931   *Anthropology*. D. Appleton & Company, New York. (Originally published in 1881)

Tyndall, John
  1869   "The Scope and Limit of Scientific Materialism." Presidential Address to the Section on Mathematics and Physics. *Report of the 38th Meeting of the British Association for the Advancement of Science, 1868*, pp. 1–6. John Murray, London.
  1871   *Fragments of Science for the Unscientific: A Series of Detached Essays, Lectures, and Reviews*. D. Appleton & Company, New York.
  1874   *Address Delivered Before the British Association at Belfast, with Additions*. Longmans, Green & Company, London.
  1903   *Lectures and Essays*. Rationalist Press Association, London.

Tyson, Neil deGrasse
  2003   "An Astrophysicist Ponders the God Question." In *Science and Religion: Are They Compatible?* edited by Paul Kurtz, pp. 73–79. Prometheus Books, Amherst, NY.

Unsigned
  1910a   "Deism." In *Encyclopaedia Britannica*, 11th edition, Vol. 7, pp. 933–937.
  1910b   "Chambers, Robert." In *Encyclopaedia Britannica*, 11th edition, Vol. 5, pp. 820–821.
  1910c   "Atheism." In *Encyclopaedia Britannica*, 11th edition, Vol. 2, pp. 827–828.
  1910d   "Büchner, Friedrich Karl Christian Ludwig." In *Encyclopaedia Britannica*, 11th edition, Vol. 4, p. 719.
  1911a   "Holbach, Paul Heinrich Dietrich." In *Encyclopaedia Britannica*, 11th edition, Vol. 13, p. 577.
  1911b   "Pantheism." In *Encyclopaedia Britannica*, 11th edition, Vol. 20, pp. 682–683.
  1911c   "Oversoul." In *Encyclopaedia Britannica*, 11th edition, Vol. 20, p. 384.

1911d   "Paley, William." In *Encyclopaedia Britannica*, 11th edition, Vol. 20, pp. 628–629.

Updike, John
  1998   "The Immortal Isaac." *The New Yorker*, March 30, pp. 114–122.

Upton, Charles B.
  1909   "Atheism and Anti-Theistic Theories." In *Encyclopaedia of Religion and Ethics*, edited by James Hastings, Vol. 2, pp. 173–183. T. & T. Clark, Edinburgh, UK.

Urbach, Peter, and John Gibson
  1994   Editors' Introduction to *Novum Organum* by Francis Bacon. Open Court, Chicago.

Vartanian, Aram
  1967a   "La Mettrie, Julien Offray de." In *The Encyclopedia of Philosophy*, edited by Paul Edwards. Vol. 4, pp. 379–382. Macmillan Publishing Company, New York.
  1967b   "Stahl, Georg Ernst." In *The Encyclopedia of Philosophy*, edited by Paul Edwards, Vol. 8, p. 4. Macmillan Publishing Company, New York.

Wald, George
  1965   "Determinacy, Individuality, and the Problem of Free Will." In *New Views of the Nature of Man*, edited by John R. Platt, pp. 16–46. University of Chicago Press, Chicago.

Wallace, Alfred Russel
  1905   *My Life: A Record of Events and Opinions.* 2 vols. Dodd, Mead & Company, New York.

Ward, Henshaw
  1943   *Charles Darwin and the Theory of Evolution.* New Home Library, New York. (Originally published in 1927)

Ward, James
  1911   "Naturalism." In *Encyclopaedia Britannica,* 11th edition, Vol. 19, pp. 274–275.

Ward, Lester F.
  1883   *Dynamic Sociology.* 2 vols. D. Appleton & Company, New York.
  1909   "The Career of Herbert Spencer." *Popular Science Monthly*, Vol. 74, pp. 5–18.

Warnock, G. J.
  1958   *English Philosophy Since 1900*. Oxford University Press, London.

Watson, James D.
  2003   *DNA: The Secret of Life*. Alfred A. Knopf, New York.

Weinberg, Steven
  1992   *Dreams of a Final Theory*. Pantheon Books, New York.

West, Geoffrey
  1938   *Charles Darwin: A Portrait*. Yale University Press, New Haven, CT.

Wheen, Francis
  2001   *Karl Marx: A Life*. W. W. Norton & Company, New York.

White, Andrew D.
  1899   *A History of the Warfare of Science with Theology in Christendom*. 2 vols. D. Appleton & Company, New York.

White, Hayden
  1967   "Feuerbach, Ludwig Andreas." In *The Encyclopedia of Philosophy*, edited by Paul Edwards, Vol. 3, pp. 190–192. Macmillan Publishing Company, New York.

White, Leslie A.
  1987   *Ethnological Essays*. Edited by Beth Dillingham and Robert L. Carneiro. University of New Mexico Press, Albuquerque.

  2005   *The Science of Culture*. 2nd edition. Percheron Press/Eliot Werner Publications, Clinton Corners, NY. (First edition published in 1949)

Whitehead, Alfred North
  1963   "Religion and Science." In *Great Essays in Science*, edited by Martin Gardner, pp. 206–218. Washington Square Press, New York.

Williams, Bernard
  1967   "Descartes, René." In *The Encyclopedia of Philosophy*, edited by Paul Edwards, Vol. 1, pp. 344–354. Macmillan Publishing Company, New York.

Wilson, Arthur M.
  1967   "Encyclopédie." In *The Encyclopedia of Philosophy*, edited by

Paul Edwards, Vol. 2, pp. 505–508. Macmillan Publishing Company, New York.

Wilson, Edward O.
  1978   *On Human Nature*. Harvard University Press, Cambridge, MA.
  2006   *Nature Revealed: Selected Writings, 1949–2006*. Johns Hopkins University Press, Baltimore, MD.

Winschuttle, Keith
  1997   "The Real Stuff of History." *New Criterion*, Vol. 15, pp. 4–16.

Wooldridge, Dean E.
  1966   *The Machinery of Life*. McGraw-Hill Book Company, New York.

Youngert, S. G.
  1911   "Cosmogony and Cosmology (Teutonic)." In *Encyclopaedia of Religion and Ethics*, edited by James Hastings, Vol. 4, pp. 176–179. T. & T. Clark, Edinburgh, UK.

INDEX